# THE DISCOVERY OF INDIA

JAWAHARLAL NEHRU was born in 1889 to a wealthy Brahman family. He was educated in England, attending first Harrow, then Trinity College, Cambridge, where he studied natural science, and finally Inner Temple, London, where he studied law. He returned to India in 1912 to practice law and joined the then moderate Indian National Congress. The Amritsar Massacre of 1919 changed his outlook; he abandoned law and became a notable follower of Gandhi, eventually second in importance to him. He was imprisoned by the British for his political activities first in 1922 and several times thereafter. When the Interim Government was set up in 1946 he was made Premier, and the following year, when India became fully independent, Prime Minister and Minister of External Affairs.

The Editor, ROBERT I. CRANE, associate professor of history at the University of Michigan, was born in Delhi, India. He was formerly a fellow of the American Council of Learned Societies, and is now a member of its Committee on Asia and the editor of *Newsletters*, the publication of the Association for Asian Studies. He has written on India for many scholarly publications and worked on the India-Iran-Afghanistan desk of the Department of State's Division of Cultural Relations.

# THE DISCOVERY OF

# INDIA

## *JAWAHARLAL NEHRU*

EDITED, WITH A FOREWORD AND
COMMENTS BY ROBERT I. CRANE

Anchor Books
Doubleday & Company, Inc.,
Garden City, New York

To my colleagues and co-prisoners in the Ahmadnagar Fort prison camp from August 9, 1942 to March 28, 1945

The Discovery of India was originally published by The John Day Company in 1946. The Anchor Books edition is published by arrangement with The John Day Company, Inc.

Anchor Books edition: 1960

Cover photograph of Jaipur, a peasant cart near the entrance to the Purana Ghat, by Henri Cartier-Bresson. Cover design by Diana Klemin. Typography by Edward Gorey.

# FOREWORD

In preparing the present edition of Jawaharlal Nehru's *Discovery of India*, it has been necessary to cut out portions of the original text. Some comments seem appropriate with respect to the criteria I have used in making these emendations.

To begin with, the effort has been made to retain those portions of the original edition which seem especially valuable in giving the American reader an awareness of the mentality, personality, and viewpoint of the author, Pandit Nehru. The values and attitudes characteristic of so distinguished an Indian leader as Mr. Nehru should be more widely understood among thinking people in this country. The present volume hopes to contribute to such awareness.

In addition those passages have, in so far as possible, been retained which seem fundamental for an adequate and informed understanding of the history, culture, and institutions of India. Where a choice could be made this meant cutting the passages which dealt with specific events and which did not contribute materially to a larger understanding of India.

The attempt has also been made to retain a substantial amount of the material in the original edition which dealt with the ways in which European influence shaped life and the course of events in modern India. It has been assumed that American readers need to know how Indian life and institutions have been affected by European contact. Many of the most pressing problems of the contemporary scene arise from the complex mingling of Asian ways and values with those of Europe. Western readers can profit from the chance to ponder the case of India.

If we are to understand India or if we hope to relate to India in any meaningful and effective fashion, we need to acquire a broader and deeper understanding of Indian history, culture, and conditions. We need, in addition, to become familiar with the outlook and attitudes of India's leaders. The publication of a popular edition of *The Discovery of India* will, it is hoped, help fill such needs.

Finally, the effort has been made to retain the style and continuity of the original edition. Pandit Nehru's mastery of the English language makes reading one of his volumes a distinct pleasure. It is hoped that the editing of the present edition has not detracted in any serious fashion from the grace and readability of the original.

The reader will note that a few brief bridge passages, printed in italics, have been inserted in Mr. Nehru's text by the editor. These bridge passages provide the reader with an indication of the material in the original edition which has been left out. Bridge passages have been inserted only at those points where a fairly substantial block of pages has been omitted. Brief cuts of a few paragraphs or pages have not been so bridged.

In closing, it may be mentioned that although Prime Minister Nehru has consented to a revision of his original text for the purposes of the present edition and has approved a general indication, given in advance, of the changes which were contemplated, he has not been asked to review and approve in detail the specific deletions and emendations which have been made. Thus the editor must bear the final responsibility for the changes made in the original, widely acclaimed text.

ROBERT I. CRANE

Department of History
University of Michigan
Ann Arbor, Michigan
May 1, 1959

# PREFACE

This book was written by me in Ahmadnagar Fort prison during the five months, April to September, 1944. Some of my colleagues in prison were good enough to read the manuscript and make a number of valuable suggestions. On revising the book in prison I took advantage of these suggestions and made some additions. No one, I need hardly add, is responsible for what I have written or necessarily agrees with it. But I must express my deep gratitude to my fellow prisoners in Ahmadnagar Fort for the innumerable talks and discussions we had, which helped me greatly to clear my own mind about various aspects of Indian history and culture. Prison is not a pleasant place to live in even for a short period, much less for long years. But it was a privilege for me to live in close contact with men of outstanding ability and culture and a wide human outlook which even the passions of the moment did not obscure.

My eleven companions in Ahmadnagar Fort were an interesting cross-section of India and represented in their several ways not only politics but Indian scholarship, old and new, and various aspects of present-day India. Nearly all the principal living Indian languages, as well as the classical languages which have powerfully influenced India in the past and present, were represented, and the standard was often that of high scholarship. Among the classical languages were Sanskrit and Pali, Arabic and Persian; the modern languages were Hindu, Urdu, Bengali, Gujrati, Marathi, Telugu, Sindhi, and Oriya. I had all this wealth to draw upon, and the only limitation was my own capacity to profit by it. Though I am grateful to all my companions,

I should like to mention especially Maulana Abul Kalam Azad, whose vast erudition invariably delighted me but sometimes also rather overwhelmed me; Govind Ballabh Pant, Narendra Deva, and M. Asaf Ali.

It is a year and a quarter since I finished writing this book and some parts of it are already somewhat out of date, and much has happened since I wrote it. I have felt tempted to add and revise, but I have resisted the temptation. Indeed I could not have done otherwise, for life outside prison is of a different texture and there is no leisure for thought or writing. It has been difficult enough for me to read again what I have written. I wrote originally in longhand; this was typed after my release. I was unable to find time to read the typescript, and the publication of the book was being delayed when my daughter, Indira, came to my rescue and took this burden off my shoulders. The book remains as written in prison with no additions or changes, except for the postscript at the end.

I do not know how other authors feel about their writings, but always I have a strange sensation when I read something that I had written some time previously. That sensation is heightened when the writing had been done in the close and abnormal atmosphere of prison and the subsequent reading has taken place outside. I recognize it of course, but not wholly; it seems almost as if I am reading some familiar piece written by another, who is near to me and yet who is different. Perhaps that is the measure of the change that has taken place in me.

So I have felt about this book also. It is mine and not wholly mine, as I am constituted today; it represents rather some past self of mine which has already joined that long succession of other selves that existed for a while and faded away, leaving only a memory behind.

JAWAHARLAL NEHRU

Anand Bhawan,
Allahabad,
December 29, 1945

# CONTENTS

## VI. THE LAST PHASE: (1) CONSOLIDATION OF BRITISH RULE AND RISE OF NATIONALIST MOVEMENT

## VII. THE LAST PHASE: (2) NATIONALISM VERSUS IMPERIALISM

# THE DISCOVERY OF INDIA

"When to the sessions of sweet silent thought
I summon up remembrance of things past . . ."

# I. Ahmadnagar Fort

## I. TWENTY MONTHS

Ahmadnagar Fort. April thirteenth, nineteen forty-four. It is more than twenty months since we were brought here, more than twenty months of my ninth term of imprisonment. The new moon, a shimmering crescent in the darkening sky, greeted us on our arrival here. The bright fortnight of the waxing moon had begun. Ever since then each coming of the new moon has been a reminder to me that another month of my imprisonment is over. So it was also with my last term of imprisonment which began with the new moon, just after the Deepavali, the festival of light. The moon, ever a companion to me in prison, has grown more friendly with closer acquaintance, a reminder of the loveliness of this world, of the waxing and waning of life, of light following darkness, of death and resurrection following each other in interminable succession. Ever changing, yet ever the same, I have watched it in its different phases and its many moods in the evening, as the shadows lengthen, in the still hours of the night, and when the breath and whisper of dawn bring promise of the coming day. How helpful is the moon in counting the days and the months, for the size and shape of the moon, when it is visible, indicate the day of the month with a fair measure of exactitude. It is an easy calendar (though it must be adjusted from time to time), and for the peasant in the field the most convenient one to indicate the passage of the days and the gradual changing of the seasons.

Three weeks we spent here cut off completely from all news of the outside world. There were no contacts of any kind, no interviews, no letters, no newspapers, no radio. Even our presence here was supposed to be a state secret unknown to any except to the officials in charge of us, a poor secret, for all India knew where we were. Then newspapers were allowed and, some weeks later, letters from near relatives dealing with domestic affairs. But no interviews during these twenty months, no other contacts.

The newspapers contained heavily censored news. Yet they gave us some idea of the war that was consuming more than half the world, and how it fared with our people in India. Little we knew about these people of ours except that scores of thousands lay in prison or internment camp without trial, that thousands had been shot to death, that tens of thousands had been driven out of schools and colleges, that something indistinguishable from martial law prevailed over the whole country, that terror and frightfulness darkened the land. They were worse off, far worse than us, those scores of thousands in prison, like us, without trial, for there were not only no interviews but also no letters or newspapers for them, and even books were seldom allowed. Many sickened for lack of healthy food; some of our dear ones died for lack of proper care and treatment.

There were many thousands of prisoners of war kept in India, mostly from Italy. We compared their lot with the lot of our own people. We were told that they were governed by the Geneva Convention. But there was no convention or law or rule to govern the conditions under which Indian prisoners and *détenus* had to exist, except such ordinances as it pleased our British rulers to issue from time to time.

## II. THE WAR FOR DEMOCRACY

In Asia and Europe and Africa, and over the vast stretches of the Pacific and Atlantic and Indian oceans, war has raged in all its dreadful aspects. Nearly seven years of war in China, over four and a half years of war in Europe and Africa, and two years and four months of world war. War against fascism and nazism and attempts to gain world domination. Of these years of war I have so far spent nearly three years in prison, here and elsewhere in India.

I remember how I reacted to fascism and nazism in their early days, and not I only but many in India. How Japanese aggression in China had moved India deeply and revived the age-old friendship for China; how Italy's rape of Abyssinia had sickened us; how the betrayal of Czechoslovakia had hurt and embittered us; how the fall of republican Spain, after a struggle full of heroic endurance, had been a tragedy and a personal sorrow for me and others.

It was not merely the physical acts of aggression which fascism and nazism indulged in, not only the vulgarity and brutality that accompanied them, terrible as they were, that affected us. But the principles on which they stood and which they proclaimed so loudly and blatantly, the theories of life on which they tried to fashion themselves. For these went counter to what we believed in the present and what we had held from ages past. And even if our racial memory had forsaken us and we had lost our moorings, our own experiences, even though they came to us in different garb and somewhat disguised for the sake of decency, were enough to teach us to what these nazi principles and theories of life and the state ultimately led. For our people had been the victims for long of those very principles and methods of government. So we reacted immediately and intensely against fascism and nazism.

I remember how I refused a pressing invitation from Signor Mussolini to see him in the early days of March 1936. Many of Britain's leading statesmen, who spoke harshly of the fascist Duce in later years when Italy became a belligerent, referred to him tenderly and admiringly in those days and praised his regime and methods.

Two years later, in the summer before Munich, I was invited on behalf of the Nazi government to visit Germany, an invitation to which was added the remark that they knew my opposition to nazism and yet they wanted me to see Germany for myself. I could go as their guest or privately, in my own name or incognito, as I desired, and I would have perfect freedom to go where I liked. Again I declined with thanks. Instead I went to Czechoslovakia, that "far-away country" about which England's then Prime Minister knew so little.

Before Munich I met some of the members of the British Cabinet and other prominent politicians of England and ventured to express my antifascist and antinazi views before them. I found that my views were not welcome and I was told that there were many other considerations to be borne in mind.

During the Czechoslovak crisis what I saw of Franco-British statesmanship in Prague and in the Sudetenland, in London and Paris and in Geneva, where the League Assembly was then sitting, amazed and disgusted me. Appeasement seemed to be a feeble word for it. There was behind it not only a fear of Hitler but a sneaking admiration for him.

And now, it is a curious turn of fate's wheel that I and people like me should spend our days in prison while war against fascism and nazism is raging, and many of those who used to bow to Hitler and Mussolini and approve of Japanese aggression in China should hold aloft the banner of freedom and democracy and antifascism.

In India the change is equally remarkable. There are those here as elsewhere, "governmentarians," who hover round the skirts of Government and echo the views which they think will be approved by those whose favor they continually seek. There was a time, not so long ago, when they praised Hitler and Mussolini and held them up as models and when they cursed the Soviet Union with bell, book, and candle. Not so now, for the weather has changed. They are high government and state officials, and loudly they proclaim their antifascism and antinazism and even talk of democracy, though with bated breath, as something desirable but distant. I often wonder what they would have done if events had taken a different turn. And yet there is little reason for conjecture, for they would welcome with garlands and addresses of welcome whoever happened to wield authority.

For long years before the war my mind was full of the war that was coming. I thought of it, spoke of it and wrote about it and prepared myself mentally for it. I wanted India to take an eager and active part in the mighty conflict, for I felt that high principles would be at stake and out of this conflict would come great and revolutionary changes in India and the world. At that time I did not envisage an immediate threat to India, any probability of actual invasion. Yet I wanted India to take her full share. But I was convinced that only as a free country and an equal could she function in this way.

That was the attitude of the National Congress, the one great organization in India which consistently for all these years had been antifascist and antinazi, as it had been anti-imperialist. It had stood for republican Spain, for Czecho-slovakia, and throughout for China.

And now for nearly two years the Congress has been declared illegal, outlawed and prevented from functioning in any way. The Congress is in prison. Its elected members of the provincial parliaments, its speakers of these parliaments, its ex-ministers, its mayors and presidents of municipal corporations, are in prison.

Meanwhile the war goes on for democracy and the Atlantic Charter and the Four Freedoms.

### III. TIME IN PRISON. THE URGE TO ACTION

Time seems to change its nature in prison. The present hardly exists, for there is an absence of feeling and sensation which might separate it from the dead past. Even news of the active, living and dying world outside has a certain dreamlike unreality, an immobility and an unchangeableness as of the past. The outer objective time ceases to be, the inner and subjective sense remains but at a lower level, except when thought pulls it out of the present and experiences a kind of reality in the past or in the future. We live, as Auguste Comte said, dead men's lives, encased in our pasts, but this is especially so in prison where we try to find some sustenance for our starved and locked-up emotions in memory of the past or fancies of the future.

There is a stillness and everlastingness about the past; it changes not and has a touch of eternity, like a painted picture or a statue in bronze or marble. Unaffected by the storms and upheavals of the present, it maintains its dignity and repose and tempts the troubled spirit and the tortured mind to seek shelter in its vaulted catacombs. There is peace there and security, and one may even sense a spiritual quality.

But it is not life, unless we can find the vital links between it and the present with all its conflicts and problems. It is a kind of art for art's sake without the passion and the urge to action which are the very stuff of life. Without that passion and urge, there is a gradual oozing out of hope and vitality, a settling down on lower levels of existence, a slow merging into nonexistence. We become prisoners of the past and some part of its immobility sticks to us. This passage of the mind is all the easier in prison where action is denied and we become slaves to the routine of jail life.

Yet the past is ever with us and all that we are and that we have comes from the past. We are its products and we live immersed in it. Not to understand it and feel it as something living within us is not to understand the present. To combine it with the present and extend it to the future, to break from it where it cannot be so united, to make of all this the pulsating and vibrating material for thought and action—that is life.

Any vital action springs from the depths of the being. All the long past of the individual and even of the race has prepared the background for that psychological moment of action. All the racial memories, influences of heredity and environment and training, subconscious urges, thoughts and dreams and actions from infancy and childhood onward, in their curious and tremendous mix-up, inevitably drive to that new action, which again becomes yet another factor influencing the future. Influencing the future, partly determining it, possibly even largely determining it, and yet, surely, it is not all determinism.

Aurobindo Ghose writes somewhere of the present as "the pure and virgin moment," that razor's edge of time and existence which divides the past from the future, and is, and yet, instantaneously is not. The phrase is attractive, and yet what does it mean? The virgin moment emerging from the veil of the future in all its naked purity, coming into contact with us, and immediately becoming the soiled and stale past. Is it we that soil it and violate it? Or is the moment not so virgin after all, for it is bound up with all the harlotry of the past?

Whether there is any such thing as human freedom in the philosophic sense or whether there is only an automatic determinism, I do not know. A very great deal appears certainly to be determined by the past complex of events which bear down and often overwhelm the individual. Possibly even the inner urge that he experiences, that apparent exercise of free will, is itself conditioned. As Schopenhauer says: "A man can do what he will, but not will as he will." A belief in an absolute determinism seems to me to lead inevitably to complete inaction, to death in life. All my sense of life rebels against it, though of course that very rebellion may itself have been conditioned by previous events.

I do not usually burden my mind with such philosophical or metaphysical problems, which escape solution. Sometimes they come to me almost unawares in the long silences of prison, or even in the midst of an intensity of action, bringing with them a sense of detachment or consolation in the face of some painful experience. But usually it is action and the thought of action that fill me, and when action is denied, I imagine that I am preparing for action.

The call of action has long been with me; not action divorced from thought, but rather flowing from it in one continuous sequence. And when, rarely, there has been full harmony between the two, thought leading to action and finding its fulfillment in it, action leading back to thought and a fuller understanding—then I have sensed a certain fullness of life and a vivid intensity in that moment of existence. But such moments are rare, very rare, and usually one outstrips the other and there is a lack of harmony, and vain efforts to bring the two in line. There was a time, many years ago, when I lived for considerable periods in a state of emotional exaltation, wrapped up in the action which absorbed me. Those days of my youth seem far away now, not merely because of the passage of years but far more so because of the ocean of experience and painful thought that separates them from today. The old exuberance is much less now, the almost uncontrollable impulses have toned down, and passion and feeling are more in check. The burden of thought is often a hindrance, and in the mind where there was once certainty, doubt creeps in. Perhaps it is just age, or the common temper of our day.

And yet, even now, the call of action stirs strange depths within me and, after a brief tussle with thought, I want to experience again "that lovely impulse of delight" which turns to risk and danger and faces and mocks at death. I am not enamored of death, though I do not think it frightens me. I do not believe in the negation of or abstention from life. I have loved life and it attracts me still, and in my own way I seek to experience it, though many invisible barriers have grown up which surround me. But that very desire leads me to play with life, to peep over its edges, not to be a slave to it, so that we may value each other all the more. Perhaps I ought to have been an aviator, so that when the slowness and dullness of life overcame me I could have rushed into the tumult of the clouds and said to myself:

> I balanced all, brought all to mind,
> The years to come seemed waste of breath,
> A waste of breath the years behind
> In balance with this life, this death.

## IV. LIFE'S PHILOSOPHY

Six or seven years ago an American publisher asked me to write an essay on my philosophy of life for a symposium he was preparing. I was attracted to the idea but I hesitated, and the more I thought over it, the more reluctant I grew. Ultimately I did not write that essay.

What was my philosophy of life? I did not know. Some years earlier I would not have been so hesitant. There was a definiteness about my thinking and objectives then which has faded away since. The events of the past few years in India, China, Europe, and all over the world have been confusing, upsetting and distressing, and the future has become vague and shadowy and has lost that clearness of outline which it once possessed in my mind.

This doubt and difficulty about fundamental matters did not come in my way in regard to immediate action, except that it blunted somewhat the sharp edge of that activity. No longer could I function, as I did in my younger days, as an arrow flying automatically to the target of my choice, ignoring all else but that target. Yet I functioned, for the urge to action was there and a real or imagined co-ordination of that action with the ideals I held. But a growing distaste for politics, as I saw them, seized me, and gradually my whole attitude to life seemed to undergo a transformation.

The ideals and objectives of yesterday were still the ideals of today but they had lost some of their luster, and even as one seemed to go toward them, they lost the shining beauty which had warmed the heart and vitalized the body. Evil triumphed often enough, but what was far worse was the coarsening and distortion of what had seemed so right. Was human nature so essentially bad that it would take ages of training, through suffering and misfortune, before it could behave reasonably and raise man above that creature of lust and violence and deceit that he now was? And meanwhile was every effort to change it

radically in the present or the near future doomed to
failure?

Ends and means: were they tied up inseparably, acting
and reacting on each other, the wrong means distorting and
sometimes even destroying the end in view? But the right
means might well be beyond the capacity of infirm and
selfish human nature. What then was one to do? Not to act
was a complete confession of failure and a submission to
evil; to act meant often enough a compromise with some
form of that evil, with all the untoward consequences that
such compromises result in.

My early approach to life's problems had been more or
less scientific, with something of the easy optimism of the
science of the nineteenth and early twentieth century. A
secure and comfortable existence, and the energy and self-
confidence I possessed, increased that feeling of optimism.
A kind of vague humanism appealed to me.

Religion, as I saw it practiced, and accepted even by
thinking minds, whether it was Hinduism or Islam or
Buddhism or Christianity, did not attract me. It seemed to
be closely associated with superstitious practices and dogmatic beliefs, and behind it lay a method of approach to
life's problems which was certainly not that of science.
There was an element of magic about it, an uncritical
credulousness, a reliance on the supernatural.

Yet it was obvious that religion had supplied some
deeply felt inner need of human nature, and that the vast
majority of people all over the world could not do without some form of religious belief. It had produced many
fine types of men and women, as well as bigoted, narrow-
minded, cruel tyrants. It had given a set of values to human life, and though some of these values had no application today, or were even harmful, others were still the
foundation of morality and ethics.

In the wider sense of the word, religion dealt with the
uncharted regions of human experience, uncharted, that is,
by the scientific positive knowledge of the day. In a sense
it might be considered an extension of the known and
charted region, though the methods of science and religion
were utterly unlike each other, and to a large extent they

had to deal with different kinds of media. It was obvious that there was a vast unknown region all around us, and science, with its magnificent achievements, knew little enough about it, though it was making tentative approaches in that direction. Probably also the normal methods of science, its dealings with the visible world and the processes of life, were not wholly adapted to the psychical, the artistic, the spiritual, and other elements of the invisible world. Life does not consist entirely of what we see and hear and feel, the visible world which is undergoing change in time and space. It is continually touching an invisible world of other, and possibly more stable or equally changeable elements, and no thinking person can ignore this invisible world.

Science does not tell us much, or for the matter of that, anything, about the purpose of life. It is now widening its boundaries and it may invade the so-called invisible world before long and help us to understand this purpose of life in its widest sense, or at least give us some glimpses which illumine the problem of human existence. The old controversy between science and religion takes a new form— the application of the scientific method to emotional and religious experiences.

Religion merges into mysticism and metaphysics and philosophy. There have been great mystics, attractive figures, who cannot easily be disposed of as self-deluded fools. Yet mysticism (in the narrow sense of the word) irritates me; it appears to be vague and soft and flabby, not a rigorous discipline of the mind but a surrender of mental faculties and a living in a sea of emotional experience. The experience may lead occasionally to some insight into inner and less obvious processes, but it is also likely to lead to self-delusion.

Metaphysics and philosophy, or a metaphysical philosophy, have a greater appeal to the mind. They require hard thinking and the application of logic and reasoning, though all this is necessarily based on some premises which are presumed to be self-evident, and yet which may or may not be true. All thinking persons, to a greater or less degree, dabble in metaphysics and philosophy, for not to do so is to ignore many of the aspects of this universe of ours. Some may feel more attracted to them than others, and the emphasis on them may vary in different ages. In the ancient world, both in Asia and in Europe, all the emphasis was laid on the supremacy of the inward life over things external, and this inevitably led to metaphysics and philosophy. The modern man is wrapped up much more in these things external, and yet even he, in moments of crisis and mental trouble, often turns to philosophy and metaphysical speculations.

Some vague or more precise philosophy of life we all have, though most of us accept unthinkingly the general attitude which is characteristic of our generation and environment. Most of us accept also certain metaphysical conceptions as part of the faith in which we have grown up. I have not been attracted toward metaphysics; in fact I have had a certain distaste for vague speculation. And yet I have sometimes found a certain intellectual fascination in trying to follow the rigid lines of metaphysical and philosophic thought of the ancients or the moderns. But I have never felt at ease there and have escaped from their spell with a feeling of relief.

Essentially I am interested in this world, in this life, not in some other world or a future life. Whether there is such a thing as a soul, or whether there is a survival after death or not, I do not know; and important as these questions are, they do not trouble me in the least. The environment in which I have grown up takes the soul (or rather the *atma*) and a future life, the karma theory of cause and effect, and reincarnation for granted. I have been affected by this, and so, in a sense, I am favorably disposed toward these assumptions. There might be a soul which survives the physical death of the body, and a theory of cause and effect governing life's actions seems reasonable, though it leads to obvious difficulties when one thinks of the ultimate cause. Presuming a soul, there appears to be some logic also in the theory of reincarnation.

But I do not believe in any of these or other theories and assumptions as a matter of religious faith. They are just intellectual speculations in an unknown region about which we know next to nothing. They do not affect my life, and whether they were proved right or wrong subsequently, they would make little difference to me.

Spiritualism with its séances and its so-called manifestations of spirits and the like has always seemed to me a rather absurd and impertinent way of investigating psychic phenomena and the mysteries of the afterlife. Usually it is something worse and is an exploitation of the emotions of some overcredulous people who seek relief or escape from mental trouble. I do not deny the possibility of some of these psychic phenomena having a basis of truth, but the approach appears to me to be all wrong and the conclusions drawn from scraps and odd bits of evidence to be unjustified.

Often, as I look at this world, I have a sense of mysteries, of unknown depths. The urge to understand it, in so far as I can, comes to me; to be in tune with it and to experience it in its fullness. But the way to that understanding seems to me essentially the way of science, the way of objective approach, though I realize that there can be no such thing as true objectiveness. If the subjective element is unavoidable and inevitable, it should be conditioned as far as possible by the scientific method.

What the mysterious is I do not know. I do not call it God because God has come to mean much that I do not believe in. I find myself incapable of thinking of a deity or of any unknown supreme power in anthropomorphic terms, and the fact that many people think so is continually a source of surprise to me. Any idea of a personal God seems very odd to me. Intellectually, I can appreciate to some extent the conception of monism, and I have been attracted toward the Advaita (nondualist) philosophy of the Vedanta, though I do not presume to understand it in all its depth and intricacy, and I realize that merely an intellectual appreciation of such matters does not carry one far. At the same time the Vedanta, as well as other similar approaches, rather frighten me with their vague formless incursions into infinity. The diversity and fullness of nature stir me and produce a harmony of the spirit, and I can imagine myself feeling at home in the old Indian or

Greek pagan and pantheistic atmosphere, but minus the conception of god or gods that was attached to it.

Some kind of ethical approach to life has a strong appeal for me, though it would be difficult for me to justify it logically. I have been attracted by Gandhiji's stress on right means, and I think one of his greatest contributions to our public life has been this emphasis.[1] The idea is by no means new, but this application of an ethical doctrine to large-scale public activity was certainly novel. It is full of difficulty, and perhaps ends and means are not really separable and form together one organic whole. In a world which thinks almost exclusively of ends and ignores means, this emphasis on means seems odd and remarkable. How far it has succeeded in India I cannot say. But there is no doubt that it has created a deep and abiding impression on the minds of large numbers of people.

A study of Marx and Lenin produced a powerful effect on my mind and helped me to see history and current affairs in a new light. The long chain of history and of social development appeared to have some meaning, some sequence, and the future lost some of its obscurity. The practical achievements of the Soviet Union were also tremendously impressive. Often I disliked or did not understand some development there and it seemed to me to be too closely concerned with the opportunism of the moment or the power politics of the day. But despite all these developments and possible distortions of the original passion for human betterment, I had no doubt that the Soviet revolution had advanced human society by a great leap and had lit a bright flame which could not be smothered, and that it had laid the foundations for that "new civilization" toward which the world would advance. I am too much of an individualist and believer in personal freedom to like overmuch regimentation. Yet it seemed to me obvious that in a complex social structure individual freedom had to be

[1] The suffix in the form Gandhiji is sometimes mistaken by American and English readers to be an affectionate diminutive. On the contrary, it is the simplest of numerous terms of respect used in the Hindustani language and is preferred by Gandhi over the title Mahatma. It amounts to calling him "Mr. Gandhi."—Ed.

limited, and perhaps the only way to real personal freedom was through some such limitation in the social sphere. The lesser liberties may often need limitation in the interest of the larger freedom.

Much in the Marxist philosophical outlook I could accept without difficulty: its monism and nonduality of mind and matter, the dynamics of matter and the dialectic of continuous change by evolution as well as leap, through action and interaction, cause and effect, thesis, antithesis, and synthesis. It did not satisfy me completely, nor did it answer all the questions in my mind, and almost unawares a vague idealist approach would creep into my mind, something rather akin to the Vedanta approach. It was not a difference between mind and matter but rather of something that lay beyond the mind. Also there was the background of ethics. I realized that the moral approach is a changing one and depends upon the growing mind and an advancing civilization; it is conditioned by the mental climate of the age. Yet there was something more to it than that, certain basic urges which had greater permanence. I did not like the frequent divorce in communist, as in other, practice between action and these basic urges or principles. So there was an odd mixture in my mind which I could not rationally explain or resolve. There was a general tendency not to think too much of those fundamental questions which appear to be beyond reach, and rather to concentrate on the problems of life—to understand in the narrower and more immediate sense what should be done and how. Whatever ultimate reality may be, and whether we can ever grasp it in whole or in part, there certainly appear to be vast possibilities of increasing human knowledge, even though this may be partly or largely subjective, and of applying this to the advancement and betterment of human living and social organization.

There has been in the past, and there is to a lesser extent even today among some people, an absorption in finding an answer to the riddle of the universe. This leads them away from the individual and social problems of the day, and when they are unable to solve that riddle they despair and turn to inaction and triviality, or find comfort in some dogmatic creed. Social evils, most of which are certainly capable of removal, are attributed to original sin, to the unalterableness of "human nature," or the social structure, or (in India) to the inevitable legacy of previous births. Thus one drifts away from even the attempt to think rationally and scientifically and takes refuge in irrationalism, superstition, and unreasonable and inequitable social prejudices and practices. It is true that even rational and scientific thought does not always take us as far as we would like to go. There is an infinite number of factors and relations which influence and determine events in varying degrees and it is impossible to grasp all of them. Still we can try to pick out the dominating forces at work and by observing external material reality, and by experiment and practice, trial and error, grope our way to ever-widening knowledge and truth.

For this purpose, and within these limitations, the general Marxist approach, fitting in as it more or less did with the present state of scientific knowledge, seemed to me to offer considerable help. But even accepting that approach, the consequences that flow from it and the interpretation of past and present happenings were by no means always clear. Marx's general analysis of social development seems to have been remarkably correct, and yet many developments took place later which did not fit in with his outlook for the immediate future. Lenin successfully adapted the Marxian thesis to some of these subsequent developments, and again since then further remarkable changes have taken place—the rise of fascism and nazism and all that lay behind them. The very rapid growth of technology and the practical application of vast developments in scientific knowledge are now changing the world picture with an amazing rapidity, leading to new problems.

And so while I accepted the fundamentals of the socialist theory, I did not trouble myself about its numerous inner controversies. I had little patience with leftist groups in India, spending much of their energy in mutual conflict and recrimination over fine points of doctrine which did not interest me at all. Life is too complicated, and as far as we can understand it in our present state of knowledge, too illogical for it to be confined within the four corners of a fixed doctrine.

The real problems for me remain problems of individual and social life, of harmonious living, of a proper balancing of an individual's inner and outer life, of an adjustment of the relations between individuals and between groups, of a continuous becoming something better and higher, of social development, of the ceaseless adventure of man. In the solution of these problems the way of observation and precise knowledge and deliberate reasoning, according to the method of science, must be followed. This method may not always be applicable in our quest of truth, for art and poetry and certain psychic experiences seem to belong to a different order of things and to elude the objective methods of science. Let us therefore not rule out intuition and other methods of sensing truth and reality. They are necessary even for the purposes of science. But always we must hold to our anchor of precise objective knowledge tested by reason and even more so by experiment and practice, and always we must beware of losing ourselves in a sea of speculation unconnected with the day-to-day problems of life and the needs of men and women. A living philosophy must answer the problems of today.

It may be that we of this modern age, who so pride ourselves on the achievements of our times, are prisoners of our age, just as the ancients and the men and women of medieval times were prisoners of their respective ages. We may delude ourselves, as others have done before us, that our way of looking at things is the only right way, leading to truth. We cannot escape from that prison or get rid entirely of that illusion, if illusion it is.

Yet I am convinced that the methods and approach of science have revolutionized human life more than anything else in the long course of history, and have opened doors and avenues of further and even more radical change, leading up to the very portals of what has long been considered the unknown. The technical achievements of science are obvious enough; its capacity to transform an economy of scarcity into one of abundance is evident; its invasion of many problems which have so far been the monopoly of philosophy is becoming more pronounced. Space-time and the quantum theory utterly changed the picture of the physical world. More recent researches into the nature of matter, the structure of the atom, the transmutation of the elements, and the transformation of electricity and light, either into the other, have carried human knowledge much further. Man no longer sees nature as something apart and distinct from himself. Human destiny appears to become a part of nature's rhythmic energy.

All this upheaval of thought, due to the advance of science, has led scientists into a new region verging on the metaphysical. They draw different and often contradictory conclusions. Some see in it a new unity, the antithesis of chance. Others, like Bertrand Russell, say: "Academic philosophers ever since the time of Parmenides have believed the world is unity. The most fundamental of my beliefs is that this is rubbish." Or again: "Man is the product of causes which had no prevision of the end they were achieving; his origin, his growth, his hopes and fears, his loves and beliefs are but the outcome of accidental collocations of atoms." And yet the latest developments in physics have gone a long way to demonstrate a fundamental unity in nature. "The belief that all things are made of a single substance is as old as thought itself; but ours is the generation which, first of all in history, is able to perceive the unity of Nature not as a baseless dogma or a hopeless aspiration, but a principle of science based on proof as sharp and clear as anything which is known."[2]

Old as this belief is in Asia and Europe, it is interesting to compare some of the latest conclusions of science with the fundamental ideas underlying the Advaita Vedantic theory. These ideas were that the universe is made of one substance whose form is perpetually changing, and further that the sum total of energies remains always the same. Also that "the explanations of things are to be found within their own nature, and that no external beings or

[2] Karl K. Darrow, *The Renaissance of Physics* (New York, 1936), p. 301.

existences are required to explain what is going on in the universe," with its corollary of a self-evolving universe.

It does not very much matter to science what these vague speculations lead to, for meanwhile it forges ahead in a hundred directions, in its own precise experimental way of observation, widening the bounds of the charted region of knowledge, and changing human life in the process. It may be on the verge of discovering vital mysteries, and yet they may elude it. Still it will go on along its appointed path, for there is no end to its journeying. Ignoring for the moment the *Why?* of philosophy, it will go on asking *How?*, and as it finds this out it gives greater content and meaning to life, and perhaps takes us some way to answering the why.

Or perhaps we cannot cross that barrier, and the mysterious will continue to remain the mysterious, and life with all its changes will still remain a bundle of good and evil, a succession of conflicts, a curious combination of incompatible and mutually hostile urges.

Or again, perhaps the very progress of science, unconnected with and isolated from moral discipline and ethical considerations, will lead to the concentration of power and the terrible instruments of destruction which it has made in the hands of evil and selfish men, seeking the domination of others—and thus to the destruction of its own great achievements. Something of this kind we see happening now, and behind this war there lies this internal conflict of the spirit of man.

How amazing is this spirit of man! In spite of innumerable failings, man, throughout the ages, has sacrificed his life and all he held dear for an ideal, for truth, for faith, for country and honor. That ideal may change, but that capacity for self-sacrifice continues, and because of that, much may be forgiven to man, and it is impossible to lose hope for him. In the midst of disaster he has not lost his dignity or his faith in the values he cherished. Plaything of nature's mighty forces, less than the speck of dust in this vast universe, he has hurled defiance at the elemental powers, and with his mind, cradle of revolution, sought to master them. Whatever gods there be, there is something godlike in man, as there is also something of the devil in him.

The future is dark, uncertain. But we can see part of the way leading to it and can tread it with firm steps, remembering that nothing that can happen is likely to overcome the spirit of man which has survived so many perils. Remembering also that life, for all its ills, has joy and beauty, and we can always wander, if we know how to, in the enchanted woods of nature.

> What else is Wisdom? What of man's endeavour
> Or God's high grace, so lovely and so great?
> To stand from fear set free, to breathe and wait;
> To hold a hand uplifted over Hate;
> And shall not Loveliness be loved for ever?[3]

[3] Chorus from the *Bacchae* of Euripides—Gilbert Murray's translation.

# II. The Quest

### I. THE PANORAMA OF INDIA'S PAST

During these years of thought and activity my mind has been full of India, trying to understand her and to analyze my own reactions toward her. I went back to my childhood days and tried to remember what I felt like then, what vague shape this conception took in my growing mind and how it was molded by fresh experience. Sometimes it receded into the background, but it was always there, slowly changing, a queer mixture derived from old story and legend and modern fact. It produced a sensation of pride in me as well as that of shame, for I was ashamed of much that I saw around me, of superstitious practices, of outworn ideas, and above all, our subject and poverty-stricken state.

As I grew up and became engaged in activities which promised to lead to India's freedom, I became obsessed with the thought of India. What was this India that possessed me and beckoned to me continually, urging me to action so that we might realize some vague but deeply felt desire of our hearts? The initial urge came to me, I suppose, through pride, both individual and national, and the desire, common to all men, to resist another's domination and have freedom to live the life of our choice. It seemed monstrous to me that a great country like India, with a rich and immemorial past, should be bound hand and foot to a faraway island which imposed its will upon her. It was still more monstrous that this forcible union had resulted in poverty and degradation beyond measure. That was reason enough for me and for others to act.

But it was not enough to satisfy the questioning that arose within me. What is this India, apart from her physical and geographical aspects? What did she represent in the past; what gave strength to her then? How did she lose that old strength, and has she lost it completely? Does she represent anything vital now, apart from being the home of a vast number of human beings? How does she fit in to the modern world?

## II. INDIA'S STRENGTH AND WEAKNESS

The search for the sources of India's strength and for her deterioration and decay is long and intricate. Yet the recent causes of that decay are obvious enough. She fell behind in the march of technique, and Europe, which had long been backward in many matters, took the lead in technical progress. Behind this technical progress was the spirit of science and a bubbling life and spirit which displayed itself in many activities and in adventurous voyages of discovery. New techniques gave military strength to the countries of western Europe and it was easy for them to spread out and dominate the East. That is the story not of India only but of almost the whole of Asia.

Why this should have happened so is more difficult to unravel, for India was not lacking in mental alertness and technical skill in earlier times. One senses a progressive deterioration during centuries. The urge to life and endeavor becomes less, the creative spirit fades away and gives place to the imitative. Where triumphant and rebellious thought had tried to pierce the mysteries of nature and the universe, the wordy commentator comes with his glosses and long explanations. Magnificent art and sculpture give way to a meticulous carving of intricate detail without nobility of conception or design. The vigor and richness of language, powerful yet simple, are followed by highly ornate and complex literary forms. The urge to adventure and the overflowing life which led to vast schemes of distant colonization and the transplantation of Indian culture in far lands, all these fade away and a narrow orthodoxy taboos even the crossing of the high seas. A rational spirit of inquiry, so evident in earlier times, which might well have led to the further growth of science, is replaced by irrationalism and a blind idolatry of the past. Indian life becomes a sluggish stream, living in the past, moving slowly through the accumulations of dead centuries. The heavy burden of the past crushes it and a kind of coma seizes it. It is not surprising that in this condition of mental stupor and physical weariness India should have deteriorated and remained rigid and immobile while other parts of the world marched ahead.

Yet this is not a complete or wholly correct survey. If there had only been a long and unrelieved period of rigidity and stagnation, this might well have resulted in a complete break with the past, the death of an era, and the erection of something new on its ruins. There has not been such a break and there is a definite continuity. Also from time to time vivid flashes of renascence have occurred, and some of them have been long and brilliant. Always there is visible an attempt to understand and adapt the new and harmonize it with the old, or at any rate with parts of the old which were considered worth preserving. Often that old retains an external form only, as a kind of symbol, and changes its inner content. But something vital and living continued, some urge driving the people in a direction not wholly realized, always a desire for synthesis between the old and the new. It was this urge and desire that kept them going and enabled them to absorb new ideas while retaining much of the old. Whether there was such a thing as an Indian dream through the ages, vivid and full of life or sometimes reduced to the murmurings of troubled sleep, I do not know. Every people and every nation has some such belief or myth of national destiny, and perhaps it is partly true in each case. Being an Indian, I am myself influenced by this reality or myth about India, and I feel that anything that had the power to mold hundreds of generations, without a break, must have drawn its enduring vitality from some deep well of strength, and have had the capacity to renew that vitality from age to age.

Was there some such well of strength? And if so, did it dry up, or did it have hidden springs to replenish it? What of today? Are there any springs still functioning from which we can refresh and strengthen ourselves? We are an old race, or rather an odd mixture of many races, and our racial memories go back to the dawn of history. Have we had our day and are we now living in the later afternoon or evening of our existence, just carrying on after the manner of the aged, quiescent, devitalized, uncreative, desiring peace and sleep above all else?

No people, no race continues unchanged. Continually it is mixing with others and slowly changing; it may appear to die almost and then rise again as a new people or just a variation of the old. There may be a definite break between the old people and the new, or vital links of thought and ideals may join them.

Behind the past quarter of a century's struggle for India's independence, and all our conflicts with British authority, lay in my mind and that of many others the desire to revitalize India. We felt that through action and self-imposed suffering and sacrifice, through voluntarily facing risk and danger, through refusal to submit to what we considered evil and wrong, we would recharge the battery of India's spirit and waken her from her long slumber. Though we came into conflict continually with the British government in India, our eyes were always turned toward our own people. Political advantage had value only in so far as it helped in that fundamental purpose of ours. Because of this governing motive, frequently we acted as no politician moving in the narrow sphere of politics, only, would have done, and foreign and Indian critics expressed surprise at the folly and intransigence of our ways. Whether we were foolish or not the historians of the future will judge. We aimed high and looked far. Probably we were often foolish, from the point of view of opportunist politics, but at no time did we forget that our main purpose was to raise the whole level of the Indian people, psychologically and spiritually and also, of course, politically and economically. It was the building up of that real inner strength of the people that we were after, knowing that the rest would inevitably follow. We had to wipe out the evil aftermath from some generations of shameful subservience and timid submission to an arrogant alien authority.

## III. THE SEARCH FOR INDIA

Though books and old monuments and past cultural achievements helped to produce some understanding of India, they did not satisfy me or give me the answer I was looking for. Nor could they, for they dealt with a past age, and I wanted to know if there was any real connection between that past and the present. The present for me, and for many others like me, was an odd mixture of medievalism, appalling poverty and misery, and a somewhat superficial modernism of the middle classes. I was not an admirer of my own class or kind, and yet inevitably I looked to it for leadership in the struggle for India's salvation. That middle class felt caged and circumscribed and wanted to grow and develop itself. Unable to do so within the framework of British rule, a spirit of revolt grew against this rule, and yet this spirit was not directed against the structure that crushed us. It sought to retain it and control it by displacing the British. These middle classes were too much the product of that structure to challenge it and seek to uproot it.

New forces arose that drove us to the masses in the villages, and for the first time, a new and different India rose up before the young intellectuals who had almost forgotten its existence, or attached little importance to it. It was a disturbing sight, not only because of its stark misery and the magnitude of its problems, but because it began to upset some of our values and conclusions. So began for us the discovery of India as it was, and it produced both understanding and conflict within us. Our reactions varied and depended on our previous environment and experience. Some were already sufficiently acquainted with these village masses not to experience any new sensation; they took them for granted. But for me it was a real voyage of discovery, and while I was always painfully conscious of the failings and weaknesses of my people, I found in India's countryfolk something, difficult to define, which attracted me. That something I had missed in our middle classes.

I do not idealize the conception of the masses, and as far as possible I try to avoid thinking of them as a theoretical abstraction. The people of India are very real to me in their great variety, and in spite of their vast numbers I try to think of them as individuals rather than as vague groups. Perhaps it was because I did not expect much from them that I was not disappointed; I found more than I had expected. It struck me that perhaps the reason for this, and for a certain stability and potential strength that they possessed, was the old Indian cultural tradition which was still retained by them in a small measure. Much had gone in the battering they had received during the past two hundred years. Yet something remained that was worth while, and with it so much that was worthless and evil.

During the twenties my work was largely confined to my own provinces and I traveled extensively and intensively through the towns and villages of the forty-eight districts of the United Provinces of Agra and Oudh, that heart of Hindustan as it has so long been considered, the seat and center of both ancient and medieval civilization, the melting pot of so many races and cultures, the area where the great revolt of 1857 blazed up and was later ruthlessly crushed. I grew to know the sturdy Jat of the northern and western districts, that typical son of the soil, brave and independent-looking, relatively more prosperous; the Rajput peasant and petty landholder, still proud of his race and ancestry, even though he might have changed his faith and adopted Islam; the deft and skillful artisans and cottage workers, both Hindu and Moslem; the poorer peasantry and tenants in their vast numbers, especially in Oudh and the eastern districts, crushed and ground down by generations of oppression and poverty, hardly daring to hope that a change would come to better their lot, and yet hoping and full of faith.

During the thirties, in the intervals of my life out of prison, and especially during the election campaign of 1936–37, I traveled more extensively throughout India, in towns and cities and villages alike. Except for rural Bengal, which unhappily I have only rarely visited, I toured in every province and went deep into villages. I spoke of political and economic issues, and judging from my speech I was full of politics and elections. But all this while, in a corner of my mind, lay something deeper and more vivid, and elections meant little to it, or the other excitements of the passing day. Another and a major excitement had seized me, and I was again on a great voyage of discovery and the land of India and the people of India lay spread out before me. India with all her infinite charm and variety began to grow upon me more and more, and yet the more I saw of her, the more I realized how very difficult it was for me or for anyone else to grasp the ideas she had embodied. It was not her wide spaces that eluded me, or even her diversity, but some depth of soul which I could not fathom, though I had occasional and tantalizing glimpses of it. She was like some ancient palimpsest on which layer upon layer of thought and revery had been inscribed, and yet no succeeding layer had completely hidden or erased what had been written previously. All of these existed together in our conscious or subconscious selves, though we might not be aware of them, and they had gone to build up the complex and mysterious personality of India. That sphinxlike face with its elusive and sometimes mocking smile was to be seen throughout the length and breadth of the land. Though outwardly there was diversity and infinite variety among our people, everywhere there was that tremendous impress of oneness, which had held all of us together for ages past, whatever political fate or misfortune had befallen us. The unity of India was no longer merely an intellectual conception for me: it was an emotional experience which overpowered me. That essential unity had been so powerful that no political division, no disaster or catastrophe had been able to overcome it.

It was absurd, of course, to think of India or any country as a kind of anthropomorphic entity. I did not do so. I was also fully aware of the diversities and divisions of Indian life, of classes, castes, religions, races, different degrees of cultural development. Yet I think that a country with a long cultural background and a common outlook on life develops a spirit that is peculiar to it and that is impressed on all its children, however much they may differ among themselves. Can anyone fail to see this in China, whether he meets an old-fashioned mandarin or a Communist who has apparently broken with the past? It was this spirit of India that I was after, not through idle curiosity, though I was curious enough, but because I felt that it might give me some key to the understanding of my country and people, some guidance to thought and action. Politics and elections were day-to-day affairs when we grew excited over trumpery matters. But if we were going to build the house of India's future, strong and secure and beautiful, we would have to dig deep for the foundations.

## IV. BHARAT MATA

Often as I wandered from meeting to meeting I spoke to my audience of this India of ours, of Hindustan and of Bharata, the old Sanskrit name derived from the mythical founder of the race. I seldom did so in the cities, for there the audiences were more sophisticated and wanted stronger fare. But to the peasant, with his limited outlook, I spoke of this great country for whose freedom we were struggling, of how each part differed from the other and yet was India, of common problems of the peasants from north to south and east to west, of the *Swaraj*, the self-rule that could only be for all and every part and not for some. I told them of my journeying from the Khyber Pass in the far northwest to Kanya Kumari or Cape Comorin in the distant south, and how everywhere the peasants put me identical questions, for their troubles were the same—poverty, debt, vested interests, landlord, moneylender, heavy rents and taxes, police harassment, and all these wrapped up in the structure that the foreign government had imposed upon us—and relief must also come for all. I tried to make them think of India as a whole, and even to some little extent of this wide world of which we were a part. I brought in the struggle in China, in Spain, in Abyssinia, in central Europe, in Egypt and the countries of western Asia. I told them of the wonderful changes in the Soviet Union and of the great progress made in America. The task was not easy; yet it was not so difficult as I had imagined, for our ancient epics and myth and legend, which they knew so well, had made them familiar with the conception of their country, and some there were always who had traveled far and wide to the great places of pilgrimage situated at the four corners of India. Or there were old soldiers who had served in foreign parts in World War I or other expeditions. Even my references to foreign countries were brought home to them by the consequences of the great depression of the thirties.

Sometimes as I reached a gathering, a great roar of welcome would greet me: *Bharat Mata ki Jai*—Victory to Mother India! I would ask them unexpectedly what they meant by that cry, who was this *Bharat Mata*, Mother India, whose victory they wanted? My question would amuse them and surprise them, and then, not knowing exactly what to answer, they would look at each other and at me. I persisted in my questioning. At last a vigorous Jat, wedded to the soil from immemorial generations, would say that it was the *dharti*, the good earth of India, that they meant. What earth? Their particular village patch, or all the patches in the district or province, or in the whole of India? And so question and answer went on, till they would ask me impatiently to tell them all about it. I would endeavor to do so and explain that India was all this that they had thought, but it was much more. The mountains and the rivers of India, and the forests and the broad fields, which gave us food, were all dear to us, but what counted ultimately were the people of India, people like them and me, who were spread out all over this vast land. *Bharat Mata*, Mother India, was essentially these millions of people, and victory to her meant victory to these people. You are parts of this *Bharat Mata*, I told them, you are in a manner yourselves *Bharat Mata*, and as this idea slowly soaked into their brains, their eyes would light up as if they had made a great discovery.

## V. THE VARIETY AND UNITY OF INDIA

The diversity of India is tremendous; it is obvious; it lies on the surface and anybody can see it. It concerns itself with physical appearances as well as with certain mental habits and traits. There is little in common, to outward seeming, between the Pathan of the northwest and the Tamil in the far south. Their racial stocks are not the same, though there may be common strands running through them; they differ in face and figure, food and clothing, and, of course, language. In the North-Western Frontier Province there is already the breath of central Asia, and many a custom there, as in Kashmir, reminds one of the countries on the other side of the Himalayas. Pathan popular dances are singularly like Russian Cossack dancing. Yet with all these differences, there is no mistaking the impress of India on the Pathan, as this is obvious on the Tamil. It is not surprising, for these border lands, and indeed Afghanistan also, were united with India for thousands of years. The old Turkish and other races who inhabited Afghanistan and parts of central Asia before the advent of Islam were largely Buddhists, and earlier still, during the period of the Epics, Hindus. The frontier area was one of the principal centers of old Indian culture, and it abounds still with ruins of monuments and monasteries and especially of the great university of Taxila, which was at the height of its fame two thousand years ago, attracting students from all over India as well as different parts of Asia. Changes of religion made a difference but could not change entirely the mental backgrounds which the people of those areas had developed.

The Pathan and the Tamil are two extreme examples; the others lie somewhere in between. All of them have their distinctive features, all of them have still more the distinguishing mark of India. It is fascinating to find how the Bengalese, the Marathas, the Gujratis, the Tamils, the Andhras, the Oriyas, the Assamese, the Canarese, the Malayalis, the Sindhis, the Punjabis, the Pathans, the Kashmiris, the Rajputs, and the great central bloc comprising the Hindustani-speaking people, have retained their peculiar characteristics for hundreds of years, have still more or less the same virtues and failings of which old tradition or record tells us, and yet have been throughout these ages distinctively Indian, with the same national heritage and the same set of moral and mental qualities. There was something living and dynamic about this heritage which showed itself in ways of living and a philosophical attitude to life and its problems. Ancient India, like ancient China, was a world in itself, a culture and a civilization which gave shape to all things. Foreign influences poured in and often influenced that culture and were absorbed. Disruptive tendencies gave rise immediately to an attempt to find a synthesis. Some kind of a dream of unity has occupied the mind of India since the dawn of civilization. That unity was not conceived as something imposed from outside, a standardization of externals or even of beliefs. It was something deeper, and within its fold the widest tolerance of belief and custom was practiced and every variety acknowledged and even encouraged.

Differences, big or small, can always be noticed even within a national group, however closely bound together it may be. The essential unity of that group becomes apparent when it is compared to another national group, though often the differences between two adjoining groups fade out or intermingle near the frontiers, and modern developments are tending to produce a certain uniformity everywhere. In ancient and medieval times the idea of the modern nation was nonexistent, and feudal, religious, racial or cultural bonds had more importance. Yet I think that at almost any time in recorded history an Indian would have felt more or less at home in any part of India, and would have felt as a stranger and alien in any other country. He would certainly have felt less of a stranger in countries which had partly adopted his culture or religion. Those who professed a religion of non-Indian origin and coming to India settled down there, became distinctively Indian in the course of a few generations, such as Christians, Jews, Parsees, Moslems. Indian converts to some of these religions never ceased to be Indians in spite of a change of faith. All these were looked upon in other countries as Indians and foreigners, even though there might have been a community of faith between them.

Today, when the conception of nationalism has developed much more, Indians in foreign countries inevitably form a national group and hang together for various purposes, in spite of their internal differences. An Indian Christian is looked upon as an Indian wherever he may go. An Indian Moslem is considered an Indian in Turkey or Arabia or Iran or any other country where Islam is the dominant religion.

All of us, I suppose, have varying pictures of our native land and no two persons will think exactly alike. When I think of India, I think of many things: of broad fields dotted with innumerable small villages; of towns and cities I have visited; of the magic of the rainy season which pours life into the dry, parched-up land and converts it suddenly into a glistening expanse of beauty and greenery, of great rivers and flowing water; of the Khyber Pass in all its bleak surroundings; of the southern tip of India; of people, individually and in the mass; and above all, of the Himalayas, snow-capped, or some mountain valley in Kashmir in the spring, covered with new flowers, and with a brook bubbling and gurgling through it. We make and preserve the pictures of our choice, and so I have chosen this mountain background rather than the more normal picture of a hot, subtropical country. Both pictures would be correct, for India stretches from the tropics right up to the temperate regions, from near the equator to the cold heart of Asia.

# III. The Discovery of India

## I. THE INDUS VALLEY CIVILIZATION

The Indus Valley civilization, of which impressive remains have been discovered at Mohenjo-daro in Sind and at Harappa in the western Punjab, is the earliest picture that we have of India's past. These excavations have revolutionized the conception of ancient history. Unfortunately, a few years after this work of excavation began in these areas, it was stopped, and for the last thirteen years or so nothing significant has been done. The stoppage was initially due to the great depression of the early thirties. Lack of funds was pleaded, although there was never any lack for the display of imperial pomp and splendor. The coming of World War II effectively stopped all activity, and even the work of preservation of all that has been dug out has been rather neglected. Twice I have visited Mohenjo-daro, in 1931 and in 1936. During my second visit I found that the rain and the dry sandy air had already injured many of the buildings that had been dug out. After being preserved for over five thousand years under a covering of sand and soil, they were rapidly disintegrating owing to exposure, and very little was being done to preserve these priceless relics of ancient times. The officer of the archaeological department in charge of the place complained that he was allowed practically no funds or other help or material to enable him to keep the excavated buildings as they were. What has happened during these last eight years I do not know, but I imagine that the wearing away has continued and within another few years many of the characteristic features of Mohenjo-daro will have disappeared.

That is a tragedy for which there is no excuse, and something that can never be replaced will have gone, leaving only pictures and written descriptions to remind us of what it was.

Mohenjo-daro and Harappa are far apart. It was sheer chance that led to the discovery of these ruins in these two places. There can be little doubt that there lie many such buried cities and other remains of the handiwork of ancient man in between these two areas; that, in fact, this civilization was widespread over large parts of India, certainly of north India. A time may come when this work of uncovering the distant past of India is again taken in hand and far-reaching discoveries are made. Already remains of this civilization have been found as far apart as Kathiawar in the west and the Ambala district of the Punjab, and there is reason for believing that it spread to the Gangetic valley. Thus it was something much more than an Indus Valley civilization. The inscriptions found at Mohenjo-daro have so far not been fully deciphered.

But what we know, even thus far, is of the utmost significance. The Indus Valley civilization, as we find it, was highly developed and must have taken thousands of years to reach that stage. It was, surprisingly enough, a predominantly secular civilization, and the religious element, though present, did not dominate the scene. It was clearly also the precursor of later cultural periods in India.

Sir John Marshall tells us: "One thing that stands out clear and unmistakable both at Mohenjo-daro and Harappa is that the civilization hitherto revealed at these two places is not an incipient civilization, but one already age-old and stereotyped on Indian soil, with many millennia of human endeavor behind it. Thus India must henceforth be recognized, along with Persia, Mesopotamia, and Egypt as one of the most important areas where the civilizing processes were initiated and developed." And again he says that "the Punjab and Sind, if not other parts of India as well, were enjoying an advanced and singularly uniform civilization of their own, closely alien but in some respects even superior, to that of contemporary Mesopotamia and Egypt."

These people of the Indus Valley had many contacts with the Sumerian civilization of that period, and there is even some evidence of an Indian colony, probably of merchants, at Akkad. "Manufactures from the Indus cities reached even the markets on the Tigris and Euphrates. Conversely, a few Sumerian devices in art, Mesopotamia toilet sets and a cylinder seal were copied on the Indus. Trade was not confined to raw materials and luxury articles; fish, regularly imported from the Arabian Sea coasts, augmented the food-supplies of Mohenjo-daro."[1]

Cotton was used for textiles even at that remote period in India. Marshall compares and contrasts the Indus Valley civilization with those of contemporary Egypt and Mesopotamia: "Thus, to mention only a few salient points, the use of cotton for textiles was exclusively restricted at this period to India and was not extended to the western world until 2000 or 3000 years later. Again, there is nothing that we know of in pre-historic Egypt or Mesopotamia or anywhere else in western Asia to compare with the well-built baths and commodious houses of the citizens of Mohenjo-daro. In those countries, much money and thought were lavished on the building of magnificent temples for the gods and on the palaces and tombs of kings, but the rest of the people seemingly had to content themselves with insignificant dwellings of mud. In the Indus Valley the picture is reversed, and the finest structures are those erected for the convenience of the citizens." These public and private baths, as well as the excellent drainage system we find at Mohenjo-daro, are the first of their kind yet discovered anywhere. There are also two-storied private houses, made of baked bricks, with bathrooms and a porter's lodge, as well as tenements.

Yet another quotation from Marshall, the acknowledged authority on the Indus Valley civilization, who was himself responsible for the excavations. He says that "equally peculiar to the Indus Valley and stamped with an indi-

[1] Gordon Childe, *What Happened in History* (Pelican Books, 1943), p. 112.

vidual character of their own are its art and its religion. Nothing that we know of in other countries at this period bears any resemblance, in point of style, to the faience models of rams, dogs, and other animals or to the intaglio engravings on the seals, the best of which—notably the humped and short-horn bulls—are distinguished by a breadth of treatment and a feeling for line and plastic form that have rarely been surpassed in glyptic art; nor would it be possible, until the classic age of Greece, to match the exquisitely supple modelling of the two human statuettes from Harappa. . . . In the religion of the Indus people there is much, of course, that might be paralleled in other countries. This is true of every pre-historic and most historic religions as well. But, taken as a whole, their religion is so characteristically Indian as hardly to be distinguished from still living Hinduism."

We find thus this Indus Valley civilization connected and trading with its sister civilizations of Persia, Mesopotamia, and Egypt, and superior to them in some ways. It was an urban civilization where the merchant class was wealthy and evidently played an important role. The streets, lined with stalls and what were probably small shops, give the impression of an Indian bazaar of today. Professor Childe says: "It would seem to follow that the craftsmen of the Indus cities were, to a large extent, producing 'for the market.' What, if any, form of currency and standard of value had been accepted by society to facilitate the exchange of commodities is, however, uncertain. Magazines attached to many spacious and commodious private houses mark their owners as merchants. Their number and size indicate a strong and prosperous merchant community. . . . A surprising wealth of ornaments of gold, silver, precious stones and faience, of vessels of beaten copper and of metal implements and weapons, has been collected from the ruins." Childe adds that "well-planned streets and a magnificent system of drains, regularly cleared out, reflect the vigilance of some regular municipal government. Its authority was strong enough to secure the observance of town-planning bye-laws and the maintenance

of approved lines for streets and lanes over several recon-
structions rendered necessary by floods."[2]

Between this Indus Valley civilization and today in India there are many gaps and periods about which we know
little. The links joining one period to another are not always evident, and a very great deal has of course happened and innumerable changes have taken place. But
there is always an underlying sense of continuity, of an
unbroken chain which joins modern India to the far distant
period of six or seven thousand years ago when the Indus
Valley civilization probably began. It is surprising how
much there is in Mohenjo-daro and Harappa which reminds one of persisting traditions and habits—popular ritual, craftsmanship, even some fashions in dress. Much of
this influenced western Asia.

It is interesting to note that at this dawn of India's story,
she does not appear as a puling infant, but already grown
up in many ways. She is not oblivious of life's ways, lost in
dreams of a vague and unrealizable supernatural world, but
has made considerable technical progress in the arts and
amenities of life, creating not only things of beauty, but
also the utilitarian and more typical emblems of modern
civilization—good baths and drainage systems.

## II. THE COMING OF THE ARYANS

Who were these people of the Indus Valley civilization
and whence had they come? We do not know yet. It is
quite possible, and even probable, that their culture was
an indigenous culture and its roots and offshoots may be
found even in southern India. Some scholars find an essential similarity between these people and the Dravidian
races and culture of south India. Even if there was some
ancient migration to India, this could only have taken place
some thousands of years before the date assigned to
Mohenjo-daro. For all practical purposes we can treat
them as the indigenous inhabitants of India.

[2] Gordon Childe, *What Happened in History*, pp. 113, 114.

What happened to the Indus Valley civilization and how did it end? Some people (among them Gordon Childe) say that there was a sudden end to it due to an unexplained catastrophe. The river Indus is well-known for its mighty floods which overwhelm and wash away cities and villages. Or a changing climate might lead to a progressive desiccation of the land and the encroachment of the desert over cultivated areas. The ruins of Mohenjo-daro are themselves evidence of layer upon layer of sand being deposited, raising the ground level of the city and compelling the inhabitants to build higher on the old foundations. Some excavated houses have the appearance of two- or three-storied structures, and yet they represent a periodic raising of the walls to keep pace with the rising level. The province of Sind, we know, was rich and fertile in ancient times, but from medieval times onward it has been largely desert.

It is probable therefore that these climatic changes had a marked effect on the people of those areas and their ways of living. But that effect could only have been gradual and not catastrophic. And in any event climatic changes must have affected only a relatively small part of the area of this widespread urban civilization, which, as we have now reason to believe, spread right up to the Gangetic valley, and possibly even beyond. We have really no sufficient data to judge. Sand, which probably overwhelmed and covered some of these ancient cities, also preserved them; while other cities and evidences of the old civilization gradually decayed and went to pieces in the course of ages. Perhaps future archaeological discoveries might disclose more links with later ages.

While there is a definite sense of continuity between the Indus Valley civilization and later periods, there is also a kind of break or a gap, not only in point of time but also in the kind of civilization that came next. This latter was probably more agricultural to begin with, though towns existed and there was some kind of city life also. This emphasis on the agricultural aspect may have been given to it by the newcomers, the Aryans who poured into India in successive waves from the northwest.

The Aryan migrations are supposed to have taken place about a thousand years after the Indus Valley period; and yet it is possible that there was no considerable gap and tribes and peoples came to India from the northwest from time to time, as they did in later ages, and became absorbed in India. We might say that the first great cultural synthesis and fusion took place between the incoming Aryans and the Dravidians, who were probably the representatives of the Indus Valley civilization. Out of this synthesis and fusion grew the Indian races and the basic Indian culture, which had distinctive elements of both. In the ages that followed there came many other races: Iranians, Greeks, Parthians, Bactrians, Scythians, Huns, Turkis or Turks (before Islam), early Christians, Jews, Zoroastrians; they came, made a difference, and were absorbed. India was, according to Dodwell, "infinitely absorbent like the ocean." It is odd to think of India with her caste system and exclusiveness having this astonishing inclusive capacity to absorb foreign races and cultures. Perhaps it was due to this that she retained her vitality and rejuvenated herself from time to time. The Moslems, when they came, were also powerfully affected by her. "The foreigners (Muslim Turks)," says Vincent Smith, "like their fore-runners the Sakas and the Yueh-chi, universally yielded to the wonderful assimilative power of Hinduism, and rapidly became Hinduised."

## III. THE EARLIEST RECORDS
### SCRIPTURE AND MYTHOLOGY

Before the discovery of the Indus Valley civilization, the Vedas were supposed to be the earliest records we possess of Indian culture. There was much dispute about the chronology of the Vedic period, European scholars usually giving later dates and Indian scholars much earlier ones. It was curious, this desire on the part of Indians to go as far back as possible and thus enhance the importance of our ancient culture. Professor Winternitz thinks that the beginnings of Vedic literature go back to 2000 B.C. or even 2500 B.C. This brings us very near the Mohenjo-daro period.

The usual date accepted by most scholars today for the hymns of the *Rig Veda* is 1500 B.C., but there is a tendency, ever since the Mohenjo-daro excavations, to date further back these early Indian scriptures. Whatever the exact date may be, it is probable that this literature is earlier than that of either Greece or Israel; that, in fact, it represents some of the earliest documents of the human mind that we possess. Max Müller has called it: "the first word spoken by the Aryan man."

The Vedas were the outpourings of the Aryans as they streamed into the rich land of India. They brought their ideas with them from that common stock out of which grew the Avesta in Iran, and elaborated them in the soil of India. Even the language of the Vedas bears a striking resemblance to that of the Avesta, and it has been remarked that the Avesta is nearer the Veda than the Veda is to its own epic Sanskrit.

How are we to consider the scripture of various religions, much of it believed by its votaries to be revealed scripture? To analyze it and criticize it and look upon it as a human document is often to offend the true believers. Yet there is no other way to consider it.

I have always hesitated to read books of religion. The totalitarian claims made on their behalf did not appeal to me. The outward evidences of the practice of religion that I saw did not encourage me to go to the original sources. Yet I had to drift to these books, for ignorance of them was not a virtue and was often a severe drawback. I knew that some of them had powerfully influenced humanity, and anything that could have done so must have some inherent power and virtue in it, some vital source of energy. I found great difficulty in reading through many parts of them, for try as I would, I could not rouse up sufficient interest; but the sheer beauty of some passages would hold me. And then a phrase or a sentence would suddenly leap up and electrify me and make me feel the presence of the really great. Some words of the Buddha or of Christ would shine out with deep meaning and seem to me applicable as much today as when they were uttered two thousand or more years ago. There was a compelling reality about them, a permanence which time and space could not touch. So I felt sometimes when I read about Socrates or the Chinese philosophers, and also when I read the Upanishads and the *Bhagavad Gita*. I was not interested in the metaphysics, or the description of ritual, or the many other things which apparently had no relation to the problems that faced me. Perhaps I did not understand the inner significance of much that I read, and sometimes indeed a second reading threw more light. I made no real effort to understand mysterious passages, and I passed by those which had no particular significance for me. Nor was I interested in long commentaries and glossaries. I could not approach these books, or any books, as Holy Writ which must be accepted in their totality without challenge or demur. Indeed this approach of Holy Writ usually resulted in my mind's being closed to what they contained. I was much more friendly and open to them when I could consider them as having been written by human beings, very wise and far-seeing, but nevertheless ordinary mortals, and not incarnations or mouthpieces of a divinity about whom I had no knowledge or surety whatever.

It has always seemed to me a much more magnificent and impressive thing that a human being should rise to great heights, mentally and spiritually, and should then seek to raise others up, than that he should be the mouthpiece of a divine or superior power. Some of the founders of religions were astonishing individuals, but all their glory vanishes in my eyes when I cease to think of them as human beings. What impresses me and gives me hope is the growth of the mind and spirit of man, and not his being used as an agent to convey a message.

Mythology affected me in much the same way. If people believed in the factual contents of these stories, the whole thing was absurd and ridiculous. But as soon as one ceased believing in them, they appeared in a new light, a new beauty, a wonderful flowering of a richly endowed imagination, full of human lessons. No one believes now in the

stories of Greek gods and goddesses, and so, without any
difficulty, we can admire them and they become part of
our mental heritage. But if we had to believe in them,
what a burden it would be, and how, oppressed by this
weight of belief, we would often miss their beauty! Indian
mythology is richer, vaster, very beautiful and full of meaning. I have often wondered what manner of men and
women they were who gave shape to these bright dreams
and lovely fancies, and from what gold mine of thought
and imagination they dug them out.

Looking at scripture then as a product of the human
mind, we have to remember the age in which it was written, the environment and mental climate in which it grew,
the vast distance in time and thought and experience that
separates it from us. We have to forget the trappings of
ritual and religious usage in which it was wrapped, and remember the social background in which it expanded. Many
of the problems of human life have a permanence and a
touch of eternity about them, and hence the abiding interest in these ancient books. But there were other problems also, strictly limited to that particular age, which have
no living interest for us now.

## IV. THE VEDAS

Many Hindus look upon the Vedas as revealed scripture.
This seems to me to be peculiarly unfortunate, for thus we
miss their real significance—the unfolding of the human
mind in the earliest stages of thought. And what a wonderful mind it was! The Vedas (from the root *vid*, to know)
were simply meant to be a collection of the existing knowledge of the day; they are a jumble of many things: hymns,
prayers, ritual for sacrifice, magic, magnificent nature poetry. There is no idolatry in them; no temples for the gods.
The vitality and affirmation of life pervading them are extraordinary. The early Vedic Aryans were so full of the zest
for life that they paid little attention to the soul. In a

vague way they believed in some kind of existence after death.

Gradually the conception of God grows: there are the Olympian type of gods, and then monotheism, and later, rather mixed with it, the conception of monism. Thought carries them to strange realms, and brooding on nature's mystery comes, and the spirit of inquiry. These developments take place in the course of hundreds of years, and by the time we reach the end of the Veda, the Vedanta (*Veda* plus *anta*, end), we have the philosophy of the Upanishads.

The *Rig Veda*, the first of the Vedas, is probably the earliest book that humanity possesses. In it we can find the first outpourings of the human mind, the glow of poetry, the rapture at nature's loveliness and mystery. And in these early hymns there are, as Dr. Macnicol says, the beginnings of "the brave adventures, made so long ago and recorded here, of those who seek to discover the significance of our world and of man's life within it. . . . India here set out on a quest which she has never ceased to follow."

Yet behind the *Rig Veda* itself lay ages of civilized existence and thought, during which the Indus Valley and the Mesopotamian and other civilizations had grown. It is appropriate, therefore, that there should be this dedication in the *Rig Veda*: "To the Seers, our Ancestors, the First Path-Finders!"

These Vedic hymns have been described by Rabindranath Tagore "as a poetic testament of a people's collective reaction to the wonder and awe of existence. A people of vigorous and unsophisticated imagination awakened at the very dawn of civilization to a sense of the inexhaustible mystery that is implicit in life. It was a simple faith of theirs that attributed divinity to every element and force of Nature, but it was a brave and joyous one, in which the sense of mystery only gave enchantment to life, without weighing it down with bafflement—the faith of a race unburdened with intellectual brooding on the conflicting diversity of the objective universe, though now and again illumined by intuitive experience as: 'Truth is one: [though] the wise call it by various names.'"

But that brooding spirit crept in gradually till the author of the Veda cried out: "O Faith, endow us with belief," and raised deeper questions in a hymn called "The Song of Creation," to which Max Müller gave the title "To the Unknown God":

1. Then there was not non-existent nor existent: there was no realm of air, no sky beyond it.
   What covered in, and where? and what gave shelter? was water there, unfathomed depth of water?

2. Death was not then, nor was there aught immortal: no sign was there, the day's and night's divider.
   That one thing, breathless, breathed by its own nature: apart from it was nothing whatsoever.

3. Darkness there was: at first concealed in darkness, this All was undiscriminated chaos.
   All that existed then was void and formless; by the great power of warmth was born that unit.

4. Thereafter rose desire in the beginning, Desire the primal seed and germ of spirit.
   Sages who searched with their heart's thought discovered the existent's kinship in the non-existent.

5. Transversely was their severing line extended: what was above it then, and what below it?
   There were begetters, there were mighty forces, free action here and energy of yonder.

6. Who verily knows and who can here declare it, whence it was born and whence comes this creation?
   The gods are later than this world's production. Who knows, then, whence it first came into being?

7. He, the first origin of this creation, whether he formed it all or did not form it,
   Whose eye controls this world in highest heaven, he verily knows it, or perhaps he knows it not.[3]

[3] This translation has been taken from *Hindu Scriptures*, Everyman's Library.

## V. THE ACCEPTANCE AND THE NEGATION
## OF LIFE

From these dim beginnings of long ago flow out the rivers of Indian thought and philosophy, of Indian life and culture and literature, ever widening and increasing in volume, and sometimes flooding the land with their rich deposits. During this enormous span of years they changed their courses sometimes, and even appeared to shrivel up, yet they preserved their essential identity. They could not have done so if they had not possessed a sound instinct for life. That staying power need not necessarily be a virtue; it may well mean, as I think it has meant in India for a long time past, stagnation and decay. But it is a major fact to be reckoned with, especially in these days when we seem to be witnessing an undermining, in repeated wars and crises, of a proud and advanced civilization. Out of this crucible of war, wherein so much is melting, we hope that something finer will emerge for the West as well as the East, something that will retain all the great achievements of humanity and add to them what they lacked. But this repeated and widespread destruction not only of material resources and human lives but of essential values that have given meaning to life is significant. Was it that in spite of astonishing progress in numerous directions and the higher standards, undreamed of in previous ages, that came in its train, our modern highly industrialized civilization did not possess some essential ingredient, and the seeds of self-destruction lay within it?

As a man grows to maturity he is not entirely engrossed in or satisfied with the external objective world. He seeks also some inner meaning, some psychological and psychical satisfactions. So also with peoples and civilizations as they mature and grow adult. Every civilization and every people exhibit these parallel streams of an external life and an internal life. Where they meet or keep close to each other, there is an equilibrium and stability. When they diverge, conflict arises, and the crises that torture the mind and spirit.

We see from the period of the *Rig Veda* hymns onward the development of both these streams of life and thought. The early ones are full of the external world, of the beauty and mystery of nature, of joy in life and an overflowing vitality. The gods and goddesses, like those of Olympus, are very human; they are supposed to come down and mix with men and women; there is no hard and fast line dividing the two. Then thought comes and the spirit of inquiry, and the mystery of a transcendental world deepens. Life still continues in abundant measure but there is also a turning away from its outward manifestations, and a spirit of detachment grows as the eyes are turned to things invisible, which cannot be seen or heard or felt in the ordinary way. What is the object of it all? Is there a purpose in the universe? And if so, how can man's life be put in harmony with it? Can we bring about a harmonious relation between the visible and invisible worlds, and thus find out the right conduct of life?

So we find in India, as elsewhere, these two streams of thought and action—the acceptance of life and the abstention from it—developing side by side, with the emphasis on the one or the other varying in different periods. Yet the basic background of that culture was not one of other-worldliness or world-worthlessness. Even when, in philosophical language, it discussed the world as *maya*, or what is popularly believed to be illusion, that very conception was not an absolute one but relative to what was thought of as ultimate reality (something like Plato's shadow of reality), and it took the world as it is and tried to live its life and enjoy its manifold beauty. Probably Semitic culture, as exemplified in many religions that emerged from it, and certainly early Christianity, was far more otherworldly. T. E. Lawrence says that "the common base of all Semitic creeds, winners or losers, was the ever present idea of world-worthlessness." And this often led to an alternation of self-indulgence and self-denial.

In India we find during every period when her civilization bloomed an intense joy in life and nature, a pleasure in the act of living, the development of art and music and literature and song and dancing and painting and the theater, and even a highly sophisticated inquiry into the sex relation. It is inconceivable that a culture or view of life based on otherworldliness or world-worthlessness could have produced all these manifestations of vigorous and varied life. Indeed it should be obvious that any culture that was basically otherworldly could not have carried on for thousands of years.

Yet some people have thought that Indian thought and culture represent essentially the principle of life negation and not of life affirmation. Both principles are, I suppose, present in varying degrees in all the old religions and cultures. But I should have thought that Indian culture, taken as a whole, never emphasized the negation of life, though some of its philosophies did so; it seems to have done so much less than Christianity. Buddhism and Jainism rather emphasized the abstention from life, and in certain periods of Indian history there was a running away from life on a big scale, as, for instance, when large numbers of people joined the Buddhist viharas or monasteries. What the reason for this was I do not know. Instances equally or more significant can be found during the Middle Ages in Europe, when a widespread belief existed that the world was coming to an end. Perhaps the ideas of renunciation and life-negation are caused or emphasized by a feeling of frustration due to political and economic factors.

Buddhism, in spite of its theoretical approach, or rather approaches, for there are several, as a matter of fact avoids extremes; it is the doctrine of the golden mean, the Middle Path. Even the idea of nirvana was very far from being a kind of nothingness, as it is sometimes supposed to be; it was a positive condition, but because it was beyond the range of human thought, negative terms were used to describe it. If Buddhism, a typical product of Indian thought and culture, had merely been a doctrine of life negation or denial, it would surely have had some such effect on the hundreds of millions who profess it. Yet as a matter of fact the Buddhist countries are full of evidence to the contrary, and the Chinese people are an outstanding example of what affirmation of life can be.

The confusion seems to have arisen from the fact that Indian thought was always laying stress on the ultimate purpose of life. It could never forget the transcendent element in its make-up. And so, while affirming life to the full, it refused to become a victim and a slave of life. Indulge in right action with all your strength and energy, it said, but keep above it, and do not worry much about the results of such action. Thus it taught detachment in life and action, not abstention from them. This idea of detachment runs through Indian thought and philosophy, as it does through most other philosophies. It is another way of saying that a right balance and equilibrium should be kept between the visible and invisible worlds, for if there is too much attachment to action in the visible world, the other world is forgotten and fades away, and that action itself becomes without ultimate purpose.

There is an emphasis on truth, a dependence on it, a passion for it, in these early adventures of the Indian mind. Dogma or revelation are passed by as something for lesser minds who cannot rise above them. The approach was one of experiment based on personal experience. That experience, when it dealt with the invisible world, was, like all emotional and psychic experiences, different from the experience of the visible, external world. It seemed to go out of the three-dimensional world we know into some different and vaster realm, and was thus difficult to describe in terms of three dimensions. What that experience was, and whether it was a vision or realization of some aspect of truth and reality, or was merely a phantasm of the imagination, I do not know. Probably it was often self-delusion. What interests me more is the approach, which was not authoritarian or dogmatic but was an attempt to discover for one's self what lay behind the external aspect of life.

## VI. SYNTHESIS AND ADJUSTMENT
### THE BEGINNINGS OF THE CASTE SYSTEM

The coming of the Aryans into India raised new problems —racial and political. The conquered race, the Dravidians, had a long background of civilization behind them, but there is little doubt that the Aryans considered themselves vastly superior to them and a wide gulf separated the two. Then there were also some backward aboriginal tribes, nomads or forest dwellers. Out of this conflict and inter-action of races gradually rose the caste system, which, in the course of succeeding centuries, was going to affect Indian life so profoundly. Probably this was neither Aryan nor Dravidian. It was an attempt at the social organization of different races, a rationalization of the facts as they existed at the time. It brought degradation in its train afterward, and it is still a burden and a curse. But we can hardly judge it from subsequent standards or later developments. It was in keeping with the spirit of the times, and some such grading took place in most of the ancient civilizations, though apparently China was free from it. There was a fourfold division in that other branch of the Aryans, the Iranians, during the Sassanian period, but it did not petrify into caste. Many of these old civilizations, including that of Greece, were entirely dependent on mass slavery. There was no such mass or large-scale labor slavery in India, although there were relatively small numbers of domestic slaves. Plato in his *Republic* refers to a division similar to that of the four principal castes. Medieval Catholicism knew this division also.

Caste began with a hard and fast division between Aryans and non-Aryans, the latter again being divided into the Dravidian races and the aboriginal tribes. The Aryans, to begin with, formed one class, and there was hardly any specialization. The word *Arya* comes from a root word meaning to till, and the Aryans as a whole were agricul-turists and agriculture was considered a noble occupation.

The tiller of the soil functioned also as priest, soldier, or trader, and there was no privileged order of priests. The caste divisions, originally intended to separate the Aryans from the non-Aryans, reacted on the Aryans themselves, and as division of functions and specialization increased, the new classes took the form of castes.

Thus at a time when it was customary for the conquerors to exterminate or enslave the conquered races, caste enabled a more peaceful solution which fitted in with the growing specialization of functions. Life was graded and out of the mass of agriculturists evolved the *Vaishyas*, the agriculturists, artisans, and merchants; the *Kshatriyas*, or rulers and warriors; and the *Brahmans*, priests and thinkers who were supposed to guide policy and preserve and maintain the ideals of the nation. Below these three there were the *Shudras* or laborers and unskilled workers other than the agriculturists. Among the indigenous tribes many were gradually assimilated and given a place at the bottom of the social scale, that is among the Shudras. This process of assimilation was a continuous one. The castes must have been in a fluid condition; rigidity came in much later. Probably the ruling class had always great latitude, and any person who by conquest or otherwise assumed power, could, if he so willed, join the hierarchy as a Kshatriya and get the priests to manufacture an appropriate genealogy connecting him with some ancient Aryan hero.

The word *Arya* ceased to have any racial significance and came to mean "noble," just as *unarya* meant ignoble and was usually applied to nomadic tribes, forest dwellers, etc.

The Indian mind was extraordinarily analytical and had a passion for putting ideas and concepts, and even 'life's activities, into compartments. The Aryans not only divided society into four main groups but also divided the individual's life into four parts: the first part consisted of growth and adolescence, the student period of life, acquiring knowledge, developing self-discipline and self-control, continence; the second was that of the householder and man of the world; the third was that of the elder statesman, who had attained a certain poise and objectivity, and could devote himself to public work without the selfish desire to profit by it; and the last stage was that of the recluse, who lived a life largely cut off from the world's activities. In this way also they adjusted the two opposing tendencies which often exist side by side in man—the acceptance of life in its fullness and the rejection of it.

In India, as in China, learning and erudition have always stood high in public esteem, for learning was supposed to imply both superior knowledge and virtue. Before the learned man, the ruler and the warrior have always bowed. The old Indian theory was that those who were concerned with the exercise of power could not be completely objective. Their personal interests and inclinations would come into conflict with their public duties. Hence the task of determining values and the preservation of ethical standards was allotted to a class or group of thinkers who were freed from material cares and were as far as possible without obligations, so that they could consider life's problems in a spirit of detachment. This class of thinkers or philosophers was thus supposed to be at the top of the social structure, honored and respected by all. The men of action, the rulers and warriors, came after them, and however powerful they might be, did not command the same respect. The possession of wealth was still less entitled to honor and respect. The warrior class, though not at the top, held a high position, and was not, as in China, looked upon with contempt.

This was the theory, and to some extent it may be found elsewhere, as in Christendom in medieval Europe, when the Roman church assumed the functions of leadership in all spiritual, ethical, and moral matters, and even in the general principles underlying the conduct of the state. In practice Rome became intensely interested in temporal power, and the princes of the church were rulers in their own right. In India the Brahman class, in addition to supplying the thinkers and the philosophers, became a powerful and entrenched priesthood, intent on preserving its vested interests. Yet this theory, in varying degrees, has influenced Indian life profoundly, and the ideal has continued to be of a man full of learning and charity, essentially good, self-disciplined, and capable of sacrificing himself for the sake of others. The Brahman class has shown all the vices of a privileged and entrenched class in the past, and large numbers of them have possessed neither learning nor virtue. Yet they have largely retained the esteem of the public, not because of temporal power or possession of money, but because they have produced a remarkable succession of men of intelligence and their record of public service and personal sacrifice for the public good has been a notable one. The whole class profited by the example of its leading personalities in every age, and yet the public esteem went to the qualities rather than to any official status. The tradition was one of respecting learning and goodness in any individual who possessed them. There are innumerable examples of non-Brahmans, and even persons belonging to the depressed classes, being so respected and sometimes considered saints. Official status and military power never commanded the same measure of respect, though it may have been feared.

Even today, in this money age, the influence of this tradition is marked, and because of it Gandhi (who is not a Brahman) can become the supreme leader of India and move the hearts of millions without force or compulsion or official position or possession of money. Perhaps this is as good a test as any of a nation's cultural background and its conscious or subconscious objective: to what kind of a leader does it give its allegiance?

The central idea of old Indian civilization, or Indo-Aryan culture, was that of *dharma*, which was something much more than religion or creed. It was a conception of obligations, of the discharge of one's duties to one's self and to others. This dharma itself was part of *rita*, the fundamental moral law governing the functioning of the universe and all it contained. If there was such an order, then man was supposed to fit into it and he should function in such a way as to remain in harmony with it. If man did his duty and was ethically right in his action, the right consequences would inevitably follow. Rights as such were not emphasized. That, to some extent, was the old outlook everywhere. It stands out in marked contrast with the modern assertion of rights, rights of individuals, of groups, of nations.

## VII. THE CONTINUITY OF INDIAN CULTURE

Thus in these very early days we find the beginnings of the civilization and culture which were to flower so abundantly and richly in subsequent ages, and which have continued, in spite of many changes, to our own day. The basic ideals, the governing concepts are taking shape, and literature and philosophy, art and drama, and all other activities of life were conditioned by these ideals and world-view. Also we see the seeds of that exclusiveness and touch-me-notism which were to grow and grow till they became rigid, octopus-like, with their grip on everything—the caste system of recent times. Fashioned for a particular day, intended to stabilize the then organization of society and give it strength and equilibrium, it developed into a prison for that social order and for the mind of man. Security was purchased in the long run at the cost of ultimate progress.

Yet it was a very long run, and even within that framework the vital original impetus for advancement in all directions was so great that it spread out all over India and over the eastern seas, and its stability was such that it survived repeated shock and invasion. Professor Macdonell in his *History of Sanskrit Literature* tells us that "the importance of Indian literature as a whole consists in its originality. When the Greeks towards the end of the 4th century B.C. invaded the north-west, the Indians had already worked out a national culture of their own, unaffected by foreign influences. And in spite of successive waves of invasion and conquest by Persians, Greeks, Scythians, Muhammadans, the national development of the life and literature of the Indo-Aryan race remained practically unchecked and unmodified from without down to the era of British occupation. No other branch of the Indo-European stock has experienced an isolated evolution like this. No other country except China can trace back its language and literature, its religious beliefs and rites, its dramatic and social customs through an uninterrupted development of more than three thousand years."

Still India was not isolated, and throughout this long period of history she had continuous and living contacts with Iranians and Greeks and Chinese and central Asians and others. If her basic culture survived these contacts, there must have been something in that culture itself which gave it the dynamic strength to do so, some inner vitality and understanding of life. For this three or four thousand years of cultural growth and continuity is remarkable. Max Müller, the famous scholar and Orientalist, emphasizes this: "There is, in fact, an unbroken continuity between the most modern and the most ancient phases of Hindu thought, extending over more than three thousand years." Carried away by his enthusiasm, he said (in his lectures delivered before the University of Cambridge, England, in 1882): "If we were to look over the whole world to find out the country most richly endowed with all the wealth, power and beauty that nature can bestow—in some parts a very paradise on earth—I should point to India. If I were asked under what sky the human mind has most fully developed some of its choicest gifts, has most deeply pondered over the greatest problems of life, and has found solutions of some of them which well deserve the attention even of those who have studied Plato and Kant—I should point to India. And if I were to ask myself from what literature, we here in Europe, we who have been nurtured almost exclusively on the thoughts of Greeks and Romans, and of one Semitic race, the Jewish, may draw the corrective which is most wanted in order to make our inner life more perfect, more comprehensive, more universal, in fact more truly human a life, not for this life only, but a transfigured and eternal life—again I should point to India."

## VIII. THE UPANISHADS

The Upanishads, dating from about 800 B.C., take us a step further in the development of Indo-Aryan thought, and it is a big step. The Aryans have long been settled down, and a stable, prosperous civilization has grown up, a mixture of the old and the new, dominated by Aryan thought and ideals, but with a background of more primitive forms of worship. The Vedas are referred to with respect but also in a spirit of gentle irony. The Vedic gods no longer satisfy, and the ritual of the priests is made fun of. But there is no attempt to break with the past; that is taken as a starting point for further progress.

The Upanishads are instinct with a spirit of inquiry, of mental adventure, of a passion for finding out the truth about things. The search for this truth is of course not by the objective methods of modern science, yet there is an element of the scientific method in that approach. No dogma is allowed to come in the way. There is much that is trivial and without any meaning or relevance for us today. The emphasis is essentially on self-realization, on knowledge of the individual self and the Absolute Self, both of which are said to be the same in essence. The objective external world is not considered unreal but real in a relative sense, an aspect of the inner reality.

There are many ambiguities in the Upanishads, and different interpretations have been made. But that is a matter for the philosopher or scholar. The general tendency is toward monism, and the whole approach is evidently intended to lessen the differences that must have existed then, leading to fierce debate. It is the way of synthesis. Interest in magic and suchlike supernatural knowledge is sternly discouraged, and ritual and ceremonies without enlightenment are said to be vain—"those engaged in them, considering themselves men of understanding and learned, stagger along aimlessly like blind men led by the blind, and fail to reach the goal." Even the Vedas are treated as the lower knowledge; the higher one being that of the inner mind. There is a warning given against philosophical learning without discipline of conduct. And there is a continuous attempt to harmonize social activity with spiritual adventure. The duties and obligations imposed by life were to be carried out, but in a spirit of detachment.

Probably the ethic of individual perfection was overemphasized and hence the social outlook suffered. "There is nothing higher than the person," say the Upanishads. Society must have been considered stabilized, and hence the mind of man was continually thinking of individual perfection, and in quest of this it wandered about in the heavens and in the innermost recesses of the heart. This old Indian approach was not a narrow nationalistic one, though there must have been a feeling that India was the hub of the world, just as China and Greece and Rome have felt at various times. "The whole world of mortals is an interdependent organism," says the *Mahabharata*.

The dominating characteristic of the Upanishads is the dependence on truth. "Truth wins ever, not falsehood. With truth is paved the road to the Divine." And the famous invocation is for light and understanding: "Lead me from the unreal to the real! Lead me from darkness to light! Lead me from death to immortality."

Again and again the restless mind peeps out, ever seeking, ever questioning: "At whose behest doth mind light on its perch? At whose command doth life, the first, proceed? At whose behest do men send forth this speech? What god, indeed, directed eye and ear?" And again: "Why cannot the wind remain still? Why has the human mind no rest? Why, and in search of what, does the water run out and cannot stop its flow even for a moment?" It is the adventure of man that is continually calling and there is no resting on the way and no end of the journey. In the *Aitereya Brahmana* there is a hymn about this long, endless journey which we must undertake, and every verse ends with the refrain: *Charaiveti, charaiveti*—"Hence, O Traveler, march along, march along!"

There is no humility about all this quest, the humility before an all-powerful deity, so often associated with religion. It is the triumph of mind over the environment. "My body will be reduced to ashes and my breath will join the restless and deathless air, but not I and my deeds. O Mind, remember this always, remember this." In a morning prayer the sun is addressed thus: "O Sun of refulgent glory, I am the same Person as makes thee what thou art!" What superb confidence!

What is the soul? It cannot be described or defined except negatively: "It is not this, not this." Or, in a way, positively: "That thou art!" The individual soul is like a spark thrown out and reabsorbed by the blazing fire of the Absolute Soul. "As fire, though one, entering the world, takes a separate form according to whatever it burns, so does the inner Self within all things become different, according to whatever it enters, yet itself is without form." This realization that all things have that same essence removes the barriers which separate us from them and produces a sense of unity with humanity and nature, a unity which underlies the diversity and manifoldness of the external world. "Who knoweth all things are Self; for him what grief existeth, what delusion, when [once] he gazeth on the oneness?" "Aye, who so seeth all things in that Self, and Self in everything; from That he'll no more hide."

It is interesting to compare and contrast the intense individualism and exclusiveness of the Indo-Aryans with this all-embracing approach, which overrides all barriers of caste and class and every other external and internal difference. This latter is a kind of metaphysical democracy. "He who sees the One Spirit in all, and all in the One Spirit, henceforth can look with contempt on no creature." Though this was theory only, there can be no doubt that it must have affected life and produced that atmosphere of tolerance and reasonableness, that acceptance of free thought in matters of faith, that desire and capacity to live and let live, which are dominant features of Indian culture, as they are of the Chinese. There was no totalitarianism in religion or culture, and they indicate an old and wise civilization with inexhaustible mental reserves.

There is a question in the Upanishads to which a very curious and yet significant answer is given. "The question is: 'What is this universe? From what does it arise? Into what does it go?' And the answer is: 'In freedom it rises, in freedom it rests, and into freedom it melts away.'" What exactly this means I am unable to understand, except that the authors of the Upanishads were passionately attached to the idea of freedom and wanted to see everything in terms of it. Swami Vivekananda was always emphasizing this aspect.

It is not easy for us, even imaginatively, to transplant ourselves to this distant period and enter the mental climate of that day. The form of writing itself is something that we are unused to, odd-looking, difficult to translate, and the background of life is utterly different. We take for granted so many things today because we are used to them, although they are curious and unreasonable enough. But what we are not used to at all is much more difficult to appreciate or understand. In spite of all these difficulties and almost insuperable barriers, the message of the Upanishads has found willing and eager listeners throughout Indian history and has powerfully molded the national mind and character. "There is no important form of Hindu thought, heterodox Buddhism included, which is not rooted in the Upanishads," says Bloomfield.

### IX. THE ADVANTAGES AND DISADVANTAGES OF AN INDIVIDUALISTIC PHILOSOPHY

There is, in the Upanishads, a continual emphasis on the fitness of the body and clarity of the mind, on the discipline of both body and mind, before effective progress can be made. The acquisition of knowledge, or any achievement, requires restraint, self-suffering, self-sacrifice. This idea of some kind of penance, *tapasya*, is inherent in Indian thought, both among the thinkers at the top and the unread masses below. It is present today as it was present some thousands of years ago, and it is necessary to appreciate it in order to understand the psychology underlying the mass movements which have convulsed India under Gandhiji's leadership.

It is obvious that the ideas of the authors of the Upanishads, the rarefied mental atmosphere in which they moved, were confined to a small body of the elect who were capable of understanding them. They were entirely beyond the comprehension of the vast mass of the people. A creative minority is always small in numbers, but if it is in tune with the majority, and is always trying to pull the latter up and make it advance, so that the gap between the two is lessened, a stable and progressive culture results. Without that creative minority a civilization must inevitably decay. But it may also decay if the bond between a creative minority and the majority is broken and there is a loss of social unity in society as a whole, and ultimately that minority itself loses its creativeness and becomes barren and sterile. Or else it gives place to another creative or vital force which society throws up.

It is difficult for me, as for most others, to visualize the period of the Upanishads and to analyze the various forces that were at play. I imagine, however, that in spite of the vast mental and cultural difference between the small thinking minority and the unthinking masses, there was a bond between them or, at any rate, there was no obvious gulf. The graded society in which they lived had its mental gradations also, and these were accepted and provided for. This led to some kind of social harmony, and conflicts were avoided. Even the new thought of the Upanishads was interpreted for popular purposes so as to fit in with popular prejudices and superstitions, thereby losing much of its essential meaning. The graded social structure was not touched; it was preserved. The conception of monism became transformed into one of monotheism for religious purposes, and even lower forms of belief and worship were not only tolerated but encouraged, as suited to a particular stage of development.

Thus the ideology of the Upanishads did not permeate to any marked extent to the masses, and the intellectual separation between the creative minority and the majority became more marked. In course of time this led to new movements—a powerful wave of materialistic philosophy, agnosticism, atheism. Out of this again grew Buddhism and Jainism, and the famous Sanskrit epics, the *Ramayana* and the *Mahabharata*, wherein yet another attempt was made to bring about a synthesis between rival creeds and ways of thought. The creative energy of the people, or of the creative minority, is very evident during these periods, and again there appears to be a bond between that minority and the majority. On the whole they pull together.

In this way period succeeds period with bursts of creative effort in the fields of thought and action, in literature and the drama, in sculpture and architecture, and in cultural, missionary, and colonial enterprises far from India's borders. In between, there are periods of disharmony and conflict, due both to inner causes and intrusions from outside. Yet they are ultimately overcome and a fresh period of creative energy supervenes. The last great period of such activity in a variety of directions was the classical epoch which began in the fourth century after Christ. By about 1000 A.D. or earlier, signs of inner decay in India are very evident, although the old artistic impulse continued to function and produce fine work. The coming of new races with a different background brought a new driving force to India's tired mind and spirit, and out of that impact arose new problems and new attempts at solution.

It seems that the intense individualism of the Indo-Aryans led, in the long run, to both the good and the evil that their culture produced. It led to the production of very superior types, not in one particular limited period of history, but again and again, age after age. It gave a certain idealist and ethical background to the whole culture, which persisted and still persists, though it may not influence practice much. With the help of this background and by sheer force of example at the top, they held together the social fabric and repeatedly rehabilitated it when it threatened to go to pieces. They produced an astonishing flowering of civilization and culture which, though largely confined to the upper circles, inevitably spread to some extent to the masses. By their extreme tolerance of other beliefs and other ways than their own, they avoided the conflicts that have so often torn society asunder, and managed to maintain, as a rule, some kind of equilibrium. By allowing, within the larger framework, considerable freedom to people to live the life of their choice, they showed the wisdom of an old and experienced race. All these were very remarkable achievements.

But that very individualism led them to attach little importance to the social aspect of man, of man's duty to society. For each person life was divided and fixed up, a bundle of duties and responsibilities within his narrow sphere in the graded hierarchy. He had no duty to, or conception of, society as a whole, and no attempt was made to make him feel his solidarity with it. This idea is perhaps largely a modern development and cannot be found in any ancient society. It is unreasonable, therefore, to expect it in ancient India. Still the emphasis on individualism, or exclusiveness, on graded castes is much more evident in India. In later ages it was to grow into a very prison for the mind of our people—not only for the lower castes, who suffered most from it, but for the higher ones also. Throughout our history it was a weakening factor, and one might perhaps say that along with the growth of rigidity in the caste system grew rigidity of mind, and the creative energy of the race faded away.

Another curious fact seems to stand out. The extreme tolerance of every kind of belief and practice, every superstition and folly, had its injurious side also, for this perpetuated many an evil custom and prevented people from getting rid of the traditional burdens that prevented growth. The growing priesthood exploited this situation to their own advantage and built up their powerful vested interests on the foundation of the superstitions of the masses. That priesthood was probably never quite so powerful as in some branches of the Christian church, for there were always spiritual leaders who condemned its practices, and there was a variety of beliefs to choose from; but it was strong enough to hold and exploit the masses.

So this mixture of free thought and orthodoxy lived side by side, and out of them scholasticism grew, and a puritanical ritualism. The appeal was always made to the ancient authorities, but little attempt was made to interpret their truths in terms of changing conditions. The creative and spiritual forces weakened, and only the shell of what used to be so full of life and meaning remained. Aurobindo Ghose has written: "If an ancient Indian of the time of the Upanishad, of the Buddha, or the later classical age were to be set down in modern India . . . he would see his race clinging to forms and shells and rags of the past and missing nine-tenths of its nobler meaning . . . he would be amazed by the extent of the mental poverty, the immobility, the static repetition, the cessation of science, the long sterility of art, the comparative feebleness of the creative intuition."

*Mr. Nehru continues the discussion of the varieties and complexities of Indian philosophical thought. He then comments on the probable development of the two great epics of ancient India—the* Ramayana *and the* Mahabharata. *This leads him to a discussion of the* Bhagavad Gita, *which is a part of the* Mahabharata.

## X. THE BHAGAVAD GITA

The *Bhagavad Gita* is part of the *Mahabharata*, an episode in the vast drama. But it stands apart and is complete in itself. It is a relatively small poem of seven hundred verses —"the most beautiful, perhaps the only true philosophical song existing in any known tongue," so Wilhelm von Humboldt described it. Its popularity and influence have not waned ever since it was composed and written in the pre-Buddhistic age, and today its appeal is as strong as ever in India. Every school of thought and philosophy looks up to it and interprets it in its own way. In times of crisis, when the mind of man is tortured by doubt and is torn by the conflict of duties, it has turned all the more to the Gita for light and guidance. For it is a poem of crisis, of political and social crisis, and even more so of crisis in the spirit of man. Innumerable commentaries on the Gita have appeared in the past, and they continue to come out with unfailing regularity. Even the leaders of thought and action of the present day—Tilak, Aurobindo Ghose, Gandhi—have written on it, each giving his own interpretation. Gandhiji bases his firm belief in nonviolence on it; others justify violence and warfare for a righteous cause.

The poem begins with a conversation between Arjuna and Krishna on the very field of battle before the great war begins. Arjuna is troubled, his conscience revolts at the thought of the war and the mass murder that it involves, the killing of friends and relatives—for what purpose? What conceivable gain can outweigh this loss, this sin? All his old standards fail him, his values collapse. Arjuna becomes the symbol of the tortured spirit of man, which from age to age has been torn by conflicting obligations and moralities. From this personal conversation we are taken step by step to higher and more impersonal regions of individual duty and social behavior, of the application of ethics to human life, of the spiritual outlook that should govern all. There is much that is metaphysical in it, and an attempt to reconcile and harmonize the three ways for human advancement: the path of the intellect or knowledge, the path of action, and the path of faith. Probably more emphasis is laid on faith than on the others, and even a personal God emerges, though he is considered as a manifestation of the Absolute. The Gita deals essentially with the spiritual background of human existence, and it is in this context that the practical problems of everyday life appear. It is a call to action to meet the obligations and duties of life, but always keeping in view that spiritual background and the larger purpose of the universe. Inaction is condemned, and action and life have to be in accordance with the highest ideals of the age, for these ideals themselves may vary from age to age. The *yugadharma*, the ideal of the particular age, has always to be kept in view.

Because modern India is full of frustration and has suffered from too much quietism, this call to action makes a special appeal. It is also possible to interpret that action in modern terms as action for social betterment and social service, practical, altruistic, patriotic, and humanitarian.

Such action is desirable, according to the Gita, but behind it must lie the spiritual ideal. And action must be in a spirit of detachment, not much concerned with its results. Right action must necessarily yield right results, though these might not be immediately apparent, for the law of cause and effect holds good under all circumstances.

The message of the Gita is not sectarian or addressed to any particular school of thought. It is universal in its approach for everyone, Brahman or outcaste: "All paths lead to Me," it says. It is because of this universality that it has found favor with all classes and schools. There is something in it which seems to be capable of being constantly renewed and not to become out of date with the passing of time—an inner quality of earnest inquiry and search, of contemplation and action, of balance and equilibrium in spite of conflict and contradiction. There is a poise in it and a unity in the midst of disparity, and its temper is one of supremacy over the changing environment, not by seeking escape from it but fitting in with it. During the two thousand five hundred years since it was written, Indian humanity went repeatedly through the processes of change and development and decay; experience succeeded experience, thought followed thought, but it always found something living in the Gita, something that fitted into the developing thought and had a freshness and applicability to the spiritual problems that afflict the mind.

## XI. LIFE AND WORK IN ANCIENT INDIA

A great deal has been done by scholars and philosophers to trace the development of philosophic and metaphysical thought in the India of the past; much has also been done to fix the chronology of historic events and draw in broad outline political maps of those periods. But not much has so far been done to investigate the social and economic conditions of those days, how people lived, carried on their work, what they produced and how, and the way trade functioned. Greater attention is being paid to these vital questions now, and some works by Indian scholars, and one by an American, have appeared. But a great deal remains to be done. The *Mahabharata* itself is a storehouse of sociological and other data, and many other books will no doubt yield useful information. But they have to be critically examined from this particular point of view. One book of inestimable value is Kautilya's *Arthashastra* of the fourth century B.C., which gives details of the political, social, economic, and military organization of the Maurya empire.

An earlier account, which definitely takes us back to the pre-Buddhist period in India, is contained in the collection of the Jataka tales. These Jatakas were given their present shape sometime after the Buddha. They are supposed to deal with the previous incarnations of the Buddha and have become an important part of Buddhist literature. But the stories are evidently much older, and they deal with the pre-Buddhistic period and give us much valuable information about life in India in those days. Professor Rhys Davids has described them as the oldest, most complete and most important collection of folklore extant. Many of the subsequent collections of animal and other stories which were written in India and found their way to western Asia and Europe can be traced to the Jatakas.

The Jatakas deal with the period when the final amalgamation of the two principal races of India, the Dravidians and the Aryans, was taking place. They reveal "a multiform and chaotic society which resists more or less every attempt at classification and about which there can be no talk of an organization according to caste in that age."[4] The Jatakas may be said to represent the popular tradition as contrasted with the priestly or Brahmanic tradition and the Kshatriya or ruling class tradition.

There are chronologies and genealogies of various kingdoms and their rulers. Kingship, originally elective, becomes hereditary, according to the rule of primogeniture.

---

[4] Richard Fick, *The Social Organization in North-East India in Buddha's Time* (Calcutta, 1920), p. 286. A more recent book, chiefly based on the Jataka stories, is Ratilal Mehta's *Pre-Buddhist India* (Bombay, 1939). I am indebted to this latter book for most of my facts.

Women are excluded from this succession, but there are exceptions. As in China, the ruler is held responsible for all misfortunes; if anything goes wrong the fault must lie with the king. There was a council of ministers, and there are also references to some kind of state assembly. Nevertheless the king was an autocratic monarch, though he had to function within established conventions. The high priest had an important position in court as an adviser and person in charge of religious ceremonies. There are references to popular revolts against unjust and tyrannical kings, who are sometimes put to death for their crimes.

Village assemblies enjoyed a measure of autonomy. The chief source of revenue was from the land. The land tax was supposed to represent the king's share of the produce, and it was usually, but not always, paid in kind. Probably this tax was about one-sixth of the produce. It was predominantly an agricultural civilization, and the basic unit was the self-governing village. The political and economic structure was built up from these village communities which were grouped in tens and hundreds. Horticulture, rearing of livestock, and dairy farming were practiced on an extensive scale. Gardens and parks were common, and fruits and flowers were valued. The list of flowers mentioned is a long one; among the favorite fruits were the mango, fig, grape, plantain, and the date. There were evidently many shops of vegetable and fruit sellers in the cities, as well as of florists. The flower garland was then, as now, a favorite of the Indian people.

Hunting was a regular occupation chiefly for the food it provided. Flesh-eating was common and included poultry and fish; venison was highly esteemed. There were fisheries and slaughterhouses. The principal articles of diet were, however, rice, wheat, millet, and corn. Sugar was extracted from sugar cane. Milk and its various products were then, as they are now, highly prized. There were liquor shops, and liquor was apparently made from rice, fruits, and sugar cane.

There was mining for metals and precious stones. Among the metals mentioned are: gold, silver, copper, iron, lead, tin, and brass. Among the precious stones were diamonds, rubies, corals; also pearls. Gold, silver, and copper coins are referred to. There were partnerships for trade, and loans were advanced on interest.

Among the manufactured goods are silks, woolens, and cotton textiles; rugs, blankets, and carpets. Spinning, weaving, and dyeing were flourishing and widespread industries. The metallurgical industry produced weapons of war. The building industry used stone, wood, and bricks. Carpenters made a variety of furniture, etc., including carts, chariots, ships, bedsteads, chairs, benches, chests, toys, etc. Cane workers made mattresses, baskets, fans, and sunshades. Potters functioned in every village. From flowers and sandalwood a number of perfumes, oils and "beauty" products were made, including sandalwood powder. Various medicines and drugs were manufactured and dead bodies were sometimes embalmed.

Apart from the many kinds of artisans and craftsmen who are mentioned, various other professions are referred to: teachers, physicians and surgeons, merchants and traders, musicians, astrologers, greengrocers, actors, dancers, itinerant jugglers, acrobats, puppet players, peddlers.

Domestic slavery appears to have been fairly common, but agricultural and other work was done with the help of hired labor. There were even then some untouchables—the chandalas, as they were called, whose chief business was the disposal of dead bodies.

Trade associations and craft guilds had already assumed importance. "The existence of trade associations," says Fick, "which grew partly for economical reasons, better employment of capital, facilities of intercourse, partly for protecting the legal interest of their class, is surely to be traced to an early period of Indian culture." The Jatakas say that there were eighteen craft unions, but they actually mention only four: the woodworkers and the masons, the smiths, the leatherworkers, and the painters.

Even in the Epics there are references to trade and craft organizations. The *Mahabharata* says: "The safeguard of corporations [guilds] is union." It is said that "the merchant-guilds were of such authority that the king was not allowed to establish any laws repugnant to these trade unions. The heads of guilds are mentioned next after priests as objects of a king's anxious concern."[5] The chief of the merchants, the *shreshthi* (modern seth) was a man of very considerable importance.

One rather extraordinary development emerges from the Jataka accounts. This is the establishment of special settlements or villages of people belonging to particular crafts. Thus there was a carpenters' village, consisting, it is said, of a thousand families, a smiths' village, and so on. These specialized villages were usually situated near a city, which absorbed their special products and which provided them with the other necessaries of life. The whole village apparently worked on co-operative lines and undertook large orders. Probably out of this separate living and organization the caste system developed and spread out. The example set by the Brahmans and the nobility was gradually followed by the manufacturers' corporations and trade guilds.

Great roads, with travelers' rest houses and occasional hospitals, covered north India and connected distant parts of the country. Trade flourished not only in the country itself but between India and foreign countries. There was a colony of Indian merchants living at Memphis in Egypt about the fifth century B.C. as the discovery of modeled heads of Indians there has shown. Probably there was trade also between India and the islands of southeast Asia. Overseas trade involved shipping, and it is clear that ships were built in India both for the inland waterways and ocean traffic. There are references in the Epics to shipping duties being paid by "merchants coming from afar."

The Jatakas are full of references to merchants' voyages. There were overland caravans across deserts going westward to the seaport of Broach and north toward Gandhara and central Asia. From Broach ships went to the Persian Gulf for Babylon (Baveru). There was a great deal of river traffic, and according to the Jatakas, ships traveled from Benares, Patna, Champa (Bhagalpur), and other places to the sea and thence to southern ports and Ceylon and Ma-

[5] Prof. E. Washburn Hopkins in *Cambridge History of India*, Vol. I, p. 269.

laya. Old Tamil poems tell us of the flourishing port of Kaveri-pattinam on the Kaveri River in the south, which was a center of international trade. These ships must have been fairly large, as it is said in the Jatakas that "hundreds" of merchants and emigrants embarked on a ship.

In the "Milinda" (this is of the first century A.D.; Milinda is the Greek Bactrian king of north India who became an ardent Buddhist) it is said: "As a shipowner who has become wealthy by constantly levying freight in some seaport town, will be able to traverse the high seas, and go to Vanga (Bengal) or Takkola, or China or Sovira, or Surat or Alexandria, or the Koromandel coast, or Further India, or any other place where ships do congregate."[6]

Among the exports from India were: "Silks, muslins, the finer sorts of cloth, cutlery and armour, brocades, embroideries and rugs, perfumes and drugs, ivory and ivory work, jewelry and gold (seldom silver):—these were the main articles in which the merchant dealt."[7]

India, or rather north India, was famous for her weapons of war, especially for the quality of her steel, her swords and daggers. In the fifth century B.C. a large body of Indian troops, cavalry and infantry, accompanied the Persian army to Greece. When Alexander invaded Persia, it is stated in the famous Persian epic poem Firdausi's *Shah Namah* that swords and other weapons were hurriedly sent for by the Persians from India. The old (pre-Islamic) Arabic word for sword is *muhannad* which means "from Hind," or Indian. This word is in common use still.

Ancient India appears to have made considerable progress in the treatment of iron. There is an enormous Iron Pillar near Delhi which has baffled modern scientists, who have been unable to discover by what process it was made, which has enabled it to withstand oxidization and other atmospheric changes. The inscription on it is in the Gupta script which was in use from the fourth to the seventh century A.D. Some scholars are, however, of opinion that

[6] Quoted by Mrs. C. A. F. Rhys Davids in *Cambridge History of India*, Vol. I, p. 212.

[7] Rhys Davids, *Buddhist India*, p. 98.

the pillar itself is much older than this inscription, which was added later.

Writing in India goes back to the most ancient times. Old pottery belonging to the Neolithic period is inscribed with writing in the Brahmi characters. Mohenjo-daro has inscriptions which have not so far been wholly deciphered. The Brahmi inscriptions found all over India are undoubtedly the basic script from which Devanagari and others have arisen in India. Some of Ashoka's inscriptions are in the Brahmi script; others, in the northwest, are in the Kharoshti script.

As early as the sixth or seventh century B.C., Panini wrote his great grammar of the Sanskrit language.[8] He mentions previous grammars, and already in his time Sanskrit had crystallized and become the language of an ever-growing literature. Panini's book is something more than a mere grammar. It has been described by the Soviet professor Th. Tscherbatsky of Leningrad as "one of the greatest productions of the human mind." Panini is still the standard authority on Sanskrit grammar, though subsequent grammarians have added to it and interpreted it. It is interesting to note that Panini mentions the Greek script. This indicates that there were contacts of some kind between India and the Greeks long before Alexander came to the East.

The study of astronomy was especially pursued, and it often merged into astrology. Medicine had its textbooks, and there were hospitals. Dhanwantari is the legendary founder of the Indian science of medicine. The best-known old textbooks, however, date from the early centuries of the Christian era. These are by Charak on medicine and Sushruta on surgery. Charak is supposed to have been the royal court physician of Kanishka, who had his capital in the northwest. These textbooks enumerate a large number of diseases and give methods of diagnosis and treatment. They deal with surgery, obstetrics, baths, diet, hygiene, infant-feeding, and medical education. There is an experi-

---

[8] Keith and some others place Panini at c. 300 B.C. But the balance of authority seems to be clear that Panini lived and wrote before the commencement of the Buddhist period.

mental approach, and dissection of dead bodies was practiced in the course of surgical training. Various surgical
instruments are mentioned by Sushruta, as well as operations, including amputation of limbs, abdominal, caesarian
section, cataract, etc. Wounds were sterilized by fumiga-
tion. In the third or fourth century B.C. there were also
hospitals for animals. This was probably due to the influence of Jainism and Buddhism with their emphasis on
nonviolence.

In mathematics the ancient Indians made some epoch-
making discoveries, notably that of the zero sign, of the
decimal place-value system, of the use of the minus sign,
and the use in algebra of letters of the alphabet to denote
unknown quantities. It is difficult to date these as there
was always a big time-lag between the discovery and its
practical application. But it is clear that the beginnings of
arithmetic, algebra, and geometry were laid in the earliest
period. Ten formed the basis of enumeration in India even
at the time of the *Rig Veda*. The time and number sense
of the ancient Indians was extraordinary. They had a long
series of number names for very high numerals. The
Greeks, Romans, Persians, and Arabs had apparently no
terminology for denominations above the thousand or at
most the myriad ($10^4 = 10000$). In India there were eighteen specific denominations ($10^{18}$), and there are even
longer lists. In the story of Buddha's early education he is
reported to have named denominations up to $10^{50}$.

At the other end of the scale there was a minute division
of time, of which the smallest unit was approximately one-
seventeenth of a second, and the smallest lineal measure
is given as something which approximates to $1.3 \times 7^{-10}$
inches. All these big and small figures were no doubt
entirely theoretical and used for philosophical purposes.
Nevertheless the old Indians, unlike other ancient nations,
had vast conceptions of time and space. They thought in
a big way. Even their mythology deals with ages of hundreds of millions of years. To them the vast periods of
modern geology or the astronomical distances of the stars
would not have come as a surprise. Because of this background in India, Darwin's and other similar theories could

not create here the turmoil and inner conflict which they produced in Europe in the middle of the nineteenth century. The popular mind in Europe was used to a time scale which did not go beyond a few thousand years.

In the *Arthashastra* we are given the weights and measures which were in use in north India in the fourth century B.C. There used to be careful supervision of the weights in the market places.

In the Epic period we have frequent mention of some kind of forest universities, situated not far from a town or city, where students gathered round well-known scholars for training and education, which comprised a variety of subjects, including military training. These forest abodes were preferred so as to avoid the distractions of city life and enable the students to lead a disciplined and continent life. After some years of this training they were supposed to go back and live as householders and citizens. Probably these forest schools consisted of small groups, though there are indications that a popular teacher would attract large numbers.

Benares has always been a center of learning, and even in Buddha's day it was old and known as such. It was in the Deer Park near Benares that Buddha preached his first sermon. But Benares does not appear to have been at any time anything like a university, such as existed, then and later, in other parts of India. There were numerous groups there consisting of a teacher and his disciples, and often between rival groups there was fierce debate and argument.

But in the northwest, near modern Peshawar, there was an ancient and famous university at Takshashila or Taxila. This was particularly noted for science, especially medicine, and the arts, and people went to it from distant parts of India. The Jataka stories are full of instances of sons of nobles and Brahmans traveling, unattended and unarmed, to Taxila to be educated. Probably students came also from central Asia and Afghanistan, as it was conveniently situated. It was considered an honor and a distinction to be a graduate of Taxila. Physicians who had studied in the school of medicine there were highly thought of, and it is related that whenever Buddha felt unwell, his admirers brought to him a famous physician who had graduated from Taxila. Panini, the great grammarian of the sixth or seventh century B.C., is said to have studied there.

Taxila was thus a pre-Buddhist university and a seat of Brahmanical learning. During the Buddhist period it became also a center of Buddhist scholarship and attracted Buddhist students from all over India and across the border. It was the headquarters of the northwestern province of the Maurya empire.

The legal position of women, according to Manu, the earliest exponent of the law, was definitely bad. They were always dependent on somebody—on the father, the husband, or the son. Almost they were treated in law as chattels. And yet from the numerous stories in the Epics, this law was not applied very rigidly and they held an honored place in the home and in society. The old lawgiver, Manu, himself says: "Where women are honored, the Gods dwell." There is no mention of women students at Taxila or any of the old universities. But some of them did function as students somewhere, for there is repeated mention of learned and scholarly women. In later ages also there were a number of eminent women scholars. Bad as the legal position of women was in ancient India, judged by modern standards, it was far better than in ancient Greece, Rome, early Christianity, the Canon Law of medieval Europe, and indeed till right up to comparatively modern times at the beginning of the nineteenth century.

The exponents of the law from Manu onward refer to forms of partnership in business. Manu refers chiefly to priests; Yagnavalkya includes trade and agriculture. A later writer, Narada, says: "Loss, expense, profit of each partner are equal to, more than, or less than those of other partners according as his share [invested] is equal, greater or less. Storage, food, charges [tolls], loss, freightage, expense of keeping, must be paid by each partner in accordance with the terms of agreement."

Manu's conception of a state was evidently that of a small kingdom. This conception was, however, growing and changing, leading to the vast Maurya empire of the fourth century B.C. and to international contacts with the Greek world.

Megasthenes, the Greek ambassador in India in the fourth century B.C., totally denies the existence of slavery in India. But in this he was wrong, as there were certainly domestic slaves and there are references in Indian books of the period to improving the lot of the slaves. It is clear, however, that there were no large-scale slavery and no slave gangs for labor purposes, as were common in many countries then, and this may have led Megasthenes to believe that slavery was completely absent. It was laid down that "Never shall an Arya be subjected to slavery." Who exactly was an Arya and who was not, it is difficult to say, but the Aryan fold at that time had come to mean rather vaguely all the four basic castes, including the shudras but not the untouchables.

## XII. MAHAVIRA AND BUDDHA. CASTE

Some such background existed in north India from the time of the Epics onward to the early Buddhist period. It was ever changing politically and economically, and the processes of synthesis and amalgamation, as well as the specialization of labor, were taking place. In the realm of ideas there was continuous growth and often conflict. The early Upanishads had been followed by the development of thought and activity in many directions; they were themselves a reaction against priestcraft and ritualism. Men's minds had rebelled against much that they saw, and out of that rebellion had grown these early Upanishads as well as, a little later, the strong current of materialism, and Jainism and Buddhism, and the attempt to synthesize various forms of belief in the *Bhagavad Gita*. Out of all this again grew the six systems of Indian philosophy. Yet behind all this mental conflict and rebellion lay a vivid and growing national life.

Both Jainism and Buddhism were breakaways from the Vedic religion and its offshoots, though in a sense they had grown out of it. They deny the authority of the Vedas, and, most fundamental of all matters, they deny or say nothing about the existence of a first cause. Both lay emphasis on nonviolence and build up organizations of celibate monks and priests. There is a certain realism and rationalism in their approach, though inevitably this does not carry one very far in dealings with the invisible world. One of the fundamental doctrines of Jainism is that truth is relative to our standpoints. It is a rigorous ethical and nontranscendental system laying a special emphasis on the ascetic aspect of life and thought.

Mahavira, the founder of Jainism, and Buddha were contemporaries, and both came from the Kshatriya warrior class. Buddha died at the age of eighty in 544 B.C., and the Buddhist era begins then. (This is the traditional date. Historians give a later date, 487 B.C. But now they are inclined to accept the traditional date as more correct.) It is an odd coincidence that I am writing this on the Buddhist New Year's Day 2488—the day of the full moon of the month of Vaisakha—the *Vaisakhi Purnima*, as it is called. It is stated in Buddhist literature that Buddha was born on this full moon day of Vaisakha (May-June), that he attained enlightenment and finally died also on the same day of the year.

Buddha had the courage to attack popular religion, superstition, ceremonial, and priestcrafts, and all the vested interests that clung to them. He condemned also the metaphysical and theological outlook, miracles, revelations, and dealings with the supernatural. His appeal was to logic, reason, and experience; his emphasis was on ethics, and his method was one of psychological analysis, a psychology without a soul. His whole approach comes like the breath of the fresh wind from the mountains after the stale air of metaphysical speculation.

Buddha did not attack caste directly, yet in his own order he did not recognize it, and there is no doubt that his whole attitude and activity weakened the caste system. Probably caste was very fluid in his day and for some centuries later. It is obvious that a caste-ridden community could not indulge in foreign trade or other foreign adventures, and yet for fifteen hundred years or more after Buddha, trade was developing between India and neighboring countries, and Indian colonies flourished. Foreign elements continued to stream into India from the northwest and were absorbed.

It is interesting to observe this process of absorption which worked at both ends. New castes were formed at the bottom of the scale, and any successful invading element became transformed soon into Kshatriyas, the ruling class. Coins of the period just before and after the beginning of the Christian era show this rapid change in the course of two or three generations. The first ruler has a foreign name. His son or grandson appears with a Sanskrit name and is crowned according to the traditional rites meant for Kshatriyas.

Many of the Rajput Kshatriya clans date back to the Shaka, or Scythian invasions which began about the second century B.C.; or from the later invasion of the White Huns. All these accepted the faith and institutions of the country and then tried to affiliate themselves to the famous heroes of the Epics. Thus the Kshatriya group depended more on status and occupation rather than on descent, and so it was much easier for foreigners to be incorporated into it.

It is curious and significant that throughout the long span of Indian history there have been repeated warnings given by great men against priestcraft and the rigidity of the caste system, and powerful movements have risen against them; yet slowly, imperceptibly, almost, it seems, as if it were the inevitable course of destiny, caste has grown and spread and seized every aspect of Indian life in its strangling grip. Rebels against caste have drawn many followers, and yet in course of time their group has itself become a caste. Jainism, a rebel against the parent religion and in many ways utterly different from it, was yet tolerant to caste and adapted itself to it; and so it survives and continues in India, almost as an offshoot of Hinduism. Buddhism, not adapting itself to caste, and more independent in its thought and outlook, ultimately passes away from India, though it influences India and Hinduism profoundly. Christianity comes here eighteen hundred years ago and settles down and gradually develops its own castes. The Moslem social structure in India, in spite of its vigorous denunciation of all such barriers within the community, is also partly affected.

In our own period numerous movements to break the tyranny of caste have arisen among the middle classes, and they have made a difference, but not a vital one, so far as the masses were concerned. Their method was usually one of direct attack. Then Gandhi came and tackled the problem, after the immemorial Indian fashion, in an indirect way, and his eyes were on the masses. He has been direct enough, aggressive enough, persistent enough, but without challenging the original basic functional theory underlying the four main castes. He has attacked the rank undergrowth and overgrowth, knowing well that he was undermining the whole caste structure thereby.[9] He has already shaken the foundations, and the masses have been powerfully affected. For them the whole structure holds or breaks all together. But an even greater power than he is at work: the conditions of modern life—and it seems that at last this hoary and tenacious relic of past times must die.

But while we struggle with caste in India (which, in its origin, was based on color), new and exclusive overbearing castes have arisen in the West with doctrines of racial exclusiveness, sometimes clothed in political and economic terms, and even speaking in the language of democracy.

Before the Buddha, seven hundred years before Christ, a great Indian, the sage and lawgiver Yagnavalkya, is reported to have said: "It is not our religion, still less the

[9] Gandhiji's references to caste have been progressively stronger and more pointed, and he has made it repeatedly clear that caste as a whole and as it exists must be eliminated. Referring to the constructive program which he has placed before the nation, he says: "It has undoubtedly independence, political, social and economic, as its aim. It is a moral, non-violent revolution in all the departments of life of a big nation, at the end of which caste and untouchability and such other superstitions must vanish, differences between Hindu and Muslim become things of the past, enmity against Englishmen or Europeans must be wholly forgotten. . . ." And again quite recently: "The caste system, as we know, is an anachronism. It must go if both Hinduism and India are to live and grow from day to day."

color of our skin, that produce virtue; virtue must be practiced. Therefore let no one do to others what he would not have done to himself."

## XIII. CHANDRAGUPTA AND CHANAKYA
### THE MAURYA EMPIRE ESTABLISHED

Buddhism spread gradually in India. Although in origin a Kshatriya movement and representing a conflict between the ruling class and the priests, its ethical and democratic aspect, and more especially its fight against priestcraft and ritualism, appealed to the people. It developed as a popular reform movement attracting even some Brahman thinkers. But generally Brahmans opposed it and called Buddhists heretics and rebels against the established faith. More important than the outward progress was the interaction of Buddhism and the older faith on each other, and the continuous undermining of Brahmans. Two and a half centuries later, the emperor Ashoka became a convert to the faith and devoted all his energies to spreading it by peaceful missionary efforts in India and foreign countries.

These two centuries saw many changes in India. Various processes had long been going on to bring about racial fusion and to amalgamate the petty states and small kingdoms and republics; the old urge to build up a united centralized state had been working, and out of all this emerged a powerful and highly developed empire. Alexander's invasion of the northwest gave the final push to this development, and two remarkable men arose who could take advantage of the changing conditions and mold them according to their will. These men were Chandragupta Maurya, and his friend and minister and counselor the Brahman Chanakya. This combination functioned well. Both had been exiled from the powerful Nanda kingdom of Magadha, which had its headquarters at Pataliputra (the modern Patna); both went to Taxila in the northwest and came in contact with the Greeks stationed there by Alexander. Chandragupta met Alexander himself; he heard of his conquests and glory and was fired by ambition to emulate him. Both of them watched and prepared themselves; they hatched great and ambitious schemes and waited for the opportunity to realize them.

Soon news came of Alexander's death at Babylon in 323 B.C., and immediately Chandragupta and Chanakya raised the old and ever new cry of nationalism and roused the people against the foreign invader. The Greek garrison was driven away and Taxila captured. The appeal to nationalism had brought allies to Chandragupta, and he marched with them across north India to Pataliputra. Within two years of Alexander's death, he was in possession of that city and kingdom and the Maurya empire had been established.

Alexander's general Seleucus, who had inherited after his chief's death the countries from Asia Minor to India, tried to re-establish his authority in northwest India and crossed the Indus with an army. He was defeated and had to cede a part of Afghanistan, up to Kabul and Herat, to Chandragupta, who also married the daughter of Seleucus. Except for south India, Chandragupta's empire covered the whole of India, from the Arabian Sea to the Bay of Bengal, and extended in the north to Kabul. For the first time in recorded history a vast centralized state had arisen in India. The city of Pataliputra was the capital of this great empire.

What was this new state like? Fortunately we have full accounts, both Indian and Greek. Megasthenes, the ambassador sent by Seleucus, has left a record; and much more important is that contemporary account—Kautilya's *Arthashastra*, the "Science of Polity," to which reference has already been made. Kautilya is another name for Chanakya, and thus we have a book written not only by a great scholar but a man who played a dominating part in the establishment, growth, and preservation of the empire. Chanakya has been called the Indian Machiavelli, and to some extent the comparison is justified. But he was a much bigger person in every way, greater in intellect and action. He was no mere follower of a king, a humble adviser of an all-powerful emperor. A picture of him emerges from an old Indian play—the *Mudra-Rakshasa*—which deals with their period. Bold and scheming, proud and revengeful, never forgetting a slight, never forgetting his purpose, availing himself of every device to delude and defeat the enemy, he sat with the reins of empire in his hands and looked upon the emperor more as a loved pupil than as a master. Simple and austere in his life, uninterested in the pomp and pageantry of high position, when he had redeemed his pledge and accomplished his purpose, he wanted to retire, Brahman-like, to a life of contemplation.

There was hardly anything Chanakya would have refrained from doing to achieve his purpose; he was unscrupulous enough; yet he was also wise enough to know that this very purpose may be defeated by means unsuited to the end. Long before Clausewitz, he is reported to have said that war is only a continuance of state policy by other means. But, he adds, war must always serve the larger ends of policy and not become an end in itself; the statesman's objective must always be the betterment of the state as a result of the war, not the mere defeat and destruction of the enemy. If the war involves both parties in a common ruin, that is the bankruptcy of statesmanship. War had to be conducted by armed forces, but much more important than the force of arms was the high strategy which sapped the enemy's morale and disrupted his forces and brought about his collapse, or took him to the verge of collapse, before armed attack. Unscrupulous and rigid as Chanakya was in the pursuit of his aim, he never forgot that it was better to win over an intelligent and high-minded enemy than to crush him. His final victory was obtained by sowing discord in the enemy's ranks, and in the very moment of this victory, so the story goes, he induced Chandragupta to be generous to his rival chief. Chanakya himself is said to have handed over the insignia of his own high office to the minister of that rival, whose intelligence and loyalty to his old chief had impressed him greatly. So the story ends not in the bitterness of defeat and humiliation, but in reconciliation and in laying the firm and enduring foundations of a state which had not only defeated but won over its chief enemy.

The Maurya empire maintained diplomatic relations with the Greek world, both with Seleucus and his successors and with Ptolemy Philadelphus. These relations rested on the solid foundation of mutual commercial interest. Strabo tells us that the Oxus River in central Asia formed a link in an important chain along which Indian goods were carried to Europe by way of the Caspian and the Black Sea. This route was popular in the third century B.C. Central Asia then was rich and fertile. More than a thousand years later it began to dry up. The *Arthashastra* mentions that the king's stud had "Arabian steeds."

## XIV. THE ORGANIZATION OF THE STATE

What was this new state like that arose in 321 B.C. and covered far the greater part of India, right up to Kabul in the north? It was an autocracy, a dictatorship at the top, as most empires were and still are. There was a great deal of local autonomy in the towns and village units, and elective elders looked after these local affairs. This local autonomy was greatly prized, and hardly any king or supreme ruler interfered with it. Nevertheless, the influence and many-sided activities of the central government were all-pervasive, and in some ways this Mauryan state reminds one of modern dictatorships. There could have been then, in a purely agricultural age, nothing like the control of the individual by the state which we see today. But, in spite of limitations, an effort was made to control and regulate life. The state was very far from being just a police state, interested in keeping external and internal peace and collecting revenue.

There was a widespread and rigid bureaucracy, and there are frequent references to espionage. Agriculture was regulated in many ways; so were rates of interest. Regulation and periodical inspection took place of food, markets, manufacturers, slaughterhouses, cattle raising, water rights, sports, courtesans, and drinking saloons. Weights and measures were standardized. The cornering and adulteration of foodstuffs were rigorously punished. Trade was taxed, and so also, in some respects, the practice of religion.

When there was a breach of regulation or some other misdemeanor, the temple moneys were confiscated. If rich people were found guilty of embezzlement or of profiting from national calamity, their property was also confiscated. Sanitation and hospitals were provided, and there were medical men at the chief centers. The state gave relief to widows, orphans, the sick and the infirm. Famine relief was a special care of the state, and half the stores in all the state warehouses were always kept in reserve for times of scarcity and famine.

All these rules and regulations were probably applied far more to the cities than to the villages; and it is also likely that practice lagged far behind theory. Nevertheless even the theory is interesting. The village communities were practically autonomous.

Chanakya's *Arthashastra* deals with a vast variety of subjects and covers almost every aspect of the theory and practice of government. It discusses the duties of the king, of his ministers and councilors, of council meetings, of departments of government, of diplomacy, of war and peace. It gives details of the vast army which Chandragupta had, consisting of infantry, cavalry, chariots, and elephants.[10] And yet Chanakya suggests that mere numbers do not count for much; without discipline and proper leadership they may become a burden. Defense and fortifications are also dealt with.

Among the other matters discussed in the book are trade and commerce, law and law courts, municipal government, social customs, marriage and divorce, rights of women, taxation and revenue, agriculture, the working of mines and factories, artisans, markets, horticulture, manufacturers, irrigation and waterways, ships and navigation, corporations, census operations, fisheries, slaughterhouses, passports, and jails. Widow remarriage is recognized; also divorce under certain circumstances.

[10] The game of chess, which had its origin in India, probably developed from this fourfold conception of the army. It was called *chaturanga*, four-limbed, from which came the word *shatrang*. Alberuni gives an account of this game as played in India by four players.

There is a reference to *chinapatta*, silk fabrics of China manufacture, and a distinction is made between these and the silk made in India. Probably the latter was of a coarser variety. The importation of Chinese silk indicates trade contacts with China at least as early as the fourth century B.C.

The king, at the time of his coronation, had to take the oath of service to the people—"May I be deprived of heaven, of life, and of offspring if I oppress you." "In the happiness of his subjects lies his happiness; in their welfare, whatever pleases himself he shall consider as not good, but whatever pleases his subjects, he shall consider as good." "If a king is energetic, his subjects will be equally energetic." Public work could not suffer or await king's pleasure; he had always to be ready for it. And if the king misbehaved, his people had the right to remove him and put another in his place.

There was an irrigation department to look after the many canals, and a navigation department for the harbors, ferries, bridges, and the numerous boats and ships that went up and down the rivers and crossed the seas to Burma and beyond. There was apparently some kind of a navy, too, as an adjunct of the army.

Trade flourished in the empire and great roads connected the distant parts, with frequent rest houses for travelers. The chief road was named the King's Way, and this went right across the country from the capital to the northwest frontier. Foreign merchants are especially mentioned and provided for, and seem to have enjoyed a kind of extraterritoriality. It is said that the old Egyptians wrapped their mummies in Indian muslins and dyed their cloth with indigo obtained from India. Some kind of glass has also been discovered in the old remains. Megasthenes, the Greek ambassador, tells us that the Indians loved finery and beauty, and even notes the use of the shoe to add to one's height.

There was a growth of luxury in the Maurya empire. Life becomes more complicated, specialized, and organized. "Inns, hostelries, eating houses, serais, and gaming-houses are evidently numerous; sects and crafts have their meeting places and the latter their public dinners. The business of entertainment provides a livelihood for various classes of dancers, singers, and actors. Even the villages are visited by them, and the author of the Arthashastra is inclined to discourage the existence of a common hall used for their shows as too great a distraction from the life of the home and the fields. At the same time there are penalties for refusal to assist in organizing public entertainment. The king provides in amphitheatres constructed for the occasion dramatic, boxing, and other contests of men and animals, and also spectacles with displays of pictured objects of curiosity . . . not seldom the streets were lighted for festivals."[11] There were also royal processions and hunts.

There were many populous cities in this vast empire, but the chief of them was the capital, Pataliputra, a magnificent city spread out along the banks of the Ganga, where the Sone River meets it (the modern Patna). Megasthenes describes it thus: "At the junction of this river [Ganges] with another is situated Palibothra a city of eighty stadia [9.2 miles] in length and fifteen stadia [1.7 miles] in breadth. It is of a shape of a parallelogram and is girded with a wooden wall, pierced with loopholes for the discharge of arrows. It has a ditch in front for defense and for receiving the sewage of the city. This ditch which encompassed it all round is six hundred feet in breadth and thirty cubits in depth, and the wall is crowned with 570 towers and has four and sixty gates."

Not only this great wall was made of wood but most of the houses also. Apparently this was a precaution against earthquakes, as that area was peculiarly liable to them. In 1934 the great Bihar earthquake forcibly reminded us of this fact. Because the houses were of wood, very elaborate precautions against fire were taken. Every householder had to keep ladders, hooks, and vessels full of water.

Pataliputra had a municipality elected by the people. It had thirty members, divided up into six committees of five members each, dealing with industries and handicrafts, deaths and births, manufactures, arrangements for travelers

[11] Dr. F. W. Thomas in the *Cambridge History of India*, Vol. I, p. 480.

and pilgrims, etc. The whole municipal council looked after finance, sanitation, water supply, public buildings and gardens.

## XV. ASHOKA

The contacts between India and the western world which Chandragupta Maurya had established continued during the reign of his son Bindusara. Ambassadors came to the court at Pataliputra from Ptolemy of Egypt and Antiochus, the son and successor of Seleucus Nicator of western Asia. Ashoka, grandson of Chandragupta, added to these contacts and India became in his time an important international center, chiefly because of the rapid spread of Buddhism.

Ashoka succeeded to this great empire about 273 B.C. He had previously served as viceroy in the northwestern province of which Taxila, the university center, was the capital. Already the empire included far the greater part of India and extended right into central Asia. Only the southeast and a part of the south were beyond its sway. The old dream of uniting the whole of India under one supreme government fired Ashoka, and forthwith he undertook the conquest of Kalinga on the east coast, which corresponds roughly with modern Orissa and part of Andhra. His armies triumphed in spite of the brave and obstinate resistance of the people of Kalinga. There was a terrible slaughter in this war, and when news of this reached Ashoka he was stricken with remorse and disgusted with war. Unique among the victorious monarchs and captains in history, he decided to abandon warfare in the full tide of victory. The whole of India acknowledged his sway, except for the southern tip, and that tip was his for the taking. But he refrained from any further aggression, and his mind turned, under the influence of Buddha's gospel, to conquests and adventures in other fields.

What Ashoka felt and how he acted are known to us in his own words in the numerous edicts he issued, carved in rock and metal. Those edicts, spread out all over India, are still with us, and they conveyed his messages not only to his people but to posterity. In one of the edicts it is said that:

"Kalinga was conquered by His Sacred and Gracious Majesty when he had been consecrated eight years. One hundred and fifty thousand persons were thence carried away as captive, one hundred thousand were there slain, and many times that number died.

"Directly after the annexation of the Kalingas began His Sacred Majesty's zealous protection of the Law of Piety, his love of that Law, and his inculcation of that Law dharma. Thus arose His Sacred Majesty's remorse for having conquered the Kalingas, because the conquest of a country previously unconquered involves the slaughter, death and carrying away captive of the people. That is a matter of profound sorrow and regret to His Sacred Majesty."

No longer, goes on the edict, would Ashoka tolerate any more killing or taking into captivity, not even of a hundredth or a thousandth part of the number killed and made captive in Kalinga. True conquest consists of the conquest of men's hearts by the Law of Duty or Piety, and, adds Ashoka, such real victories had already been won by him, not only in his own dominions, but in distant kingdoms. Moreover, the edict further says,

"Moreover, should anyone do him wrong, that too must be borne with by His Sacred Majesty, so far as it can possibly be borne with. Even upon the forest folk in his dominions His Sacred Majesty looks kindly and he seeks to make them think aright, for, if he did not, repentance would come upon His Sacred Majesty. For His Sacred Majesty desires that all animate beings should have security, self-control, peace of mind, and joyousness."

This astonishing ruler, beloved still in India and in many other parts of Asia, devoted himself to the spread of Buddha's teaching, of righteousness and good will, and to public works for the good of the people. He was no passive spectator of events, lost in contemplation and self-improvement. He labored hard at public business and declared that he was always ready for it: "at all times and at all places, whether I am dining or in the ladies' apartments, in my bedroom or in my closet, in my carriage or in my palace gardens, the official reporters should keep me informed of the people's business. . . . At any hour and at any place, work I must for the commonweal."

His messengers and ambassadors went to Syria, Egypt, Macedonia, Cyrene, and Epirus, conveying his greeting and Buddha's message. They went to central Asia also and to Burma and Siam, and he sent his own son and daughter, Mahendra and Sanghamitra, to Ceylon in the south. Everywhere an appeal was made to the mind and the heart; there was no force or compulsion. Ardent Buddhist as he was, he showed respect and consideration for all other faiths. He proclaimed in an edict:

"All sects deserve reverence for one reason or another. By thus acting a man exalts his own sect and at the same time does service to the sects of other people."

Buddhism spread rapidly in India from Kashmir to Ceylon. It penetrated into Nepal and later reached Tibet and China and Mongolia. In India one of the consequences of this was the growth of vegetarianism and abstention from alcoholic drinks. Till then both Brahmans and Kshatriyas often ate meat and took wine. Animal sacrifice was forbidden.

Because of the growth of foreign contacts and missionary enterprises, trade between India and other countries must have also grown. We have records of an Indian colony in Khotan (now in Sinkiang, central Asia). The Indian universities, especially Taxila, also attracted more students from abroad.

Ashoka was a great builder, and it has been suggested that he employed foreign craftsmen to assist in building some of his huge structures. This inference is drawn from the designs of some clustered columns, which remind one of Persepolis. But even in these early sculptures and other remains the characteristically Indian art tradition is visible.

Ashoka's famous many-pillared hall in his palace at Pataliputra was partly dug out by archaeologists about thirty years ago. Dr. Spooner of the Archaeological Department of India in his official report said that this was "in almost incredible state of preservation, the logs which formed it being as smooth and perfect as the day they were laid, more than two thousand years ago." He says further that the "marvellous preservation of the ancient wood, whose edges were so perfect that the very lines of jointure were indistinguishable, evoked admiration of all who witnessed the experiment. The whole was built with a precision and reasoned care that could not possibly be excelled today. . . . In short, the construction was absolute perfection of such work."

In other excavated buildings also in different parts of the country wooden logs and rafters have been found in an excellent state of preservation. This would be surprising anywhere, but in India it is more so, for the climate wears them away and all manner of insects eat them up. There must have been some special treatment for the wood; what this was is still, I believe, a mystery.

Between Pataliputra (Patna) and Gaya there lie the impressive remains of Nalanda university, which was to become famous in later days. It is not clear when this began functioning, and there are no records of it in Ashoka's time.

Ashoka died in 232 B.C. after ruling strenuously for forty-one years. Of him H. G. Wells says in his *Outline of History:* "Amidst the tens of thousands of names of monarchs that crowd the columns of history, their majesties and graciousnesses and serenities and royal highnesses and the like, the name of Ashoka shines, and shines almost alone, a star. From the Volga to Japan his name is still honoured. China, Tibet, and even India, though it has left his doctrine, preserve the tradition of his greatness. More living men cherish his memory today than have ever heard the names of Constantine or Charlemagne."

# IV. Through the Ages

## I. NATIONALISM AND IMPERIALISM
### UNDER THE CUPTAS

The Maurya empire faded away and gave place to the Sunga dynasty, which ruled over a much smaller area. In the south great states were rising, and in the north the Bactrians, or Indo-Greeks, were spreading out from Kabul to the Punjab. Under Menander they threatened Pataliputra itself but were defeated and repelled. Menander himself succumbed to the spirit and atmosphere of India and became a Buddhist, a famous one, known as King Milinda, popular in Buddhist legend and regarded almost as a saint. From the fusion of Indian and Greek cultures rose the Graeco-Buddhist art of Gandhara, the region covering Afghanistan and the frontier.

There is a granite pillar, called the Heliodorus Column, dating from the first century B.C., at Besnagar near Sanchi in central India, bearing an inscription in Sanskrit. This gives us a glimpse of the process of indianization of the Greeks who had come to the frontier, and their absorption of Indian culture. The inscription has been translated thus:

This Garuda column of Vasudeva [Vishnu], the God of gods, was erected by Heliodorus, a worshiper of Vishnu, the son of Dion, and an inhabitant of Taxila, who came as Greek ambassador from the Great King Antialcidas to King Kashiputra Bhagabhadra, the Saviour, then reigning in the fourteenth year of his kingship.

Three immortal precepts, when practised well, lead to Heaven—self-restraint, self-sacrifice [charity], conscientiousness.

In central Asia the Shakas or Scythians (Seistan = Shakasthan) had established themselves in the Oxus Valley. The Yueh Chih, coming from farther east, drove them out and pushed them into north India. These Shakas became converts to Buddhism and Hinduism. Among the Yueh Chih, one of the clans, the Kushans, established their supremacy and then extended their sway over northern India. They defeated the Shakas and pushed them still farther south, the Shakas going to Kathiawar and the Deccan. The Kushans thereupon established an extensive and durable empire over the whole of north India and a great part of central Asia. Some of them became converts to the Hindu faith but most of them became Buddhists, and their most famous king, Kanishka, is also one of the heroes of Buddhist legend, which records his great deeds and public works. Buddhist though he was, it appears that the state religion was a mixed affair to which even Zoroastrianism had contributed. This borderland state, called the Kushan empire, with its seat near modern Peshawar, and the old university of Taxila near by, became the meeting place of men from many nations. There the Indians met the Scythians, the Yueh Chih, the Iranians, the Bactrian Greeks, the Turks, and the Chinese, and the various cultures reacted on each other. A vigorous school of sculpture and painting arose as a result of their interactions. It was during this period that, historically, the first contacts took place between China and India, and a Chinese embassy came to India in 64 A.D. Minor but very welcome gifts of China to India at that time were the peach and the pear trees. Right on the borders of the Gobi Desert, at Turfan and Kucha, rose fascinating amalgams of Indian, Chinese, and Iranian cultures.

During the Kushan period a great schism divided Buddhism into two sections—the Mahayana and the Hinayana—and controversy raged between them, and, as has been India's way, the issue was put to debate in great assemblies, to which representatives came from all over the country. Kashmir was situated near the center of the empire and was full of this debate and of cultural activities. One name stands out in this controversy, that of Nagarjuna, who lived in the first century A.D. He was a towering personality, great in Buddhist scholarship and Indian philosophy, and it was largely because of him that Mahayana triumphed in India. It was the Mahayana doctrine that spread to China, while Ceylon and Burma adhered to Hinayana.

The Kushans had indianized themselves and had become patrons of Indian culture. Yet an undercurrent of nationalist resistance to their rule continued, and when, later, fresh tribes poured into India, this nationalist and antiforeign movement took shape at the beginning of the fourth century A.D. Another great ruler, also named Chandragupta, drove out the new intruders and established a powerful and widespread empire.

Thus began the age of the imperial Guptas in 320 A.D. which produced a remarkable succession of great rulers, successful in war and in the arts of peace. Repeated invasions had produced a strong antiforeign feeling, and the old Brahman-Kshatriya element in the country was forced to think in terms of defense both of their homeland and of their culture. The foreign elements which had been absorbed were accepted, but all newcomers met with a vigorous resistance, and an attempt was made to build up a homogeneous state based on old Brahmanic ideals. But the old self-assurance was going, and these ideals began to develop a rigidity which was foreign to their nature. India seemed to draw into her shell, both physically and mentally.

Yet that shell was deep enough and wide enough. Previously, in the ages since the Aryans had come down to what they called Aryavarta or Bharatvarsha, the problem that faced India was to produce a synthesis between this new race and culture and the old race and civilization of the land. To that the mind of India devoted itself, and it produced an enduring solution built on the strong foundations of a joint Indo-Aryan culture. Other foreign elements came and were absorbed. They made little difference. Though

India had many contacts with other countries through trade and otherwise, essentially she was absorbed in herself and paid little attention to what happened elsewhere. But now periodic invasion by strange peoples with strange customs had shaken her up, and she could no longer ignore these irruptions, which not only broke up her political structure but endangered her cultural ideals and social structure also. The reaction was essentially a nationalist one, with the strength as well as the narrowness of nationalism. That mixture of religion and philosophy, history and tradition, custom and social structure, which in its wide fold included almost every aspect of the life of India then, and which might be called Brahmanism or (to use a later word) Hinduism, became the symbol of nationalism. It was indeed a national religion with its appeal to all those deep instincts, racial and cultural, which form the basis everywhere of nationalism today. Buddhism, child of Indian thought, had its nationalist background also. India was to it the holy land where Buddha had lived and preached and died, where famous scholars and saints had spread the faith. But Buddhism was essentially international, a world religion, and as it developed and spread, it became increasingly so. Thus it was natural for the old Brahmanic faith to become the symbol, again and again, of nationalist revivals.

That faith and philosophy were tolerant and chivalrous to the various religions and racial elements in India, and they still continued to absorb them into their wide-flung structure, but they became increasingly aggressive toward the outsider and sought to protect themselves against his impact. In their doing so, the spirit of nationalism they had roused often took on the semblance of imperialism, as it frequently does when it grows in strength. The age of the Guptas, enlightened, vigorous, highly cultured and full of vitality as it was, rapidly developed these imperialistic tendencies. One of its great rulers, Samudragupta, has been called the Indian Napoleon. From a literary and artistic point of view it was a brilliant period.

From early in the fourth century onward for about a hundred and fifty years the Guptas ruled over a powerful and prosperous state in the north. For almost another century and a half their successors continued, but they were on the defensive now and the empire shrank and became smaller and smaller. New invaders from central Asia were pouring into India and attacking them. These were the White Huns, as they are called, who ravaged the land, as under Attila they were ravaging Europe. Their barbarous behavior and fiendish cruelty at last roused the people, and a united attack by a confederacy under Yashovarman was made on them. The Hun power was broken and their chief, Mahiragula, was made a prisoner. But the descendant of the Guptas, Baladitya, in accordance with his country's customs, treated him with generosity and allowed him to leave India. Mahiragula responded to this treatment by returning later and making a treacherous attack on his benefactor.

But the Hun rule in northern India was of brief duration—about half a century. Many of them, however, remained in the country as petty chiefs, giving trouble occasionally, and being absorbed into the sea of Indian humanity. Some of these chiefs became aggressive early in the seventh century A.D. They were crushed by the king of Kanauj, Harshavardhana, who thereafter built up a powerful state right across northern and central India. He was an ardent Buddhist, but his Buddhism was of the Mahayana variety which was akin in many ways to Hinduism. He encouraged both Buddhism and Hinduism. It was in his time that the famous Chinese pilgrim Hsuan Tsang (or Yuan Chwang) came to India (in 629 A.D.). Harshavardhana was a poet and dramatist and he gathered round his court many artists and poets, making his capital, Ujjayini, a famous center of cultural activities. Harsha died in 648 A.D., just about the time when Islam was emerging from the deserts of Arabia, to spread out rapidly across Africa and Asia.

*There follows a description, in some detail, of Indian history and culture during the period after the imperial Guptas. Included is material on Indian contacts with premodern Iran and Greece, with emphasis on the similarities of Indian and classical Greek culture. Mr. Nehru then turns to the early Indian theater.*

## II. THE OLD INDIAN THEATER

The discovery by Europe of the old Indian drama led immediately to suggestions that it had its origin in, or had been greatly influenced by, Greek drama. There was some plausibility in the theory, for till then no other ancient drama had been known to exist, and after Alexander's raid Hellenized states were established on the frontiers of India. These states continued to function for several centuries, and Greek theatrical representations must have been known there. This question was closely scrutinized and debated by European scholars throughout the nineteenth century. It is now generally admitted that the Indian theater was entirely independent in its origins, in the ideas which governed it, and in its development. Its earliest beginnings can be traced back to the hymns and dialogues of the *Rig Veda* which have a certain dramatic character. There are references to nataka, or the drama, in the *Ramayana* and the *Mahabharata*. It began to take shape in the songs and music and dances of the Krishna legends. Panini, the great grammarian of the sixth or seventh century B.C., mentions some dramatic forms.

A treatise on the art of the theater—the *Natyashastra*— is said to date from the third century A.D., but this was evidently based on previous books on the subject. Such a book could only be written when the dramatic art was fully developed and public representations were common. A considerable literature must have preceded it, and behind it must lie many centuries of gradual progress. Recently an ancient playhouse, dating from the second century B.C., has been unearthed in the Ramgarh Hills in Chota Nagpur. It is significant that this playhouse fits in with the general description of theaters given in the *Natyashastra*.

It is now believed that the regular Sanskrit drama was

fully established by the third century B.C., though some scholars take the date back to the fifth century. In the plays that we have, mention is often made of earlier authors and plays which have not so far been found. One such lost author was Bhasa, highly praised by many subsequent dramatists. Early in this century a bunch of thirteen of his plays was discovered. Probably the earliest Sanskrit plays so far discovered are those of Ashvaghosa, who lived just before or after the beginning of the Christian era. These are really fragments only of manuscripts on palm leaf, and they were discovered, strangely enough, at Turfan on the borders of the Gobi Desert. Ashvaghosa was a pious Buddhist and wrote also the *Buddhacarita*, a life of the Buddha, which was well known and had long been popular in India and China and Tibet. The Chinese translation, made in a past age, was by an Indian scholar.

Europe first learned of the old Indian drama from Sir William Jones's translation of Kalidasa's *Shakuntala* published in 1789. Something in the nature of a commotion was created among European intellectuals by this discovery, and several editions of the book followed. Translations also appeared (made from Sir William Jones's translation) in German, French, Danish, and Italian. Goethe was powerfully impressed, and he paid a magnificent tribute to *Shakuntala*. The idea of giving a prologue to Faust is said to have originated from Kalidasa's prologue, which was in accordance with the usual tradition of the Sanskrit drama.[1]

[1] There is a tendency on the part of Indian writers, to which I have also partly succumbed, to give selected extracts and quotations from the writings of European scholars in praise of old Indian literature and philosophy. It would be equally easy, and indeed much easier, to give other extracts giving an exactly opposite view. The discovery by the European scholars of the eighteenth and nineteenth centuries of Indian thought and philosophy led to an outburst of admiration and enthusiasm. There was a feeling that these filled a need, something that European culture had been unable to do. Then there was a reaction away from this attitude, and criticism and skepticism grew. This was caused by a feeling that the philosophy was formless and diffuse, and a dislike of the rigid caste structure of Indian society. Both these reactions, in favor and against, were based on very incomplete knowledge of old Indian literature. Goethe himself moved from

Kalidasa wrote other plays also and some long poems. His date is uncertain, but very probably he lived toward the end of the fourth century A.D. at Ujjayini during the reign of Chandragupta II, Vikramaditya of the Gupta dynasty. Tradition says that he was one of the nine gems of his court, and there is no doubt that his genius was appreciated and he met with full recognition during his life. He was among the fortunate whom life treated as a cherished son and who experienced its beauty and tenderness more than its harsh and rough edges. His writings betray this love of life and a passion for nature's beauty.

One of Kalidasa's long poems is the *Meghaduta*, the *Cloud Messenger*. A lover, made captive and separated from his beloved, asks a cloud, during the rainy season, to carry his message of desperate longing to her. To this poem and to Kalidasa, the American scholar Ryder has paid a splendid tribute. He refers to the two parts of the poem and says: "The former half is a description of external nature, yet interwoven with human feeling; the latter half is a picture of a human heart, yet the picture is framed in natural beauty. So exquisitely is the thing done that none can say which half is superior. Of those who read this perfect poem in the original text, some are moved by the one, some by the other. Kalidasa understood in the fifth century what Europe did not learn until the nineteenth, and even now comprehends only imperfectly, that the world was not made for man, that man reaches his full stature only as he realizes the dignity and worth of life that is not human. That Kalidasa seized this truth is a magnificent tribute to his intellectual power, a quality quite as necessary to great

one opinion to the other, and while he acknowledged the tremendous stimulus of Indian thought on Western civilization, he refused to submit to its far-reaching influence. This dual and conflicting approach has been characteristic of the European mind in regard to India. In recent years that great European and typical product of the best European culture, Romain Rolland, made a more synthetic and very friendly approach to the basic foundations of Indian thought: for him East and West represented different phases of the eternal struggle of the human soul. On this subject —Western reaction to Indian thought—Mr. Alex Aronson of Santiniketan University has written with learning and ability.

poetry as perfection of form. Poetical fluency is not rare; intellectual grasp is not very uncommon; but the combination has not been found perhaps more than a dozen times since the world began. Because he possessed this harmonious combination, Kalidasa ranks not with Anacreon and Horace and Shelley but with Sophocles, Virgil, Milton."

Probably long before Kalidasa, another famous play was produced—Shudraka's *Mricchakatika* or *The Clay Cart*, a tender, rather artificial play, and yet with a reality which moves us and gives us a glimpse into the mind and civilization of the day. About 400 A.D., also during the reign of Chandragupta II, yet another notable play was produced: Vishaka-datta's *Mudra-Rakshasa* or *The Signet Ring*. This is a purely political play with no love motive or story from mythology. It deals with the times of Chandragupta Maurya, and his chief minister Chanakya, the author of the *Arthashastra*, is the hero. In some ways it is a remarkably topical play today.

Harsha, the king, who established a new empire early in the seventh century A.D., was also a playwright, and we have three plays written by him. About 700 A.D. there lived Bhavabhuti, another shining star in Sanskrit literature. He does not yield himself easily to translation, for his beauty is chiefly of language, but he is very popular in India and only Kalidasa has precedence over him. Wilson, who used to be professor of Sanskrit at Oxford University, has said of these two: "It is impossible to conceive language so beautifully musical, or so magnificently grand, as that of the verses of Bhavabhuti and Kalidasa."

The stream of Sanskrit drama continued to flow for centuries, but after Murari, early in the ninth century, there is a marked decline in the quality. That decline, and a progressive decay, were becoming visible also in other forms of life's activities. It has been suggested that this decline of the drama may be partly due to the lack of royal patronage during the Indo-Afghan and Moghul periods and to the Islamic disapproval of the drama as an art form, chiefly because of its intimate association with the national religion. For this literary drama, apart from the popular aspects which continued, was highbrow and sophisticated and dependent on aristocratic patronage. But there is little substance in this argument, though it is possible that political changes at the top had some indirect effect. As a matter of fact the decline of the Sanskrit drama is obvious long before those political changes took place. And even those changes were confined for some centuries to north India, and if this drama had any vitality left, it could have continued its creative career in the south. The record of the Indo-Afghan, Turkish, and Moghul rulers, apart from some brief puritanical periods, is one of definite encouragement of Indian culture, occasionally with variations and additions to it. Indian music was adopted as a whole and with enthusiasm by the Moslem courts and nobility, and some of its greatest masters have been Moslems. Literature and poetry were also encouraged, and among the noted poets in Hindi are Moslems. Ibrahim Adil Shah, the ruler of Bijapur, wrote a treatise in Hindi on Indian music. Both Indian poetry and music were full of references to the Hindu gods and goddesses, and yet they were accepted and the old allegories and metaphors continued. It might be said that except in regard to actual image-making no attempt was made by Moslem rulers, apart from a few exceptions, to suppress any art form.

The Sanskrit drama declined because much in India was declining in those days and the creative spirit was lessening. It declined long before the Afghans and Turks established themselves on the throne of Delhi. Subsequently Sanskrit had to compete to some extent as the learned language of the nobility with Persian. But one obvious reason appears to have been the ever-widening gap between the language of the Sanskrit drama and the languages of day-to-day life. By 1000 A.D. the popular spoken languages, out of which our modern languages have grown, were beginning to take literary forms.

Sanskrit plays were undoubtedly meant for acting, and elaborate stage directions are given, and rules for seating the audience. Unlike the practice in ancient Greece, actresses took part in the presentation. In both Greek and Sanskrit there is a sensitive awareness of nature and a feeling of being a part of that nature. There is a strong lyric element, and poetry seems to be an integral part of life, full of meaning and significance. It was frequently recited. Reading the Greek drama, one comes across many customs and ways of thought and life which suddenly remind one of old Indian customs. Nevertheless Greek drama is essentially different from the Sanskrit.

The essential basis of the Greek drama is tragedy, the problem of evil. Why does man suffer? Why is there evil in the world? The enigma of religion, of God. What a pitiful thing is man, child of a day, with his blind and aimless strivings against all-powerful fate—"The Law that abides and changes not, ages long . . ." Man must learn by suffering, and, if he is fortunate, he will rise above his striving:

> Happy be, on the weary sea
> Who hath fled the tempest and won the haven.
> Happy whoso has risen, free,
> Above his striving. For strangely graven
> Is the art of life, that one and another
> In gold and power may outpass his brother.
> And men in their millions float and flow
> And seethe with a million hopes as leaven;
> And they win their Will, or they miss their Will,
> And the hopes are dead or are pined for still;
> But whoever can know,
> As the long days go,
> That to Live is happy, hath found his Heaven!

Man learns by suffering; he learns how to face life, but he learns also that the ultimate mystery remains and he cannot find an answer to his questions or solve the riddle of good and evil.

> There be many shapes of mystery;
> And many things God brings to be,
> Past hope or fear.
> And the end men looked for cometh not,
> And a path is there where no man thought.[2]

[2] These two quotations are from Professor Gilbert Murray's translations from Euripides. The first one is from *The Bacchae* and the second from *Alcestis*.

There is nothing comparable to the power and majesty of Greek tragedy in Sanskrit. Indeed there is no tragedy at all, for a tragic ending was not permitted. No such fundamental questions are discussed there, for the commonly held patterns of religious faith were accepted by the dramatists. Among these were the doctrines of rebirth and cause and effect. Accident or evil without cause were ruled out, for what happens now is the necessary result of some previous happening in a former life. There is no intervention of blind forces acting blindly against which man has to fight though his struggles are of no avail. The philosophers and the thinkers were not satisfied by these simple explanations and they were continually going behind them in their search for final causes and fuller explanations. But life was generally governed by these beliefs, and the dramatists did not challenge them. The plays and Sanskrit poetry in general were in full accord with the Indian spirit and there are few traces of any rebellion against it. The rules laid down for dramatic writing were strict, and it was not easy to break them. Yet there is no meek submission to fate; the hero is always a man of courage who faces all hazards. "The ignorant rely on Providence," says Chanakya contemptuously in the *Mudra-Rakshasa*, "they look to the stars for help instead of relying on themselves." Some artificiality creeps in: the hero is always the hero, the villain almost always acts villainously; there are few intermediate shades.

Yet there are powerful dramatic situations and moving scenes and a background of life which seems like a picture in a dream, real and yet unreal, all woven together by a poet's fancy in magnificent language. It almost seems, though it may not have been so, that life in India was more peaceful, more stable then, as if it had discovered its roots and found answer to its questions. It flows along serenely and even strong winds and passing storms ruffle its surface only. There is nothing like the fierce tempests of Greek tragedy. But it is very human, and there is an aesthetic harmony and a logical unity about it. The nataka, the Indian drama, says Sylvain Lévi, still remains the happiest invention of the Indian genius.

Professor A. Berriedale Keith says also that "the Sanskrit

drama may legitimately be regarded as the highest product of Indian poetry, and as summing up in itself the final conception of literary art achieved by the very self-conscious creators of Indian literature. . . . The Brahmin, in fact, much abused as he has been in this as in other matters, was the source of the intellectual distinction of India. As he produced Indian philosophy, so by another effort of his intellect he evolved the subtle and effective form of the drama."

An English translation of Shudraka's *Mricchakatika* was staged in New York in 1924. Mr. Joseph Wood Krutch, the dramatic critic of the *Nation*, wrote of it as follows: "Here, if anywhere, the spectator will be able to see a genuine example of that 'pure art theatre' of which theorists talk, and here, too, he will be led to meditate upon that real wisdom of the East which lies not in esoteric doctrine but in a tenderness far deeper and truer than that of the traditional Christianity which has been so thoroughly corrupted by the hard righteousness of Hebraism. . . . A play wholly artificial yet profoundly moving because it is not realistic but real. . . . Who ever the author may have been, and whether he lived in the fourth century or the eighth, he was a man good and wise with the goodness and wisdom which come not from the lips or the smoothly flowing pen of the moralist but from the heart. An exquisite sympathy with the fresh beauty of youth and love tempered his serenity, and he was old enough to understand that lighthearted story of ingenious complication could be made the vehicle of tender humanity and confident goodness. . . . Such a play can be produced only by a civilization which has reached stability; when a civilization has thought its way through all the problems it faces, it must come to rest upon something calm and naive like this. Macbeth and Othello, however great and stirring they might be, are barbarous heroes because the passionate tumult of Shakespeare is the tumult produced by the conflict between a newly awakened sensibility and a series of ethical concepts inherited from the savage age. The realistic drama of our own time is a product of a like confusion; but when problems are settled, and when passions are reconciled with

the decisions of an intellect, then form alone remains. . . .
Nowhere in our European past do we find, this side the
classics, a work more completely civilized."[3]

## III. THE VITALITY AND PERSISTENCE
## OF SANSKRIT

Sanskrit is a language amazingly rich, efflorescent, full of
luxuriant growth of all kinds, and yet precise and strictly
keeping within the framework of grammar which Panini
laid down two thousand six hundred years ago. It spread
out, added to its richness, became fuller and more ornate,
but always it stuck to its original roots. In the years of the
decline of Sanskrit literature, it lost some of its power and
simplicity of style and became involved in highly complex
forms and elaborate similes and metaphors. The grammati-
cal rule which enabled words to be joined together became
in the hands of the epigones a mere device to show off
their cleverness by combining whole strings of words running into many lines.

Sir William Jones observed as long ago as 1784: "The
Sanskrit language, whatever be its antiquity, is of a wonderful structure; more perfect than the Greek, more copi-
ous than the Latin and more exquisitely refined than
either: yet bearing to both of them a stronger affinity, both
in the roots of verbs, and in the forms of grammar, than
could possibly have been produced by accident; so strong
indeed, that no philologer could examine them all without
believing them to have sprung from *some common source*
which perhaps no longer exists. . . ."

William Jones was followed by many other European
scholars, English, French, German, and others, who studied
Sanskrit and laid the foundations of a new science—com-

[3] I have taken this long quotation from R. S. Pandit's preface
to his translation of the *Mudra-Rakshasa*. This translation contains many interesting notes and appendices. I have frequently
consulted Sylvain Lévi's *Le théâtre Indien* (Paris, 1890) and
A. Berriedale Keith's *The Sanskrit Drama* (Oxford, 1924), and
some quotations have been taken from these two books.

parative philology. German scholarship forged ahead in this new domain, and it is to these German scholars of the nineteenth century that the greatest credit must go for research in Sanskrit. Practically every German university had a Sanskrit department with one or two professors in charge of it. Indian scholarship, which was considerable, was of the old style, uncritical and seldom acquainted with foreign classical languages, except Arabic and Persian. A new type of scholarship arose in India under European inspiration, and many Indians went to Europe (usually to Germany) to train themselves in the new methods of research and critical and comparative study. These Indians had an advantage over the Europeans, and yet there was a disadvantage also. The disadvantage was due to certain preconceived notions, inherited beliefs, and traditions, which came in the way of dispassionate criticism. The advantage, and it was great, was the capacity to enter into the spirit of the writing, to picture the environment in which it grew and thus to be more in tune with it.

A language is something infinitely greater than grammar and philology. It is the poetic testament of the genius of a race and a culture, and the living embodiment of the thoughts and fancies that have molded them. Words change their meanings from age to age and old ideas transform themselves into new, often keeping their old attire. It is difficult to capture the meaning, much less the spirit, of an old word or phrase. Some kind of romantic and poetical approach is necessary if we are to have a glimpse into that old meaning and into the minds of those who used the language in former days. The richer and more abundant the language, the greater the difficulty. Sanskrit, like other classical languages, is full of words which have not only poetic beauty but a deep significance, a host of associated ideas, which cannot be translated into a language foreign in spirit and outlook. Even its grammar, its philosophy have a strong poetic content; one of its old dictionaries is in poetic form.

It is no easy matter even for those of us who have studied Sanskrit to enter into the spirit of this ancient tongue and to live again in its world of long ago. Yet we may do so to a small extent, for we are the inheritors of old traditions and that old world still clings to our fancies. Our modern languages in India are children of Sanskrit and to it owe most of their vocabulary and their forms of expression. Many rich and significant words in Sanskrit poetry and philosophy, untranslatable in foreign languages, are still living parts of our popular languages. And Sanskrit itself, though long dead as a language of the people, has still an astonishing vitality. But for foreigners, however learned, the difficulties become greater. Unfortunately scholars and learned men are seldom poets, and it is the scholar-poet who is required to interpret a language. From these scholars we usually get, as M. Barth has pointed out, *"traductions infidèles à force d'être littérales."*

So while the study of comparative philology has progressed and much research work has been done in Sanskrit, it is rather barren and sterile from the point of view of a poetic and romantic approach to this language. There is hardly any translation in English or any other foreign language from the Sanskrit which can be called worthy or just to the original. Both Indians and foreigners have failed in this work for different reasons. That is a great pity, and the world misses something that is full of beauty and imagination and deep thinking, something that is not merely the heritage of India but should be the heritage of the human race.

The hard discipline, reverent approach, and insight of the English translators of the Authorised Version of the Bible not only produced a noble book but gave to the English language strength and dignity. Generations of European scholars and poets have labored lovingly over Greek and Latin classics and produced fine translations in various European languages. And so even common folk can share to some extent in those cultures and, in their drab lives, have glimpses of truth and loveliness. Unfortunately this work has yet to be done with the Sanskrit classics. When it will be done, or whether it will be done at all, I do not know. Our scholars grow in numbers and grow in scholarship and we have our poets too; but between the two there is a wide and ever-growing gap. Our creative tendencies are turned in a different direction, and the many demands that the world of today makes upon us hardly give us time for the leisured study of the classics. Especially in India we have to look another way and make up for long lost time; we have been too much immersed in the classics in the past, and because we lost our own creative instincts, we ceased to be inspired even by those classics which we claimed to cherish so much. Translations, I suppose, from the Indian classics will continue to appear and scholars will see to it that the Sanskrit words and names are properly spelled and have all the necessary diacritical marks, and there are plenty of notes and explanations and comparisons; there will be everything, in fact, literally and conscientiously rendered, only the living spirit will be missing. What was a thing of life and joy, so lovely and musical and full of imaginative daring, will become old and flat and stale, with neither youth nor beauty, but with only the dust of the scholar's study and the smell of midnight oil.

For how long Sanskrit has been a dead language, in the sense of not being popularly spoken, I do not know. Even in the days of Kalidasa it was not the people's language, though it was the language of educated people throughout India. So it continued for centuries and even spread to the Indian colonies in southeast Asia and central Asia. There are records of regular Sanskrit recitations, and possibly plays also, in Cambodia in the seventh century A.D. Sanskrit is still used for some ceremonial purposes in Thailand (Siam). In India the vitality of Sanskrit has been amazing. When the Afghan rulers had established themselves on the throne of Delhi, about the beginning of the thirteenth century, Persian became the court language over the greater part of India, and gradually many educated people took to it in preference to Sanskrit. The popular languages also grew and developed literary forms. Yet in spite of all this, Sanskrit continued, though it declined in quality. Speaking at the Oriental Conference held in 1937 at Trivandrum, over which he presided, Dr. F. F. Thomas pointed out what a great unifying force Sanskrit had been in India and how widespread its use still was. He actually suggested that a simple form of Sanskrit, a kind of Basic Sanskrit, should be encouraged as a common all-India language to-day! He quoted, agreeing with him, what Max Müller had said previously: "Such is the marvellous continuity be-tween the past and the present in India, that in spite of repeated social convulsions, religious reforms, and foreign invasions, Sanskrit may be said to be still the only lan-guage spoken over the whole extent of that vast country. . . . Even at the present moment, after a century of Eng-lish rule and English teaching, I believe that Sanskrit is more widely understood in India than Latin was in Europe at the time of Dante."

I have no idea of the number of people who understood Latin in the Europe of Dante's time; nor do I know how many understand Sanskrit in India today. But the number of these latter is still large, especially in the south. Simple spoken Sanskrit is not very difficult to follow for those who know well any of the present-day Indo-Aryan languages—Hindi, Bengali, Marathi, Gujrati, etc. Even present-day Urdu, itself wholly an Indo-Aryan language, probably con-tains 80 per cent words derived from Sanskrit. It is often difficult to say whether a word has come from Persian or Sanskrit, as the root words in both of these languages are alike. Curiously enough the Dravidian languages of the south, though entirely different in origin, have borrowed and adopted such masses of words from the Sanskrit that nearly half their vocabulary is very nearly allied to Sanskrit.

The ancient Indians attached a great deal of importance to sound, and hence their writing, poetry or prose, had a rhythmic and musical quality. Special efforts were made to insure the correct enunciation of words, and elaborate rules were laid down for this purpose. This became all the more necessary as, in the old days, teaching was oral and whole books were committed to memory and thus handed down from generation to generation. The significance at-tached to the sound of words led to attempts to co-ordinate the sense with the sound, resulting sometimes in delightful combinations, and at other times in crude and artificial mixtures. E. H. Johnstone has written about this: "The classical poets of India have a sensitiveness to variations of sound, to which the literatures of other countries afford few parallels, and their delicate combinations are a source of never-failing joy. Some of them, however, are inclined to attempt to match the sense with the sound in a way that is decidedly lacking in subtlety, and they have perpetrated real atrocities in the manufacture of verses with a limited number of consonants or even only one."[4]

Recitations from the Vedas, even in the present day, are done according to the precise rules for enunciation laid down in ancient times.

The modern Indian languages descended from the Sanskrit, and therefore called Indo-Aryan languages, are: Hindi-Urdu, Bengali, Marathi, Gujrati, Oriya, Assamese, Rajasthani (a variation of Hindi), Punjabi, Sindhi, Pashto, and Kashmiri. The Dravidian languages are: Tamil, Telugu, Canarese, and Malayalam. These fifteen languages cover the whole of India, and of these Hindi, with its variation Urdu, is far the most widespread and is understood even where it is not spoken. Apart from these, there are only some dialects and some undeveloped languages spoken, in very limited areas, by some backward hill and forest tribes. The oft-repeated story of India's having five hundred or more languages is a fiction of the philologist's and the census commissioner's mind, who note down every variation in dialect and every petty hill-tongue on the Assam-Bengal frontier with Burma as a separate language, although sometimes it is spoken only by a few hundred or a few thousand persons. Most of these so-called hundreds of languages are confined to this eastern frontier of India and to the eastern border tracts of Burma. According to the method adapted by census commissioners, Europe has hundreds of languages and Germany was, I think, listed as having about sixty.

The real language question in India has nothing to do with this variety. It is practically confined to Hindi-Urdu, one language with two literary forms and two scripts. As spoken, there is hardly any difference; as written, especially in literary style, the gap widens. Attempts have been, and are being, made to lessen this gap and develop a common

[4] From E. H. Johnstone's translation of Ashvaghosa's *Buddhacarita* (Lahore, 1936).

form, which is usually styled Hindustani. This is developing into a common language understood all over India.

Pashto, one of the Indo-Aryan languages derived from Sanskrit, is the popular language in the North-West Frontier Province as well as in Afghanistan. It has been influenced, more than any of our other languages, by Persian. This frontier area has in the past produced a succession of brilliant thinkers, scholars, and grammarians in Sanskrit.

The language of Ceylon is Singhalese. This is also an Indo-Aryan language derived directly from Sanskrit. The Singhalese people have not only got their religion, Buddhism, from India, but are racially and linguistically akin to Indians.

Sanskrit, it is now well recognized, is allied to the European classical and modern languages. Even the Slavonic languages have many common forms and roots with Sanskrit. The nearest approach to Sanskrit in Europe is made by the Lithuanian language.

*Mr. Nehru next writes of Buddhist philosophy and the effect of Buddhism on Hinduism. The problem of why Buddhism failed in India is considered in the context of a discussion of the six systems of Hindu philosophy, which he describes. Mr. Nehru then turns to a consideration of Indian contacts with pre-modern China associated with the spread of Buddhism to the latter country. He also summarizes the spread of Hindu art outside the sub-continent. From that follows a discussion of the characteristics of Hindu art.*

### IV. OLD INDIAN ART

The amazing expansion of Indian culture and art to other countries has led to some of the finest expressions of this art being found outside India. Unfortunately many of our old monuments and sculptures, especially in northern India, have been destroyed in the course of the ages. "To know Indian art in India alone," says Sir John Marshall, "is to know but half its story. To apprehend it to the full, we must follow it in the wake of Buddhism, to central Asia, China and Japan; we must watch it assuming new forms and breaking into new beauties as it spreads over Tibet and Burma and Siam; we must gaze in awe at the unexampled grandeur of its creations in Cambodia and Java. In each of these countries, Indian art encounters a different racial genius, a different local environment, and under their modifying influence it takes on a different garb."[5]

Indian art is so intimately associated with Indian religion and philosophy that it is difficult to appreciate it fully unless one has some knowledge of the ideals that governed the Indian mind. In art, as in music, there is a gulf which separates Eastern from Western conceptions. Probably the great artists and builders of the middle ages in Europe would have felt more in tune with Indian art and sculpture than modern European artists, who derive part of their inspiration at least from the Renaissance period and after. For in Indian art there is always a religious urge, a looking beyond, such as probably inspired the builders of the great cathedrals of Europe. Beauty is conceived as subjective, not objective; it is a thing of the spirit, though it may also take lovely shape in form or matter. The Greeks loved beauty for its own sake and found not only joy but truth in it; the ancient Indians loved beauty also, but always they sought to put some deeper significance in their work, some vision of the inner truth as they saw it. In the supreme examples of their creative work they extort admiration, even though one may not understand what they were aiming at or the ideas that governed them. In lesser examples, this lack of understanding, this not being in tune with the artist's mind, becomes a bar to appreciation. There is a vague feeling of discomfort, even of irritation, at something one cannot grasp, and this leads to the conclusion that the artist did not know his job and has failed. Sometimes there is even a feeling of repulsion.

[5] From the foreword to Reginald Le May's *Buddhist Art in Siam* (Cambridge, 1938), quoted by Ghosal in *Progress of Greater Indian Research* (Calcutta, 1943).

I know nothing about art, Eastern or Western, and am not competent to say anything about it. I react to it as any untutored layman might do. Some painting or sculpture or building fills me with delight, or moves me and makes me feel a strange emotion; or it just pleases me a little; or it does not affect me at all and I pass it by almost unnoticed; or it repels me. I cannot explain these reactions or speak learnedly about the merits or demerits of works of art. The Buddha statue at Anuradhapura in Ceylon moved me greatly, and a picture of it has been my companion for many years. On the other hand some famous temples in south India, heavy with carving and detail, disturb me and fill me with unease.

Europeans, trained in the Greek tradition, at first examined Indian art from the Grecian point of view. They recognized something they knew in the Graeco-Buddhist art of Gandhara and the frontier and considered other forms in India as degraded types of this. Gradually a new approach was made, and it was pointed out that Indian art was something original and vital and in no way derived from this Graeco-Buddhist art, which was a pale reflection of it. This new approach came more from the continent of Europe than from England. It is curious that Indian art, and this applies to Sanskrit literature also, has been more appreciated on the continent than in England. I have often wondered how far this has been conditioned by the unfortunate political relationship existing between India and England. Probably there is something in that, though there must be other and more basic causes of difference also. There are of course many Englishmen, artists and scholars and others, who have come near to the spirit and outlook of India and helped to discover our old treasures and interpret them to the world. There are many also to whom India is grateful for their warm friendship and service. Yet the fact remains that there is a gulf, and an ever-widening gulf, between Indians and Englishmen. On the Indian side this is easier to understand, at any rate for me, for a great deal has happened in recent years that has cut deep into our souls. On the other side perhaps some similar reactions have taken place for different reasons, among them being anger at being put in the wrong before the world when, according to them, the fault was not theirs. But the feeling is deeper than politics and it comes out unawares, and most of all it seems to affect English intellectuals. The Indian, to them, appears to be a special manifestation of original sin and all his works bear this mark. A popular English author, though hardly representative of English thought or intelligence, has recently written a book which is full of a malicious hatred and disgust for almost everything Indian. A more eminent and representative English author, Mr. Osbert Sitwell says in his book *Escape With Me* (1941) that "the idea of India, despite its manifold and diverse marvels, continued to be repellent." He refers also to "that repulsive, greasy quality that so often mars Hindu works of art."

Mr. Sitwell is perfectly justified in holding those opinions about Indian art or India generally. I am sure he feels that way. I am myself repelled by much in India, but I do not feel that way about India as a whole. Naturally, for I am an Indian and I cannot easily hate myself, however unworthy I might be. But it is not a question of opinions or views on art; it is much more a conscious and subconscious dislike and unfriendliness to a whole people. Is it true that those whom we have injured, we dislike and hate?

Among the Englishmen who have appreciated Indian art and applied new standards of judgment to it have been Lawrence Binyon and E. B. Havell. Havell is particularly enthusiastic about the ideals of Indian art and the spirit underlying them. He emphasizes that a great national art affords an intimate revelation of national thought and character, but it is only to be appreciated if the ideals behind it are understood. An alien governing race misapprehending and depreciating those ideals sows the seeds of intellectual antipathy. Indian art, he says, was not addressed to a narrow coterie of literati. Its intention was to make the central ideas of religion and philosophy intelligible to the masses. "That Hindu art was successful in its educational purpose may be inferred from the fact, known to all who have intimate acquaintance with Indian life, that the Indian peasantry, though illiterate in the Western sense, are among the most cultured of their class anywhere in the world."[6]

In art, as in Sanskrit poetry and Indian music, the artist was supposed to identify himself with nature in all her moods, to express the essential harmony of man with nature and the universe. That has been the keynote of all Asiatic art, and it is because of this that there is a certain unity about the art of Asia, in spite of its great variety and the national differences that are so evident. There is not much of old painting in India, except for the lovely frescoes of Ajanta. Perhaps much of it has perished. It was in her sculpture and architecture that India stood out, just as China and Japan excelled in painting.

Indian music, which is so different from European music, was highly developed in its own way, and India stood out in this respect and influenced Asiatic music considerably, except for China and the Far East. Music thus became another link with Persia, Afghanistan, Arabia, Turkestan, and to some extent with other areas where Arab civilization flourished, for instance North Africa. Indian classical music will probably be appreciated in all these countries.

An important influence in the development of art in India, as elsewhere in Asia, was the religious prejudice against graven images. The Vedas were against image worship, and it was only at a comparatively late period in Buddhism that Buddha's person was represented in sculpture and painting. In the Mathura Museum there is a huge stone figure of the Bodhisattva which is full of strength and power. This belongs to the Kushan period about the beginning of the Christian era.

The early period of Indian art is full of a naturalism which may partly be due to Chinese influences. Chinese influence is visible at various stages of Indian art history, chiefly in the development of this naturalism, just as Indian idealism went to China and Japan and powerfully influenced them during some of their great periods.

During the Gupta period, fourth to sixth centuries A.D.,

6 E. B. Havell, *The Ideals of Indian Art* (1920), p. xix.

the Golden Age of India as it is called, the caves of Ajanta were dug out and the frescoes painted. Bagh and Badami are also of this period. The Ajanta frescoes, very beautiful though they are, have, ever since their discovery, exercised a powerful influence on our present-day artists, who have turned away from life and sought to model their style on that of Ajanta, with unhappy results.

Ajanta takes one back into some distant, dreamlike and yet very real world. These frescoes were painted by the Buddhist monks. Keep away from women, do not even look at them, for they are dangerous, had said their Master long ago. And yet we have here women in plenty, beautiful women, princesses, singers, dancers, seated and standing, beautifying themselves, or in procession. The women of Ajanta have become famous. How well those painter-monks must have known the world and the moving drama of life, how lovingly they have painted it, just as they have painted the Bodhisattva in his calm and otherworldly majesty.

In the seventh and eighth centuries the mighty caves of Ellora were carved out of solid rock with the stupendous Kailasa temple in the center; it is difficult to imagine how human beings conceived this, or having conceived it, gave body and shape to their conception. The caves of Elephanta, with the powerful and subtle Trimurti, date also from this period. Also the group of monuments at Mamallapuram in south India.

In the Elephanta caves there is a broken statue of Shiva Nataraja, Shiva dancing. Even in its mutilated condition, Havell says that it is a majestic conception and an embodiment of titanic power: "Though the rock itself seems to vibrate with the rhythmic movement of the dance, the noble head bears the same look of serene calm and dispassion which illuminate the face of the Buddha!"

There is another Shiva Nataraja in the British Museum, and of this Epstein has written: "Siva dances, creating the world and destroying it, his large rhythms conjure up vast aeons of time, and his movements have a relentless magical power of incantation. A small group of the British Museum is the most tragic summing up of the death in love motive ever seen, and it epitomises, as no other work, the fatal element in human passion. Our European allegories are banal and pointless by comparison with these profound works, devoid of the trappings of symbolism, concentrating on the essential, the essentially plastic."[7]

There is a head of a Bodhisattva from Borobudur in Java which has been taken to the Glyptotek in Copenhagen. It is beautiful, in the sense of formal beauty, but, as Havell says, there is something deeper in it revealing, as in a mirror, the pure soul of the Bodhisattva. "It is a face which incarnates the stillness of the depths of ocean; the serenity of an azure, cloudless sky; a beatitude beyond mortal ken."

"Indian art in Java," adds Havell, "has a character of its own which distinguishes it from that of the continent from whence it came. There runs through both the same strain of deep serenity, but in the divine ideal of Java we lose the austere feeling which characterizes the Hindu sculpture of Elephanta and Mamallapuram. There is more of human contentment and joy in Indo-Javanese art, an expression of that peaceful security which the Indian colonists enjoyed in their happy island home, after the centuries of storm and struggle which their forefathers had experienced on the mainland."[8]

## V. INDIA'S FOREIGN TRADE

Throughout the first millennium of the Christian era India's trade was widespread and Indian merchants controlled many foreign markets. It was dominant in the eastern seas, and it reached out also to the Mediterranean. Pepper and other spices went from India or via India to the West, often on Indian and Chinese bottoms, and it is said that Alaric the Goth took away three thousand pounds of pepper from Rome. Roman writers bemoaned the fact that gold flowed from Rome to India and the East in exchange for various luxury articles.

This trade was largely, in India as elsewhere at the time,

---

[7] Epstein, *Let There Be Sculpture* (1942), p. 193.
[8] Havell, *The Ideals of Indian Art* (1920), p. 169.

one of give and take of materials found and developed locally. India was a fertile land and rich in some of the materials that other countries lacked, and the seas being open to her, she sent these materials abroad. She also obtained them from the eastern islands and profited as a merchant carrier. But she had further advantages. She had been manufacturing cloth from the earliest ages, long before other countries did so, and a textile industry had developed. Indian textiles went to far countries. Silk was also made from very early times, though probably it was not nearly as good as Chinese silk, which began to be imported as early as the fourth century B.C. The Indian silk industry may have developed subsequently, though it does not seem to have gone far. An important advance was made in the dyeing of cloth, and special methods were discovered for the preparation of fast dyes. Among these was indigo, a word derived from India through Greek. It was probably this knowledge of dyeing that gave a great impetus to India's trade with foreign countries.

It is difficult to say how far mechanical appliances had developed then, but shipbuilding was a flourishing industry and there is frequent reference to various kinds of "machines," especially for purposes of war. This has led some enthusiastic and rather credulous Indians to imagine all kinds of complicated machines. It does seem, however, that India at that time was not behind any country in the making and use of tools and in the knowledge of chemistry and metallurgy. It was this that gave her an advantage in trade and enabled her for several centuries to control a number of foreign markets.

Possibly she had one other advantage also—the absence of slave labor, which handicapped Greek and other early civilizations and came in the way of their progress. The caste system, with all its evils, which progressively increased, was infinitely better than slavery even for those lowest in the scale. Within each caste there was equality and a measure of freedom; each caste was occupational and applied itself to its particular work. This led to a high degree of specialization and skill in handicrafts and craftsmanship.

## VI. MATHEMATICS IN ANCIENT INDIA

Highly intellectual and given to abstract thinking as they were, one would expect the ancient Indians to excel in mathematics. Europe got its early arithmetic and algebra from the Arabs—hence the "Arabic numerals"—but the Arabs themselves had previously taken them from India. The astonishing progress that the Indians had made in mathematics is now well known, and it is recognized that the foundations of modern arithmetic and algebra were laid long ago in India. The clumsy method of using a counting frame, and the use of Roman and suchlike numerals, had long retarded progress when the ten Indian numerals, including the zero sign, liberated the human mind from these restrictions and threw a flood of light on the behavior of numbers. These number symbols were unique and entirely different from all other symbols that had been in use in other countries. They are common enough today, and we take them for granted; yet they contained the germs of revolutionary progress in them. It took many centuries for them to travel from India, via Baghdad, to the Western world.

A hundred and fifty years ago, during Napoleon's time, La Place wrote: "It is India that gave us the ingenuous method of expressing all numbers by means of ten symbols, each symbol receiving a value of position, as well as an absolute value; a profound and important idea which appears so simple to us now that we ignore its true merit, but its very simplicity, the great ease which it has lent to all computations, puts our arithmetic in the first rank of useful inventions; and we shall appreciate the grandeur of this achievement when we remember that it escaped the genius of Archimedes and Apollonius, two of the greatest men produced by antiquity."[9]

[9] Quoted in Hogben's *Mathematics for the Million* (London, 1942).

The origins of geometry, arithmetic, and algebra in India go back to remote periods. Probably to begin with there was some kind of geometrical algebra used for making figures for Vedic altars. Mention is made in the most ancient books of the geometrical method for the transformation of a square into a rectangle having a given side: $ax = c$. Geometrical figures are even now commonly used in Hindu ceremonies. Geometry made progress in India, but in this respect Greece and Alexandria went ahead. It was in arithmetic and algebra that India kept the lead. The inventor or inventors of the decimal place-value system and the zero mark are not known. The earliest use of the zero symbol, so far discovered, is in one of the scriptural books dated about 200 B.C. It is considered probable that the place-value system was invented about the beginning of the Christian era. The zero, called *shunya* or nothing, was originally a dot, and later it became a small circle. It was considered a number like any other. Professor Halsted thus emphasizes the vital significance of this invention: "The importance of the creation of the zero mark can never be exaggerated. This giving to airy nothing, not merely a local habitation and a name, a picture, a symbol, but helpful power, is the characteristic of the Hindu race from whence it sprang. It is like coining the Nirvana into dynamos. No single mathematical creation has been more potent for the general on-go of intelligence and power."[10]

Yet another modern mathematician has grown eloquent over this historic event. Dantzig in his *Number* writes: "This long period of nearly five thousand years saw the rise and fall of many a civilization, each leaving behind it a heritage of literature, art, philosophy, and religion. But what was the net achievement in the field of reckoning, the earliest art practised by man? An inflexible numeration so crude as to make progress wellnigh impossible, and a calculating device so limited in scope that even elementary calculations called for the services of an expert. . . . Man used these devices for thousands of years without con-

---

[10] G. B. Halsted, *On the Foundation and Technique of Arithmetic* (Chicago, 1912), p. 20; quoted in *History of Hindu Mathematics* by B. Datta and A. N. Singh (1935).

tributing a single important idea to the system. . . . Even when compared with the slow growth of ideas during the dark ages, the history of reckoning presents a peculiar picture of desolate stagnation. When viewed in this light, the achievements of the unknown Hindu, who some time in the first centuries of our era discovered the principle of position, assumes the importance of a world event."[11]

Dantzig is puzzled at the fact that the great mathematicians of Greece did not stumble on this discovery. "Is it that the Greeks had such a marked contempt for applied science, leaving even the instruction of their children to slaves? But if so, how is it that the nation that gave us geometry, and carried this science so far, did not create even a rudimentary algebra? Is it not equally strange that algebra, that cornerstone of modern mathematics, also originated in India, and at about the same time that positional numeration did?"

The answer to this question is suggested by Professor Hogben. "The difficulty of understanding why it should have been the Hindus who took this step, why it was not taken by the mathematicians of antiquity, why it should first have been taken by practical man, is only insuperable if we seek for the explanation of intellectual progress in the genius of a few gifted individuals, instead of in the whole social framework of custom and thought which circumscribes the greatest individual genius. What happened in India about A.D. 100 had happened before. May be it is happening now in Soviet Russia. . . . To accept it [this truth] is to recognize that every culture contains within itself its own doom, unless it pays as much attention to the education of the mass of mankind as to the education of the exceptionally gifted people."[12]

We must assume then that these momentous inventions were not just due to the momentary illumination of an erratic genius, much in advance of his time, but that they were essentially the product of the social milieu and

11 Quoted in L. Hogben's *Mathematics for the Million* (London, 1942).
12 Hogben, *Mathematics for the Million* (London, 1942), p. 285.

that they answered some insistent demand of the times. Genius of a high order was certainly necessary to find this out and fulfill this demand, but if that demand had not been there, the urge to find some way out would have been absent, and even if the invention had been made, it would have been forgotten or put aside till circumstances more propitious for its use arose. It seems clear from the early Sanskrit works on mathematics that the demand was there, for these books are full of problems of trade and social relationship involving complicated calculations. There are problems dealing with taxation, debt, and interest; problems of partnership, barter and exchange, and the calculation of the fineness of gold. Society had grown complex, and large numbers of people were engaged in governmental operations and in an extensive trade. It was impossible to carry on without simple methods of calculation.

In the eighth century, during the reign of the khalifa Al-Mansur (753–74), a number of Indian scholars went to Baghdad, and among the books they took with them were works on mathematics and astronomy. Probably even earlier than this, Indian numerals had reached Baghdad, but this was the first systematic approach, and Aryabhata's and other books were translated into Arabic. They influenced the development of mathematics and astronomy in the Arab world, and Indian numerals were introduced. Baghdad was then a great center of learning, and Greek and Jewish scholars had gathered there bringing with them Greek philosophy, geometry, and science. The cultural influence of Baghdad was felt throughout the Moslem world from central Asia to Spain, and a knowledge of Indian mathematics in their Arabic translations spread all over this vast area. The numerals were called by the Arabs "figures of Hind" (or India), and the Arabic word for a number is *Hindsah,* meaning "from Hind."

From this Arab world the new mathematics traveled to European countries, probably through the Moorish universities of Spain, and became the foundation for European mathematics. There was opposition in Europe to the use of the new numbers, as they were considered infidel symbols, and it took several hundred years before they were in common use. The earliest known use is in a Sicilian coin of 1134; in Britain the first use is in 1490.

It seems clear that some knowledge of Indian mathematics, and especially of the place-value system of numbers, had penetrated into western Asia even before the formal embassy carried books to Baghdad. There is an interesting passage in a complaint made by a Syrian scholar-monk who was hurt at the arrogance of some Greek scholars who looked down on Syrians. Severus Sebokht was his name, and he lived in a convent situated on the Euphrates. He writes in 662 A.D. and tries to show that the Syrians were in no way inferior to the Greeks. By way of illustration he refers to the Indians: "I will omit all discussion of the science of the Hindus, a people not the same as the Syrians, their subtle discoveries in the science of astronomy, discoveries that are more ingenious than those of the Greeks and the Babylonians; their computing that surpasses description. I wish only to say that this computation is done by means of nine signs. If those who believe, because they speak Greek, that they have reached the limits of science, should know of these things, they would be convinced that there are also others who know something."[13]

Mathematics in India inevitably makes one think of one extraordinary figure of recent times. This was Srinivasa Ramanujam. Born in a poor Brahman family in south India, having no opportunities for a proper education, he became a clerk in the Madras Port Trust. But he was bubbling over with some irrepressible quality of instinctive genius and played about with numbers and equations in his spare time. By a lucky chance he attracted the attention of a mathematician who sent some of his amateur work to Cambridge in England. People there were impressed, and a scholarship was arranged for him. So he left his clerk's job and went to Cambridge and during a very brief period there did work of profound value and amazing originality. The Royal Society of England went rather out of their way and made him a fellow, but he died two years later, probably

[13] Quoted in *History of Hindu Mathematics* by B. Datta and A. N. Singh (1935). I am indebted to this book for much information on this subject.

of tuberculosis, at the age of thirty-three. Professor Julian Huxley has, I believe, referred to him somewhere as the greatest mathematician of the century.

Ramanujam's brief life and death are symbolic of conditions in India. Of our millions how few get any education at all, how many live on the verge of starvation; of even those who get some education, how many have nothing to look forward to but a clerkship in some office on pay that is usually far less than the unemployment dole in England. If life opened its gates to them and offered them food and healthy conditions of living and education and opportunities of growth, how many among these millions would be eminent scientists, educationists, technicians, industrialists, writers and artists, helping to build a new India and a new world?

## VII. GROWTH AND DECAY

During the first thousand years of the Christian era, there are many ups and downs in India, many conflicts with invading elements and internal troubles. Yet it is a period of a vigorous national life, bubbling over with energy and spreading out in all directions. Culture develops into a rich civilization flowering out in philosophy, literature, drama, art, science, and mathematics. India's economy expands, the Indian horizon widens and other countries come within its scope. Contacts grow with Iran, China, the Hellenic world, central Asia, and above all there is a powerful urge toward the eastern seas which leads to the establishment of Indian colonies and the spread of Indian culture far beyond India's boundaries. During the middle period of this millennium, from early in the fourth to the sixth century, the Gupta empire flourishes and becomes the patron and symbol of this widespread intellectual and artistic activity. That is called the Golden or Classical Age of India, and in the writings of that period, which form the classics of Sanskrit literature, there is a quiet serenity, a confidence in themselves, and a glow of pride at being privileged to be alive in that high noon of civilization, and with this there is the urge to use their great intellectual and artistic powers to the utmost.

Yet even before that Golden Age had come to a close, signs of weakness and decay become visible. The White Huns come from the northwest in successive hordes and are repeatedly pushed back. But they come again and again and eat their way slowly into north India. For a half century they even establish themselves as a ruling power all over the north. But then, with a great effort, the last of the great Guptas, joining up in a confederacy with Yashovarman, a ruler of central India, drives out the Huns. This long-drawn-out conflict weakened India politically and militarily, and probably the settlement of large numbers of these Huns all over northern India gradually produced an inner change in the people. They were absorbed as all foreign elements had so far been absorbed, but they left their impress and weakened the old ideals of the Indo-Aryan races. Old accounts of the Huns are full of their excessive cruelty and barbarous behavior which were so foreign to Indian standards of warfare and government.

In the seventh century there was a revival and renascence under Harsha, both political and cultural. Ujjayini (modern Ujjain), which had been the brilliant capital of the Guptas, again became a center of art and culture and the seat of a powerful kingdom. But in the centuries that followed, this too weakens and fades off. In the ninth century Mihira Bhoja of Gujrat consolidates a unified state in north and central India with his capital at Kanauj. There is another literary revival, of which the central figure is Rajashekhara. Again, at the beginning of the eleventh century, another Bhoja stands out as a powerful and attractive figure, and Ujjayini again becomes a great capital. This Bhoja was a remarkable man who distinguished himself in many fields. He was a grammarian and a lexicographer, and interested in medicine and astronomy. He was a builder and a patron of art and literature, and was himself a poet and a writer to whom many works are attributed. His name has become a part of popular fable and legend as a symbol of greatness, learning, and generosity.

And yet for all these bright patches, an inner weakness seems to seize India which affects not only her political status but her creative activities. There is no date for this, for the process was a slow and creeping one, and it affected north India earlier than the south. The south indeed becomes more important both politically and culturally. Perhaps this was due to the south having escaped the continuous strain of fighting waves of invaders; perhaps many of the writers and artists and master builders migrated to the south to escape from the unsettled conditions in the north. The powerful kingdoms of the south, with their brilliant courts, must have attracted these people and given them opportunities for creative work which they lacked elsewhere.

But though the north did not dominate India, as it had often done in the past, and was split up into small states, life was still rich there and there were many centers of cultural and philosophic activity. Benares, as ever, was the heart of religious and philosophical thought, and every person who advanced a new theory, or a new interpretation of an old theory, had to come there to justify himself. Kashmir was for long a great Sanskrit center of Buddhist and Brahmanical learning. The great universities flourished, Nalanda most famous of all, respected for its scholarship all over India. To have been to Nalanda was a hallmark of culture. It was not easy to enter that university, for admission was restricted to those who had already attained a certain standard. It specialized in postgraduate study and attracted students from China, Japan, and Tibet, and even, it is said, from Korea and Mongolia and Bokhara. Apart from religious and philosophical subjects (both Buddhist and Brahmanical), secular and practical subjects were also taught. There was a school of art and a department for architecture; a medical school; an agricultural department; dairy farms and cattle. The intellectual life of the university is said to have been one of animated debates and discussions. The spread of Indian culture abroad was largely the work of scholars from Nalanda.

Then there was the Vikramshila university, near modern Bhagalpur in Bihar, and Vallabhi in Kathiawar. During the period of the Guptas, the Ujjayini university rose into prominence. In the south there was the Amravati university.

Yet, as the millennium approached its end, all this appears to be the afternoon of a civilization; the glow of the morning had long faded away, high noon was past. In the south there was still vitality and vigor, and this lasted for some centuries more; in the Indian colonies abroad there was aggressive and full-blooded life right up to the middle of the next millennium. But the heart seems to petrify, its beats are slower, and gradually this petrifaction and decay spread to the limbs. There is no great figure in philosophy after Shankara in the eighth century, though there is a long succession of commentators and dialecticians. Even Shankara came from the south. The sense of curiosity and the spirit of mental adventure give place to a hard and formal logic and a sterile dialectic. Both Brahmanism and Buddhism deteriorate and degraded forms of worship grow up, especially some varieties of tantric worship and perversions of the Yoga system.

In literature, Bhavabhuti (eighth century) is the last great figure. Many books continued to be written, but their style becomes more and more involved and intricate; there is neither freshness of thought nor of expression. In mathematics Bhaskara II (twelfth century) is the last great name. In art, E. B. Havell takes us rather beyond this period. He says that the form of expression was not artistically perfected until about the seventh and eighth centuries, when most of the great sculpture and painting in India was produced. From the seventh or eighth to the fourteenth century, according to him, was the great period of Indian art, corresponding to the highest development of Gothic art in Europe. He adds that it was in the sixteenth century that the creative impulse of the old Indian art began markedly to diminish. How far this judgment is correct I do not know, but I imagine that even in the field of art it was south India that carried on the old tradition for a longer period than the north.

The last of the major emigrations for colonial settlement took place from south India in the ninth century, but the

Cholas in the south continued to be a great sea power till the eleventh century, when they defeated and conquered Srivijaya.

We thus see that India was drying up and losing her creative genius and vitality. The process was a slow one and lasted several centuries, beginning in the north and finally reaching the south. What were the causes of this political decline and cultural stagnation? Was this due to age alone, that seems to attack civilizations as it does individuals, or to a kind of tidal wave with its forward and backward motion? Or were external causes and invasions responsible for it? Radhakrishnan says that Indian philosophy lost its vigor with the loss of political freedom. Sylvain Lévi writes: *"La culture sanscrite a fine avec la liberté de l'Inde; des langues nouvelles, des littératures nouvelles ont envahi la territoire aryen et l'en ont chassée; elle s'est réfugié dans les collèges et y a pris un air pédantesque."*

All this is true, for the loss of political freedom leads inevitably to cultural decay. But why should political freedom be lost unless some kind of decay has preceded it? A small country might easily be overwhelmed by superior power, but a huge, well-developed and highly civilized country like India cannot succumb to external attack unless there is internal decay, or the invader possesses a higher technique of warfare. That internal decay is clearly evident in India at the close of these thousand years.

There are repeatedly periods of decay and disruption in the life of every civilization, and there had been such periods in Indian history previously. But India had survived them and rejuvenated herself afresh, sometimes retiring into her shell for a while and emerging again with fresh vigor. There always remained a dynamic core which could renew itself with fresh contacts and develop again, something different from the past and yet intimately connected with it. Had that capacity for adaptation, that flexibility of mind which had saved India so often in the past, left her now? Had her fixed beliefs and the growing rigidity of her social structure made her mind also rigid? For if life ceases to grow and evolve, the evolution of thought also ceases. India had all along been a curious combination of conservatism in practice and explosive thought. Inevitably that thought affected the practice, though it did so in its own way without irreverence for the past. "*Mais si leur yeux suivaient les mots anciens, leur intelligence y voyait des idées nouvelles. L'Inde s'est transformèe à son insu.*" But when thought lost its explosiveness and creative power and became a tame attendant on an outworn and meaningless practice, mumbling old phrases and fearful of everything new, then life became stagnant and tied and constrained in a prison of its own making.

We have many examples of the collapse of a civilization, and perhaps the most notable of these is that of the European classical civilization which ended with the fall of Rome. Long before Rome fell to the invaders from the north, it had been on the verge of collapse from its own internal weaknesses. Its economy, once expanding, had shrunk and brought all manner of difficulties in its train. Urban industries decayed, flourishing cities grew progressively smaller and impoverished, and even fertility rapidly declined. The emperors tried many expedients to overcome their ever-increasing difficulties. There was compulsory state regulation of merchants, craftsmen, and workers, who were tied down to particular employments. Many kinds of employees were even forbidden to marry outside their own group of workers. Thus some occupations were practically converted into castes. The peasantry became serfs. But all these superficial attempts to check the decline failed and even worsened conditions; and the Roman Empire collapsed.

There was and has been no such dramatic collapse of Indian civilization, and it has shown an amazing staying power despite all that has happened. But a progressive decline is visible. It is difficult to specify in any detail what the social conditions in India were at the end of the first millennium after Christ. But it may be said with some assurance that the expanding economy of India had ended and there was a strong tendency to shrink. Probably this was the inevitable result of the growing rigidity and exclusiveness of the Indian social structure as represented chiefly by the caste system. Where Indians had gone abroad, as in southeast Asia, they were not so rigid in mind or customs or in their economy, and they had opportunities for growth and expansion. For another four or five hundred years they flourished in these colonies and displayed energy and creative vigor. But in India herself the spirit of exclusiveness sapped the creative faculty and developed a narrow, small-group, and parochial outlook. Life became all cut up into set frames where each man's job was fixed and permanent and he had little concern with others. It was the Kshatriya's business to fight in defense of the country, and others were not interested or were not even allowed to do so. The Brahman and the Kshatriya looked down on trade and commerce. Education and opportunities of growth were withheld from the lower castes, who were taught to be submissive to those higher up in the scale. In spite of a well-developed urban economy and industries, the structure of the state was in many ways feudal. Probably even in the technique of warfare India had fallen behind. No marked progress was possible under these conditions without changing that structure and releasing fresh sources of talent and energy. The caste system was a barrier to such a change. For all its virtues and the stability it had given to Indian society, it carried within it the seeds of destruction.

The Indian social structure (and I shall consider this more fully later) had given amazing stability to Indian civilization. It had given strength and cohesion to the group, but this came in the way of expansion and a larger cohesion. It developed crafts and skill and trade and commerce, but always within each group separately. Thus particular types of activity became hereditary, and there was a tendency to avoid new types of work and activity and to confine oneself to the old groove, to restrict initiative and the spirit of innovation. It gave a measure of freedom within a certain limited sphere, but at the expense of the growth of a larger freedom and at the heavy price of keeping large numbers of people permanently at the bottom of the social ladder, deprived of the opportunities of growth. So long as that structure afforded avenues for growth and expansion, it was progressive; when it reached the limits of expansion open to it, it became stationary, unprogressive, and, later, inevitably regressive.

Because of this there was decline all along the line—intellectual, philosophical, political, in technique and methods of warfare, in knowledge of and contacts with the outside world, in shrinking economy, and there was a growth of local sentiments and feudal and small-group feeling at the expense of the larger conception of India as a whole. Yet, as later ages were to show, there was yet vitality in the old structure and an amazing tenacity, as well as some flexibility and capacity for adaptation. Because of this it managed to survive and to profit by new contacts and waves of thought, and even progress in some ways. But that progress was always tied down to and hampered by far too many relics of the past.

# V. New Problems

## I. THE ARABS AND THE MONGOLS

While Harsha was reigning over a powerful kingdom in north India and Hsuan Tsang, the Chinese scholar-pilgrim, was studying at Nalanda university, Islam was taking shape in Arabia. Islam was to come to India both as a religious and a political force and create many new problems, but it is well to remember that it took a long time before it made much difference to the Indian scene. It took nearly six hundred years before it reached the heart of India, and when it came to the accompaniment of political conquest, it had already changed much and its standard-bearers were different. The Arabs who, in a fine frenzy of enthusiasm and with a dynamic energy, had spread out and conquered from Spain to the borders of Mongolia, carrying with them a brilliant culture, did not come to India proper. They stopped at its northwestern fringe and remained there. Arab civilization gradually decayed, and various Turkish tribes came into prominence in central and western Asia. It was these Turkis and Afghans from the Indian borderland who brought Islam as a political force to India.

Some dates might help to bring these facts home to us. Islam may be said to begin with the *Hijrah*, the departure of the prophet Mohammed from Mecca to Medina, in 622 A.D. Mohammed died ten years later. Some time was spent in consolidating the position in Arabia, and then the astounding series of events took place which carried the Arabs, with the banner of Islam, right across central Asia in the East and across the whole north African continent to Spain and France in the West. In the seventh century and by the beginning of the eighth, they had spread over Iraq, Iran, and central Asia. In 712 A.D. they reached and occupied Sind in the northwest of India and stopped there. A great desert separated this area from the more fertile parts of India. In the West, the Arabs crossed the narrow straits between Africa and Europe (since called the Straits of Gibraltar) and entered Spain in 711 A.D. They occupied the whole of Spain and crossed the Pyrenees into France. In 732 they were defeated and checked by Charles Martel at Tours in France.

This triumphant career of a people whose homelands were the deserts of Arabia and who had thus far played no notable part in history is most remarkable. They must have derived their vast energy from the dynamic and revolutionary character of their Prophet and his message of human brotherhood. And yet it is wrong to imagine that Arab civilization suddenly rose out of oblivion and took shape after the advent of Islam. There has been a tendency on the part of Islamic scholars to decry the pre-Islamic past of the Arab people and to refer to it as the period of *jahiliyat,* a kind of dark age of ignorance and superstition. Arab civilization, like others, had a long past, intimately connected with the development of the Semitic race, the Phoenicians, Cretans, Chaldeans, Hebrews. The Israelites became more exclusive and separated themselves from the more catholic Chaldeans and others. Between them and other Semitic races there were conflicts. Nevertheless all over the Semitic area there were contacts and interchanges and to some extent a common background. Pre-Islamic Arab civilization grew up, especially in Yemen. Arabic was a highly developed language at the time of the Prophet, with a mixture of Persian and even some Indian words. Like the Phoenicians, the Arabs went far across the seas in search of trade. There was an Arab colony in south China, near Canton, in pre-Islamic days.

Nevertheless it is true that the Prophet of Islam vitalized his people and filled them with faith and enthusiasm. Considering themselves the standard-bearers of a new cause,

they developed the zeal and self-confidence which sometimes fills a whole people and changes history. Their success
was also undoubtedly due to the decay of the states in
western and central Asia and in north Africa. North Africa
was torn by internecine conflicts between rival Christian
factions leading often to bloody struggles for mastery. The
Christianity that was practiced there at the time was narrow and intolerant, and the contrast between this and the
general toleration of the Moslem Arabs, with their message of human brotherhood, was marked. It was this that
brought whole peoples, weary of Christian strife, to their
side.

The culture that the Arabs carried with them to distant
countries was itself continuously changing and developing.
It bore the strong impress of the new ideas of Islam, and yet
to call it Islamic civilization is confusing and probably incorrect. With their capital at Damascus, they soon left
their simple ways of living and developed a more sophisticated culture. That period might be called one of Arab-
Syrian civilization. Byzantine influences came to them, but
most of all, when they moved to Baghdad the traditions of
old Iran affected them and they developed the Arab-
Persian civilization which became dominant over all the
vast areas they controlled.

Widespread and apparently easy as the Arab conquests
were, they did not go far beyond Sind in India, then or
later. Was this due to the fact that India was still strong
enough to resist effectively the invader? Probably so, for it
is difficult to explain otherwise the lapse of several centuries
before a real invasion took place. Partly it may have been
due to the internal troubles of the Arabs. Sind fell away
from the central authority at Baghdad and became a small
independent Moslem state. But though there was no invasion, contacts between India and the Arab world grew,
travelers came to and fro, embassies were exchanged, Indian books, especially on mathematics and astronomy,
were taken to Baghdad and were translated into Arabic.
Many Indian physicians went to Baghdad. These trade and
cultural relations were not confined to north India. The
southern states of India also participated in them, espe-

cially the Rashtrakutas on the west coast of India, for purposes of trade.

This frequent intercourse inevitably led to Indians getting to know the new religion, Islam. Missionaries also came to spread this new faith, and they were welcomed. Mosques were built. There was no objection raised either by the state or the people, nor were there any religious conflicts. It was the old tradition of India to be tolerant to all faiths and forms of worship. Thus Islam came as a religion to India several centuries before it came as a political force.

## II. MAHMUD OF GHAZNI AND THE AFGHANS

Early in the eighth century, in 712, the Arabs had reached Sind and occupied it. They stopped there. Even Sind fell away from the Arab empire within half a century or so, though it continued as a small independent Moslem state. For nearly three hundred years there was no further invasion of or incursion into India. About 1000 A.D. Sultan Mahmud of Ghazni in Afghanistan, a Turk who had risen to power in central Asia, began his raids into India. There were many such raids, and they were bloody and ruthless and on every occasion Mahmud carried away with him a vast quantity of treasure. A scholar-contemporary, Alberuni of Khiva, describes these raids: "The Hindus became like the atoms of dust scattered in all directions and like a tale of old in the mouths of people. Their scattered remains cherish of course the most inveterate aversion towards all Moslems." This poetic description gives us some idea of the devastation caused by Mahmud, and yet it is well to remember that Mahmud touched and despoiled only a part of north India, chiefly along the lines of his marches. The whole of central, eastern and south India escaped from him completely.

South India at that time and later was dominated by the powerful Chola empire which controlled the sea routes and had reached as far as Srivijaya in Java and Sumatra. The

Indian colonies in the eastern seas were also flourishing and strong. Sea power was shared between them and south India. But this did not save north India from a land invasion.

Mahmud annexed the Punjab and Sind to his dominions and returned to Ghazni after each raid. He was unable to conquer Kashmir. This mountain country succeeded in checking and repulsing him. He met with a severe defeat also in the Rajputana desert regions on his way back from Somnath in Kathiawar.[1] This was his last raid, and he did not return.

Mahmud was far more a warrior than a man of faith, and like many other conquerors, he used and exploited the name of religion for his conquests. India was to him just a place from which he could carry off treasure and material to his homeland. He enrolled an army in India and placed it under one of his noted generals, Tilak by name, who was an Indian and a Hindu. This army he used against his own coreligionists in central Asia. He was anxious to make his own city of Ghazni rival the great cities of central and western Asia, and he carried off from India large numbers of artisans and master builders. Building interested him, and he was much impressed by the city of Mathura (modern Muttra) near Delhi. About this he wrote: "There

---

[1] There is a curious passage relating to this defeat in an old chronicle in Persian, the *Tarikh-i-Sorath* (Trans. by Ranchodji Amarji, Bombay, 1882, p. 112): "Shah Mahmud took to his heels in dismay and saved his life, but many of his followers of both sexes were captured. . . . Turks, Afghans and Mughal female prisoners, if they happened to be virgins, were accepted as wives by the Indian soldiers. . . . The bowels of the others, however, were cleansed by means of emetics and purgatives, and thereafter the captives were married to men of similar rank. . . . Low females were joined to low men. Respectable men were compelled to shave off their beards, and were enrolled among the Shekhavat and the Wadhel tribes of Rajputs; whilst the lower kinds were allotted to the castes of Kolis, Khantas, Babrias and Mers." I am not myself acquainted with the *Tarikh-i-Sorath* and do not know how far it can be considered reliable. I have taken this quotation from K. M. Munshi's *The Glory That Was Gurjardesa*, Part III, p. 140. What is especially interesting is the way foreigners are said to have been absorbed into the Rajput clans and even marriages to have taken place. The cleansing process mentioned is novel.

are here a thousand edifices as firm as the faith of the faithful; nor is it likely that this city has attained its present condition but at the expense of many millions of dinars, nor could such another be constructed under a period of two hundred years."

In the intervals of his fighting, Mahmud was interested in encouraging cultural activities in his own homeland, and he gathered together a number of eminent men. Among these was the famous Persian poet Firdausi, author of the *Shah Namah*, who later fell out with Mahmud. Alberuni, a scholar and a traveler, was a contemporary, and in his books he gives us a glimpse into other aspects of life in central Asia then. Born near Khiva, but of Persian descent, he came to India and traveled a great deal. He tells us of the great irrigation works in the Chola kingdom in the south, though it is doubtful if he visited them himself or went to south India. He learned Sanskrit in Kashmir and studied the religion, philosophy, science, and arts of India. He had previously learned Greek in order to study Greek philosophy. His books are not only a storehouse of information, but tell us how, behind war and pillage and massacre, patient scholarship continued, and how the people of one country tried to understand those of another even when passion and anger had embittered their relations. That passion and anger no doubt clouded the judgments on either side, and each considered his own people superior to the other. Of the Indians, Alberuni says that they are "haughty, foolishly vain, self-contained and stolid" and that they believe "that there is no country like theirs, no nation like theirs, no kings like theirs, no science like theirs." Probably a correct enough description of the temper of the people.

Mahmud's raids are a big event in Indian history, though politically India as a whole was not greatly affected by them and the heart of India remained untouched. They demonstrated the weakness and decay of north India, and Alberuni's accounts throw further light on the political disintegration of the North and West. These repeated incursions from the northwest brought many new elements in India's closed thought and economy. Above all they brought Islam, for the first time, to the accompaniment of ruthless military conquest. So far, for over three hundred years, Islam had come peacefully as a religion and taken its place among the many religions of India without trouble or conflict. The new approach produced powerful psychological reactions among the people and filled them with bitterness. There was no objection to a new religion, but there was strong objection to anything which forcibly interfered with and upset their way of life.

India was, it must be remembered, a country of many religions, in spite of the dominance of the Hindu faith in its various shapes and forms. Apart from Jainism and Buddhism, which had largely faded away and been absorbed by Hinduism, there were Christianity and the Hebrew religion. Both of these had reached India probably during the first century after Christ, and both had found a place in the country. There were large numbers of Syrian Christians and Nestorians in south India, and they were as much part of the country as anyone else. So were the Jews. And so too was the small community of the Zoroastrians who had come to India from Iran in the seventh century. So also were many Moslems on the west coast and in the northwest.

Mahmud came as a conqueror, and the Punjab became just an outlying province of his dominions. Yet when he had established himself as a ruler there, an attempt was made to tone down his previous methods in order to win over the people of the province to some extent. There was less of interference with their ways, and Hindus were appointed to high office in the army and the administration. Only the beginnings of this process are noticeable in Mahmud's time; it was to grow later.

Mahmud died in 1030. More than a hundred and sixty years passed after his death without any other invasion of India or an extension of Turkish rule beyond the Punjab. Then an Afghan, Shahab-ud-Din Ghuri, captured Ghazni and put an end to the Ghaznavite empire. He marched to Lahore and then to Delhi. But the king of Delhi, Prithvi Raj Chauhan, defeated him utterly. Shahab-ud-Din retired to Afghanistan and came back next year with another army.

This time he triumphed, and in 1192 he sat on the throne of Delhi.

Prithvi Raj is a popular hero, still famous in song and legend, for reckless lovers are always popular. He had carried away the girl he loved and who loved him from the very palace of her father, Jaichandra, king of Kanauj, defying an assembled host of princelings who had come to offer court to her. He won his bride for a brief while, but at the cost of a bitter feud with a powerful ruler and the lives of the bravest on both sides. The chivalry of Delhi and central India engaged in internecine conflict, and there was much mutual slaughter. And so, all for the love of a woman, Prithvi Raj lost his life and throne, and Delhi, that seat of empire, passed into the hands of an invader from outside. But his love story is sung still and he is a hero, while Jaichandra is looked upon almost as a traitor.

This conquest of Delhi did not mean the subjugation of the rest of India. The Cholas were still powerful in the south, and there were other independent states. It took another century and a half for Afghan rule to spread over the greater part of the south. But Delhi was significant and symbolic of the new order.

### III. THE INDO-AFGHANS—SOUTH INDIA— VIJAYANAGAR—BABAR—SEA POWER

Indian history has usually been divided by English as well as some Indian historians into three major periods: ancient or Hindu; Moslem; and the British period. This division is neither intelligent nor correct; it is deceptive and gives a wrong perspective. It deals more with the more superficial changes at the top than with the essential changes in the political, economic, and cultural development of the Indian people. The so-called ancient period is vast and full of change, of growth and decay and then growth again. What is called the Moslem or medieval period brought another change, and an important one, and yet it was more or less confined to the top and did not vitally affect the essential continuity of Indian life. The invaders who came to India from the northwest, like so many of their predecessors in more ancient times, became absorbed into India and part of her life. Their dynasties became Indian dynasties, and there was a great deal of racial fusion by intermarriage. A deliberate effort was made, apart from a few exceptions, not to interfere with the ways and customs of the people. They looked to India as their home country and had no other affiliations. India continued to be an independent country.

The coming of the British made a vital difference, and the old system was uprooted in many ways. They brought an entirely different impulse from the West, which had slowly developed in Europe from the times of the Renaissance, Reformation, and political revolution in England, and was taking shape in the beginnings of the Industrial Revolution. The American and French revolutions were to carry this further. The British remained outsiders, aliens and misfits in India and made no attempt to be otherwise. Above all, for the first time in India's history, her political control was exercised from outside and her economy was centered in a distant place. They made India a typical colony of the modern age, a subject country for the first time in her long history.

Mahmud of Ghazni's invasion of India was certainly a foreign Turkish invasion and resulted in the Punjab's being separated from the rest of India for a while. The Afghans who came at the end of the twelfth century were different. They were an Indo-Aryan race closely allied to the people of India. Indeed for long stretches of time Afghanistan had been, and was destined to be, a part of India. Their language, Pashto, was basically derived from Sanskrit. There are few places in India or outside which are so full of ancient monuments and remains of Indian culture, chiefly of the Buddhist period, as Afghanistan. More correctly, the Afghans should be called the Indo-Afghans. They differed in many ways from the people of the Indian plains, just as the people of the mountain valleys of Kashmir differed from the dwellers of the warmer and flatter regions below. But in spite of this difference Kashmir had always been and continued to be an important seat of Indian learning and culture. The Afghans differed also from the more highly cultured and sophisticated Arabs and Persians. They were hard and fierce like their mountain fastnesses, rigid in their faith, warriors not inclined toward intellectual pursuits or adventures of the mind. They behaved, to begin with, as conquerors over a rebellious people and were cruel and harsh.

But soon they toned down. India became their home and Delhi was their capital, not distant Ghazni as in Mahmud's time. Afghanistan, where they came from, was just an outlying part of their kingdom. The process of indianization was rapid, and many of them married women of the country. One of their great rulers, Alauddin Khilji, himself married a Hindu lady, and so did his son. Some of the subsequent rulers were racially Turks, such as Qutb-ud-Din Aibak, the Sultana Razia, and Iltutmish; but the nobility and army continued to be mainly Afghan. Delhi flourished as an imperial capital. Ibn Batuta, a famous Arab traveler from Morocco who visited many countries and saw many cities from Cairo and Constantinople to China, described it in the fourteenth century, perhaps with some exaggeration, as "one of the greatest cities in the universe."

The Delhi sultanate spread southward. The Chola kingdom was declining, but in its place a new seafaring power had grown. This was the Pandya kingdom, with its capital at Madura and its port at Kayal on the east coast. It was a small kingdom but a great center of trade. Marco Polo twice visited this port on his way from China, in 1288 and 1293, and described it as "a great and noble city," full of ships from Arabia and China. He also mentions the very fine muslins, which "look like tissues of a spider's web," and which were made on the east coast of India. Marco Polo tells us also of an interesting fact. Large numbers of horses were imported by sea from Arabia and Persia into south India. The climate of south India was not suited to horse breeding, and horses, apart from their other uses, were necessary for military purposes. The best breeding grounds for horses were in central and western Asia, and this may well explain, to some extent, the superiority of the central Asian races in warfare. Chingiz Khan's Mongols were magnificent horsemen and were devoted to their horses. The Turks were also fine horsemen, and the love of the Arab for his horse is well known. In north and west India there are some good breeding grounds for horses, especially in Kathiawar, and the Rajputs are very fond of their horses. Many a petty war was waged for a famous charger. There is a story of a Delhi sultan admiring the charger of a Rajput chief and asking him for it. The Hara chief replied to the Lodi king: "There are three things you must not ask of a Rajput: his horse, his mistress, or his sword," and he galloped away. There was trouble afterward.

Late in the fourteenth century, Timur, the Turk or Turco-Mongol, came down from the north and smashed up the Delhi sultanate. He was only a few months in India; he came to Delhi and went back. But all along his route he created a wilderness adorned with pyramids of skulls of those he had slain; and Delhi itself became a city of the dead. Fortunately he did not go far, and only some parts of the Punjab and Delhi had to suffer this terrible affliction.

It took many years for Delhi to wake up from this sleep of death, and even when it woke up it was no longer the capital of a great empire. Timur's visit had broken that empire, and out of it had arisen a number of states in the south. Long before this, early in the fourteenth century, two great states had risen—Gulbarga, called the Bahmani kingdom;[2] and the Hindu kingdom of Vijayanagar. Gulbarga now split up into five states, one of these being Ahmadnagar. Ahmad Nizam Shah, the founder of Ahmadnagar in 1490, was the son of Nizam-ul-Mulk Bhairi, a minister of the Bahmani kings. This Nizam-ul-Mulk was the son of a Brahman accountant named Bhairu (from which his name Bhairi). Thus the Ahmadnagar dynasty was of indigenous origin, and Chand Bibi, the heroine of

[2] The name and origin of the Bahmani kingdom of the south is interesting. The founder of this state was an Afghan Moslem who had a Hindu patron in his early days—Gangu Brahman. In gratitude to him he even took his name and his dynasty was called the Bahmani (from Brahman) dynasty.

Ahmadnagar, had mixed blood. All the Moslem states in the south were indigenous and indianized.

After Timur's sack of Delhi, north India remained weak and divided up. South India was better off, and the largest and most powerful of the southern kingdoms was Vijayanagar. This state and city attracted many of the Hindu refugees from the north. From contemporary accounts, it appears that the city was rich and very beautiful—"The city is such that eye has not seen nor ear heard of any place resembling it upon the whole earth," says Abdur-Razzak from central Asia. There were arcades and magnificent galleries for the bazaars, and rising above them all was the palace of the king surrounded by "many rivulets and streams flowing through channels of cut stone, polished and even." The whole city was full of gardens, and because of them, as an Italian visitor in 1420, Nicolo Conti, writes, the circumference of the city was sixty miles. A later visitor was Paes, a Portuguese who came in 1522 after having visited the Italian cities of the Renaissance. The city of Vijayanagar, he says, is as "large as Rome and very beautiful to the sight"; it is full of charm and wonder with its innumerable lakes and waterways and fruit gardens. It is "the best-provided city in the world" and "everything abounds." The chambers of the palace were a mass of ivory, with roses and lotuses carved in ivory at the top—"it is so rich and beautiful that you would hardly find anywhere another such." Of the ruler, Krishna Deva Raya, Paes writes: "He is the most feared and perfect King that could possibly be, cheerful of disposition and very merry; he is one that seeks to honor foreigners, and receives them kindly, asking about all their affairs whatever their condition may be."

While Vijayanagar was flourishing in the south, the petty sultanate of Delhi had to meet a new foe. Yet another invader came down from the northern mountains, and on the famous battlefield of Panipat, near Delhi, where so often India's fate has been decided, he won the throne of Delhi in 1526. This was Babar, a Turco-Mongol and a prince of the Timurid line in central Asia. With him begins the Moghul empire of India.

Babar's success was probably due not only to the weakness of the Delhi sultanate but to his possessing a new and improved type of artillery which was not in use in India then. From this period onward India seems to lag behind in developing the science of warfare. It would be more correct to say that the whole of Asia remained where it was while Europe was advancing in this science. The great Moghul empire, powerful as it was in India for two hundred years, probably could not compete on equal terms with European armies from the seventeenth century onward. But no European army could come to India unless it had control over the sea routes. The major change that was taking place during these centuries was the development of European sea power. With the fall of the Chola kingdom in the south in the thirteenth century, Indian sea power declined rapidly. The small Pandya state, though intimately connected with the sea, was not strong enough. The Indian colonies, however, still continued to hold command over the Indian Ocean till the fifteenth century, when they were ousted by the Arabs, who were soon to be followed by the Portuguese.

## IV. SYNTHESIS AND GROWTH OF MIXED CULTURE
### PURDAH
#### KABIR—GURU NANAK—AMIR KHUSRAU

It is thus wrong and misleading to talk of a Moslem invasion of India or of the Moslem period in India, just as it would be wrong to refer to the coming of the British to India as a Christian invasion, or to call the British period in India a Christian period. Islam did not invade India; it had come to India some centuries earlier. There was a Turkish invasion (Mahmud's), and an Afghan invasion, and then a Turco-Mongol or Moghul invasion; and of these the two latter were important. The Afghans might well be considered a border Indian group, hardly strangers to India, and the period of their political dominance should be called the Indo-Afghan period. The Moghuls were outsiders and strangers to India, and yet they fitted into the Indian structure with remarkable speed and began the Indo-Moghul period.

Through choice or circumstance or both, the Afghan rulers and those who had come with them merged into India. Their dynasties became completely indianized with their roots in India, looking upon India as their homeland and the rest of the world as foreign. In spite of political conflict they were generally considered as such, and many even of the Rajput princes accepted them as their overlords. But there were other Rajput chiefs who refused to submit, and there were fierce conflicts. Feroze Shah, one of the well-known sultans of Delhi, had a Hindu mother; so had Ghyas-ud-Din Tughlak. Such marriages between the Afghan, Turkish, and the Hindu nobility were not frequent but they did take place. In the south the Moslem ruler of Gulbarga married a Hindu princess of Vijayanagar with great pomp and ceremony.

It appears that in the Moslem countries of central and western Asia, Indians had a good reputation. As early as the eleventh century—that is, before the Afghan conquest —a Moslem geographer, Idrisi, wrote: "The Indians are naturally inclined to justice, and never depart from it in their actions. Their good faith, honesty and fidelity to their engagements are well known, and they are so famous for these qualities that people flock to their country from every side."[3]

An efficient administration grew up and communications were especially improved, chiefly for military reasons. Government was more centralized now, though it took care not to interfere with local customs. Sher Shah (who intervened during the early Moghul period) was the ablest among the Afghan rulers. He laid the foundations of a revenue system which was later to be expanded by Akbar. Raja Todar Mal, Akbar's famous revenue minister, was first employed by Sher Shah. Hindu talent was increasingly used by the Afghan rulers.

The effect of the Afghan conquest on India and Hin-

[3] From Elliot's *History of India*, Vol. I, p. 88.

duism was twofold, each development contradicting the other. The immediate reaction was an exodus of people to the south, away from the areas under Afghan rule. Those who remained became more rigid and exclusive, retired into their shells, and tried to protect themselves from foreign ways and influences by hardening the caste system. On the other hand, there was a gradual and hardly conscious approach toward these foreign ways both in thought and life. A synthesis worked itself out: new styles of architecture arose: food and clothing changed, and life was affected and varied in many other ways. This synthesis was especially marked in music, which, following its old Indian classical pattern, developed in many directions. The Persian language became the official court language, and many Persian words crept into popular use. At the same time the popular languages were developed.

Among the unfortunate developments that took place in India was the growth of purdah or the seclusion of women. Why this should have been so is not clear, but somehow it did result from the interaction of the new elements on the old. In India there had been previously some segregation of the sexes among the aristocracy, as in many other countries and notably in ancient Greece. Some such segregation existed in ancient Iran also, and to some extent all over western Asia. But nowhere was there any strict seclusion of women. Probably this started in the Byzantine court circles where eunuchs were employed to guard the women's apartments. Byzantine influence traveled to Russia, where there was a fairly strict seclusion of women right up to Peter the Great's time. This had nothing to do with the Tartars, who, it is well established, did not segregate their womenfolk. The mixed Arab-Persian civilization was affected in many ways by Byzantine customs, and possibly the segregation of upper-class women grew to some extent. Yet, even so, there was no strict seclusion of women in Arabia or in other parts of western or central Asia. The Afghans who crowded into northern India after the capture of Delhi had no strict purdah. Turkish and Afghan princesses and ladies of the court often went riding, hunting, and paying visits. It is an old Islamic custom, still to be observed, that women must keep their faces unveiled during the Haj pilgrimage to Mecca. Purdah seems to have grown in India during Moghul times, when it became a mark of status and prestige among both Hindus and Moslems. This custom of seclusion of women spread especially among the upper classes of those areas where Moslem influence had been most marked—in the great central and eastern block comprising Delhi, the United Provinces, Rajputana, Bihar, and Bengal. And yet it is odd that purdah has not been very strict in the Punjab and in the Frontier Province, which are predominantly Moslem. In the south and west of India there has been no such seclusion of women, except to some extent among the Moslems.

I have no doubt at all that among the causes of India's decay in recent centuries, purdah or the seclusion of women holds an important place. I am even more convinced that the complete ending of this barbarous custom is essential before India can have a progressive social life. That it injures woman is obvious enough, but the injury to man, to the growing child who has to spend much of its time among women in purdah, and to social life generally is equally great. Fortunately this evil practice is fast disappearing among the Hindus, more slowly among the Moslems. The strongest factor in this liquidation of purdah has been the Congress political and social movements which have drawn tens of thousands of middle-class women into some kind of public activity. Gandhiji has been, and is, a fierce opponent of purdah and has called it a "vicious and brutal custom" which has kept woman backward and undeveloped. "I thought of the wrong being done by men to the women of India by clinging to a barbarous custom which, whatever use it might have had when it was first introduced, had now become totally useless and was doing incalculable harm to the country." Gandhi urged that women should have the same liberty and opportunity for self-development as man. "Good sense must govern the relations between the two sexes. There should be no barrier erected between them. Their mutual behaviour should be natural and spontaneous." Gandhi has indeed written and spoken with pas-

sion in favor of women's equality and freedom, and has
bitterly condemned their domestic slavery.

I have digressed and made a sudden jump to modern
times, and must go back to the medieval period after the
Afghans had established themselves in Delhi and a synthesis was working itself out between old ways and new. Most
of these changes took place at the top, among the nobility
and upper classes, and did not affect the mass of the population, especially the rural masses. They originated in court
circles and spread in the cities and urban areas. Thus began a process which was to continue for several centuries,
of developing a mixed culture in north India. Delhi, and
what are known now as the United Provinces, became the
center of this, just as they had been, and still continued
to be, the center of the old Aryan culture. But much of
this Aryan culture drifted to the south, which became a
stronghold of Hindu orthodoxy.

After the Delhi sultanate had weakened owing to Timur's incursion, a small Moslem state grew up in Jaunpur
(in the United Provinces). Right through the fifteenth
century this was a center of art and culture and toleration
in religion. The growing popular language, Hindi, was encouraged, and an attempt was even made to bring about
a synthesis between the religious faiths of the Hindus and
the Moslems. About this time in far Kashmir in the north
an independent Moslem king, Zainaulabdin, also became
famous for his toleration and his encouragement of Sanskrit learning and the old culture.

All over India this new ferment was working and new
ideas were troubling people's minds. As of old, India was
subconsciously reacting to the new situation, trying to absorb the foreign element and herself changing somewhat
in the process. Out of this ferment arose new types of reformers who deliberately preached this synthesis and often
condemned or ignored the caste system. There was the
Hindu Ramanand in the south, in the fifteenth century,
and his still more famous disciple Kabir, a Moslem weaver
of Benares. Kabir's poems and songs became, and still are,
very popular. In the north there was Guru Nanak, who is
considered the founder of Sikhism. The influence of these

reformers went far beyond the limits of the particular sects that grew up after them. Hinduism as a whole felt the impact of the new ideas, and Islam in India also became somewhat different from what it was elsewhere. The fierce monotheism of Islam influenced Hinduism, and the vague pantheistic attitude of the Hindu had its effect on the Indian Moslem. Most of these Indian Moslems were converts bred up in and surrounded by the old traditions; only a comparatively small number of them had come from outside. Moslem mysticism, and Sufism, which probably had had its beginnings in neo-Platonism, grew.

Perhaps the most significant indication of the growing absorption of the foreign element in India, was its use of the popular language of the country, even though Persian continued to be the court language. There are many notable books written by the early Moslems in Hindi. The most famous of these writers was Amir Khusrau, a Turk whose family had settled in the United Provinces for two or three generations and who lived in the fourteenth century during the reigns of several Afghan sultans. He was a poet of the first rank in Persian, and he knew Sanskrit also. He was a great musician and introduced many innovations in Indian music. He is also said to have invented the sitar, the popular stringed instrument of India. He wrote on many subjects, and in particular in praise of India, enumerating the various things in which India excelled. Among these were religion, philosophy, logic, language and grammar (Sanskrit), music, mathematics, science, and the mango fruit!

But his fame in India rests, above all, on his popular songs, written in the ordinary spoken dialect of Hindi. Wisely he did not choose the literary medium which would have been understood by a small coterie only; he went to the villager not only for his language but for his customs and ways of living. He sang of the different seasons, and each season, according to the old classical style of India, had its own appropriate tune and words; he sang of life in its various phases, of the coming of the bride, of separation from the beloved, of the rains when life springs anew from the parched earth. Those songs are still widely sung

and may be heard in any village or town in northern and
central India. Especially when the rainy season begins and
in every village big swings are hung from the branches of
the mango or the pipal trees, and all the village girls and
boys gather together to celebrate the occasion.

Amir Khusrau was the author also of innumerable riddles and conundrums which are very popular with children
as well as grownups. Even during his long life Khusrau's
songs and riddles had made him famous. That reputation
has continued and grown. I do not know if there is any
other instance anywhere of songs written six hundred years
ago maintaining their popularity and their mass appeal and
being still sung without any change of words.

## V. THE INDIAN SOCIAL STRUCTURE
### IMPORTANCE OF THE GROUP

Almost everyone who knows anything at all about India has
heard of the caste system; almost every outsider and many
people in India condemn it or criticize it as a whole. Probably there is hardly anyone left even in India who approves
of it in all its present ramifications and developments,
though there are undoubtedly many still who accept its
basic theory and large numbers of Hindus adhere to it in
their lives. Some confusion arises in the use of the word
caste, for different people attach a different meaning to it.
The average European, or an Indian who is allied to him
in thought and approach, thinks of it as just a petrifaction
of classes, an ingenious method to preserve a certain hierarchy of classes, to keep the upper classes permanently at
the top and the lower ones permanently at the bottom of
the scale. There is truth in that, and in its origin it was
probably a device to keep the Aryan conquerors apart from
and above the conquered peoples. Undoubtedly in its
growth it has acted in that way, though originally there may
have been a good deal of flexibility about it. Yet that is
only a part of the truth, and it does not explain its power
and cohesiveness and the way it has lasted down to our

present day. It survived not only the powerful impact of Buddhism and many centuries of Afghan and Moghul rule and the spread of Islam, but also the strenuous efforts of innumerable Hindu reformers who raised their voices against it. It is only today that it is seriously threatened and its very basis has been attacked. That is not chiefly because of some powerful urge to reform itself which has arisen in Hindu society, though such an urge is undoubtedly present, nor is it because of ideas from the West, though such ideas have certainly exerted their influence. The change that is taking place before our eyes is due essentially to basic economic changes which have shaken up the whole fabric of Indian society and are likely to upset it completely. Conditions of life have changed and thought-patterns are changing so much that it seems impossible for the caste system to endure. What will take its place is more than I can say, for something much more than the caste system is at stake. The conflict is between two approaches to the problem of social organization which are diametrically opposed to each other: the old Hindu conception of the group being the basic unit of organization, and the excessive individualism of the West, emphasizing the individual above the group.

That conflict is not of India only; it is of the West also and of the entire world, though it takes different forms there. The nineteenth-century civilization of Europe, taking shape in democratic liberalism and its extensions in the economic and social fields, represented the high-water mark of that individualism. That nineteenth-century ideology with its social and political organization has extended itself and flowed into the twentieth century, but it seems wholly out of date now and is cracking under stress of crisis and war. The importance of the group and the community is emphasized more now, and the problem is to reconcile the respective claims of the individual and the group. The solution of that problem may take different forms in different countries, yet there will be an ever-increasing tendency for one basic solution to apply to all.

The caste system does not stand by itself; it is a part, and an important part, of a much larger scheme of social organization. It may be possible to remove some of its obvious abuses and to lessen its rigidity, and yet to leave the system intact. But that is highly unlikely, as the social and economic forces at play are not much concerned with this superstructure; they are attacking it at the base and undermining the other supports which held it up. Indeed, much of that support is already gone or is rapidly going, and more and more of the caste system is left stranded by itself. It has ceased to be a question of whether we like caste or dislike it. Changes are taking place in spite of our likes and dislikes. But it is certainly in our power to mold those changes and direct them, so that we can take full advantage of the character and genius of the Indian people as a whole, which have been so evident in the cohesiveness and stability of the social organization they built up.

Sir George Birdwood has said somewhere: "So long as the Hindus hold to the caste system, India will be India; but from the day they break from it, there will be no more India. That glorious peninsula will be degraded to the position of a bitter 'East End' of the Anglo-Saxon Empire." With caste or without it, we have long been degraded to that position in the British Empire. And in any event, whatever our future position is likely to be, it will not be confined within the bounds of that empire. But there is some truth in what Sir George Birdwood said, though probably he did not look at it from this point of view. The breakup of a huge and long-standing social organization may well lead to a complete disruption of social life, resulting in absence of cohesion, mass suffering, and the development on a vast scale of abnormalities in individual behavior, unless some other social structure, more suited to the times and to the genius of the people, takes its place. Perhaps disruption is inevitable during the transition period; there is enough of this disruption all over the world today. Perhaps it is only through the pain and suffering that accompany such disruption that a people grow and learn the lessons of life and adapt themselves anew to changing conditions.

Nevertheless we cannot just disrupt and hope for something better without having some vision of the future we are working for, however vague that vision may be. We cannot just create a vacuum, or else that vacuum will fill itself up in a way that we may have to deplore. In the constructive schemes that we may make, we have to pay attention to the human material we have to deal with, to the background of its thought and urges, and to the environment in which we have to function. To ignore all this and to fashion some idealistic scheme in the air, or merely to think in terms of imitating what others have done elsewhere, would be folly. It becomes desirable therefore to examine and understand the old Indian social structure which has so powerfully influenced our people.

This structure was based on three concepts: the autonomous village community; caste; and the joint family system. In all these three it is the group that counts; the individual has a secondary place. There is nothing very unique about all this separately, and it is easy to find something equivalent to any of these three in other countries, especially in medieval times. Like the old Indian republics, there were primitive republics elsewhere. There was also a kind of primitive communism. The old Russian mir might be comparable in some way to the Indian village community. Caste has been essentially functional and similar to the medieval trade guilds of Europe. The Chinese family system bears a strong resemblance to the Hindu joint family. I do not know enough of all these to carry the comparison far, and in any case this is not important for my purpose. Taken as a whole the entire Indian structure was certainly unique, and as it developed, it became more so.

### VI. VILLAGE SELF-GOVERNMENT
#### THE SHUKRA NITISARA

There is an old book, of the tenth century, which gives us some idea of Indian polity as it was conceived prior to the Turkish and Afghan invasions. This is the *Nitisara*, the *Science of Polity*, by Shukracharya. It deals with the organization of the central government as well as of town and village life; of the King's Council of State and various departments of government. The village panchayat or elected council had large powers, both executive and judicial, and its members were treated with the greatest respect by the king's officers. Land was distributed by this panchayat, which also collected taxes out of the produce and paid the government's share on behalf of the village. Over a number of these village councils there was a larger panchayat or council to supervise and interfere if necessary.

Some old inscriptions further tell us how the members of the village councils were elected and what their qualifications and disqualifications were. Various committees were formed, elected annually, and women could serve on them. In case of misbehavior a member could be removed. A member could be disqualified if he failed to render accounts of public funds. An interesting rule to prevent nepotism is mentioned: near relatives of members were not to be appointed to public office.

These village councils were very jealous of their liberties, and it was laid down that no soldier could enter the village unless he had a royal permit. If the people complained of an official, the *Nitisara* says that the king "should take the side not of his officers but of his subjects." If many complained, then the official was to be dismissed, "for who does not get intoxicated by drinking of the vanity of office?" The king was to act in accordance with the opinion of the majority of the people. "Public opinion is more powerful than the king as the rope made of many fibres is strong enough to drag a lion." "In making official appointments work, character and merit were to be regarded—neither caste nor family," and "neither through colour nor through ancestors can the spirit worthy of a Brahmin be generated."

In the larger towns there were many artisans and merchants, and craft guilds, mercantile associations, and banking corporations were formed. Each of these controlled its own domestic affairs.

All this information is very fragmentary, but it does appear from this and many other sources that there was a widespread system of self-government in towns and vil-

lages and the central government seldom interfered, so
long as its quota of taxes was paid. Customary law was
strong, and the political or military power seldom interfered with rights based on customs. Originally the agrarian
system was based on a co-operative or collective village. Individuals and families had certain rights as well as certain
obligations, both of which were determined and protected
by customary law.

There was no theocratic monarchy in India. In Indian
polity if the king is unjust or tyrannical, the right to rebel
against him is admitted. What the Chinese philosopher
Mencius said two thousand years ago might apply to India:
"When a ruler treats his subjects like grass and dirt, then
the subjects should treat him as a bandit and an enemy."
The whole conception of monarchical power differed from
that of European feudalism, where the king had authority
over all persons and things in his domain. This authority
he delegated to lords and barons, who vowed allegiance to
him. Thus a hierarchy of authority was built up. Both the
land and the people connected with it belonged to the
feudal lord and through him to the king. This was the development of the Roman conception of dominium. In India there was nothing of this kind. The king had the right
to collect certain taxes from the land and this revenue-
collecting power was all he could delegate to others. The
peasant in India was not the lord's serf. There was plenty
of land available, and there was no advantage in dispos-
sessing the peasant. Thus in India there was no landlord
system, as known in the West, nor was the individual peasant the full owner of his patch of land. Both these concepts
were introduced much later by the British with disastrous
results.

Foreign conquests brought war and destruction, revolts
and their ruthless suppression, and new ruling classes relying chiefly on armed force. This ruling class could often
ignore the numerous constitutional restraints which had
always been part of the customary law of the country. Important consequences followed and the power of the self-
governing village communities decreased, and later various
changes were introduced in the land revenue system. Never-

theless the Afghan and Moghul rulers took special care not to interfere with old customs and conventions, and no fundamental changes were introduced, and the economic and social structure of Indian life continued as before. Ghyas-ud-Din Tughlak issued definite instructions to his officials to preserve customary law and to keep the affairs of the state apart from religion, which was a personal matter of individual preference. But changing times and conflicts, as well as the increasing centralization of government, slowly but progressively lessened the respect given to customary law. The village self-governing community, however, continued. Its breakup began only under British rule.

## VII. THE THEORY AND PRACTICE OF CASTE
## THE JOINT FAMILY

"In India," says Havell, "religion is hardly a dogma, but a working hypothesis of human conduct, adapted to different stages of spiritual development and different conditions of life." In the ancient days when Indo-Aryan culture first took shape, religion had to provide for the needs of men who were as far removed from each other in civilization and intellectual and spiritual development as it is possible to conceive. There were primitive forest dwellers, fetishists, totem worshipers and the believers in every kind of superstition, and there were those who had attained the highest flights of spiritual thought. In between, there was every shade and gradation of belief and practice. While the highest forms of thought were pursued by some, these were wholly beyond the reach of many. As social life grew, certain uniformities of belief spread; but even so, many differences, cultural and temperamental, remained. The Indo-Aryan approach was to avoid the forcible suppression of any belief or the destruction of any claim. Each group was left free to work out its ideals along the plane of its mental development and understanding. Assimilation was attempted, but there was no denial or suppression.

A similar and even more difficult problem had to be

faced in social organization: how to combine these utterly different groups in one social system, each group co-
operating with the whole and yet retaining its own freedom
to live its own life and develop itself. In a sense—though
the comparison is farfetched—this may be compared to the
numerous minority problems of today which afflict so many
countries and are still far from solution. The United States
of America solves its minority problems, more or less, by
trying to make every citizen a 100 per cent American. They
make everyone conform to a certain type. Other countries,
with a longer and more complicated past, are not so favorably situated. Even Canada has its strong race-, religion-, and
language-conscious French group. In Europe the barriers
are higher and deeper. And yet all this applies to Europeans, or those who have spread from Europe; people who
have a certain common background and similarity of culture. Where non-Europeans come in, they do not fit this
pattern. In the United States, Negroes, though they may
be a hundred per cent American, are a race apart, deprived
of many opportunities and privileges which others have as a
matter of course. There are innumerable worse examples
elsewhere. Only Soviet Russia is said to have solved its
problem of nationalities and minorities by creating what
is called a multinational state.

If these difficulties and problems pursue us even today
with all our knowledge and progress, how much harder they
must have been in the ancient days when the Indo-Aryans
were evolving their civilization and social structure in a land
full of variety and different types of human beings. The
normal way to deal with these problems then and later was
to exterminate or enslave the conquered populations. This
way was not followed in India, but it is clear that every
precaution was taken to perpetuate the superior position
of the upper groups. Having insured that superiority, a kind
of multiple-community state was built up, in which, within
certain limits and subject to some general rules, freedom
was given to each group to follow its avocation and live its
own life in accordance with its own customs or desires. The
only real restriction was that it must not interfere or come
into conflict with another group. This was a flexible and

expanding system, for new groups could always be formed either by newcomers or by dissident members of an old group, provided they were numerous enough to do so. Within each group there was equality and democracy, and the elected leaders guided it and frequently consulted the entire group whenever any important question arose.

These groups were almost always functional, each specializing in a particular trade or craft. They became thus some kind of trade union or craft guild. There was a strong sense of solidarity within each, which not only protected the group but sheltered and helped an individual member who got into trouble or was in economic distress. The functions of each group or caste were related to the functions of other castes, and the idea was that if each group functioned successfully within its own framework, then society as a whole worked harmoniously. Over and above this, a strong and fairly successful attempt was made to create a common national bond which would hold all these groups together—the sense of a common culture, common traditions, common heroes and saints, and a common land to the four corners of which people went on pilgrimage. This national bond was of course very different from present-day nationalism; it was weak politically, but socially and culturally it was strong. Because of its political lack of cohesiveness it facilitated foreign conquest; because of its social strength it made recovery easy, as well as assimilation of new elements. It had so many heads that they could not be cut off, and they survived conquest and disaster.

Thus caste was a group system based on services and functions. It was meant to be an all-inclusive order without any common dogma and allowing the fullest latitude to each group. Within its wide fold there was monogamy, polygamy and celibacy; they were all tolerated, just as other customs, beliefs, and practices were tolerated. Life was to be maintained at all levels. No minority need submit to a majority, for it could always form a separate autonomous group, the only test being: Is it a distinctive group large enough to function as such? Between two groups there could be any amount of variation of race, religion, color, culture, and intellectual development.

An individual was only considered as a member of a group; he could do anything he liked so long as he did not interfere with the functioning of the group. He had no right to upset that functioning, but if he was strong enough and could gather enough supporters, it was open to him to form another group. If he could not fit in with any group, that meant that he was out of joint so far as the social activities of the world were concerned. He could then become a *sanyasi* who had renounced caste, every group and the world of activity, and could wander about and do what he liked.

It must be remembered that while the Indian social tendency was to subordinate the individual to the claims of the group and society, religious thought and spiritual seeking have always emphasized the individual. Salvation and knowledge of the ultimate truth were open to all, to the member of every caste, high or low. This salvation or enlightenment could not be a group affair; it was highly individualistic. In the search for this salvation also there were no inflexible dogmas, and all doors were supposed to lead to it.

Though the group system was dominant in the organization of society, leading to caste, there has always been an individualistic tendency in India. A conflict between the two approaches is often in evidence. Partly that individualism was the result of the religious doctrine which laid emphasis on the individual. Social reformers who criticized or condemned the caste system were usually religious reformers, and their main argument was that the divisions of the caste system came in the way of spiritual development and that intense individualism to which religion pointed. Buddhism was a breakaway from the group-caste ideal toward some kind of individualism as well as universalism. But this individualism became associated with a withdrawal from normal social activities. It offered no effective alternative social structure to caste, and so caste continued then and later.

What were the main castes? If we leave out for a moment those who were considered outside the pale of caste, the untouchables, there were the Brahmans, the priests,

teachers, intellectuals; the Kshatriyas or the rulers and warriors; the Vaishyas or merchants, traders, bankers, etc.; and
the Shudras, who were the agricultural and other workers.
Probably the only closely knit and exclusive caste was that
of the Brahmans. The Kshatriyas were frequently adding
to their numbers both from foreign incoming elements and
others in the country who rose to power and authority. The
Vaishyas were chiefly traders and bankers and also engaged
in a number of other professions. The main occupations of
the Shudras were cultivation and domestic service. There
was always a continuous process of new castes being formed,
as new occupations developed and for other reasons, and
older castes were always trying to go up in the social scale.
These processes have continued to our day. Some of the
lower castes suddenly take to wearing the sacred thread
which is supposed to be reserved for the upper castes. All
this really made little difference, as each caste continued
to function in its own ambit and pursued its own trade or
occupation. It was merely a question of prestige. Occasionally men of the lower classes, by sheer ability, attained
to positions of power and authority in the state, but this
was very exceptional.

The organization of society being, generally speaking,
noncompetitive and nonacquisitive, these divisions into
castes did not make as much difference as they might otherwise have done. The Brahman at the top, proud of his intellect and learning and respected by others, seldom had
much in the way of worldly possessions. The merchant,
prosperous and rich, had no very high standing in society
as a whole.

The vast majority of the population consisted of the agriculturists. There was no landlord system, nor was there any
peasant proprietorship. It is difficult to say who owned the
land in law; there was nothing like the present doctrine of
ownership. The cultivator had the right to till his land, and
the only real question was as to the distribution of the
produce of the land. The major share went to the cultivator; the king or the state took a share (usually one-sixth);
and every functional group in the village which served the
people in any way had its share—the Brahman priest and

teacher, the merchant, the blacksmith, the carpenter, the cobbler, the potter, the builder, the barber, the scavenger, etc. Thus, in a sense, every group from the state to the scavenger was a shareholder in the produce.

Who were the depressed classes and the untouchables? The "depressed classes" is a new designation applying rather vaguely to a number of castes near the bottom of the scale. There is no hard and fast line to separate them from the others. The untouchables are more definite. In north India only a very small number, engaged in scavenging or unclean work, are considered untouchable. Fa Hien tells us that when he came, the persons who removed human feces were untouchable. In south India the numbers are much larger. How they began and grew to such numbers, it is difficult to say. Probably those who were engaged in occupations considered unclean were so treated; later landless agricultural labor might have been added.

The idea of ceremonial purity has been extraordinarily strong among the Hindus. This has led to one good consequence and many bad ones. The good one is bodily cleanliness. A daily bath has always been an essential feature of a Hindu's life, including most of the depressed classes. It was from India that this habit spread to England and elsewhere. The average Hindu, and even the poorest peasant, takes some pride in his shining pots and pans. This sense of cleanliness is not scientific, and the man who bathes twice a day will unhesitatingly drink water that is unclean and full of germs. Nor is it corporate, at any rate now. The individual will keep his own hut fairly clean but throw all the rubbish in the village street in front of his neighbor's house. The village is usually very dirty and full of garbage heaps. It is also noticeable that cleanliness is not thought of as such but as a consequence of some religious sanction. When that religious sanction goes, there is marked deterioration in the standards of cleanliness.

The evil consequence of ceremonial purity was a growth of exclusiveness, touch-me-notism, and of not eating and drinking with people of other castes. This grew to fantastic lengths unknown in any other part of the world. It led also to certain classes being considered untouchable because they had the misfortune to do some kinds of essential work which were considered unclean. The practice of normally feeding with one's own caste people spread to all castes. It became a sign of social status, and the lower castes stuck to it even more rigidly than some of the higher ones. This practice is breaking up now among the higher castes, but it still continues among these lower castes, including the depressed classes.

If interdining was taboo, much more so was intermarriage between castes. Some mixed marriages inevitably took place, but on the whole it is extraordinary how each caste kept to itself and propagated its own kind. The continuation of racial identity through long ages is an illusion, and yet the caste system in India has to some extent managed to preserve distinctive types, especially among the higher castes.

Some groups at the bottom of the scale are sometimes referred to as outside the caste groups. As a matter of fact no group, not even the untouchables, is outside the framework of the caste system. The depressed classes and the untouchables form their own castes and have their panchayats or caste councils for settling their own affairs. But many of these have been made to suffer cruelly by excluding them from the common life of the village.

The autonomous village community and the caste system were thus two of the special features of the old Indian social structure. The third was the joint family, where all the members were joint sharers in the common property and inheritance went by survivorship. The father or some other elder was the head, but he functioned as a manager and not as the old Roman paterfamilias. A division of property was permitted under certain circumstances and if the parties concerned so desired. The joint property was supposed to provide for the needs of all the members of the family, workers or nonworkers. Inevitably this meant a guaranteed minimum for all of them, rather than high rewards for some. It was a kind of insurance for all, including even the subnormal and the physically or mentally deficient. Thus while there was security for all, there was a certain leveling down of the standard of service demanded as well as of the recompense given. Emphasis was not laid on personal advantage or ambition but on the group's, that is the family's, advantage. The fact of growing up and living in a large family minimized the egocentric attitude of the child and tended to develop an aptitude for socialization.

All this is the very opposite of what happens in the highly individualistic civilization of the West and more especially of America, where personal ambition is encouraged and personal advantage is almost the universal aim, and all the plums go to the bright and pushing, and the weak, timid, or second-rate go to the wall. The joint family system is rapidly breaking up in India and individualistic attitudes are developing, leading not only to far-reaching changes in the economic background of life but also to new problems of behavior.

All the three pillars of the Indian social structure were thus based on the group and not on the individual. The aim was social security: stability and continuance of the group; that is, of society. Progress was not the aim, and progress therefore had to suffer. Within each group, whether this was the village community, the particular caste, or the large joint family, there was a communal life shared together, a sense of equality, and democratic methods. Even now caste panchayats function democratically. It surprised me at one time to see the eagerness of a villager, sometimes illiterate, to serve on elected committees for political or other purposes. He soon got into the way of it and was a helpful member whenever any question relating to his life came up, and was not easily subdued. But there was an unfortunate tendency for small groups to split up and quarrel among themselves.

The democratic way was not only well known but was a common method of functioning in social life, in local government, trade guilds, religious assemblies, etc. Caste, with all its evils, kept up the democratic habit in each group. There used to be elaborate rules of procedure, election, and debate. The Marquis of Zetland has referred to some of these in writing about the early Buddhist assemblies: "And it may come as a surprise to many to learn that in the Assemblies of the Buddhists in India two thousand or more years ago are to be found the rudiments of our own parliamentary practice of the present day. The dignity of the Assembly was preserved by the appointment of a special officer—the embryo of 'Mr. Speaker' in the House of Commons. A second officer was appointed whose duty it was to see that when necessary a quorum was secured—the prototype of the Parliamentary Chief Whip in our own system. A member initiating business did so in the form of a motion which was then open to discussion. In some cases this was done once only, in others three times, thus anticipating the practice of Parliament in requiring that a Bill be read a third time before it becomes law. If discussion disclosed a difference of opinion the matter was decided by the vote of the majority, the voting being by ballot."[4]

The old Indian social structure had thus some virtues, and indeed it could not have lasted so long without them. Behind it lay the philosophic ideal of Indian culture—the integration of man and the stress on goodness, beauty, and truth rather than acquisitiveness. An attempt was made to prevent the joining together and concentration of honor, power, and wealth. The duties of the individual and the group were emphasized, not their rights. The Smritis (Hindu religious books) give lists of dharmas, functions and duties, of various castes, but none of them contains an inventory of rights. Self-sufficiency was aimed at in the group, especially in the village and, in a different sense, in the caste. It was a closed system, allowing a certain adaptability, change, and freedom within its outer framework, but inevitably growing more and more exclusive and rigid. Progressively it lost its power to expand and tap new sources of talent. Powerful vested interests prevented any radical change and kept education from spreading to other classes. The old superstitions, known to be such by many among the upper classes, were preserved and new ones were added to them. Not only the national economy but thought itself became stationary, traditional, rigid, unexpansive and unprogressive.

[4] Quoted by Professor Rawlinson in *The Legacy of India*, 1937, p. xi.

The conception and practice of caste embodied the aristocratic ideal and was obviously opposed to democratic conceptions. It had its strong sense of *noblesse oblige*, provided people kept to their hereditary stations and did not challenge the established order. India's success and achievements were on the whole confined to the upper classes; those lower down in the scale had very few chances, and their opportunities were strictly limited. These upper classes were not a small limited group but large in numbers, and there was a diffusion of power, authority, and influence. Hence they carried on successfully for a very long period. But the ultimate weakness and failing of the caste system and the Indian social structure were that they degraded a mass of human beings and gave them no opportunities to get out of that condition—educationally, culturally, or economically. That degradation brought deterioration all along the line, including in its scope even the upper classes. It led to that petrifaction which became a dominant feature of India's economy and life. The contrasts between this social structure and those existing elsewhere in the past were not great, but with the changes that have taken place all over the world during the past few generations they have become far more pronounced. In the context of society today, the caste system and much that goes with it are wholly incompatible, reactionary, restrictive, and barriers to progress. There can be no equality in status and opportunity within its framework, nor can there be political democracy, and much less, economic democracy. Between these two conceptions conflict is inherent, and only one of them can survive.

## VIII. BABAR AND AKBAR
### THE PROCESS OF INDIANIZATION

To go back. The Afghans had settled down in India and had become indianized. Their rulers had to face first the problem of lessening the hostility of the people and then of winning them over. So, as a deliberate policy, they toned down their early ruthless methods, became more tolerant, invited co-operation, and tried to function not as conquerors from outside but as Indians born in and bred in the land. What was at first a policy gradually became an inevitable trend as the Indian environment influenced these people from the northwest and absorbed them. While the process continued at the top, more powerful currents arose spontaneously among the people, aiming at a synthesis of thought and ways of living. The beginnings of a mixed culture began to appear, and foundations were laid on which Akbar was to build.

Akbar was the third of the Moghul dynasty in India, yet it was in effect by him that the empire was consolidated. His grandfather, Babar, had won the throne of Delhi in 1526, but he was a stranger to India and continued to feel so. He had come from the north where the Timurid renaissance was flourishing in his homelands in central Asia and the influence of the art and culture of Iran was strong. He missed the friendly society he was used to, the delights of conversation, the amenities and refinements of life which had spread from Baghdad and Iran. He longed for the snow and ice of the northern highlands, for the good flesh and flowers and fruits of Ferghana. Yet with all his disappointment at what he saw, he says that Hindustan is a remarkably fine country. Babar died within four years of his coming to India, and much of his time was spent in fighting and in laying out a splendid capital at Agra, for which he obtained the services of a famous architect from Constantinople. Those were the days of Suleiman the Magnificent in Constantinople, when fine buildings were rising up in that city.

Akbar won many people to his side and kept them there, but he failed to subdue the proud and indomitable spirit of Rana Pratap of Mewar in Rajputana, who preferred to lead a hunted life in the jungle rather than give even formal allegiance to one he considered a foreign conqueror.

Round himself Akbar collected a brilliant group of men, devoted to him and his ideals. Among these were the two famous brothers Fyzee and Abul Fazl, Birbal, Raja Man Singh, and Abdur Rahim Khankhana. His court became a meeting place for men of all faiths and all who had some new idea or new invention. His toleration of views and his encouragement of all kinds of beliefs and opinions went so far as to anger some of the more orthodox Moslems. He even tried to start a new synthetic faith to suit everybody. It was in his reign that the cultural amalgamation of Hindu and Moslem in north India took a long step forward. Akbar himself was certainly as popular with the Hindus as with the Moslems. The Moghul dynasty became firmly established as India's own.

## IX. THE CONTRAST BETWEEN ASIA AND EUROPE IN MECHANICAL ADVANCE AND CREATIVE ENERGY

Akbar was full of curiosity, ever seeking to find out about things, both spiritual and temporal. He was interested in mechanical contrivances and in the science of war. He prized war elephants especially, and they formed an important part of his army. The Portuguese Jesuits of his court tell us that "he was interested in, and curious to learn about many things, and possessed an intimate knowledge not only of military and political matters, but many of the mechanical arts." In "his eagerness for knowledge" he "tried to learn everything at once, like a hungry man trying to swallow his food at a single gulp."

And yet it is very curious how his curiosity stopped at a point and did not lead him to explore certain obvious avenues which lay open before him. With all his great prestige as the Grand Moghul and his strength as a land power, he was powerless at sea. Vasco da Gama had reached Calicut, via the Cape, in 1498; Albuquerque had seized Malacca in 1511 and established Portuguese sea power in the Indian Ocean. Goa on the western coast of India had become a Portuguese possession. All this did not bring the Portuguese into direct conflict with Akbar. But Indian pilgrims going to Mecca by sea, and these sometimes included members of the imperial family, or of the nobility, were often held up for ransom by the Portuguese. It was obvious that however powerful Akbar might be on land, the Portuguese were masters of the sea. It is not difficult to understand that a continental power did not attach much importance to sea power, although, as a matter of fact, India's greatness and importance in the past had been partly due to her control of the sea routes. Akbar had a vast continent to conquer and had little time to spare for the Portuguese, to whom he attached no importance even though they stung him occasionally. He did think of building ships once, but this was looked upon more as a pastime than a serious naval development.

Again in the matter of artillery the Moghul armies, as well as those of other states in India at the time, chiefly relied on foreign experts, who were usually Turks from the Ottoman dominions. The master of the artillery came to be known by the title of Rumi Khan—Rum being Eastern Rome; that is, Constantinople. These foreign experts trained local men, but why did not Akbar or anyone else send his own men abroad for training or interest himself in improvement by encouraging research work?

Yet another very significant thing: the Jesuits presented Akbar with a printed Bible and perhaps one or two other printed books. Why did he not get curious about printing, which would have been of tremendous advantage to him in his governmental activities as well as his vast enterprises?

Again, clocks. These were very popular with the Moghul nobility, and they were brought by the Portuguese and later by the English from Europe. They were regarded as luxuries for the rich, the ordinary people being content with sundials and sand and water clocks. No attempt was made to understand how these spring clocks were made and to get them made here. This lack of mechanical bent is remarkable, especially as there were very fine craftsmen and artisans in India.

It is not in India alone that this paralysis of creative energy and the inventive faculty is visible during this period. The whole of western and central Asia suffered from it even more. I do not know about China, but I imagine that some such stagnation affected her also. It must be remembered that both in India and China, during earlier periods, there was considerable progress in various departments of science. Shipbuilding and an extensive sea trade acted as a constant spur even to mechanical improvements. It is true that no major mechanical development took place in either of these countries or in any other country at the time. The world of the fifteenth century was, from this point of view, not very different from what it had been a thousand or two thousand years earlier.

## X. DEVELOPMENT OF A COMMON CULTURE

Akbar had built so well that the edifice he had erected lasted for another hundred years in spite of inadequate successors. After almost every Moghul reign there were wars between the princes for the throne, weakening the central power. But the court continued to be brilliant, and the fame of the Grand Moghul spread all over Asia and Europe. Beautiful buildings combining the old Indian ideals in architecture with a new simplicity and a nobility of line grew up in Agra and Delhi. This Indo-Moghul art was in marked contrast with the decadent, overelaborate, and heavily ornamented temples and other buildings of the north and south. Inspired architects and builders put up with loving hands the Taj Mahal at Agra.

The last of the so-called Grand Moghuls, Aurungzeb, tried to put back the clock, and in this attempt stopped it and broke it up. The Moghul rulers were strong as long as they put themselves in line with the genius of the nation and tried to work for a common nationality and a synthesis of the various elements in the country. When Aurungzeb began to oppose this movement and suppress it and to function more as a Moslem than an Indian ruler, the Moghul empire began to break up. The work of Akbar, and to some extent his successors, was undone, and the various forces that had been kept in check by Akbar's policy broke loose and challenged that empire. New movements arose, narrow in outlook but representing a resurgent nationalism, and though they were not strong enough to build permanently, and circumstances were against them, they were capable of destroying the empire of the Moghuls.

The impact of the invaders from the northwest and of Islam on India had been considerable. It had pointed out and shown up the abuses that had crept into Hindu society —the petrifaction of caste, untouchability, exclusiveness carried to fantastic lengths. The idea of the brotherhood of Islam and of the theoretical equality of its adherents made a powerful appeal, especially to those in the Hindu fold who were denied any semblance of equal treatment. From this ideological impact grew up various movements aiming at a religious synthesis. Many conversions also took place, but the great majority of these were from the lower castes, especially in Bengal. Some individuals belonging to the higher castes also adopted the new faith, either because of a real change of belief or, more often, for political and economic reasons. There were obvious advantages in accepting the religion of the ruling power.

In spite of these widespread conversions, Hinduism, in all its varieties, continued as the dominant faith of the land, solid, exclusive, self-sufficient, and sure of itself. The upper castes had no doubt about their own superiority in the realm of ideas and thought, and considered Islam as a rather crude approach to the problems of philosophy and metaphysics. Even the monotheism of Islam they found in their own religion, together with monism, which was the basis of much of their philosophy. Each person could take his choice of these or of more popular and simpler forms of worship. He could be a Vaishnavite and believe in a personal God and pour out his faith to him. Or, more philosophically inclined, he could wander in the tenuous realms of metaphysics and high philosophy. Though all their social structure was based on the group, in matters of religion they were highly individualistic, not believing in proselyting themselves, and caring little if some people were converted to another faith. What was objected to was an interference with their own social structure and ways of living. If another group wanted to function in its own way, it was at liberty to do so. It is worth noting that, as a rule, conversions to Islam were group conversions, so powerful was the influence of the group. Among the upper castes individuals might change their religion, but lower down the scale a particular caste in a locality, or almost an entire village, would be converted. Thus their group life as well as their functions continued as before with only minor variations as regards worship, etc. Because of this we find today particular occupations and crafts almost entirely monopolized by Moslems. Thus the class of weavers is predominantly, and in large areas entirely, Moslem. So also used to be shoe merchants and butchers. Tailors are almost always Moslems. Various kinds of artisans and craftsmen are Moslems. Owing to the breaking up of the group system, many individuals have taken to other occupations, and this has somewhat obliterated the line dividing the various occupational groups. The destruction of crafts and village industries, originally deliberately undertaken under early British rule and later resulting from the development of a new colonial economy, led to vast numbers of these artisans and craftsmen, more especially the weavers, being deprived of their occupations and livelihood. Those who survived this catastrophe drifted to the land and became landless laborers or shared a tiny patch of land with their relatives.

Conversions to Islam in those days, whether individual or group, probably aroused no particular opposition, except when force or some kind of compulsion was used. Friends and relatives or neighbors might disapprove, but the Hindu community as such apparently attached little importance to this. In contrast with this indifferent attitude, conversions today attract widespread attention and are resented, whether they are to Islam or Christianity. This is largely due to political factors and especially to the introduction of separate religious electorates. Each convert is supposed to be a gain to the communal group, leading ultimately to greater representation and more political power. Attempts are even made to manipulate the census to this end. Apart from political reasons, there has also been a growth in Hinduism of a tendency to proselytize and convert non-Hindus to Hinduism. This is one of the direct effects of

Islam on Hinduism, though in practice it brings it into conflict with Islam in India. Orthodox Hindus still do not approve of it.

In Kashmir a long-continued process of conversion to Islam had resulted in 95 per cent of the population becoming Moslems, though they retained many of their old Hindu customs. In the middle nineteenth century the Hindu ruler of the state found that very large numbers of these people were anxious or willing to return *en bloc* to Hinduism. He sent a deputation to the pundits of Benares inquiring if this could be done. The pundits refused to countenance any such change of faith, and there the matter ended.

The Moslems who came to India from outside brought no new technique or political and economic structure. In spite of a religious belief in the brotherhood of Islam, they were class bound and feudal in outlook. In technique and in the methods of production and industrial organization they were inferior to what prevailed then in India. Thus their influence on the economic life of India and the social structure was very little. This life continued as of old, and all the people, Hindu or Moslem or others, fitted into it.

The position of women deteriorated. Even the ancient laws had been unfair to them in regard to inheritance and their position in the household—though even so they were fairer than nineteenth-century English law. Those laws of inheritance derived from the Hindu joint family system and sought to protect joint property from transfer to another family. A woman by marriage changed her family. In an economic sense she was looked upon as a dependent of her father or husband or son, but she could and did hold property in her own right. In many ways she was honored and respected and had a fair measure of freedom, taking part in social and cultural activities. Indian history is full of the names of famous women, including thinkers and philosophers, rulers and warriors. This freedom grew progressively less. Islam had a fairer law of inheritance, but this did not affect Hindu women. What did affect many of them to their great disadvantage, as it affected Moslem women to a much greater degree, was the intensification of the custom of seclusion of women. This spread among the upper classes all over the north and in Bengal, but the south and west of India escaped this degrading custom. Even in the north, only the upper classes indulged in it and the masses were happily free from it. Women now had less chances of education, and their activities were largely confined to the household.[5] Lacking most other ways of distinguishing themselves, living a confined and restricted life, they were told that their supreme virtue lay in chastity and the supreme sin in a loss of it. Such was the man-made doctrine, but man did not apply it to himself. Tulsidas in his deservedly famous poem, the Hindi Ramayana, written during Jehengir's time, painted a picture of woman which is grossly unfair and prejudiced.

Partly because the great majority of Moslems in India were converts from Hinduism, partly because of long contact, Hindus and Moslems in India developed numerous common traits, habits, ways of living and artistic tastes, especially in northern India—in music, painting, architecture, food, clothes, and common traditions. They lived together peacefully as one people, joined each other's festivals and celebrations, spoke the same language, lived in more or less the same way, and faced identical economic problems. The nobility and the landed gentry and their numerous hangers-on took their cue from the court. (These people were not landlords or owners of the land. They did not take rent but were allowed to collect and retain the state revenue for a particular area. These grants were usually for life.) They developed a highly intricate and sophisticated common culture. They wore the same kind of clothes, ate the same type of food, had common artistic pursuits, military pastimes, hunting, chivalry, and games. Polo was a favorite game, and elephant fights were popular.

All this intercourse and common living took place in spite of the caste system which prevented fusion. There were no intermarriages except in rare instances, and even

[5] And yet many instances of notable women, scholars as well as rulers, occur even during this period and later. In the eighteenth century Lakshmi Devi wrote a great legal commentary on the *Mitakshara*, a famous lawbook of the medieval period.

then it was not fusion but usually the transfer of a Hindu woman to the Moslem fold. Nor was there interdining, but this was not so strict. The seclusion of women prevented the development of social life. This applied even more to Muslims *inter se*, for purdah among them was stricter. Though Hindu and Moslem men met each other frequently, such opportunities were lacking to the women of both groups. These women of the nobility and upper classes were thus far more cut off from each other and developed much more marked separate ideological groups, each largely ignorant of the other.

Among the common people in the villages, and that means the vast majority of the population, life had a much more corporate and joint basis. Within the limited circle of the village there was an intimate relationship between the Hindus and Moslems. Caste did not come in the way, and the Hindus looked upon the Moslems as belonging to another caste. Most of the Moslems were converts who were still full of their old traditions. They were well acquainted with the Hindu background, mythology, and epic stories. They did the same kind of work, lived similar lives, wore the same kind of clothes, spoke the same language. They joined each other's festivals, and some semireligious festivals were common to both. They had common folk songs. Mostly these people were peasants and artisans and craftsmen.

The third large group, in between the nobility and the peasantry and artisans, was the merchant and trader class. This was predominantly Hindu, and though it had no political power, the economic structure was largely under its control. This class had fewer intimate contacts with the Moslems than any other class, above it or below. The Moslems who had come from outside India were feudal in outlook and did not take kindly to trade. The Islamic prohibition against the taking of interest also came in the way of trade. They considered themselves the ruling class, the nobility, and functioned as state officials, holders of grants of land, or as officers in the army. There were also many scholars attached to the court or in charge of theological and other academies.

During the Moghul period large numbers of Hindus wrote books in Persian, which was the official court language. Some of these books have become classics of their kind. At the same time Moslem scholars translated Sanskrit books into Persian and wrote in Hindi. Two of the best-known Hindi poets are Malik Mohammad Jaisi, who wrote the *Padmavat*, and Abdur Rahim Khankhana, one of the premier nobles of Akbar's court and son of his guardian. Khankhana was a scholar in Arabic, Persian, and Sanskrit, and his Hindi poetry is of a high quality. For some time he was the commander-in-chief of the imperial army, and yet he has written in praise and admiration of Rana Pratap of Mewar, who was continually fighting Akbar and never submitted to him. Khankhana admires and commends the patriotism and high sense of honor and chivalry of his enemy on the battlefield.

It was this chivalrous and friendly approach on which Akbar based his policy and which many of his counselors and ministers learned from him. He was particularly attached to the Rajputs, for he admired in them qualities which he himself possessed—reckless courage, a sense of honor and chivalry, and an adherence to the pledged word. He won over the Rajputs; but the Rajputs, for all their admirable qualities, represented a medieval type of society which was already becoming out of date as new forces were arising. Akbar was not conscious of these new forces, for he himself was a prisoner of his own social inheritance.

Akbar's success is astonishing, for he created a sense of oneness among the diverse elements of north and central India. There was the barrier of a ruling class, mainly of foreign origin, and there were the barriers of religion and caste, a proselytizing religion opposed to a static but highly resistant system. These barriers did not disappear, but in spite of them that feeling of oneness grew. It was not merely an attachment to his person; it was an attachment to the structure he had built. His son and grandson, Jehangir and Shah Jehan, accepted that structure and functioned within its framework. They were men of no outstanding ability, but their reigns were successful because they continued on the lines so firmly laid down by Akbar.

The next comer, Aurungzeb, much abler but of a different mold, swerved and left that beaten track, undoing Akbar's work. Yet not entirely, for it is extraordinary how, in spite of him and his feeble and pitiful successors, that feeling of reverence for that structure continued. That feeling was largely confined to the north and center; it did not extend to the south or west. And it was from western India, therefore, that the challenge to it came.

## XI. AURUNGZEB PUTS THE CLOCK BACK
### GROWTH OF HINDU NATIONALISM
### SHIVAJI

Shah Jehan was a contemporary of Louis XIV of France, the grand monarch, and the Thirty Years' War was ravaging central Europe then. As Versailles took shape, the Taj Mahal and the Pearl Mosque grew up in Agra, and the Jame Masjid of Delhi and the Diwan-i-Am and the Diwan-i-Khas in the imperial palace. These lovely buildings with a fairy-like beauty represent the height of Moghul splendor. The Delhi court, with its Peacock Throne, was more magnificent and luxurious than Versailles, but, like Versailles, it rested on a poverty-stricken and exploited people. There was a terrible famine in Gujrat and the Deccan.

Meanwhile the naval power of England was rising and spreading. The only Europeans that Akbar knew were the Portuguese. During his son Jehangir's time the British navy defeated the Portuguese in Indian seas, and Sir Thomas Roe, an ambassador of James I of England, presented himself at Jehangir's court in 1615. He succeeded in getting permission to start factories. The Surat factory was started, and Madras was founded in 1639. For over a hundred years no one in India attached any importance to the British. The fact that the British now controlled the sea routes and had practically driven away the Portuguese had no significance for the Moghul rulers or their advisers. When the Moghul empire was visibly weakening during Aurungzeb's reign, the British made an organized attempt to increase their possessions in India by war. This was in 1685. Aurungzeb, weak as he was growing and beset by enemies, succeeded in defeating the British. Even before this the French had established footholds in India. The overflowing energies of Europe were spreading out in India and the East just when India's political and economic condition was rapidly declining.

In France, Louis XIV was still continuing his long reign, laying the seeds of future revolution. In England the rising middle classes had cut off the head of their king, Cromwell's brief-lived republic had flourished, Charles II had come and gone, and James II had run away. Parliament, representing to a large extent a new mercantile class, had curbed the king and established its supremacy.

It was during this period that Aurungzeb succeeded to the throne of the Moghuls after a civil war and having imprisoned his own father, Shah Jehan. Only an Akbar might have understood the situation and controlled the new forces that were rising. Perhaps even he could have only postponed the dissolution of his empire unless his curiosity and thirst for knowledge had led him to understand the significance of the new techniques that were arising, and of the shift in economic conditions that was taking place. Aurungzeb, far from understanding the present, failed even to appreciate the immediate past; he was a throwback, and for all his ability and earnestness, he tried to undo what his predecessors had done. A bigot and an austere puritan, he was no lover of art or literature. He infuriated the great majority of his subjects by imposing the old hated *jeziya* poll tax on the Hindus and destroying many of their temples. He offended the proud Rajputs who had been the props and pillars of the Moghul empire. In the north he roused the Sikhs, who, from being a peaceful sect representing some kind of a synthesis of Hindu and Islamic ideas, were converted by repression and persecution into a military brotherhood. Near the west coast of India he angered the warlike Marathas, descendants of the ancient Rashtrakutas, just when a brilliant captain had risen among them.

All over the widespread domains of the Moghul empire

there was a ferment and a growth of a revivalist sentiment, which was a mixture of religion and nationalism. That nationalism was certainly not of the modern secular type, nor did it, as a rule, embrace the whole of India in its scope. It was colored by feudalism, by local sentiment and sectarian feeling. The Rajputs, more feudal than the rest, thought of their clan loyalties; the Sikhs, a comparatively small group in the Punjab, were absorbed in their own self-defense and could hardly look beyond the Punjab. Yet the religion itself had a strong national background, and all its traditions were connected with India. "The Indians," writes Professor Macdonell, "are the only division of the Indo-European family which has created a great national religion—Brahmanism—and a great world religion—Buddhism; while all the rest far from displaying originality in this sphere have long since adopted a foreign faith." That combination of religion and nationalism gained strength and cohesiveness from both elements, and yet its ultimate weakness and insufficiency were also derived from that mixture. For it could only be an exclusive and partial nationalism, not including the many elements in India that lay outside that religious sphere. Hindu nationalism was a natural growth from the soil of India, but inevitably it comes in the way of the larger nationalism which rises above differences of religion or creed.

It is true that during this period of disruption when a great empire was breaking up and many adventurers, Indian and foreign, were trying to carve out principalities for themselves, nationalism, in its present sense, is hardly in evidence at all. Each individual adventurer sought to augment his own power; each group fended for itself. Such history as we have only tells us of these adventurers, attaching more importance to them than to more significant happenings below the surface of events. Yet there are glimpses to show that it was not all adventurism, though many adventurers held the field. The Marathas, especially, had a wider conception, and as they grew in power this conception also grew. Warren Hastings wrote in 1784: "The Marathahs possess, alone of all the people of Hindostan and Deccan, a principle of national attachment, which is strongly impressed on the minds of all individuals of the nation, and would probably unite their chiefs, as in one common cause, if any great danger were to threaten the general state." Probably this national sentiment of theirs was largely confined to the Marathi-speaking area. None the less the Marathas were catholic in their political and military system as well as their habits, and there was a certain internal democracy among them. All this gave strength to them. Shivaji, though he fought Aurungzeb, freely employed Moslems.

An equally important factor in the breakup of the Moghul empire was the cracking up of the economic structure. There were repeated peasant risings, some of them on a big scale. From 1669 onward the Jat peasantry, not far from the capital itself, rose again and again against the Delhi government. Yet another revolt of poor people was that of the Satnamis, who were described by a Moghul noble as "a gang of bloody miserable rebels, goldsmiths, carpenters, sweepers, tanners, and other ignoble beings." Thus far revolts had been confined to princes and nobles and others of high degree. Quite another class was now experimenting with them.

While the empire was rent by strife and revolt, the new Maratha power was growing and consolidating itself in western India. Shivaji, born in 1627, was the ideal guerrilla leader of hardened mountaineers, and his cavalry went far and wide, sacking the city of Surat, where the English had their factory, and enforcing the *chowth* tax payment over distant parts of the Moghul dominions. Shivaji was the symbol of a resurgent Hindu nationalism, drawing inspiration from the old classics, courageous, and possessing high qualities of leadership. He built up the Marathas as a strong, unified fighting group, gave them a nationalist background, and made them a formidable power which broke up the Moghul empire. He died in 1680, but the Maratha power continued to grow till it dominated India.

## XII. THE MARATHAS AND THE BRITISH
### STRUGGLE FOR SUPREMACY
### TRIUMPH OF THE BRITISH

The hundred years that followed the death of Aurungzeb in 1707 saw a complicated and many-sided struggle for mastery over India. The Moghul empire rapidly fell to pieces and the imperial viceroys and governors began to function as semi-independent rulers, though so great was the prestige of the descendant of the Moghuls in Delhi that a formal allegiance was paid to him even when he was powerless and a prisoner of others. These satrapies had no real power or importance, except in so far as they helped or hindered the main protagonists for power. The Nizam of Hyderabad, by virtue of the strategic position of his state in the south, appeared to have a certain importance in the beginning. But it soon transpired that this importance was entirely fictitious and the state was "straw-stuffed and held upright" by external forces. It showed a peculiar capacity for duplicity and for profiting by the misfortunes of others while avoiding all risk and danger. Sir John Shore described it as "incorrigibly depraved, devoid of energy . . . consequently liable to sink into vassalage." The Marathas looked upon the Nizam as one of their subordinate chieftains paying tribute to them. An attempt by him to avoid this and to show independence met with swift retribution, and the Marathas put to flight his feeble and none-too-brave army. He took refuge under the protecting wings of the growing power of the British East India Company and survived as a state because of this vassalage. Indeed the Hyderabad state enlarged its area considerably, without any remarkable effort on its part, by the British victory over Tipu Sultan of Mysore.

Warren Hastings, writing in 1784, refers to the Nizam of Hyderabad: "His dominions are of small extent and scanty revenue; his military strength is represented to be most contemptible; nor was he at any period of his life distinguished for personal courage or the spirit of enterprise. On the contrary, it seems to have been his constant and ruling maxim to foment the incentives of war among his neighbours, to profit by their weakness and embarrassments, but to avoid being a party himself in any of their contests, and to submit even to humiliating sacrifices rather than subject himself to the chances of war."[6]

The real protagonists for power in India during the eighteenth century were four: two of these were Indian and two foreign. The Indians were the Marathas and Haider Ali and his son Tipu Sultan in the south; the foreigners were the British and the French. Of these, it appeared almost inevitable, during the first half of the century, that the Marathas were destined to establish their supremacy over India as a whole and to be the successors of the Moghul empire. Their troops appeared at the very gates of Delhi as early as 1737, and there was no power strong enough to oppose them.

Just then (in 1739) a new eruption took place in the northwest and Nadir Shah of Persia swept down to Delhi, killing and plundering, and carrying off enormous treasure including the famous Peacock Throne. It was an easy raid for him, for the Delhi rulers were effete and effeminate, wholly unused to warfare, and Nadir Shah did not come into conflict with the Marathas. In a sense, his raid facilitated matters for the Marathas who in subsequent years spread to the Punjab. Again Maratha supremacy of India was in sight.

Nadir Shah's raid had two consequences. He put an end completely to any pretensions that the Delhi Moghul rulers had to power and dominion; henceforth they became vague shadows enjoying a ghostly sovereignty, puppets in the hands of anyone who was strong enough to hold them. To a large extent they had arrived at that stage even before Nadir Shah came; he completed the process. And yet, so strong is the hold of tradition and long-established custom, the British East India Company, as well as others, continued to send humble presents to them in token of tribute

[6] Quoted in Thompson's *The Making of the Indian Princes* (1943), p. 1.

right up to the eve of Plassey; and even afterward for a long time the company considered itself and functioned as the agent of the Delhi emperor, in whose name money was coined till 1835.

The second consequence of Nadir Shah's raid was the separation of Afghanistan from India. Afghanistan, which for long ages past had been part of India, was now cut off and became part of Nadir Shah's dominions. Sometime afterward a local rebellion resulted in the murder of Nadir Shah by a group of his own officers, and Afghanistan became an independent state.

The Marathas had in no way been weakened by Nadir Shah, and they continued to spread in the Punjab. But in 1761 they met with a crushing defeat at Panipat from an Afghan invader, Ahmad Shah Durrani, who was ruling Afghanistan then. The flower of the Maratha forces perished in this disaster, and for a while their dreams of empire faded away. They recovered gradually, and the Maratha dominions were divided into a number of independent states joined together in a confederacy under the leadership of the Peshwa at Poona. The chiefs of the bigger states were Scindhia of Gwalior, Holkar of Indore, and the Gackwar of Baroda. This confederacy still dominated a vast area in western and central India. But the Panipat defeat of the Marathas by Ahmad Shah had weakened them just when the English company was emerging as an important territorial power in India.

In Bengal, Clive, by promoting treason and forgery and with very little fighting, had won the battle of Plassey in 1757, a date which is sometimes said to mark the beginning of the British Empire in India. It was an unsavory beginning, and something of that bitter taste has clung to it ever since. Soon the British held the whole of Bengal and Bihar, and one of the early consequences of their rule was a terrible famine which ravaged these two provinces in 1770, killing over a third of the population of this rich, vast, and densely populated area.

In south India, the struggle between the English and the French, a part of the world struggle between the two, ended in the triumph of the English, and the French were almost eliminated from India.

With the elimination of the French power from India, three contestants for supremacy remained—the Maratha confederacy, Haider Ali in the south, and the British. In spite of their victory at Plassey and their spreading out over Bengal and Bihar, few, if any, people in India then looked upon the British as a dominant power destined to rule over the whole of India. An observer would still have given the first place to the Marathas, who sprawled all over western and central India right up to Delhi, and whose courage and fighting qualities were well known. Haider Ali and Tipu Sultan were formidable adversaries who inflicted a severe defeat on the British and came near to breaking the power of the East India Company. But they were confined to the south and did not directly affect the fortunes of India as a whole. Haider Ali was a remarkable man and one of the notable figures in Indian history. He had some kind of a national ideal and possessed the qualities of a leader with vision. Continually suffering from a painful disease, his self-discipline and capacity for hard work were astonishing. He realized, long before others did so, the importance of sea power and the growing menace of the British based on naval strength. He tried to organize a joint effort to drive them out, and for this purpose sent envoys to the Marathas, the Nizam, and Shuja-ud-Dowla of Oudh. But nothing came of this. He started building his own navy, and capturing the Maldive Islands, made them his headquarters for shipbuilding and naval activities. He died by the wayside as he was marching with his army. His son Tipu continued strengthening his navy. Tipu also sent messages to Napoleon and to the sultan in Constantinople.

In the north a Sikh state under Ranjit Singh was growing up in the Punjab, to spread later to Kashmir and the North-West Frontier Province. But that, too, was a marginal state not affecting the real struggle for supremacy. That struggle, it became clear as the eighteenth century approached its end, lay between the only two powers that counted—the Marathas and the British. All the other states and principalities were subordinate and subsidiary to these two.

Tipu Sultan of Mysore was finally defeated by the British in 1799, and that left the field clear for the final contest between the Marathas and the British East India Company. Charles Metcalfe, one of the ablest of the British officials in India, wrote in 1806: "India contains no more than two great powers, British and Mahratta, and every other state acknowledges the influence of one or the other. Every inch that we recede will be occupied by them." But there was rivalry among the Maratha chieftains, and they fought and were defeated separately by the British. They won some notable victories and especially inflicted a severe defeat on the British near Agra in 1804. But by 1818 the Maratha power was finally crushed, and the great chiefs that represented it in central India submitted and accepted the overlordship of the East India Company. The British became then the unchallenged sovereigns of a great part of India, governing the country directly or through puppet and subsidiary princes. The Punjab and some outlying parts were still beyond their control, but the British Empire in India had become an established fact and subsequent wars with the Sikhs and Gurkhas and in Burma merely rounded it off on the map.

## XIII. THE BACKWARDNESS OF INDIA AND THE SUPERIORITY OF THE ENGLISH IN ORGANIZATION AND TECHNIQUE

Looking back over this period, it almost seems that the British succeeded in dominating India by a succession of fortuitous circumstances and lucky flukes. With remarkably little effort, considering the glittering prize, they won a great empire and enormous wealth which helped to make them the leading power in the world. It seems easy for a slight turn in events to have taken place which would have dashed their hopes and ended their ambitions. They were defeated on many occasions—by Haider Ali and Tipu, by the Marathas, by the Sikhs and by the Gurkhas. A little less of good fortune and they might have lost their foothold in India, or at the most, held on to certain coastal territories only.

And yet a closer scrutiny reveals, in the circumstances then existing, a certain inevitability in what happened. Good fortune there certainly was, but there must be an ability to profit by good fortune. India was then in a fluid and disorganized state, following the breakup of the Moghul empire; for many centuries it had not been so weak and helpless. Organized power having broken down, the field was left open to adventurers and new claimants for dominion. Among these adventurers and claimants, the British, and the British alone at the time, possessed many of the qualities necessary for success. Their major disadvantage was that they were foreigners coming from a far country. Yet that very disadvantage worked in their favor, for no one took them very seriously or considered them as possible contestants for the sovereignty of India. It is extraordinary how this delusion lasted till long after Plassey, and their functioning in formal matters as the agents of the shadow emperor at Delhi helped to further this false impression. The plunder that they carried away from Bengal and their peculiar methods of trade led to the belief that these foreigners were out for money and treasure and not so much for dominion; that they were a temporary though painful infliction, rather like Timur or Nadir Shah who came and plundered and went back to his homelands.

The East India Company had originally established itself for trading purposes, and its military establishment was meant to protect this trade. Gradually, and almost unnoticed by others, it had extended the territory under its control, chiefly by taking sides in local disputes, helping one rival against another. The company's troops were better trained and were an asset to any side, and the company extracted heavy payment for the help. So the company's power grew and its military establishment increased. People looked upon these troops as mercenaries to be hired. When it was realized that the British were playing nobody's game but their own and were out for the political domination of India, they had already established themselves firmly in the country.

Antiforeign sentiment there undoubtedly was, and this grew in later years. But this was far removed from any general or widespread national feeling. The background was feudal, and loyalty went to the local chief. Widespread distress, as in China during the days of the war lords, compelled people to join any military leader who offered regular pay or opportunities of loot. The East India Company's armies largely consisted of Indian sepoys. Only the Marathas had some national sentiment, something much more than loyalty to a leader, behind them; but even this was narrow and limited. They managed to irritate the brave Rajputs by their treatment of them. Instead of gaining them as allies, they had to deal with them as opponents or as grumbling and dissatisfied feudatories. Among the Maratha chiefs themselves there was bitter rivalry and occasionally civil war, in spite of a vague alliance under the Peshwa's leadership. At critical moments they failed to support each other, and were separately defeated.

Yet the Marathas produced a number of very able men, statesmen and warriors, among them being Nana Farnavis, the Peshwa Baji Rao I, Mahadaji Scindhia of Gwalior and Yaswant Rao Holkar of Indore, as also that remarkable woman, Princess Ahalya Bai of Indore. Their rank and file was good, seldom deserting a post and often facing certain death unmoved. But behind all this courage there was often an adventurism and amateurishness, both in peace and war, which are surprising. Their ignorance of the world was appalling and even their knowledge of India's geography was strictly limited. What is worse, they did not take the trouble to find out what was happening elsewhere and what their enemies were doing. There could be no farsighted statesmanship or effective strategy with these limitations. Their speed of movement and mobility often surprised and unnerved the enemy, but essentially war was looked upon as a series of gallant charges and little more. They were ideal guerrilla fighters. Later they reorganized their armies on more orthodox lines, with the result that what they gained in armor they lost in speed and mobility, and they could not adjust themselves easily to these new conditions. They considered themselves clever, and so they were, but it was not difficult to overreach them in peace or war, for their thought was imprisoned in an old and out-of-date framework and could not go beyond it.

The superiority in discipline and technique of foreign-trained armies had of course been noticed at an early stage by Indian rulers. They employed French and English officers to train their own armies, and the rivalry between these two helped to build up Indian armies. Haider Ali and Tipu also had some conception of the importance of sea power, and they tried, unsuccessfully and too late, to build up a fleet in order to challenge the British on sea. The Marathas also made a feeble attempt in this direction. India was then a shipbuilding country, but it was not easy to build up a navy within a short time and in the face of constant opposition. With the elimination of the French, many of their officers in the armies of the Indian powers had to go. The foreign officers who remained, chiefly British, often deserted their employers at critical stages, and on some occasions betrayed them, surrendering and marching over to their enemies (the British) with their armies and treasure. This reliance on foreign officers not only indicates the backwardness of the army organization of the Indian powers but was also a constant source of danger owing to their unreliability. The British often had a powerful fifth column both in the administration and the armies of the Indian rulers.

If the Marathas, with their homogeneity and group patriotism, were backward in civil and military organization, much more so were the other Indian powers. The Rajputs, for all their courage, functioned in the old feudal way, romantic but thoroughly inefficient, and were rent among themselves by tribal feuds. Many of them, from a sense of feudal loyalty to an overlord, and partly as a consequence of Akbar's policy in the past, sided with the vanishing power of Delhi. But Delhi was too feeble to profit by this, and the Rajputs deteriorated and became the playthings of others, ultimately falling into the orbit of Scindhia, the Maratha. Some of their chiefs tried to play a careful balancing game in order to save themselves. The various Moslem rulers and chiefs in northern and central India were as feudal and backward in their ideas as the Rajput. They made no real difference, except to add to the confusion and the misery of the mass of the people. Some of them acknowledged the suzerainty of the Marathas.

The Gurkhas of Nepal were splendid and disciplined soldiers, the equals, if not the superiors, of any troops that the East India Company could produce. Although completely feudal in organization, their attachment to their homelands was great and this sentiment made them formidable fighters in its defense. They gave a fright to the British but made no difference to the issue of the main struggle in India.

The Marathas did not consolidate themselves in the vast areas in northern and central India where they had spread. They came and went, taking no root. Perhaps nobody could take root just then, owing to the alternating fortunes of war; and indeed many territories under British control, or acknowledging British suzerainty, were in a far worse condition, and the British or their administration had not taken root there.

If the Marathas (and much more so the other Indian powers) were amateurish and adventurist in their methods, the British in India were thoroughly professional. Many of the British leaders were adventurous enough, but they were in no way adventurist in their policy, for which they all worked in their separate spheres. "The East India Company's Secretariat," writes Edward Thompson, "was served in the courts of Native India by a succession and galaxy of men such as even the British Empire has hardly ever possessed together at any other time." One of the chief duties of the British residents at these courts was to bribe and corrupt the ministers and other officials. Their spy system was perfect, says a historian. They had complete information of the courts and armies of their adversaries, while those adversaries lived in ignorance of what the British were doing or were going to do. The fifth column of the British functioned continuously, and in moments of crisis and in the heat of war there would be defections in their favor which made a great difference. They won most of their battles before the actual fighting took place. That had been so at Plassey, and that was repeated again and again right up to the Sikh wars. A notable instance of desertion was that of a high officer in the service of Scindhia of Gwalior, who had secretly come to terms with the British and went over to them with his entire array at the moment of battle. He was rewarded for this later by being made the ruler of a new Indian state carved out of the territories of Scindhia whom he had betrayed. That state still exists, but the man's name became a byword for treason and treachery, just as Quisling's in recent years.

The British thus represented a higher political and military organization, well knit together and having very able leaders. They were far better informed than their adversaries, and they took full advantage of the disunity and rivalries of the Indian powers. Their command of the seas gave them safe bases and opportunities to add to their resources. Even when temporarily defeated, they could recuperate and assume the offensive again. Their possession of Bengal after Plassey gave them enormous wealth and resources to carry on their warfare with the Marathas and others, and each fresh conquest added to these resources. For the Indian powers, defeat often meant a disaster which could not be remedied.

This period of war and conquest and plunder converted central India and Rajputana and some parts of the south and west into derelict areas full of violence and unhappiness and misery. Armies marched across them and in their train came highway robbers, and no one cared for the miserable human beings who lived there, except to despoil them of their money and goods. Parts of India became rather like central Europe during the Thirty Years' War. Conditions were bad almost everywhere, but they were worst of all in the areas under British control or suzerainty— ". . . Nothing could be more fantastic than the picture presented by Madras or by the vassal States of Oudh and Hyderabad, a seething delirium of misery. In comparison, the regions where the Nana [Farnavis, the

Maratha statesman] governed were an oasis of gentle security"—so writes Edward Thompson.

Just prior to this period, large parts of India were singularly free from disorder, in spite of the disruption of the
Moghul empire. In Bengal during the long reign of Allawardi, the semi-independent Moghul viceroy, peaceful and
orderly government prevailed and trade and business flourished, adding to the great wealth of the province. Some
little time after Allawardi's death the battle of Plassey
(1757) took place and the East India Company constituted themselves the agents of the Delhi emperor, though
in reality they were completely independent and could do
what they willed. Then began the pillage of Bengal on behalf of the company and its agents and factors. Some years
after Plassey began the reign of Ahalya Bai of Indore in
central India, and it lasted for thirty years (1765–95).
This has become almost legendary as a period during which
perfect order and good government prevailed and the people prospered. She was a very able ruler and organizer,
highly respected during her lifetime, and considered as a
saint by a grateful people after her death. Thus during
the very period when Bengal and Bihar, under the new
rule of the East India Company, deteriorated and there
was organized plunder and political and economic chaos,
leading to terrible famines, central India as well as many
other parts of the country was in a prosperous condition.

The British had power and wealth but felt no responsibility for good government or any government. The merchants of the East India Company were interested in dividends and treasure and not in the improvement or even
protection of those who had come under their sway. In
particular, in the vassal states there was a perfect divorce
between power and responsibility.

When the British had finished with the Marathas and
were secure in their conquests, they turned their minds
toward civil government and some kind of order was
evolved. In the subsidiary states, however, the change was
very slow, for in those so-called protected areas there was
a permanent divorce between responsibility and power.

We are often reminded, lest we forget, that the British

rescued India from chaos and anarchy. That is true in so
far as they established orderly government after this period,
which the Marathas have called "the time of terror." But
that chaos and anarchy were partly, at least, due to the
policy of the East India Company and their representatives
in India. It is also conceivable that even without the good
offices of the British, so eagerly given, peace and orderly
government might have been established in India after the
conclusion of the struggle for supremacy. Such developments had been known to have taken place in India, as in
other countries, in the course of her five thousand years of
history.

## XIV. RANJIT SINGH AND JAI SINGH

It seems clear that India became a prey to foreign conquest
because of the inadequacy of her own people and because
the British represented a higher and advancing social order.
The contrast between the leaders on both sides is marked;
the Indians, for all their ability, functioned in a narrow,
limited sphere of thought and action, unaware of what was
happening elsewhere and therefore unable to adapt themselves to changing conditions. Even if the curiosity of individuals was roused, they could not break the shell which
held them and their people prisoners. The Englishmen,
on the other hand, were much more worldly wise, shaken
up and forced to think by events in their own country and
in France and America. Two great revolutions had taken
place. The campaigns of the French revolutionary armies
and of Napoleon had changed the whole science of war.
Even the most ignorant Englishman who came to India
saw different parts of the world in the course of his journey.
In England itself great discoveries were being made herald-
ing the Industrial Revolution, though perhaps few realized
their far-reaching significance at the time. But the leaven
of change was working powerfully and influencing the people. Behind it all was the expansive energy which sent the
British to distant lands.

Those who have recorded the history of India are so full of wars and tumults and the political and military leaders of the day, that they tell us very little of what was happening in the mind of India and how social and economic processes were at work. Only occasional and accidental glimpses emerge from this sordid record. It appears that during this period of terror the people generally were crushed and exhausted, passively submitting to the decrees of a malevolent fate, dazed and devoid of curiosity. There must have been many individuals, however, who were curious and who tried to understand the new forces at play, but they were overwhelmed by the tide of events and could not influence them.

One of the individuals who was full of curiosity was Maharaja Ranjit Singh, a Jat Sikh, who had built up a kingdom in the Punjab, which subsequently spread to Kashmir and the Frontier Province. He had failings and vices; nevertheless he was a remarkable man. The Frenchman Jacquemont calls him "extremely brave" and "almost the first inquisitive Indian I have seen, but his curiosity makes up for the apathy of the whole nation." "His conversation is like a nightmare."[7] It must be remembered that Indians, as a rule, are a reserved people, and more so the intellectuals among them. Very few of these would have cared to associate then with the foreign military leaders and adventurers in India, many of whose actions filled them with horror. So these intellectuals tried to preserve their dignity by keeping as far as possible from the foreign elements, and met them only on formal occasions when circumstances compelled them to do so. The Indians whom Englishmen and other foreigners usually met were of the opportunist and servile class that surrounded them, or the ministers, frequently corrupt and intriguing, of the Indian courts.

Ranjit Singh was not only intellectually curious and inquisitive, he was remarkably humane at a time when India and the world seethed with callousness and inhumanity. He built up a kingdom and a powerful army and yet he

[7] Quoted by Thompson, p. 158.

disliked bloodshed. "Never was so large an empire founded by one man with so little criminality," says Prinsep. He abolished the death sentence for every crime, however heinous it might be, when in England even petty pilferers had to face death. "Except in actual warfare," writes Osborne who visited him, "he has never been known to take life, though his own has been attempted more than once, and his reign will be found freer from any striking acts of cruelty and oppression than those of many more civilized monarchs."[8]

Another but a different type of Indian statesman was Sawai Jai Singh of Jaipur in Rajputana. He belongs to a somewhat earlier period; he died in 1743. He lived during the period of disruption following Aurungzeb's death. He was clever and opportunist enough to survive the many shocks and changes that followed each other in quick succession. He acknowledged the suzerainty of the Delhi emperor. When he found that the advancing Marathas were too strong to be checked, he came to terms with them on behalf of the emperor. But it is not his political or military career that interests me. He was a brave warrior and an accomplished diplomat, but he was something much more than this. He was a mathematician and an astronomer, a scientist and a town planner, and he was interested in the study of history.

Jai Singh built big observatories at Jaipur, Delhi, Ujjain, Benares, and Mathura. Learning through Portuguese missionaries of the progress of astronomy in Portugal, he sent his own men, with one of the missionaries, to the court of the Portuguese king Emmanuel. Emmanuel sent his envoy, Xavier da Silva, with De la Hire's tables to Jai Singh. On comparing these with his own tables, Jai Singh came to the conclusion that the Portuguese tables were less exact and had several errors. He attributed these to the "inferior diameters" of the instruments used.

Jai Singh was of course fully acquainted with Indian mathematics; he had studied the old Greek treatises and also knew of recent European developments in mathemat-

[8] Quotations taken from Thompson, pp. 157, 158.

ics. He had some of the Greek books (Euclid, etc.) as well as European works on plane and spherical trigonometry and the construction and use of logarithms translated into Sanskrit. He also had Arabic books on astronomy translated.

He founded the city of Jaipur. Interested in town planning, he collected the plans of many European cities of the time and then drew up his own plan. Many of these plans of the old European cities of the time are preserved in the Jaipur museum. The city of Jaipur was so well and wisely planned that it is still considered a model of town planning.

Jai Singh did all this and much more in the course of a comparatively brief life and in the midst of perpetual wars and court intrigues, in which he was himself often involved. Nadir Shah's invasion took place just four years before Jai Singh's death. Jai Singh would have been a remarkable man anywhere and at any time. The fact that he rose and functioned as a scientist in the typically feudal milieu of Rajputana and during one of the darkest periods of Indian history, when disruption and war and tumults filled the scene, is very significant. It shows that the spirit of scientific inquiry was not dead in India and there was some ferment at work which might have yielded rich results if only an opportunity had been given to it to fructify. Jai Singh was no anachronism or solitary thinker in an unfriendly and uncomprehending environment. He was a product of his age and he collected a number of scientific workers to work with him. Out of these he sent some in the embassy to Portugal, and social customs or taboo did not deter him from doing so. It seems probable that there was plenty of good material for scientific work in the country, both theoretical and technical, if only it were given a chance to function. That opportunity did not come for a long time. Even when the troubles and disorders were over, there was no encouragement of scientific work by those in authority.

## XV. THE ECONOMIC BACKGROUND OF INDIA
### THE TWO ENGLANDS

What was the economic background of India when all these far-reaching political changes were taking place? V. Anstey has written that right up to the eighteenth century "Indian methods of production and of industrial and commercial organization could stand comparison with those in vogue in any other part of the world." India was a highly developed manufacturing country exporting her manufactured products to Europe and other countries. Her banking system was efficient and well organized throughout the country, and the hundis or bills of exchange issued by the great business or financial houses were honored everywhere in India, as well as in Iran, and Kabul and Herat and Tashkent and other places in central Asia. Merchant capital had evolved, and there was an elaborate network of agents, jobbers, brokers, and middlemen. The shipbuilding industry was flourishing; one of the flagships of an English admiral during the Napoleonic wars had been built by an Indian firm in India. India was, in fact, as advanced industrially, commercially, and financially as any country prior to the Industrial Revolution. No such development could have taken place unless the country had enjoyed long periods of stable and peaceful government and the highways were safe for traffic and trade.

Foreign adventurers originally came to India because of the excellence of her manufactures, which had a big market in Europe. The chief business of the British East India Company in its early days was to trade with Indian goods in Europe, and very profitable trading it was, yielding enormous dividends. So efficient and highly organized were Indian methods of production, and such was the skill of India's artisans and craftsmen, that they could compete successfully even with the higher techniques of production which were being established in England. When the big machine age began in England, Indian goods continued to pour in and had to be stopped by very heavy duties, and in some cases by outright prohibition.

Clive described Murshidabad in Bengal in 1757, the very year of Plassey, as a city "as extensive, populous, and rich as the city of London, with this difference that there are individuals in the first possessing infinitely greater property than in the last." The city of Dacca in eastern Bengal was famous for its fine muslins. These two cities, important as they were, were near the periphery of Hindustan. All over the vast land there were greater cities and large numbers of big manufacturing and trading centers, and a very rapid and ingenious system of communicating news and market prices had been evolved. The great business houses often received news, even of the wars that were going on, long before dispatches reached the officials of the East India Company. The economy of India had thus advanced to as high a stage as it could reach prior to the Industrial Revolution. Whether it had the seeds of further progress in it or was too much bound up with the rigid social structure, it is difficult to say. It seems quite possible, however, that under normal conditions it would have undergone that change and begun to adapt itself, in its own way, to the new industrial conditions. And yet, though it was ripe for a change, that change itself required a revolution within its own framework. Perhaps some catalytic agent was necessary to bring about that change. It is clear that howsoever highly organized and developed its preindustrial economy was, it could not compete for long with the products of industrialized countries. It had to industrialize itself or submit to foreign economic penetration, which would have led to political interferences. As it happened, foreign political domination came first and this led to a rapid destruction of the economy she had built up, without anything positive or constructive taking its place. The East India Company represented both British political power and British vested interests and economic power. It was supreme, and being a company of merchants, it was intent on making money. Just when it was making money with amazing rapidity and in fantastic quantities, Adam Smith wrote about it in *The Wealth of Nations* in 1776: "The government of an exclusive company of merchants is perhaps the worst of all governments for any country whatever."

Though the Indian merchant and manufacturing classes were rich and spread out all over the country, and even controlled the economic structure, they had no political power. Government was despotic and still largely feudal. In fact, it was probably more feudal than it had been at some previous stages of Indian history. Hence there was no middle class strong enough to seize power, or even consciously of thinking of doing so, as in some Western countries. The people generally had grown apathetic and servile. There was thus a gap which had to be filled before any revolutionary change could take place. Perhaps this gap had been produced by the static nature of Indian society which refused to change in a changing world, for every civilization which resists change declines. That society, as constituted, had no more creative part to play. A change was overdue.

The British, at that time, were politically much more advanced. They had had their political revolution and had established the power of Parliament over that of the king. Their middle classes, conscious of their new power, were full of the impulse to expand. That vitality and energy, proof of a growing and progressive society, are indeed very evident in England. They show themselves in many ways, and most of all in the inventions and discoveries which heralded the Industrial Revolution.

And yet, what was the British ruling class then? Charles and Mary Beard, the eminent American historians, tell us how the success of the American revolution removed suddenly from the royal provinces in America the "British ruling class—a class accustomed to a barbarous criminal code, a narrow and intolerant university system, a government conceived as a huge aggregation of jobs and privileges, a contempt of men and women who toiled in field and shop, a denial of education to the masses, an Established religion forced alike on dissenters and Catholics, a dominion of squire and parson in countries and villages, callous brutality in army and navy, a scheme of primogeniture buttressing the rule of the landed gentry, a swarm of hungry placemen offering sycophancy to the king in exchange for offices, sinecures, and pensions, and a constitution of church and state so ordered as to fasten upon the masses this immense pile of pride and plunder. From the weight of this mountain the American revolutionists delivered the colonial subjects of the British Crown. Within a decade or two after that emancipation they accomplished reforms in law and policy which required a hundred years or more of persistent agitation to effect in the mother country—reforms which gave to the statesmen who led in the agitation their title to immortality in English history."[9]

The American Declaration of Independence, that landmark in freedom's history, was signed in 1776, and six years later the colonies separated from England and began their real intellectual, economic, and social revolution. The land system, that had grown up under British inspiration and after the model of England, was completely transformed. Many privileges were abolished and the large estates confiscated and then distributed in small lots. A stirring period of awakening and intellectual and economic activity followed. Free America, rid of feudal relics and foreign control, marched ahead with giant strides.

In France, the great revolution smashed the Bastille, symbol of the old order, and swept away the king and feudalism and declared the rights of man to the world.

And in England then? Frightened by these revolutionary changes in America and France, England became even more reactionary, and her fierce and barbarous penal code became even more savage. When George III came to the English throne in 1760 there were about 160 offenses for which men, women, and children were put to death. By the time his long reign ended in 1820, nearly a hundred new offenses carrying the death penalty were added to this terrible list. The ordinary soldier in the British army was treated worse than a beast of the field, with a brutality and inhumanity that horrify. Death sentences were common, and commoner still was flogging, inflicted in public, flogging up to several hundred lashes, till death sometimes

[9] *The Rise of American Civilization* (1928), Vol. I, p. 292.

intervened or the mangled body of the sufferer, just surviving, told the story to his dying day.

In this matter as in many others involving humanity and respect for the individual and the group, India was far more advanced and had a higher civilization. There was more literacy in India then than in England or the rest of Europe, though the education was strictly traditional. Probably there were more civic amenities also. The general condition of the masses in Europe was very backward and deplorable and compared unfavorably with the conditions prevailing in India. But there was this vital difference: new forces and living currents were working invisibly in western Europe, bringing changes in their train; in India conditions were far more static.

England came to India. When Queen Elizabeth gave a charter to the East India Company in 1600, Shakespeare was alive and writing. In 1611 the authorized English edition of the Bible was issued; in 1608 Milton was born. There followed Hampden and Cromwell and the political revolution. In 1660 the Royal Society of England, which was to advance the cause of science so much, was organized. A hundred years later, in 1760, the flying shuttle was invented, and there followed in quick succession the spinning jenny, the steam engine, and the power loom.

Which of these two Englands came to India? The England of Shakespeare and Milton, of noble speech and writing and brave deeds, of political revolution and the struggle for freedom, of science and technical progress, or the England of the savage penal code and brutal behavior, of entrenched feudalism and reaction? For there were two Englands, just as in every country there are these two aspects of national character and civilization. "The discrepancy in England," writes Edward Thompson, "between the highest and the ordinary levels of our civilization, has always been immense; I doubt if there is anything like it in any country with which we should wish to be compared and it is a discrepancy that lessens so slowly that it often seems hardly to lessen at all."[10]

[10] *The Making of the Indian Princes* (1943), p. 264.

The two Englands live side by side, influencing each other, and cannot be separated; nor could one of them come to India forgetting completely the other. Yet in every major action one plays the leading role, dominating the other, and it was inevitable that the wrong England should play that role in India and should come in contact with and encourage the wrong India in the process.

The independence of the United States of America is more or less contemporaneous with the loss of freedom by India. Surveying the past century and a half, an Indian looks somewhat wistfully and longingly at the vast progress made by the United States during this period and compares it with what has been done and what has not been done in his own country. It is true no doubt that the Americans have many virtues and we have many failings, that America offered a virgin field and almost a clean slate to write upon while we were cluttered up with ancient memories and traditions. And yet perhaps it is not inconceivable that if Britain had not undertaken this great burden in India and, as she tells us, endeavored for so long to teach us the difficult art of self-government, of which we had been so ignorant, India might not only have been freer and more prosperous but also far more advanced in science and art and all that makes life worth living.

# VI. The Last Phase:
# (1) Consolidation of British Rule
# and Rise of Nationalist Movement

## I. THE IDEOLOGY OF EMPIRE
### THE NEW CASTE

"Our writing of India's history is perhaps resented more than anything else we have done"—so writes an Englishman well acquainted with India and her history. It is difficult to say what Indians have resented most in the record of British rule in India; the list is long and varied. But it is true that British accounts of India's history, more especially of what is called the British period, are bitterly resented. History is almost always written by the victors and conquerors and gives their view. Or, at any rate, the victors' version is given prominence and holds the field. Very probably all the early records we have of the Aryans in India, their epics and traditions, glorify the Aryans and are unfair to the people of the country whom they subdued. No individual can wholly rid himself of his racial outlook and cultural limitations, and when there is conflict between races and countries even an attempt at impartiality is considered a betrayal of one's own people. War, which is an extreme example of this conflict, results in a deliberate throwing overboard of all fairness and impartiality so far as the enemy nation is concerned; the mind coarsens and becomes closed to almost all avenues of approach except one. The overpowering need of the moment is to justify one's own actions and condemn and blacken those of the enemy. Truth hides somewhere at the bottom of the deepest well, and falsehood, naked and unashamed, reigns almost supreme.

Even when actual war is not being waged there are often

potential war and conflicts between rival countries and interests. In a country dominated by an alien power, that conflict is inherent and continuous and affects and perverts people's thoughts and actions; the war mentality is never wholly absent. In the old days when war and its consequences, brutality and conquest and enslavement of a people, were accepted as belonging to the natural order of events, there was no particular need to cover them or justify them from some other point of view. With the growth of higher standards the need for justification has arisen, and this leads to a perversion of facts, sometimes deliberate, often unconscious. Thus hypocrisy pays its tribute to virtue and a false and sickening piety allies itself to evil deeds.

In any country, and especially in a huge country like India with its complicated history and mixed culture, it is always possible to find facts and trends to justify a particular thesis, and then this becomes the accepted basis for a new argument. America, it is said, is a land of contradictions, in spite of its standardization and uniformity. How much more then must India be full of contradictions and incongruities. We shall find there, as elsewhere, what we seek, and on this preconceived basis we can build up a structure of belief and opinion. And yet that structure will have untrue foundations and will give a false picture of reality.

Recent Indian history—that is, the history of the British period—is so connected with present-day happenings that the passions and prejudices of today powerfully influence our interpretation of it. Englishmen and Indians are both likely to err, though their errors will lie in opposite directions. Far the greater part of the records and papers out of which history takes shape and is written come from British sources and inevitably represents the British point of view. The very circumstances of defeat and disruption prevented the Indian side of the story from being properly recorded, and many of the records that existed suffered destruction during the great revolt of 1857. The papers that survived were hidden away in family archives and could not be published for fear of consequences. They remained dispersed, little known, and many perished in the manuscript stage from the incursions of termites and other insects which abound in this country. At a later stage when some of these papers were discovered, they threw a new light on many historical incidents. Even British-written Indian history had to be somewhat modified, and the Indian conception, often very different from the British, took shape. Behind this conception lay also a mass of tradition and memories, not of the remote past but of a period when our grandfathers and great-grandfathers were the living witnesses, and often the victims, of events. As history this tradition may have little value, but it is important as it enables us to understand the background of the Indian mind today. The villain of the British in India is often a hero to Indians, and those whom the British have delighted to honor and reward are often traitors and Quislings in the eyes of the great majority of the Indian people. That taint clings to their descendants.

The history of the American revolution has been differently written by Englishmen and Americans, and even today when old passions have subsided and there is friendship between the two peoples, each version is resented by the other party. In our own day Lenin was a monster and a brigand to many English statesmen of high repute; yet millions have considered him as a savior and the greatest man of the age. These comparisons will give us some faint idea of the resentment felt by Indians at being forced to study in their schools and colleges so-called histories which disparage India's past in every way, vilify those whose memory they cherish and honor, and glorify the achievements of British rule in India.

Gopal Krishna Gokhale once wrote in his gently ironical way of the inscrutable wisdom of Providence which had ordained the British connection for India. Whether it was due to this inscrutable wisdom or some process of historic destiny or just chance, the coming of the British to India brought two very different races together. Or at any rate, it should have brought them together, but as it happened they seldom approached each other and their contacts were indirect. English literature and English political thought influenced a tiny fringe of those who had learned English.

But this political thought, though dynamic in its context, had no reality in India then. The British who came to India were not political or social revolutionaries; they were conservatives representing the most reactionary social class in England, and England was in some ways one of the most conservative countries of Europe.

The impact of Western culture on India was the impact of a dynamic society, of a "modern" consciousness, on a static society wedded to medieval habits of thought, which, however sophisticated and advanced in its own way, could not progress because of its inherent limitations. And yet, curiously enough, the agents of this historic process were not only wholly unconscious of their mission in India but, as a class, actually represented no such process. In England their class fought this historic process, but the forces opposed to them were too strong for them and could not be held back. In India they had a free field and were successful in applying the brakes to that very change and progress which, in the larger context, they represented. They encouraged and consolidated the position of the socially reactionary groups in India, and opposed all those who worked for political and social change. If change came, it was in spite of them or as an incidental and unexpected consequence of their other activities. The introduction of the steam engine and the railway was a big step toward a change of the medieval structure, but it was intended to consolidate their rule and facilitate the exploitation, for their own benefit, of the interior of the country. This contradiction between the deliberate policy of the British authorities in India and some of its unintended consequences produces a certain confusion and masks that policy itself. Change came to India because of this impact of the West, but it came almost in spite of the British in India. They succeeded in slowing down the pace of that change to such an extent that even today the transition is very far from complete.

The feudal landlords and their kind who came from England to rule over India had the landlord's view of the world. To them India was a vast estate belonging to the East India Company, and the landlord was the best and the natural representative of his estate and his tenants. That view continued even after the East India Company handed over its estate of India to the British crown, being paid very handsome compensation at India's cost. (Thus began the public debt of India. It was India's purchase money, paid by India.) The British government of India then became the landlords (or landlords' agents). For all practical purposes they considered themselves "India," just as the Duke of Devonshire might be considered "Devonshire" by his peers. The millions of people who lived and functioned in India were just some kind of landlord's tenants who had to pay their rents and cesses and to keep their place in the natural feudal order. For them a challenge to that order was an offense against the very moral basis of the universe and a denial of a divine dispensation.

This somewhat metaphysical conception of British rule in India has not changed fundamentally, though it is expressed differently now. The old method of obvious rack-renting gave place to more subtle and devious devices. It was admitted that the landlord should be benevolent toward his tenantry and should seek to advance their interests. It was even agreed that some of the more loyal and faithful among the tenants should be promoted to the estate office and share in a subordinate way in the administration. But no challenge to the system of landlordism could be tolerated. The estate must continue to function as it used to, even when it changed hands. When pressure of events made some change inevitable, it was stipulated that all the faithful employees in the estate office should continue, all the old and new friends, followers, and dependents of the landlord should be provided for, the old pensioners should continue to draw their pensions, the old landlord himself should now function as a benevolent patron and adviser of the estate, and thus all attempts to bring about essential changes should be frustrated.

This sense of identifying India with their own interests was strongest in the higher administrative services, which were entirely British. In later years these developed in that close and well-knit corporation called the Indian Civil Service, "the world's most tenacious trade union," as it has been called by an English writer. They ran India, they were India, and anything that was harmful to their interests must of necessity be injurious to India. From the Indian Civil Service and the kind of history and record of current events that was placed before them, this conception spread in varying degrees to the different strata of the British people. The ruling class naturally shared it in full measure, but even the worker and the farmer were influenced by it to some slight extent and felt, in spite of their own subordinate position in their own country, the pride of possession and empire. That same worker or farmer if he came to India inevitably belonged to the ruling class here. He was totally ignorant of India's history and culture and he accepted the prevailing ideology of the British in India for he had no other standards to judge by or apply. At the most a vague benevolence filled him, but that was strictly conditioned within that framework. For a hundred years this ideology permeated all sections of the British people and became, as it were, a national heritage, a fixed and almost unalterable notion which governed their outlook on India and imperceptibly affected even their domestic outlook. In our own day that curious group which has no fixed standards or principles or much knowledge of the outside world, the leaders of the British Labour party, have usually been the staunchest supporters of the existing order in India. Sometimes a vague sense of uneasiness fills them at a seeming contradiction between their domestic and colonial policies, between their professions and practice; but regarding themselves above all as practical men of common sense, they sternly repress all these stirrings of conscience. Practical men must necessarily base themselves on established and known practice, on existing conditions, and not take a leap into the dark unknown merely because of some principle or untested theory.

Viceroys who come to India direct from England have to fit in with and rely upon the Indian Civil Service structure. Belonging to the possessing and ruling class in England, they have no difficulty whatever in accepting the prevailing I.C.S. outlook, and their unique position of absolute authority, unparalleled elsewhere, leads to subtle changes in their ways and methods of expression. Authority corrupts and absolute authority corrupts absolutely, and no man in the wide world today has had or has such absolute authority over such large numbers of people as the British viceroy of India. The viceroy speaks in a manner such as no prime minister of England or president of the United States can adopt. The only possible parallel would be that of Hitler. And not the viceroy only but the British members of his council, the governors, and even the smaller fry who function as secretaries of departments or magistrates. They speak from a noble and unattainable height, secure not only in the conviction that what they say and do is right but that it will have to be accepted as right, whatever lesser mortals may imagine, for theirs is the power and glory.

Some members of the Viceroy's Council are appointed direct from England and do not belong to the Indian Civil Service. There is usually a marked difference in their ways and utterances from those of the civil service. They function easily enough in that framework, but they cannot quite develop that superior and self-satisfied air of assured authority. Much less can the Indian members of the council (a fairly recent addition), who are obvious supers, whatever their numbers or intelligence. Indians belonging to the civil service, whatever their rank in the official hierarchy, do not belong to the charmed circle. A few of them try to ape the manners of their colleagues without much success; they become rather pompous and ridiculous.

The new generation of British members of the Indian Civil Service are, I believe, somewhat different in mind and texture from their predecessors. They do not easily fit into the old framework; but all authority and policy flow from the senior members, and the newcomers make no difference. They have either to accept the established church or, as has sometimes happened, resign and return to their homeland.

I remember that when I was a boy the British-owned newspapers in India were full of official news and utterances; of service news, transfers, and promotions; of the doings of English society, of polo, races, dances, and amateur theatricals. There was hardly a word about the people of India, about their political, cultural, social, or economic life. Reading them, one would hardly suspect that they existed.

In Bombay there used to be quadrangular cricket matches between four elevens made up respectively of Hindus, Moslems, Parsis, and Europeans. The European eleven was called "Bombay Presidency"; the others were just Hindus, Moslems, Parsis. Bombay was thus essentially represented by the Europeans; the others, one would imagine, were foreign elements who were recognized for this purpose. These quadrangular matches still take place, though there is much argument about them and a demand that elevens should not be chosen on religious lines. I believe that the "Bombay Presidency" team is now called "European."

English clubs in India usually have territorial names—the Bengal Club, the Allahabad Club, etc. They are confined to Britishers, or rather to Europeans. There need be no objection to territorial designation or even to a group of persons having a club for themselves and not approving of outsiders joining it. But this designation is derived from the old British habit of considering that they are the real India that counts, the real Bengal, the real Allahabad. Others are just excrescences, useful in their own way, if they know their place, but otherwise a nuisance. The exclusion of non-Europeans is far more a racial affair than a thoroughly justifiable way for people having cultural affinities meeting together in their leisure moments for play and social intercourse, and disliking the intrusion of other elements. For my part I have no objection to exclusive English or European clubs, and very few Indians would care to join them. But when this social exclusiveness is clearly based on racialism and on a ruling class always exhibiting its superiority and unapproachability, it bears another aspect. In Bombay there is a well-known club which did not allow, and so far as I know, does not allow, an Indian (except as a servant) even in its visitors' room, even though he might be a ruling prince or a captain of industry.

Racialism in India is not so much English versus Indian.

It is European as opposed to Asiatic. In India every European, be he German or Pole or Rumanian, is automatically a member of the ruling race. Railway carriages, station retiring rooms, benches in parks, are marked "For Europeans Only." This is bad enough in South Africa or elsewhere, but to have to put up with it in one's own country is a humiliating and exasperating reminder of our enslaved condition.

It is true that a gradual change has been taking place in these external manifestations of racial superiority and imperial arrogance. But the process is slow, and frequent instances occur to show how superficial it is. Political pressure and the rise of a militant nationalism enforce change and lead to a deliberate attempt to tone down the former racialism and aggressiveness; and yet that very political movement, when it reaches a stage of crisis and is sought to be crushed, leads to a resurgence of all the old imperialist and racial arrogance in its extremest form.

The English are a sensitive people, and yet when they go to foreign countries, there is a strange lack of awareness about them. In India, where the relation of ruler and ruled makes mutual understanding difficult, this lack of awareness is peculiarly evident. Almost, one would think, it is deliberate, so that they may see only what they want to see and be blind to all else. But facts do not vanish because they are ignored, and when they compel attention, there is a feeling of displeasure and resentment at the unexpected happening, as of some trick having been played.

In this land of caste the British, and more especially the Indian Civil Service, have built up a caste which is rigid and exclusive. Even the Indian members of the service do not really belong to that caste, though they wear its insignia and conform to its rules. That caste has developed something in the nature of a religious faith in its own paramount importance, and round that faith has grown an appropriate mythology which helps to maintain it. A combination of faith and vested interests is a powerful one, and any challenge to it arouses the deepest passions and fierce indignation.

## II. THE PLUNDER OF BENGAL HELPS THE
## INDUSTRIAL REVOLUTION IN ENGLAND

The East India Company had received permission from the Moghul emperor to start a factory at Surat early in the seventeenth century. Some years later they purchased a patch of land in the south and founded Madras. In 1662 the island of Bombay was presented to Charles II of England by way of dowry from Portugal, and he transferred it to the company. In 1690 the city of Calcutta was founded. Thus by the end of the seventeenth century the British had gained a number of footholds in India and established some bridgeheads on the Indian coast line. They spread inland slowly. The battle of Plassey in 1757 for the first time brought a vast area under their control, and within a few years Bengal, Bihar, Orissa, and the east coast were subject to them. The next big step forward was taken about forty years later, at the beginning of the nineteenth century. This brought them to the gates of Delhi. The third major advance took place after the last defeat of the Marathas in 1818; the fourth, in 1849, after the Sikh wars, completed the picture.

Thus the British have been in the city of Madras a little over 300 years; they have ruled Bengal, Bihar, etc. for almost 200 years; they extended their domination over the south roughly 150 years ago; they established themselves in the United Provinces (as they are now called), central and western India about 125 years ago; and they spread to the Punjab not quite 100 years ago. Leaving out the city of Madras as too small an area, there is a difference of nearly a hundred years between their occupation of Bengal and of the Punjab. During this period British policy and administrative methods changed repeatedly. These changes were dictated by new developments in England as well as the consolidation of British rule in India. The treatment of each newly acquired area varied according to these changes, and depended also on the character of the ruling group which had been defeated by the British. Thus in Bengal, where the victory had been very easy, the Moslem landed gentry were looked upon as the ruling classes and a policy was pursued to break their power. In the Punjab, on the other hand, power was seized from the Sikhs and there was no initial antagonism between the British and the Moslems. In the greater part of India the Marathas had been the opponents of the British.

A significant fact which stands out is that those parts of India which have been longest under British rule are the poorest today. Indeed some kind of chart might be drawn up to indicate the close connection between length of British rule and progressive growth of poverty. A few large cities and some new industrial areas do not make any essential difference to this survey. What is noteworthy is the condition of the masses as a whole, and there can be no doubt that the poorest parts of India are Bengal, Bihar, Orissa and parts of the Madras presidency; the mass level and standards of living are highest in the Punjab. Bengal certainly was a very rich and prosperous province before the British came. There may be many reasons for these contrasts and differences. But it is difficult to get over the fact that Bengal, once so rich and flourishing, after 187 years of British rule, accompanied, as we are told, by strenuous attempts on the part of the British to improve its condition and to teach its people the art of self-government, is today a miserable mass of poverty-stricken, starving and dying people.

Bengal had the first full experience of British rule in India. That rule began with outright plunder, and a land revenue system which extracted the uttermost farthing not only from the living but also the dead cultivators. The English historians of India, Edward Thompson and G. T. Garrett, tell us that "a gold-lust unequalled since the hysteria that took hold of the Spaniards of Cortes' and Pizarro's age filled the English mind. Bengal in particular was not to know peace again until she had been bled white. . . . For the monstrous financial immorality of the English conduct in India for many a year after this, Clive was largely responsible"[1]—Clive, the great empire builder, whose statue faces the India Office in London today. It was pure loot. The "Pagoda tree" was shaken again and again till the most terrible famines ravaged Bengal. This process was called trade later on, but that made little difference. Government was this so-called trade, and trade was plunder. There are few instances in history of anything like it. And it must be remembered that this lasted, under various names and under different forms, not for a few years but for generations. The outright plunder gradually took the shape of legalized exploitation which, though not so obvious, was in reality worse. The corruption, venality, nepotism, violence, and greed of money of these early generations of British rule in India is something which passes comprehension. It is significant that one of the Hindustani words which has become part of the English language is "loot." Says Edward Thompson, and this does not refer to Bengal only, "one remembers the early history of British India which is perhaps the world's high watermark of graft."

The result of all this, even in its early stages, was the famine of 1770 which swept away over a third of the population of Bengal and Bihar. But it was all in the cause of progress, and Bengal can take pride in the fact that she helped greatly in giving birth to the Industrial Revolution in England. The American writer Brooke Adams tells us exactly how this happened: "The influx of Indian treasure, by adding considerably to the nation's cash capital, not only increased its stock of energy, but added much to its flexibility and the rapidity of its movement. Very soon after Plassey, the Bengal plunder began to arrive in London, and the effect appears to have been instantaneous, for all authorities agree that the 'industrial revolution' began with the year 1770. . . . Plassey was fought in 1757, and probably nothing has ever equalled the rapidity of the change that followed. In 1760 the flying shuttle appeared, and coal began to replace wood in smelting. In 1764 Hargreaves invented the spinning jenny, in 1776 Crompton

[1] *Rise and Fulfilment of British Rule in India*, by Edward Thompson and G. T. Garrett (London, 1935).

contrived the mule, in 1785 Cartwright patented the power loom, and in 1768 Watt matured the steam engine. . . . But, though these machines served as outlets for the accelerating movements of the time, they did not cause the acceleration. In themselves inventions are passive, . . . waiting for a sufficient store of force to have accumulated to set them working. That store must always take the shape of money, and money not hoarded but in motion. Before the influx of the Indian treasure, and the expansion of credit which followed, no force sufficient for this purpose existed. . . . Possibly since the world began, no investment has ever yielded the profit reaped from the Indian plunder, because for nearly fifty years Great Britain stood without a competitor."[2]

## III. THE DESTRUCTION OF INDIA'S INDUSTRY AND THE DECAY OF HER AGRICULTURE

The chief business of the East India Company in its early period, the very object for which it was started, was to carry Indian manufactured goods—textiles, etc., as well as spices and the like—from the East to Europe, where there was a great demand for these articles. With the developments in industrial techniques in England a new class of industrial capitalists rose there demanding a change in this policy. The British market was to be closed to Indian products and the Indian market opened to British manufactures. The British parliament, influenced by this new class, began to take a greater interest in India and the working of the East India Company. To begin with, Indian goods were excluded from Britain by legislation, and as the company held a monopoly in the Indian export business, this exclusion influenced other foreign markets also. This was followed by vigorous attempts to restrict and crush Indian manufactures by various measures and internal duties

[2] Brooke Adams, *The Law of Civilization and Decay* (1928), pp. 259–60, quoted by Kate Mitchell, *India* (1943).

which prevented the flow of Indian goods within the country itself. British goods meanwhile had free entry. The Indian textile industry collapsed, affecting vast numbers of weavers and artisans. The process was rapid in Bengal and Bihar; elsewhere it spread gradually with the expansion of British rule and the building of railways. It continued throughout the nineteenth century, breaking up other old industries also, shipbuilding, metalwork, glass, paper, and many crafts.

To some extent this was inevitable as the older manufacturing came into conflict with the new industrial technique. But it was hastened by political and economic pressure, and no attempt was made to apply the new techniques to India. Indeed every attempt was made to prevent this happening, and thus the economic development of India was arrested and the growth of the new industry prevented. Machinery could not be imported into India. A vacuum was created in India which could only be filled by British goods, and which also led to rapidly increasing unemployment and poverty. The classic type of modern colonial economy was built up, India becoming an agricultural colony of industrial England, supplying raw materials and providing markets for England's industrial goods.

The liquidation of the artisan class led to unemployment on a prodigious scale. What were all these scores of millions, who had so far been engaged in industry and manufacture, to do now? Where were they to go? Their old profession was no longer open to them; the way to a new one was barred. They could die of course; that way of escape from an intolerable situation is always open. They did die in tens of millions. The English governor-general of India, Lord Bentinck, reported in 1834 that "the misery hardly finds a parallel in the history of commerce. The bones of the cotton-weavers are bleaching the plains of India."

But still vast numbers of them remained, and these increased from year to year as British policy affected remoter areas of the country and created more unemployment. All these hordes of artisans and craftsmen had no jobs, no work, and all their ancient skill was useless. They drifted to the land, for the land was still there. But the land was fully occupied and could not possibly absorb them profitably. So they became a burden on the land and the burden grew, and with it grew the poverty of the country, and the standard of living fell to incredibly low levels. This compulsory back-to-the-land movement of artisans and craftsmen led to an ever-growing disproportion between agriculture and industry; agriculture became more and more the sole business of the people because of the lack of occupations and wealth-producing activities.

India became progressively ruralized. In every progressive country there has been, during the past century, a shift of population from agriculture to industry; from village to town; in India this process was reversed, as a result of British policy. The figures are instructive and significant. In the middle of the nineteenth century about 55 per cent of the population is said to have been dependent on agriculture; recently this proportion was estimated to be 74 per cent. This is a prewar figure. Though there has been greater industrial employment during the war, those dependent on agriculture actually went up in the census of 1941, owing to increase of population. The growth of a few large cities (chiefly at the expense of the smaller towns) is apt to mislead the superficial observer and give him a false idea of Indian conditions.

This, then, is the real, the fundamental cause of the appalling poverty of the Indian people, and it is of comparatively recent origin. Other causes that contribute to it are themselves the result of this poverty and chronic starvation and undernourishment—like diseases and illiteracy. Excessive population is unfortunate and steps should be taken to curb it wherever necessary; but the density in India still compares favorably with that of many industrialized countries. It is only excessive for a predominantly agricultural community, and under a proper economic system the entire population can be made productive and should add to the wealth of the country. As a matter of fact, great density of population exists only in special areas, like Bengal and the Gangetic valley, and vast areas are still sparsely populated. It is worth remembering that Great Britain is more than twice as densely populated as India.

The crisis in industry spread rapidly to the land and became a permanent crisis in agriculture. Holdings became smaller and smaller, and fragmentation proceeded to an absurd and fantastic degree. The burden of agricultural debt grew, and ownership of the land often passed to moneylenders. The number of landless laborers increased by the million. India was under an industrial-capitalist regime, but her economy was largely that of the precapitalist period, minus many of the wealth-producing elements of that precapitalist economy. She became a passive agent of modern industrial capitalism, suffering all its ills and with hardly any of its advantages.

The transition from a preindustrialist economy to an economy of capitalist industrialism involves great hardship and heavy cost in human suffering borne by masses of people. This was especially so in the early days when no efforts were made to plan such a transition or to lessen its evil results and everything was left to individual initiative. There was this hardship in England during this period of transition, but taken as a whole, it was not great, as the change-over was rapid and the unemployment caused was soon absorbed by the new industries. But that did not mean that the cost in human suffering was not paid. It was indeed paid, and paid in full by others, particularly by the people of India, both by famine and death and vast unemployment. It may be said that a great part of the costs of transition to industrialism in western Europe were paid for by India, China, and the other colonial countries whose economy was dominated by the European powers.

It is obvious that there has been all along abundant material in India for industrial development—managerial and technical ability, skilled workers, even some capital in spite of the continuous drain from India. The historian Montgomery Martin, giving evidence before a committee of the British parliament in 1840, said: "India is as much a manufacturing country as an agriculturist; and he who would seek to reduce her to the position of an agricultural country, seeks to lower her in the scale of civilization."

That is exactly what the British in India sought to do, continuously and persistently, and the measure of their success is the present condition of India, after they have held despotic sway here for a century and a half. Ever since the demand for the development of modern industry arose in India (and this, I imagine, is at least a hundred years old), we have been told that India is pre-eminently an agricultural country and it is in her interest to stick to agriculture. Industrial development may upset the balance and prove harmful to her main business—agriculture. The solicitude which British industrialists and economists have shown for the Indian peasant has been truly gratifying. In view of this, as well as of the tender care lavished upon him by the British government in India, one can only conclude that some all-powerful and malign fate, some supernatural agency, has countered their intentions and measures and made that peasant one of the poorest and most miserable beings on earth.

It is difficult now for anyone to oppose industrial development in India; but even now, when any extensive and far-reaching plan is drawn up, we are warned by our British friends, who continue to shower their advice upon us, that agriculture must not be neglected and must have first place. As if any Indian with an iota of intelligence can ignore or neglect agriculture or forget the peasant! The Indian peasant is India more than anyone else, and it is on his progress and betterment that India's progress will depend. But our crisis in agriculture, grave as it is, is interlinked with the crisis in industry, out of which it arose. The two cannot be disconnected and dealt with separately, and it is essential for the disproportion between the two to be remedied.

India's ability to develop modern industry can be seen by her success in it whenever she has had the chance to build it up. Indeed such success has been achieved in spite of the strenuous opposition of the British government in India and of vested interests in Britain. Her first real chance came during the war of 1914–18 when the inflow of British goods was interrupted. She profited by it, though only to a relatively small extent because of British policy. Ever since then there has been continuous pressure on the government to facilitate the growth of Indian industry by removing the various barriers and special interests that come in the way. While apparently accepting this as its policy, the government has obstructed all real growth, especially of basic industries. Even in the Constitution Act of 1935 it was specifically laid down that Indian legislatures could not interfere with the vested interests of British industry in India. The prewar years witnessed repeated and vigorous attempts to build up basic and heavy industries, all scotched by official policy. But the most amazing instances of official obstruction have been during the present war, when war needs for production were paramount. Even that vital need was not sufficient to overcome British dislike of Indian industry. That industry has grown because of the force of events, but that growth is trivial compared to what it could have been or to the growth in many other countries.

The direct opposition of the earlier periods to the growth of Indian industry gave place to indirect methods which have been equally effective, just as direct tribute gave place to manipulation of customs and excise duties and financial and currency policies which benefited Britain at the expense of India.

Long subjection of a people and the denial of freedom bring many evils, and perhaps the greatest of these lies in the spiritual sphere—demoralization and sapping of the spirit of the people. It is hard to measure this, though it may be obvious. It is easier to trace and measure the economic decay of a nation, and as we look back on British economic policy in India, it seems that the present poverty of the Indian people is the ineluctable consequence of it. There is no mystery about this poverty; we can see the causes and follow the processes which have led to this present condition.

## IV. INDIA BECOMES FOR THE FIRST TIME A
## POLITICAL AND ECONOMIC APPENDAGE OF
## ANOTHER COUNTRY

The establishment of British rule in India was an entirely novel phenomenon for her, not comparable with any other invasion or political or economic change. "India had been conquered before, but by invaders who settled within her frontiers and made themselves part of her life." (Like the Normans in England or the Manchus in China.) "She had never lost her independence, never been enslaved. That is to say, she had never been drawn into a political and economic system whose centre of gravity lay outside her soil, never been subjected to a ruling class which was and which remained permanently alien in origin and character."[3] Every previous ruling class, whether it had originally come from outside or was indigenous, had accepted the structural unity of India's social and economic life and tried to fit into it. It had become indianized and had struck roots in the soil of the country. The new rulers were entirely different, with their base elsewhere, and between them and the average Indian there was a vast and unbridgeable gulf —a difference in tradition, in outlook, in income and ways of living. The early Britishers in India, rather cut off from England, adopted many Indian ways of living. But this was a superficial approach, and even this was deliberately abandoned with the improvement in communications between India and England. It was felt that the British ruling class must maintain its prestige in India by keeping aloof, exclusive, apart from Indians, living in a superior world of its own. There were two worlds: the world of British officials and the world of India's millions, and there was nothing in common between them except a common dislike for each other. Previously races had merged into one another

[3] K. S. Shelvankar, *The Problem of India* (Penguin Special, London, 1940).

or at least fitted into an organically interdependent structure. Now racialism became the acknowledged creed, and this was intensified by the fact that the dominant race had both political and economic power, without check or hindrance.

The world market that the new capitalism was building up would have, in any event, affected India's economic system. The self-sufficient village community, with its traditional division of labor, could not have continued in its old form. But the change that took place was not a normal development, and it disintegrated the whole economic and structural basis of Indian society. A system which had social sanctions and controls behind it and was a part of the people's cultural heritage was suddenly and forcibly changed, and another system, administered from outside the group, was imposed. India did not come into a world market but became a colonial and agricultural appendage of the British structure.

The village community, which had so far been the basis of Indian economy, was disintegrated, losing both its economic and administrative functions. In 1830 Sir Charles Metcalfe, one of the ablest of British officials in India, described these communities in words which have often been quoted: "The village communities are little republics having nearly everything they want within themselves; and almost independent of foreign relations. They seem to last where nothing else lasts. This union of the village communities, each one forming a separate little State in itself . . . is in a high degree conducive to their happiness, and to the enjoyment of a great portion of freedom and independence."

The destruction of village industries was a powerful blow to these communities. The balance between industry and agriculture was upset, the traditional division of labor was broken up, and numerous stray individuals could not be easily fitted into any group activity. A more direct blow came from the introduction of the landlord system, changing the whole conception of ownership of land. This conception had been one of communal ownership, not so much of the land as of the produce of the land. Possibly not fully appreciating this, but more probably taking the step de-liberately for reasons of their own, the British governors, themselves representing the English landlord class, intro-duced something resembling the English system in India. At first they appointed revenue-farmers for short terms, that is persons who were made responsible for the collec-tion of the revenue or land tax and payment of it to the Government. Later these revenue-farmers developed into landlords. The village community was deprived of all con-trol over the land and its produce; what had always been considered as the chief interest and concern of that com-munity now became the private property of the newly created landowner. This led to the breakdown of the joint life and corporate character of the community, and the co-operative system of services and functions began to disap-pear gradually.

The introduction of this type of property in land was not only a great economic change, but it went deeper and struck at the whole Indian conception of a co-operative group social structure. A new class, the owners of land, ap-peared; a class created by, and therefore to a large extent identified with, the British government. The breakup of the old system created new problems, and probably the be-ginnings of the new Hindu-Moslem problem can be traced to it. The landlord system was first introduced in Bengal and Bihar, where big landowners were created under the system known as the Permanent Settlement. It was later realized that this was not advantageous to the state, as the land revenue had been fixed and could not be enhanced. Fresh settlements in other parts of India were therefore made for a period only, and enhancements in revenue took place from time to time. In some provinces a kind of peas-ant proprietorship was established. The extreme rigor ap-plied to the collection of revenue resulted, especially in Bengal, in the ruin of the old landed gentry, and new peo-ple from the monied and business classes took their place. Thus Bengal became a province predominantly of Hindu landlords, while their tenants, though both Hindu and Moslem, were chiefly the latter.

Big landowners were created by the British after their

own English pattern, chiefly because it was far easier to deal with a few individuals than with a vast peasantry. The objective was to collect as much money in the shape of revenue and as speedily as possible. If an owner failed at the stipulated time, he was immediately pushed out and another took his place. It was also considered necessary to create a class whose interests were identified with the British. The fear of revolt filled the minds of British officials in India, and they referred to this repeatedly in their papers. Governor-General Lord William Bentinck said in 1829: "If security was wanting against extensive popular tumult or revolution, I should say that the Permanent Settlement, though a failure in many other respects, has this great advantage at least, of having created a vast body of rich landed proprietors deeply interested in the continuance of British Dominion and having complete command over the mass of the people."

British rule thus consolidated itself by creating new classes and vested interests who were tied up with that rule and whose privileges depended on its continuance. There were the landowners and the princes, and there were a large number of subordinate members of the services in various departments of government, from the patwari, the village headman, upward. The two essential branches of government were the revenue system and the police. At the head of both of these in each district was the collector or district magistrate who was the linchpin of the administration. He functioned as an autocrat in his district, combining in himself executive, judicial, revenue, and police functions. If there were any small Indian states adjoining the area under his control, he was also the British agent for them.

Then there was the Indian army, consisting of British and Indian troops but officered entirely by Englishmen. This was reorganized repeatedly, especially after the Mutiny of 1857, and ultimately became organizationally linked up with the British army. This was so arranged as to balance its different elements and keep the British troops in key positions. "Next to the grand counterpoise of a sufficient European force, comes the counterpoise of natives against natives," says the official report on reorganization in 1858. The primary function of these forces was to serve as an army of occupation—"Internal Security Troops" they were called, and a majority of these were British. The Frontier Province served as a training ground for the British army at India's expense. The field army (chiefly Indian) was meant for service abroad and it took part in numerous British imperial wars and expeditions, India always bearing the cost. Steps were taken to segregate Indian troops from the rest of the population.

Thus India had to bear the cost of her own conquest, and then of her transfer (or sale) from the East India Company to the British crown, and for the extension of the British Empire to Burma and elsewhere, and expeditions to Africa, Persia, etc., and for her defense against Indians themselves. She was not only used as a base for imperial purposes, without any reimbursement for this, but she had further to pay for the training of part of the British army in England—"capitation" charges these were called. Indeed India was charged for all manner of other expenses incurred by Britain, such as the maintenance of British diplomatic and consular establishments in China and Persia, the entire cost of the telegraph line from England to India, part of the expenses of the British Mediterranean fleet, and even the receptions given to the sultan of Turkey in London.

The building of railways in India, undoubtedly desirable and necessary, was done in an enormously wasteful way. The government of India guaranteed 5 per cent interest on all capital invested, and there was no need to check or estimate what was necessary. All purchases were made in England.

The civil establishment of government was also run on a lavish and extravagant scale, all the highly paid positions being reserved for Europeans. The process of indianization of the administrative machine was very slow and only became noticeable in the twentieth century. This process, far from transferring any power to Indian hands, proved yet another method of strengthening British rule. The really key positions remained in British hands, and Indians in the administration could only function as the agents of British rule.

To all these methods must be added the deliberate policy, pursued throughout the period of British rule, of creating divisions among Indians, of encouraging one group at the cost of the other. This policy was openly admitted in the early days of their rule, and indeed it was a natural one for an imperial power. With the growth of the nationalist movement, that policy took subtler and more dangerous forms, and though denied, functioned more intensively than ever.

Nearly all our major problems today have grown up during British rule and as a direct result of British policy: the princes; the minority problem; various vested interests, foreign and Indian; the lack of industry and the neglect of agriculture; the extreme backwardness in the social services; and, above all, the tragic poverty of the people. The attitude to education has been significant. In Kaye's *Life of Metcalfe* it is stated that "this dread of the free diffusion of knowledge became a chronic disease . . . continually afflicting the members of Government with all sorts of hypochondriacal day-dreams and nightmares, in which visions of the Printing Press and the Bible were making their flesh creep, and their hair to stand erect with horror. It was our policy in those days to keep the natives of India in the profoundest state of barbarism and darkness, and every attempt to diffuse the light of knowledge among the people, either of our own or of the independent states, was vehemently opposed and resented."[4]

Imperialism must function in this way or else it ceases to be imperialism. The modern type of finance imperialism added new kinds of economic exploitation which were unknown in earlier ages. The record of British rule in India during the nineteenth century must necessarily depress and anger an Indian, and yet it illustrates the superiority of the British in many fields, not least in their capacity to profit by our disunity and weaknesses. A people who are weak and who are left behind in the march of time invite trou-

[4] Quoted by Thompson.

ble and ultimately have only themselves to blame. If British imperialism with all its consequences was, in the circumstances, to be expected in the natural order of events, so also was the growth of opposition to it inevitable, and the final crisis between the two.


## V. CONTRADICTIONS OF BRITISH RULE IN INDIA
### RAM MOHAN ROY—THE PRESS
### SIR WILLIAM JONES
### ENGLISH EDUCATION IN BENGAL

One remarkable contradiction meets us at every turn in considering the record of British rule in India. The British became dominant in India, and the foremost power in the world, because they were the heralds of the new big-machine industrial civilization. They represented a new historic force which was going to change the world, and were thus, unknown to themselves, the forerunners and representatives of change and revolution. And yet they deliberately tried to prevent change, except in so far as this was necessary to consolidate their position and help them in exploiting the country and its people to their own advantage. Their outlook and objectives were reactionary, partly because of the background of the social class that came here, but chiefly because of a deliberate desire to check changes in a progressive direction as these might strengthen the Indian people and thus ultimately weaken the British hold on India. The fear of the people runs through all their thought and policy, for they did not want to and could not merge with them, and were destined to remain an isolated foreign ruling group surrounded by an entirely different and hostile humanity. Changes, and some changes in a progressive direction, did come, but they came in spite of British policy, although the impetus for that change was the impact of the new West through the British.

Individual Englishmen, educationalists, Orientalists, journalists, missionaries, and others, played an important part in bringing Western culture to India, and in their attempts to do so often came into conflict with their own government. That government feared the effects of the spread of modern education and put many obstacles in its way, and yet it was due to the pioneering efforts of able and earnest Englishmen, who gathered enthusiastic groups of Indian students around them, that English thought and literature and political tradition were introduced to India. (When I say Englishmen, I include of course people from the whole of Great Britain and Ireland, though I know this is improper and incorrect. But I dislike the word Britisher and even that probably does not include the Irish. My apologies to the Irish, the Scotch, and the Welsh. In India they have all functioned alike and have been looked upon as one indistinguishable group.) Even the British government, in spite of its dislike of education, was compelled by circumstances to arrange for the training and production of clerks for its growing establishment. It could not afford to bring out from England large numbers of people to serve in this subordinate capacity. So education grew slowly, and though it was a limited and perverted education, it opened the doors and windows of the mind to new ideas and dynamic thoughts.

The printing press and indeed all machinery were also considered dangerous and explosive for the Indian mind, not to be encouraged in any way lest they lead to the spread of sedition and industrial growth. There is a story that the Nizam of Hyderabad once expressed a desire to see European machinery, and thereupon the British resident procured for him an air pump and a printing press. The Nizam's momentary curiosity having been satisfied, these were stored away with other gifts and curiosities. But when the government in Calcutta heard of this, they expressed their displeasure to their resident and rebuked him especially for introducing a printing press in an Indian state. The resident offered to get it broken up secretly, if the government so desired.

But while private printing presses were not encouraged, government could not carry on its work without printing, and official presses were therefore started in Calcutta and

Madras and elsewhere. The first private printing press was started by the Baptist missionaries in Serampore, and the first newspaper was started by an Englishman in Calcutta in 1780.

All these and other like changes crept in, gradually influencing the Indian mind and giving rise to the "modern" consciousness. Only a small group was directly influenced by the thought of Europe, for India clung to her own philosophic background, considering it superior to that of the West. The real impact and influence of the West were on the practical side of life, which was obviously superior to the Eastern. The new techniques—the railway train, the printing press, other machinery, more efficient ways of warfare—could not be ignored, and these came up against old methods of thought almost unawares, by indirect approaches, creating a conflict in the mind of India. The most obvious and far-reaching change was the breakup of the agrarian system and the introduction of conceptions of private property and landlordism. Money economy had crept in, and "land became a marketable commodity. What had once been held rigid by custom was dissolved by money."

Bengal witnessed and experienced all these agrarian, technical, educational, and intellectual changes long before any other considerable part of India, for Bengal had a clear half-century of British rule before it spread over wider areas. During the second half of the eighteenth century and the first half of the nineteenth, Bengal therefore played a dominant role in British Indian life. Not only was Bengal the center and heart of the British administration, but it also produced the first groups of English-educated Indians, who spread out to other parts of India under the shadow of the British power. A number of very remarkable men rose in Bengal in the nineteenth century, who gave the lead to the rest of India in cultural and political matters, and out of whose efforts the new nationalist movement ultimately took shape. Bengal not only had a much longer acquaintance with British rule, but it experienced it in its earliest phases when it was both harsher and more exuberant, more fluid and less set in rigid frames.

It had accepted that rule, adapted itself to it, long before northern and central India submitted. The great Revolt of 1857 had little effect on Bengal, although the first spark appeared accidentally at Dum Dum near Calcutta.

Previous to British rule Bengal had been an outlying province of the Moghul empire, important but still rather cut off from the center. During the early medieval period many debased forms of worship and of tantric philosophy and practices had flourished among the Hindus there. Then came many Hindu reform movements affecting social customs and laws and even changing somewhat the well-recognized rules of inheritance elsewhere. Chaitanya, a great scholar who became a man of faith and emotion, established a form of Vaishnavism, based on faith, and influenced greatly the people of Bengal. The Bengalis developed a curious mixture of high intellectual attainments and equally strong emotionalism. This tradition of loving faith and service of humanity was represented in Bengal in the second half of the nineteenth century by another remarkable man of saintly character, Ramakrishna Paramahamsa. In his name an order of service was established which has an unequaled record in humanitarian relief and social work. Full of the ideal of patient loving service of the Franciscans of old, and quiet, unostentatious, efficient, rather like the Quakers, the members of the Ramakrishna Mission carry on their hospitals and educational establishments and engage in relief work, whenever any calamity occurs, all over India and even outside India.

Ramakrishna represented the old Indian tradition. Before him, in the eighteenth century, another towering personality had risen in Bengal, Raja Ram Mohan Roy, who was a new type combining in himself the old learning and the new. Deeply versed in Indian thought and philosophy, a scholar in Sanskrit, Persian, and Arabic, he was a product of the mixed Hindu-Moslem culture that was then dominant among the cultured classes of India. The coming of the British to India and their superiority in many ways led his curious and adventurous mind to find out what their cultural roots were. He learned English, but this was not enough; he learned Greek, Latin, and Hebrew also to discover the sources of the religion and culture of the West. He was also attracted by science and the technical aspects of Western civilization, though at that time these technical changes were not so obvious as they subsequently became. Being of a philosophical and scholarly bent, Ram Mohan Roy inevitably went to the older literatures. Describing him, Monier-Williams, the Orientalist, has said that he was "perhaps the first earnest-minded investigator of the science of Comparative Religion that the world has produced." And yet, at the same time, he was anxious to modernize education and take it out of the grip of the old scholasticism. Even in those early days he was in favor of the scientific method, and he wrote to the governor-general emphasizing the need for education in "mathematics, natural philosophy, chemistry, anatomy and other useful sciences."

He was more than a scholar and an investigator; he was a reformer above all. Influenced in his early days by Islam and later, to some extent, by Christianity, he stuck nevertheless to the foundations of his own faith. But he tried to reform that faith and rid it of its abuses and the evil practices that had become associated with it. It was largely because of his agitation for the abolition of sati that the British government prohibited it. This sati, or the immolation of women on the funeral pyre of their husbands, was never widespread. But rare instances continued to occur among the upper classes. Probably the practice was brought to India originally by the Scytho-Tartars, among whom the custom prevailed of vassals and liegemen killing themselves on the death of their lord. In early Sanskrit literature the sati custom is denounced. Akbar tried hard to stop it, and the Marathas also were opposed to it.

Ram Mohan Roy was one of the founders of the Indian press. From 1780 onward a number of newspapers had been published by Englishmen in India. These were usually very critical of the government and led to conflict and the establishment of a strict censorship. Among the earliest champions of the freedom of the press in India were Englishmen, and one of them, James Silk Buckingham, who is still remembered, was deported from the country.

The first Indian-owned and -edited newspaper was issued (in English) in 1818, and in the same year the Baptist missionaries of Serampore brought out a Bengali monthly and a weekly, the first periodicals published in an Indian language. Newspapers and periodicals in English and the Indian languages followed in quick succession in Calcutta, Madras, and Bombay.

Meanwhile the struggle for a free press had already begun, to continue with many ups and downs till today. The year 1818 also saw the birth of the famous Regulation III which provided for the first time for detention without trial. This regulation is still in force today and a number of people are kept in prison under this 126-year-old decree.

Ram Mohan Roy was associated with several newspapers. He brought out a bilingual, Bengali-English magazine, and later, desiring an all-India circulation, he published a weekly in Persian, which was recognized then as the language of the cultured classes all over India. But this came to grief soon after the enactment in 1823 of new measures for the control of the press. Ram Mohan and others protested vigorously against these measures and even addressed a petition to the King-in-Council in England.

Ram Mohan Roy's journalist activities were intimately connected with his reform movements. His synthetic and universalist point of view was resented by orthodox sections, who also opposed many of the reforms he advocated. But he also had staunch supporters, among them the Tagore family which played an outstanding part later in the renaissance in Bengal. Ram Mohan went to England on behalf of the Delhi emperor and died in Bristol in the early thirties of the nineteenth century.

Ram Mohan Roy and the Tagores and others studied English privately. There were no English schools or colleges, and the government's policy was definitely opposed to the teaching of English to Indians. In 1781 the Hindu College and the Calcutta Madrassa were started by government in Calcutta, the former for Sanskrit studies and the latter for Arabic. In 1791 a Sanskrit college was started in Benares. Probably in the second decade of the nineteenth century some missionary schools were teaching English.

During the twenties a school of thought arose in government circles in favor of the teaching of English, but this was opposed. However, as an experimental measure some English classes were attached to the Arabic school in Delhi and to some institutions in Calcutta. The final decision in favor of the teaching of English was embodied in Macaulay's Minute on Education of February 1835. The Presidency College was later started in Calcutta. In 1857 the universities of Calcutta, Madras, and Bombay began their career.

If the British government in India was reluctant to teach English to Indians, Brahman scholars objected even more, but for different reasons, to teaching Sanskrit to Englishmen. When Sir William Jones, already a linguist and a scholar, came to India as a judge of the Supreme Court, he expressed his desire to learn Sanskrit. But no Brahman would agree to teach the sacred language to a foreigner and an intruder, even though handsome rewards were offered. Jones ultimately, with considerable difficulty, got hold of a non-Brahman *vaidya* or medical practitioner who agreed to teach, but on his own peculiar and stringent conditions. Jones agreed to every stipulation, so great was his eagerness to learn the ancient language of India. Sanskrit fascinated him, and especially the discovery of the old Indian drama. It was through his writings and translations that Europe first had a glimpse of some of the treasures of Sanskrit literature. In 1784 Sir William Jones established the Bengal Asiatic Society, which later became the Royal Asiatic Society. To Jones and to the many other European scholars India owes a deep debt of gratitude for the rediscovery of her past literature. Much of it was known, of course, throughout every age, but the knowledge had become more and more confined to select and exclusive groups, and the dominance of Persian, as the language of culture, had diverted people's minds from it. The search for manuscripts brought out many a little-known work, and the application of modern critical methods of scholarship gave a new background to the vast literature that was revealed.

The advent and use of the printing press gave a great stimulus to the development of the popular Indian languages. Some of these languages—Hindi, Bengali, Gujrati, Marathi, Urdu, Tamil, Telugu—had not only long been in use but had also developed literatures. Many of the books in them were widely known among the masses. Almost always these books were epic in form, poems or collections of songs and verses which could easily be memorized. There was practically no prose literature in them at the time. Serious writing was almost confined to Sanskrit and Persian, and every cultured person was supposed to know one of these. These two classical languages played a dominating role and prevented the growth of the popular provincial language. The printing of books and newspapers broke the hold of the classics, and immediately prose literatures in the provincial languages began to develop. The early Christian missionaries, especially of the Baptist mission at Serampore, helped in this process greatly. The first private printing presses were set up by them, and their efforts to translate the Bible into prose versions of the Indian languages met with considerable success.

There was no difficulty in dealing with the well-known and established languages, but the missionaries went further and tackled some of the minor and undeveloped languages and gave them shape and form, compiling grammars and dictionaries for them. They even labored at the dialects of the primitive hill and forest tribes and reduced them to writing. The desire of the Christian missionaries to translate the Bible into every possible language thus resulted in the development of many Indian languages. Christian mission work in India has not always been admirable or praiseworthy, but in this respect, as well as in the collection of folklore, it has undoubtedly been of great service to India.

The reluctance of the East India Company to spread education was justified, for as early as 1830 a batch of students of the Hindu College of Calcutta (where Sanskrit was taught and no English) demanded certain reforms. They asked for restrictions on the political power of the company and provision for free and compulsory education. Free education was well known in India from the most ancient times. That education was traditional, not very good or profitable, but it was available to poor students without any payment, except some personal service to the teacher. In this respect both the Hindu and Moslem traditions were similar.

While the new education was deliberately prevented from spreading, the old education had been largely liquidated in Bengal. When the British seized power in Bengal, there were a very large number of muafis; that is, tax-free grants of land. Many of these were personal, but most were in the shape of endowments for educational institutions. A vast number of elementary schools of the old type subsisted on them, as well as some institutions for higher education, which was chiefly imparted in Persian. The East India Company was anxious to make money rapidly in order to pay dividends to its shareholders in England, and the demands of its directors were continuous and pressing. A deliberate policy was therefore adopted to resume and confiscate these muafi lands. Strict proof was demanded of the original grant, but the old sanads and papers had long been lost or eaten up by termites. So the muafis were resumed and the old holders were ejected, and the schools and colleges lost their endowments. Huge areas were involved in this way, and many old families were ruined. The educational establishments, which had been supported by the muafis, ceased to function, and a vast number of teachers and others connected with them were thrown out of employment.

This process helped in ruining the old feudal classes in Bengal, both Moslem and Hindu, as well as those classes who were dependent on them. Moslems were especially affected since they were, as a group, more feudal than the Hindus and were also the chief beneficiaries of the muafis. Among the Hindus there were far larger numbers of middle-class people engaged in trade and commerce and the professions. These people were more adaptable and took to English education more readily. They were also more useful to the British for their subordinate services. Moslems avoided English education, and in Bengal they were not looked upon with favor by the British rulers, who were afraid that the remnants of the old ruling class might give trouble. Bengali Hindus thus acquired almost a monopoly in the beginning in the subordinate government service and were sent to the northern provinces. A few Moslems, relics of the old families, were later taken into this service.

English education brought a widening of the Indian horizon, an admiration for English literature and institutions, a revolt against some customs and aspects of Indian life, and a growing demand for political reform. The new professional classes took the lead in political agitation, which consisted chiefly in sending representatives to government. English-educated people in the professions and the services formed in effect a new class, which was to grow all over India, a class influenced by Western thought and ways and rather cut off from the mass of the population. In 1852 the British Indian Association was started in Calcutta. This was one of the forerunners of the Indian National Congress, and yet a whole generation was to pass before the Congress was started in 1885. This gap represents the period of the revolt of 1857–58, its suppression, and its consequences. The great difference between the state of Bengal and that of northern and central India in the middle of the century is brought out by the fact that while in Bengal the new intelligentsia (chiefly Hindu) had been influenced by English thought and literature and looked to England for political constitutional reform, the other areas were seething with the spirit of revolt.

In Bengal one can see more clearly than elsewhere the early effects of British rule and Western influence. The breakup of the agrarian economy was complete, and the old feudal classes had almost been eliminated. In their place had come new landowners whose organic and traditional contacts with the land were far less, and who had few of the virtues and most of the failings of the old feudal landlords. The peasantry suffered famine and spoliation in many ways and were reduced to extreme poverty. The artisan class was almost wiped out. Over these disjointed and broken-up foundations rose new groups and classes, the products of British rule and connected with it in many ways. There were the merchants who were really middlemen of British trade and industry, profiting by the leavings of that industry. There were also the English-educated classes in the subordinate services and the learned professions, both looking to the British power for advancement and both influenced in varying degrees by Western thought. Among these grew up a spirit of revolt against the rigid conventions and social framework of Hindu society. They looked to English liberalism and institutions for inspiration.

This was the effect on the upper fringe of the Hindus of Bengal. The mass of the Hindus there were not directly affected, and even the Hindu leaders probably seldom thought of these masses. The Moslems were not affected at all, some individuals apart, and they kept deliberately aloof from the new education. They previously had been backward economically, and they became even more so. The nineteenth century produced a galaxy of brilliant Hindus in Bengal, and yet there is hardly a single Moslem Bengali leader of any note who stands out there during this period. So far as the masses were concerned, there was hardly any appreciable difference between the Hindus and Moslems; they were indistinguishable in habits, ways of living, language, and their common poverty and misery. Indeed nowhere in India were the religious and other differences between Hindus and Moslems of all classes so little marked as in Bengal. Probably 98 per cent of the Moslems were converts from Hinduism, usually from the lowest strata of society. In population figures there was probably a slight majority of Moslems over Hindus. (Today the proportions in Bengal are: 53% Moslems, 46% Hindus, 1% others.)

All these early consequences of the British connection, and the various economic, social, intellectual, and political movements that they gave rise to in Bengal, are noticeable elsewhere in India but in lesser and varying degrees. The breakup of the old feudal order and economy were less complete and more gradual elsewhere. In fact that order rose in rebellion, and even when crushed, survived to some extent. The Moslems in upper India were culturally and economically far superior to their coreligionists of Bengal, but even they kept aloof from Western education. The

Hindus took to this education more easily and were more influenced by Western ideas. The subordinate government services and the professions had far more Hindus than Moslems. Only in the Punjab this difference was less marked.

The revolt in 1857–58 flared up and was crushed, but Bengal was hardly touched by it. Throughout the nineteenth century the new English-educated class, mainly Hindu, looked up with admiration toward England and hoped to advance with her help and in co-operation with her. There was a cultural renaissance and a remarkable growth of the Bengali language, and the leaders of Bengal stood out as the leaders of political India.

Some glimpse of that faith in England which filled the mind of Bengal in those days, as well as of the revolt against old-established social codes, may be had from that moving message of Rabindranath Tagore which he gave on his eightieth birthday (May 1941), a few months before his death. "As I look back," he says, "on the vast stretch of years that lie behind me and see in clear perspective the history of my early development, I am struck by the change that has taken place both in my own attitude and in the psychology of my countrymen—a change that carries within it a cause of profound tragedy.

"Our direct contact with the larger world of men was linked up with the contemporary history of the English people whom we came to know in those earlier days. It was mainly through their mighty literature that we formed our ideas with regard to these newcomers to our Indian shores. In those days the type of learning that was served out to us was neither plentiful nor diverse, nor was the spirit of scientific enquiry very much in evidence. Thus their scope being strictly limited, the educated of those days had recourse to English language and literature. Their days and nights were eloquent with the stately declamations of Burke, with Macaulay's long-rolling sentences; discussions centred upon Shakespeare's drama and Byron's poetry and above all upon the large-hearted liberalism of the nineteenth-century English politics.

"At the time though tentative attempts were being made

to gain our national independence, at heart we had not lost faith in the generosity of the English race. This belief was so firmly rooted in the sentiments of our leaders as to lead them to hope that the victor would of his own grace pave the path of freedom for the vanquished. This belief was based upon the fact that England at the time provided a shelter to all those who had to flee from persecution in their own country. Political martyrs who had suffered for the honour of their people were accorded unreserved welcome at the hands of the English. I was impressed by this evidence of liberal humanity in the character of the English and thus I was led to set them on the pedestal of my highest respect. This generosity in their national character had not yet been vitiated by Imperialist pride. About this time, as a boy in England, I had the opportunity of listening to the speeches of John Bright, both in and outside Parliament. The large-hearted, radical liberalism of those speeches, overflowing all narrow national bounds, had made so deep an impression on my mind that something of it lingers even today, even in these days of graceless disillusionment.

"Certainly that spirit of abject dependence upon the charity of our rulers was no matter for pride. What was remarkable, however, was the whole-hearted way in which we gave our recognition to human greatness even when it revealed itself in the foreigner. The best and noblest gifts of humanity cannot be the monopoly of a particular race or country; its scope may not be limited nor may it be regarded as the miser's hoard buried underground. That is why English literature which nourished our minds in the past, does even now convey its deep resonance to the recesses of our heart."

Tagore proceeds to refer to the Indian ideal of proper conduct prescribed by the tradition of the race. "Narrow in themselves these time-honoured social conventions originated and held good in a circumscribed geographical area, in that strip of land, Brahmavarta by name, bound on either side by the rivers Saraswati and Drisadvati. That is how a pharisaic formalism gradually got the upper hand of free thought and the ideal 'proper conduct' which Manu found established in Brahmavarta steadily degenerated into socialized tyranny.

"During my boyhood days the attitude of the cultured and educated section of Bengal, nurtured on English learning, was charged with a feeling of revolt against these rigid regulations of society. . . . In place of these set codes of conduct we accepted the ideal of 'civilization' as represented by the English term.

"In our own family this change of spirit was welcomed for the sake of its sheer rational and moral force and its influence was felt in every sphere of our life. Born in that atmosphere, which was moreover coloured by our intuitive bias for literature, I naturally set the English on the throne of my heart. Thus passed the first chapters of my life. Then came the parting of ways accompanied with a painful feeling of disillusion when I began increasingly to discover how easily those who accepted the highest truths of civilization disowned them with impunity whenever questions of national self-interest were involved."

## VI. THE GREAT REVOLT OF 1857
### RACIALISM

After nearly a century of British rule, Bengal had accommodated itself to it; the peasantry devastated by famine and crushed by new economic burdens, the new intelligentsia looking to the West and hoping that progress would come through English liberalism. So also, more or less, in the south and in western India, in Madras and Bombay. But in the upper provinces there was no such submission or accommodation and the spirit of revolt was growing, especially among the feudal chiefs and their followers. Even in the masses discontent and an intense anti-British feeling were widespread. The upper classes keenly resented the insulting and overbearing manners of the foreigners; the people generally suffered from the rapacity and ignorance of the officials of the East India Company, who ignored their time-honored customs and paid no heed to what the people of the country thought. Absolute power over vast numbers of people had turned their heads, and they suffered no check or hindrance. Even the new judicial system they introduced became a thing of terror because of its complications and the ignorance of the judges of both the language and customs of the country.

As early as 1817 Sir Thomas Munro, writing to the governor-general, Lord Hastings, after pointing out the advantages of British rule, said: "But these advantages are dearly bought. They are purchased by the sacrifice of independence, of national character, and of whatever renders a people respectable. . . . The consequence, therefore, of the conquest of India by the British arms would be, in place of raising, to debase a whole people. There is perhaps no example of any conquest in which the Natives have been so completely excluded from all share of the government of their country as in British India."

Munro was pleading for the employment of Indians in the administration. A year later he wrote again: "Foreign conquerors have treated the natives with violence, and often with great cruelty, but none has treated them with so much scorn as we; none have stigmatized the whole people as unworthy of trust, as incapable of honesty, and as fit to be employed only where we cannot do without them. It seems to be not only ungenerous, but impolitic, to debase the character of a people fallen under our dominion."[5]

British dominion was extended to the Punjab by 1850 after two Sikh wars. Maharaja Ranjit Singh, who had held and extended the Sikh state in the Punjab, had died in 1839. In 1856 Oudh was annexed. Oudh had been virtually under British rule for half a century, for it was a vassal state, its nominal ruler being both helpless and degenerate, and the British resident all-powerful. It had sunk to the very depths of misery and illustrated all the evils of the subsidiary state system.

In May 1857 the Indian army at Meerut mutinied. The revolt had been secretly and well organized, but a premature outburst rather upset the plans of the leaders. It was

[5] Quoted by Thompson, *The Making of the Indian Princes*, pp. 273, 274.

much more than a military mutiny, and it spread rapidly and assumed the character of a popular rebellion and a war of Indian independence. As such a popular rebellion of the masses it was confined to Delhi, the United Provinces (as they are now called), and parts of central India and Bihar. Essentially it was a feudal outburst, headed by feudal chiefs and other followers and aided by the widespread antiforeign sentiment. As such, inevitably it looked up to the relic of the Moghul dynasty, still sitting in the Delhi palace, but feeble and old and powerless. Both Hindus and Moslems took full part in the revolt.

This revolt strained British rule to the utmost, and it was ultimately suppressed with Indian help. It brought out all the inherent weaknesses of the old regime which was making its last despairing effort to drive out foreign rule. The feudal chiefs had the sympathy of the masses over large areas, but they were incapable, unorganized, and with no constructive ideal or community of interest. They had already played their role in history and there was no place for them in the future. Many of their number, in spite of their sympathies, thought discretion the better part of valor, and stood apart waiting to see on which side victory lay. Many played the part of Quislings. The Indian princes as a whole kept aloof or helped the British, fearing to risk what they had acquired or managed to retain. There was hardly any national and unifying sentiment among the leaders, and a mere antiforeign feeling, coupled with a desire to maintain their feudal privileges, was a poor substitute for this.

The British got the support of the Gurkhas, and what is much more surprising, of the Sikhs also, for the Sikhs had been their enemies and had been defeated by them only a few years before. It is certainly to the credit of the British that they could win over the Sikhs in this way; whether it is to the credit or discredit of the Sikhs of those days depends upon one's point of view. It is clear, however, that there was a lack of nationalist feeling which might have bound the people of India together. Nationalism of the modern type was yet to come; India had still to go through much sorrow and travail before she learned the lesson which would give her real freedom. Not by fighting for a lost cause, the feudal order, would freedom come.

The revolt threw up some fine guerrilla leaders. Feroze Shah, a relative of Bahadur Shah of Delhi was one of them; but most brilliant of all was Tantia Topi, who harassed the British for many months even when defeat stared him in the face. Ultimately, when he crossed the Narbada River into the Maratha regions hoping to receive aid and welcome from his own people, there was no welcome, and he was betrayed. One name stands out above others and is revered still in popular memory, the name of Lakshmi Bai, Rani of Jhansi, a girl twenty years of age, who died fighting. "Best and bravest" of the rebel leaders, she was called by the English general who opposed her.

British memorials of the Mutiny have been put up in Cawnpore and elsewhere. There is no memorial for the Indians who died. The rebel Indians sometimes indulged in cruel and barbarous behavior; they were unorganized, suppressed, and often angered by reports of British excesses. But there is another side to the picture also, that impressed itself on the mind of India, and in my own province especially the memory of it persists in town and village. One would like to forget all this, for it is a ghastly and horrible picture showing man at his worst, even according to the new standards of barbarity set up by nazism and modern war. But it can only be forgotten, or remembered in a detached, impersonal way when it becomes truly the past, with nothing to connect it with the present. So long as the connecting links and reminders are present, and the spirit behind those events survives and shows itself, that memory also will endure and influence our people. Attempts to suppress that picture do not destroy it but drive it deeper in the mind. Only by dealing with it normally can its effect be lessened.

A great deal of false and perverted history has been written about the revolt and its suppression. What the Indians think about it seldom finds its way to the printed page. Savarkar wrote *The History of the War of Indian Independence* some thirty years ago, but his book was promptly banned and is banned still. Some frank and honorable

English historians have occasionally lifted the veil and allowed us a glimpse of the race mania and lynching mentality which prevailed on an enormous scale. The accounts given in Kaye and Malleson's *History of the Mutiny* and in Thompson and Garrett's *Rise and Fulfilment of British Rule in India* make one sick with horror. "Every Indian who was not actually fighting for the British became a 'murderer of women and children' . . . a general massacre of the inhabitants of Delhi, a large number of whom were known to wish us success, was openly proclaimed." The days of Timur and Nadir Shah were remembered, but their exploits were eclipsed by the new terror, both in extent and the length of time it lasted. Looting was officially allowed for a week, but it actually lasted for a month, and it was accompanied by wholesale massacre.

In my own city and district of Allahabad and in the neighborhood, General Neill held his "Bloody Assizes." "Soldiers and civilians alike were holding Bloody Assize, or slaying natives without any assize at all, regardless of age or sex. It is on the records of our British Parliament, in papers sent home by the Governor-General in Council, that 'the aged, women, and children are sacrificed as well as those guilty of rebellion.' They were not deliberately hanged, but burnt to death in villages—perhaps now and then accidentally shot. . . . Volunteer hanging parties went into the districts and amateur executioners were not wanting to the occasion. One gentleman boasted of the numbers he had finished off quite 'in an artistic manner,' with mango trees as gibbets and elephants for drops, the victim of this wild justice being strung up, as though for pastime, in the form of figures of eight." And so in Cawnpore and Lucknow and all over the place.

## VII. THE TECHNIQUES OF BRITISH RULE
### BALANCE AND COUNTERPOISE

The revolt of 1857-58 was essentially a feudal rising, though there were some nationalistic elements in it. Yet, at the same time, it was due to the abstention or active help of the princes and other feudal chiefs that the British succeeded in crushing it. Those who had joined the revolt were as a rule the disinherited and those deprived of their power and privileges by the British authority, or those who feared that some such fate was in store for them. British policy after some hesitation had decided in favor of a gradual elimination of the princes and the establishment of direct British rule. The revolt brought about a change in this policy, in favor not only of the princes but of the taluqdars or big landlords. It was felt that it was easier to control the masses through these feudal or semifeudal chiefs. These taluqdars of Oudh had been the tax-farmers of the Moghuls, but owing to the weakness of the central authority, they had begun to function as feudal landlords. Nearly all of them joined the revolt, though some took care to keep a way of escape open. In spite of their rebellion, the British authority offered to reinstate them (with a few exceptions) and confirm them in their estates on conditions of "loyalty and good service." Thus these taluqdars, who take pride in calling themselves the "Barons of Oudh," became one of the pillars of British rule.

Though the revolt had directly affected only certain parts of the country, it had shaken up the whole of India, and particularly the British administration. The government set about reorganizing their entire system; the British crown, that is the parliament, took over the country from the East India Company; the Indian army, which had begun the revolt by its mutiny, was organized afresh. The techniques of British rule, which had already been well established, were now clarified and confirmed and deliberately acted upon. Essentially these were: the creation and protection of vested interests bound up with British rule; and a policy of balancing and counterpoise of different elements, and the encouragement of fissiparous tendencies and division among them.

The princes and the big landlords were the basic vested interests thus created and encouraged. But now a new class, even more tied up with British rule, grew in importance. This consisted of the Indian members of the services,

usually in subordinate positions. Previously the employment of Indians had been avoided except when this could
not be helped, and Munro had pleaded for such employment. Experience had now demonstrated that Indians so
employed were so dependent on the British administration
and rule that they could be relied upon and treated as
agents of that rule. In the pre-Mutiny days most of the
Indian members of the subordinate services had been
Bengalis. These had spread out over the upper provinces
wherever the British administration needed clerks and the
like in its civil or military establishments. Regular colonies
of Bengalis had thus grown up at the administrative or
military centers in the United Provinces, Delhi, and even
in the Punjab. These Bengalis accompanied the British
armies and proved faithful employees to them. They became associated in the minds of the rebels with the British
power and were greatly disliked by them and given un-
complimentary titles.

Thus began the process of the indianization of the administrative machine in its subordinate ranks, all real
power and initiative being, however, concentrated in the
hands of the English personnel. As English education
spread, the Bengalis had no longer a virtual monopoly of
service, and other Indians came in both on the judicial and
executive sides of the administration. This indianization
became the most effective method of strengthening British
rule. It created a civil army and garrison everywhere, which
was more important even than the military army of occupation. There were some members of this civil army who
were able and patriotic and nationalistically inclined; but
like the soldier, who also may be patriotic in his individual
capacity, they were bound up by the army code and discipline, and the price of disobedience, desertion, and revolt was heavy. Not only was this civil army created, but
the hope and prospect of employment in it affected and
demoralized a vast and growing number of others. There
was a measure of prestige and security in it and a pension
at the end of the term of service, and if a sufficient subservience was shown to one's superior officers, other failings
did not count. These civil employees were the intermedi-

aries between the British authorities and the people, and if they had to be obsequious to their superiors, they could be arrogant and exact obedience from their own inferiors and the people at large.

The lack of other avenues of employment, other ways of making a living, added additional importance to government service. A few could become lawyers or doctors, but even so, success was by no means assured. Industry hardly existed. Trade was largely in the hands of certain hereditary classes who had a peculiar aptitude for it and who helped each other. The new education did not fit any one for trade or industry; its chief aim was government service. Education was so limited as to offer few openings for a professional career; other social services were almost nonexistent. So government service remained and, as the colleges poured out their graduates, even the growing government services could not absorb them all, and a fierce competition arose. The unemployed graduates and others formed a pool from which government could always draw; they were a potential threat to the security of even the employed. Thus the British government in India became not only the biggest employer, but for all practical purposes the sole big employer (including railways), and a vast bureaucratic machine was built up, strictly managed and controlled at the top. This enormous patronage was exercised to strengthen the British hold on the country, to crush discordant and disagreeable elements, and to promote rivalry and discord among various groups anxiously looking forward to employment in government service. It led to demoralization and conflict, and the government could play one group against the other.

The policy of balance and counterpoise was deliberately furthered in the Indian army. Various groups were so arranged as to prevent any sentiment of national unity growing up among them, and tribal and communal loyalties and slogans were encouraged. Every effort was made to isolate the army from the people, and even ordinary newspapers were not allowed to reach the Indian troops. All the key positions were kept in the hands of Englishmen, and no Indian could hold the king's commission. A raw English subaltern was senior to the oldest and most experienced Indian noncommissioned officer or those holding the so-called viceroy's commissions. No Indian could be employed in Army Headquarters except as a petty clerk in the accounts department. For additional protection the more effective weapons of warfare were not given to the Indian forces; they were reserved for the British troops in India. These British troops were always kept with the Indian regiments in all the vital centers of India to serve as "Internal Security Troops" for suppression of disorder and to overawe the people. While this internal army, with a predominance of British personnel, served as an army of occupation for the country, the greater portion of the Indian troops were part of the field army organized for service abroad. The Indian troops were recruited from special classes only, chiefly in northern India, which were called martial classes.

Again we notice in India that inherent contradiction in British rule. Having brought about the political unification of the country and thus let loose new dynamic forces which thought not only in terms of that unity but aimed at the freedom of India, the British government tried to disrupt that very unity it had helped to create. That disruption was not thought of in political terms then as a splitting up of India; it was aimed at the weakening of nationalist elements so that British rule might continue over the whole country. But it was nonetheless an attempt at disruption, by giving greater importance to the Indian states than they had ever had before, by encouraging reactionary elements and looking to them for support, by promoting divisions and encouraging one group against another, by encouraging fissiparous tendencies due to religion or province, and by organizing Quisling classes which were afraid of a change which might engulf them. All this was a natural and understandable policy for a foreign imperialist power to pursue, and it is a little naive to be surprised at it, harmful from the Indian nationalist point of view though it was. But the fact that it was so must be remembered if we are to understand subsequent developments. Out of this policy arose those "important elements in India's national life" of which we are reminded so often today; which were created and encouraged to disagree and disrupt, and are now called upon to agree among themselves.

Because of this natural alliance of the British power with the reactionaries in India, it became the guardian and upholder of many an evil custom and practice which it otherwise condemned. India was custom-ridden when the British came, and the tyranny of old custom is often a terrible thing. Yet customs change and are forced to adapt themselves to some extent to a changing environment. Hindu law was largely custom, and as custom changed, the law also was applied in a different way. Indeed there was no provision of Hindu law which could not be changed by custom. The British replaced this elastic customary law by judicial decisions based on the old texts, and these decisions became precedents which had to be rigidly followed. That was, in theory, an advantage, as it produced greater uniformity and certainty. But, in the way it was done, it resulted in the perpetuation of the ancient law unmodified by subsequent customs. Thus the old law, which in some particulars and in various places had been changed by custom and was thus out-of-date, was petrified, and every tendency to change it in the well-known customary way was suppressed. It was still open to a group to prove a custom overriding the law, but this was extraordinarily difficult in the law courts. Change could only come by positive legislation, but the British government, which was the legislating authority, had no wish to antagonize the conservative elements on whose support it counted. When later some legislative powers were given to partially elected assemblies, every attempt to promote social reform legislation was frowned upon by the authorities and sternly discouraged.

## VIII. GROWTH OF INDUSTRY
### PROVINCIAL DIFFERENCES

Slowly India recovered from the aftereffects of the revolt of 1857–58. Despite British policy, powerful forces were at work changing India and a new social consciousness was arising. The political unity of India, contact with the West, technological advances, and even the misfortune of a common subjection, led to new currents of thought, the slow development of industry, and the rise of a new movement for national freedom. The awakening of India was twofold: she looked to the West, and at the same time she looked at herself and her own past.

The coming of the railway to India brought the industrial age on its positive side; so far only the negative aspect, in the shape of manufactured goods from Britain, had been in evidence. In 1860 the duty on imported machinery, imposed so as to prevent the industrialization of India, was removed and large-scale industry began to develop, chiefly with British capital. First came the jute industry of Bengal, with its nerve center at Dundee in Scotland; much later, cotton mills grew up in Ahmadabad and Bombay, largely with Indian capital and under Indian ownership; then came mining. Obstruction from the British government in India continued, and an excise duty was put on Indian cotton goods to prevent them from competing with Lancashire textiles, even in India. Nothing, perhaps, reveals the police-state policy of the government of India more than the fact that they had no department of agriculture and no department of commerce and industry till the twentieth century. It was, I believe, chiefly due to the donation of an American visitor, given for agricultural improvement in India, that a department of agriculture was started in the central government. (Even now this department is a very small affair.) A department for commerce and industry followed soon after, in 1905. Even then these departments functioned in a very small way. The growth of industry was artificially restricted, and India's natural economic development was arrested.

Though the masses of India were desperately poor and growing poorer, a tiny fringe at the top was prospering under the new conditions and accumulating capital. It was this fringe that demanded political reform as well as opportunities for investment. On the political side, the Indian National Congress was started in 1885. Commerce and industry grew slowly, and it is interesting to note that the classes who took to them were predominantly those whose hereditary occupations for hundreds of years had been trade and commerce. Ahmadabad, the new center of the textile industry, had been a famous manufacturing and trade center during the Moghul period and even earlier, exporting its products to foreign countries. The big merchants of Ahmadabad had their own ships for this seaborne trade to Africa and the Persian Gulf. Broach, the seaport near by, was well known in Graeco-Roman times.

The people of Gujrat, Kathiawar, and Cutch were traders, manufacturers, merchants, and seafaring folk from ancient times. Many changes took place in India, but they carried on with their old businesses, adapting them to new conditions. They are now among the most prominent leaders in industry and commerce. Religion or a change of religion made no difference. The Parsis, who originally settled in Gujrat thirteen hundred years ago, may be considered as Gujratis for this purpose. (Their language has long been Gujrati.) Among the Moslems the most prominent sects in business and industry are the Khojas, Memons, and Bohras. All of these are converts from Hinduism, and all come from Gujrat, Kathiawar, or Cutch. All these Gujratis not only dominate industry and business in India but have spread out to Burma, Ceylon, east Africa, south Africa, and other foreign countries.

The Marwaris from Rajputana used to control internal trade and finance, and were to be found at all the nerve centers of India. They were the big financiers as well as the small village bankers; a note from a well-known Marwari financial house would be honored anywhere in India, and even abroad. The Marwaris still represent big finance in India, but have added industry to it now.

The Sindhis in the northwest have also an old commercial tradition, and with their headquarters at Shikarpur or Hyderabad, they used to spread out over central and western Asia and elsewhere. Today (that is, before the war) there is hardly a port anywhere in the world where one or more Sindhi shops cannot be found. Some of the Punjabis also have been traditionally in business.

The chettys of Madras have also been leaders in business, and banking especially, from ancient times. The word chetty is derived from the Sanskrit *shreshthi*, the leader of a merchant guild. The common appellation "Seth" is also derived from *shreshthi*. The Madras chettys have not only played an important part in south India but they spread out all over Burma, even in the remoter villages.

Within each province also, trade and commerce were largely in the hands of the old Vaishya class who had been engaged in business for untold generations. They were the retail and wholesale dealers and moneylenders. In each village there was a bania's shop which dealt in the necessaries of village life and advanced loans, on very profitable terms, to the villagers. The rural credit system was almost entirely in the hands of these banias. They spread even to the tribal and independent territories of the northwest and performed important functions there. As poverty grew, agricultural indebtedness also grew rapidly, and the moneylending establishments held mortgages on the land and eventually acquired much of the land. Thus the moneylender became the landlord also.

These demarcations of commercial, trading, and banking classes from others became less clearly defined as newcomers crept into various businesses. But they continued and are still marked. Whether they are due to the caste system, or the hold of tradition, or inherited capacity, or all of these together, it is difficult to specify. Undoubtedly among Brahmans and Kshatriyas business was looked down upon, and even the accumulation of money, though agreeable enough, was not a sufficient recompense. The possession of land was a symbol of social position, as in feudal times, and scholarship and learning were respected, even apart from possessions. Under British rule, government service gave prestige, security, and status, and later, when Indians were allowed to enter the Indian Civil Service, this service, called the "Heaven-born Service"—heaven being some pale shadow of Whitehall—became the Elysium of the English-educated classes. The professional classes, especially lawyers, some of whom earned large incomes in the new law courts, also had prestige and high status and attracted young men. Inevitably these lawyers took the lead in political and social reform movements.

The Bengalis were the first to take to the law, and some of them flourished exceedingly and cast a glamour over their profession. They were also the political leaders. They did not fit into the growing industry, either because of lack of aptitude or other reasons. The result has been that when industry began to play an important part in the country's life and influenced politics, Bengal lost its pre-eminence in the political field. The old current, when Bengalis poured out of their province as government servants and in other capacities, was reversed, and people from other provinces poured into Bengal, especially to Calcutta, and permeated the commercial and industrial life there. Calcutta had been and continues to be the chief center of British capital and industry, and the English and the Scotch dominate business there. But they are being caught up with by Marwaris and Gujratis. Even petty trades in Calcutta are often in non-Bengali hands. All the thousands of taxi drivers in Calcutta, almost without an exception, are Sikhs from the Punjab.

Bombay became the center and headquarters of Indian-owned industry, commerce, banking, insurance, etc. The Parsis, the Gujratis and Marwaris were the leaders in all these activities, and it is significant that the Maharashtrians or Marathas have played very little part in them. Bombay is a huge, cosmopolitan city now, but its population consists mainly of Marathas and Gujratis. The Marathas have distinguished themselves in the professions and in scholarship; they make, as one would expect, good soldiers; and large numbers of them are employed as workers in the textile mills. They are hardy and wiry and, as a province, poor; they are proud of the Shivaji tradition and of the achievements of their forefathers. The Gujratis are soft in body, gentler, richer, and perfectly at home in trade and commerce. Perhaps these differences are largely due to geography, for the Maratha country is bare and hard and mountainous, while Gujrat is rich and fertile.

It is interesting to observe these and other differences in various parts of India which continue to persist, though they tend to grow less. Madras, highly intellectual, has produced and still produces distinguished philosophers, mathematicians, and scientists. Bombay is now almost entirely devoted to business, with all its advantages and disadvantages. Bengal, rather backward in industry and business, has produced some fine scientists, and has especially distinguished itself in art and literature. The Punjab has produced no outstanding personalities but is a go-ahead province advancing in many fields; its people are hardheaded, make good mechanics, and are successful in small trades and petty industries. The United Provinces (including Delhi) are a curious amalgam, and in some ways an epitome of India. They are the seat of the old Hindu culture as well as of the Persian culture that came in Afghan and Moghul times, and hence the mixture of the two is most in evidence there, intermingled with the culture of the West. There is less of provincialism there than in any other part of India. For long they have considered themselves, and have been looked upon by others, as the heart of India. Indeed, in popular parlance, they are often referred to as Hindustan.

These differences, it must be noted, are geographical and not religious. A Bengali Moslem is far nearer to a Bengali Hindu than he is to a Punjabi Moslem; so also with others. If a number of Hindu and Moslem Bengalis happen to meet anywhere, in India or elsewhere, they will immediately congregate together and feel at home with each other. Punjabis, whether Moslem or Hindu or Sikh, will do likewise. The Moslems of the Bombay presidency (Khojas, Memons, and Bohras) have many Hindu customs; the Khojas (they are the followers of the Aga Khan) and the Bohras are not looked upon as orthodox by the Moslems of the north.

Moslems, as a whole, especially in Bengal and the north, not only kept away from English education for a long time, but also took little part in the growth of industry. Partly this was due to feudal modes of thought, partly (as in Roman Catholicism) to Islam's prohibition against usury and interest on money. But curiously enough, among the notorious moneylenders are a particular tribe of Pathans who come from near the frontier. Moslems were thus, in the second half of the nineteenth century, backward in English education and therefore in contacts with Western thought, as also in government service and in industry.

The growth of industry in India, slow and arrested as it was, gave the impression of progress and attracted attention. And yet it made practically no difference to the problem of the poverty of the masses and the overburden on the land. A few hundred thousand workers were transferred to industry out of the scores of millions of the unemployed and partially employed. This change-over was so extremely small that it did not affect the increasing ruralization of the country. Widespread unemployment and the pressure on land led to emigration of workers on a substantial scale to foreign countries, often under humiliating conditions. They went to south Africa, Fiji, Trinidad, Jamaica, Guiana, Mauritius, Ceylon, Burma, and Malaya. The small groups or individuals who found opportunities for growth and betterment under foreign rule were divorced from the masses, whose condition continued to worsen. Some capital accumulated in the hands of those groups, and conditions were gradually created for further growth. But the basic problems of poverty and unemployment remained untouched.

## IX. REFORM AND OTHER MOVEMENTS AMONG HINDUS AND MOSLEMS

The real impact of the West came to India in the nineteenth century through technical changes and their dynamic consequences. In the realm of ideas also there was shock and change, a widening of the horizon which had so long been confined within a narrow shell. The first reaction, limited to the small English-educated class, was one of admiration and acceptance of almost everything Western. Repelled by some of the social customs and practices of Hinduism, many Hindus were attracted toward Christianity, and some notable conversions took place in Bengal.

An attempt was therefore made by Raja Ram Mohan Roy to adapt Hinduism to this new environment, and he started the Brahmo Samaj on a more or less rationalist and social reform basis. His successor, Keshab Chander Sen, gave it a more Christian outlook. The Brahmo Samaj influenced the rising middle classes of Bengal, but as a religious faith it remained confined to few, among whom, however, were some outstanding persons and families. But even these families, though ardently interested in social and religious reform, tended to go back to the old Indian philosophic ideals of the Vedanta.

Elsewhere in India also the same tendencies were at work, and dissatisfaction arose at the rigid social forms and protean character of Hinduism as practiced. One of the most notable reform movements was started in the second half of the nineteenth century by a Gujrati, Swami Dayananda Saraswati, but it took root among the Hindus of the Punjab. This was the Arya Samaj, and its slogan was "Back to the Vedas." This slogan really meant an elimination of developments of the Aryan faith since the Vedas; the Vedanta philosophy as it subsequently developed, the central conception of monism, the pantheistic outlook, as well as popular and cruder developments, all alike were severely condemned. Even the Vedas were interpreted in a particular way. The Arya Samaj was a reaction to the influence of Islam and Christianity, more especially the former. It was a crusading and reforming movement from within, as well as a defensive organization for protection against external attacks. It introduced proselytism into Hinduism and thus tended to come into conflict with other proselyting religions. The Arya Samaj, which had been a close approach to Islam, tended to become a defender of everything Hindu against what it considered as the encroachments of other faiths. It is significant that it spread chiefly among the middle-class Hindus of the Punjab and the United Provinces. At one time it was considered by the government a politically revolutionary movement, but the large numbers of government servants in it made it thoroughly respectable. It has done very good work in the spread of education both among boys and girls, in improving the condition of women, and in raising the status and standards of the depressed classes.

About the same period as Swami Dayananda, a different type of person lived in Bengal and his life influenced many of the new English-educated classes. He was Shri Ramakrishna Paramahamsa, a simple man, no scholar but a man of faith, and not interested in social reform as such. He was in a direct line with Chaitanya and other Indian saints. Essentially religious and yet broad-minded, in his search for self-realization he went to Moslem and Christian mystics and lived with them for years, following their strict routines. He settled down at Dakshineshwar near Calcutta, and his extraordinary personality and character gradually attracted attention. People who went to visit him, and some who were even inclined to scoff at this simple man of faith, were powerfully influenced, and many who had been completely westernized felt that here was something they had missed. Stressing the essentials of religious faith, he linked up the various aspects of the Hindu religion and philosophy and seemed to represent all of them in his own person. Indeed he brought within his fold other religions also. Opposed to all sectarianism, he emphasized that all roads lead to truth. He was like some of the saints we read about in the past records of Asia and Europe; difficult to understand in the context of modern life, and yet fitting into India's many-colored pattern and accepted and revered by many of her people as a man with a touch of the divine fire about him. His personality impressed itself on all who saw him, and many who never saw him have been influenced by the story of his life. Among these latter is Romain Rolland, who has written a story of his life and that of his chief disciple, Swami Vivekananda.

Vivekananda, together with his brother disciples, founded the nonsectarian Ramakrishna Mission of service. Rooted in the past and full of pride in India's heritage, Vivekananda was yet modern in his approach to life's problems and was a kind of bridge between the past of India and her present. He was a powerful orator in Bengali and English and a graceful writer of Bengali prose and poetry. He was a fine figure of a man, imposing, full of poise and dignity, sure of himself and his mission, and at the same time full of a dynamic and fiery energy and a passion to push India forward. He came as a tonic to the depressed and demoralized Hindu mind and gave it self-reliance and some roots in the past. He attended the Parliament of Religions in Chicago in 1893, spent over a year in the U.S.A., traveled across Europe going as far as Athens and Constantinople, and visited Egypt, China, and Japan. Wherever he went, he created a minor sensation not only by his presence but by what he said and how he said it. Having seen this Hindu *sanyasin* once, it was difficult to forget him or his message. In America he was called the "cyclonic Hindu." He was himself greatly influenced by his travels in Western countries; he admired British perseverance, and the vitality and spirit of equality of the American people. "America is the best field in the world to carry on any idea," he wrote to a friend in India. But he was not impressed by the manifestations of religion in the West, and his faith in the Indian philosophical and spiritual background became firmer. India, in spite of her degradation, still represented to him the Light.

He preached the monism of the Advaita philosophy of the Vedanta, and was convinced that only this could be the future religion of thinking humanity. For the Vedanta was not only spiritual but rational and in harmony with scientific investigations of external nature. "This universe has not been created by any extra-cosmic God, nor is it the work of any outside genius. It is self-creating, self-dissolving, self-manifesting, One Infinite Existence, the Brahma." The Vedanta ideal was of the solidarity of man and his inborn divine nature; to see God in man is the real God-vision; man is the greatest of all beings. But "the abstract Vedanta must become living—poetic—in everyday life; out of hopelessly intricate mythology must come concrete moral forms; and out of bewildering Yogi-ism must come the most scientific and practical psychology." India had fallen because she had narrowed herself, gone into her shell and lost touch with other nations, and thus sunk into a state of "mummified" and "crystallized" civilization. Caste, which was necessary and desirable in its early forms, and meant to develop individuality and freedom, had become a monstrous degradation, the opposite of what it was meant to be, and had crushed the masses. Caste was a form of social organization which was and should be kept separate from religion. Social organizations should change with the changing times. Passionately Vivekananda condemned the meaningless metaphysical discussions and arguments about ceremonials, and especially the touch-me-notism of the upper castes. "Our religion is in the kitchen. Our God is the cooking-pot, and our religion is: 'don't touch me, I am holy.'"

He kept away from politics and disapproved of the politicians of his day. But again and again he laid stress on the necessity for liberty and equality and the raising of the masses. "Liberty of thought and action is the only condition of life, of growth and well-being. Where it does not exist, the man, the race, the nation must go." "The only hope of India is from the masses. The upper classes are physically and morally dead." He wanted to combine Western progress with India's spiritual background: "Make a European society with India's religion. . . . Become an occidental of occidentals in your spirit of equality, freedom, work and energy, and at the same time a Hindu to the very backbone in religious culture and instincts." Progressively Vivekananda grew more international in outlook: "Even in Politics and Sociology, problems that were only national twenty years ago can no longer be solved on national grounds only. They are assuming huge proportions, gigantic shapes. They can only be solved when looked at in the broader light of international grounds. International organizations, international combinations, international laws are the cry of the day. That shows solidarity. In science, every day they are coming to a similar broad view of matter." And again: "There cannot be any progress without the whole world following in the wake, and it is becoming every day clearer that the solution of any problem can never be attained on racial, or national, or narrow grounds. Every idea has to become broad till it covers the whole of this world, every aspiration must go on increasing till it has engulfed the whole of humanity, nay the whole of life, within its scope." All this fitted in with Vivekananda's view of the Vedanta philosophy, and he preached this from end to end of India. "I am thoroughly convinced that no individual or nation can live by holding itself apart from the community of others, and wherever such an attempt has been made under false ideas of greatness, policy or holiness—the result has always been disastrous to the secluding one. . . . The fact of our isolation from all the other nations of the world is the cause of our degeneration and its only remedy is getting back into the current of the rest of the world. Motion is the sign of life."

He once wrote: "I am a socialist not because I think it is a perfect system, but half a loaf is better than no bread. The other systems have been tried and found wanting. Let this one be tried—if for nothing else, for the novelty of the thing."

Vivekananda spoke of many things, but the one constant refrain of his speech and writing was *abhay*—be fearless, be strong. For him man was no miserable sinner but a part of divinity; why should he be afraid of anything? "If there is a sin in the world it is weakness; avoid all weakness, weakness is sin, weakness is death." That had been the great lesson of the Upanishads. Fear breeds evil and weeping and wailing. There had been enough of that, enough of softness. "What our country now wants are muscles of iron and nerves of steel, gigantic wills which nothing can resist, which can penetrate into the mysteries and the secrets of the universe, and will accomplish their purpose in any fashion, even if it meant going down to the bottom of the ocean and meeting death face to face." He condemned "occultism and mysticism . . . these creepy things; there may be great truths in them, but they have nearly destroyed us. . . . And here is the test of truth—anything that makes you weak physically, intellectually and spiritually, reject as poison, there is no life in it, it cannot be true. Truth is strengthening. Truth is purity, truth is all-knowledge. . . . These mysticisms, in spite of some grains of truth in them, are generally weakening. . . . Go back to your Upanishads, the shining, the strengthening, the bright philosophy, and part from all these mysterious things, all these weakening things. Take up this philosophy; the greatest truths are the simplest things in the world, simple as your own existence." And beware of superstition. "I would rather see everyone of you rank atheists than superstitious fools, for the atheist is alive, and you can make something of him. But if superstition enters, the brain is gone, the brain is softening, degradation has seized upon the life. . . . Mystery-mongering and superstition are always signs of weakness."[6]

So Vivekananda thundered from Cape Comorin on the southern tip of India to the Himalayas, and he wore himself out in the process, dying in 1902 when he was thirty-nine years of age.

A contemporary of Vivekananda, and yet belonging much more to a later generation, was Rabindranath Tagore. The Tagore family had played a leading part in various reform movements in Bengal during the nineteenth century. There were men of spiritual stature in it and fine

---

[6] Most of these extracts have been taken from *Lectures from Colombo to Almora* by Swami Vivekananda (1933) and *Letters of Swami Vivekananda* (1942), both published by the Advaita Ashrama, Mayavati, Almora, Himalayas. In the Letters, p. 390, there is a remarkable letter written by Vivekananda to a Moslem friend. In the course of this he says:

"Whether we call it Vedantism or any *ism*, the truth is that Advaitism is the last word of religion and thought and the only position from which one can look upon all religions and sects with love. We believe it is the religion of the future enlightened humanity. The Hindus may get the credit of arriving at it earlier than other races, they being an older race than either the Hebrew or the Arab; yet practical Advaitism, which looks upon and behaves to all mankind as one's own soul, is yet to be developed among the Hindus universally.

"On the other hand our experience is that if ever the followers of any religion approach to this equality in an appreciable degree in the plane of practical work-a-day life—it may be quite unconscious generally of the deeper meaning and the underlying principle of such conduct, which the Hindus as a rule so clearly perceive—it is those of Islam and Islam alone. . . .

"For our own motherland a junction of the two great systems, Hinduism and Islam—Vedanta brain and Islam body—is the only hope.

"I see in my mind's eye the future perfect India rising out of this chaos and strife, glorious and invincible, with Vedanta brain and Islam body." This letter is dated Almora, 10th June, 1898.

writers and artists, but Rabindranath towered above them all, and indeed all over India his position gradually became one of unchallenged supremacy. His long life of creative activity covered two entire generations, and he seems almost of our present day. He was no politician, but he was too sensitive and devoted to the freedom of the Indian people to remain always in his ivory tower of poetry and song. Again and again he stepped out of it, when he could tolerate some development no longer, and in prophetic language warned the British government or his own people. He played a prominent part in the Swadeshi movement that swept through Bengal in the first decade of the twentieth century, and again when he gave up his knighthood at the time of the Amritsar massacre. His constructive work in the field of education, quietly begun, has already made Santiniketan one of the focal points of Indian culture. His influence over the mind of India, and especially of successive rising generations, has been tremendous. Not Bengali only, the language in which he himself wrote, but all the modern languages of India have been molded partly by his writings. More than any other Indian, he has helped to bring into harmony the ideals of the East and the West, and broadened the bases of Indian nationalism. He has been India's internationalist par excellence, believing and working for international co-operation, taking India's message to other countries and bringing their messages to his own people. And yet with all his internationalism, his feet have always been planted firmly on India's soil and his mind has been saturated with the wisdom of the Upanishads. Contrary to the usual course of development, as he grew older he became more radical in his outlook and views. Strong individualist as he was, he became an admirer of the great achievements of the Russian revolution, especially in the spread of education, culture, health, and the spirit of equality. Nationalism is a narrowing creed, and nationalism in conflict with a dominating imperialism produces all manner of frustrations and complexes. It was Tagore's immense service to India, as it has been Gandhi's in a different plane, that he forced the people in some measure out of their narrow grooves of thought and made them think of broader issues affecting humanity. Tagore was the great humanist of India.

Tagore and Gandhi have undoubtedly been the two outstanding and dominating figures of India in this first half of the twentieth century. It is instructive to compare and contrast them. No two persons could be so different from one another in their make-up or temperaments. Tagore, the aristocratic artist, turned democrat with proletarian sympathies, represented essentially the cultural tradition of India, the tradition of accepting life in the fullness thereof and going through it with song and dance. Gandhi, more a man of the people, almost the embodiment of the Indian peasant, represented the other ancient tradition of India, that of renunciation and asceticism. And yet Tagore was primarily the man of thought, Gandhi of concentrated and ceaseless activity. Both, in their different ways, had a world outlook, and both were at the same time wholly India. They seemed to represent different but harmonious aspects of India and to complement one another.

Tagore and Gandhi bring us to our present age. But we were considering an earlier period and the effect produced on the people, and especially the Hindus, by the stress laid by Vivekananda and others on the past greatness of India and their pride in it. Vivekananda himself was careful to warn his people not to dwell too much on the past, but to look to the future. "When, O Lord," he wrote, "shall our land be free from this eternal dwelling upon the past?" But he himself and others had evoked that past, and there was a glamour in it, and no getting away from it.

This looking back to the past and finding comfort and sustenance there was helped by a renewed study of ancient literature and history, and later by the story of the Indian colonies in the eastern seas, as this unfolded itself. Mrs. Annie Besant was a powerful influence in adding to the confidence of the Hindu middle classes in their spiritual and national heritage. There was a spiritual and religious element about all this, and yet there was a strong political background to it. The rising middle classes were politically inclined and were not so much in search of a religion; but they wanted some cultural roots to cling to, something that gave them assurance of their own worth, something that would reduce the sense of frustration and humiliation that foreign conquest and rule had produced. In every country with a growing nationalism there is this search apart from religion, this tendency to go to the past. Iran, without in any way weakening in its religious faith, has deliberately gone back to its pre-Islamic days of greatness and utilized this memory to strengthen its present-day nationalism. So also in other countries. The past of India, with all its cultural variety and greatness, was a common heritage of all the Indian people, Hindu, Moslem, Christian, and others, and their ancestors had helped to build it. The fact of subsequent conversion to other faith did not deprive them of this heritage; just as the Greeks, after their conversion to Christianity, did not lose their pride in the mighty achievements of their ancestors, or the Italians in the great days of the Roman republic and early empire. If all the people of India had been converted to Islam or Christianity, her cultural heritage would still have remained to inspire them and give them that poise and dignity which a long record of civilized existence with all its mental struggles with the problems of life gives a people.

If we had been an independent nation, all of us in this country, working together in the present for a common future, would no doubt have looked to our common past with equal pride. Indeed, during the Moghul period, the emperors and their chief associates, newcomers as they were, wanted to identify themselves with that past and to share it with others. But the accidents and processes of history, helped no doubt by man's policy and weaknesses, worked differently, and the changes which came prevented normal development. One would have expected that the new middle class, which was the product of the impact from the West and of technological and economic changes, would have a common background in Hindu and Moslem alike. To some extent this was so, and yet differences arose which were not present, or were present in far lesser degree, in the feudal and semifeudal classes and the masses. The Hindu and Moslem masses were hardly distinguishable from each other; the old aristocracy had developed common ways and standards. They yet followed a common culture and had common customs and festivals. The middle classes began to diverge psychologically and later in other ways.

To begin with, the new middle classes were almost absent among the Moslems. Their avoidance of Western education, their keeping away from trade and industry, and their adherence to feudal ways gave a start to the Hindus, which they profited by and retained. British policy was inclined to be pro-Hindu and anti-Moslem, except in the Punjab, where Moslems took more easily to Western education than elsewhere. But the Hindus had got a big start elsewhere long before the British took possession of the Punjab. Even in the Punjab, though conditions were more nearly equal for the Hindu and Moslem, the Hindus had an economic advantage. Antiforeign sentiment was shared alike by the Hindu and Moslem aristocracy and the masses. The revolt of 1857 was a joint affair, but in its suppression Moslems felt strongly, and to some extent rightly, that they were the greater sufferers. This revolt also put an end finally to any dreams or fantasies of the revival of the Delhi empire. That empire had vanished long ago, even before the British arrived upon the scene. The Marathas had smashed it and controlled Delhi itself. Ranjit Singh ruled in the Punjab. Moghul rule had ended in the north without any intervention of the British, and in the south also it had disintegrated. Yet the shadow emperor sat in the Delhi palace, and though he had become a dependent and pensioner of the Marathas and the British successively, still he was a symbol of a famous dynasty. Inevitably during the revolt the rebels tried to take advantage of this symbol, in spite of his weakness and unwillingness. The ending of the revolt meant also the smashing of the symbol.

As the people recovered slowly from the horror of the Mutiny days, there was a blank in their minds, a vacuum which sought for something to fill it. Of necessity, British rule had to be accepted, but the break with the past had brought something more than a new government. It had brought doubt and confusion and a loss of faith in themselves. That break indeed had come long before the Mutiny and had led to the many movements of thought in Bengal and elsewhere to which I have already referred. But the Moslems generally had then retired into their shells far more than the Hindus, avoided Western education, and lived in daydreams of a restoration of the old order. There could be no more dreaming now, but there had to be something to which they could cling. They still kept away from the new education. Gradually and after much debate and difficulty, Sir Syed Ahmad Khan turned their minds toward English education and started the Aligarh College. That was the only avenue leading to government service, and the lure of that service proved powerful enough to overcome old resentments and prejudices. The fact that Hindus had gone far ahead in education and service was disliked and proved a powerful argument to do likewise. Parsis and Hindus were also going ahead in industry, but Moslem attention was directed to government service alone.

But even this new direction to their activities, which was really confined to comparatively few, did not resolve the doubt and confusion of their minds. Hindus, in like straits, had looked back and sought consolation in ancient times. Old philosophy and literature, art and history had brought some comfort. Ram Mohan Roy, Dayananda, Vivekananda, and others had started new movements of thought. While they drank from the rich streams of English literature, their minds were also full of ancient sages and heroes of India, their thoughts and deeds, and the myths and traditions which they had imbibed from their childhood.

Much of this was common to the Moslem masses, who were well acquainted with these traditions. But it began to be felt, especially by the Moslem upper classes, that it was not quite proper for them to associate themselves with these semireligious traditions, that any encouragement of them would be against the spirit of Islam. They searched for their national roots elsewhere. To some extent they found them in the Afghan and Moghul periods of India, but this was not quite enough to fill the vacuum. Those periods were common for Hindus and Moslems alike, and the sense of foreign intrusion had disappeared from Hindu

minds. The Moghul rulers were looked upon as Indian national rulers, though in the case of Aurungzeb there was a
difference of opinion. It is significant that Akbar, whom
the Hindus especially admired, has not been approved of
in recent years by some Moslems. Lately the four hundredth anniversary of his birth was celebrated in India;
all classes of people, including many Moslems, joined, but
the Moslem League kept aloof because Akbar was a symbol
of India's unity.

This search for cultural roots led Indian Moslems (that
is some of them of the middle class) to Islamic history
and to the periods when Islam was a conquering and
creative force in Baghdad, Spain, Constantinople, central
Asia, and elsewhere. There had always been interest in this
history and some contacts with neighboring Islamic countries. There was also the Haj pilgrimage to Mecca which
brought Moslems from various countries together. But all
such contacts were limited and superficial and did not
really affect the general outlook of Indian Moslems, which
was confined to India. The Afghan kings of Delhi, especially Muhammad Tughlak, had acknowledged the khalifa
at Cairo. The Ottoman emperors at Constantinople subsequently became the khalifas, but they were not recognized as such in India. The Moghul emperors in India
recognized no khalifa or spiritual superiors outside India.
It was only after the complete collapse of the Moghul
power early in the nineteenth century that the name of
the Turkish sultan began to be mentioned in Indian
mosques. This practice was confirmed after the Mutiny.

Thus Indian Moslems sought to derive some psychological satisfaction from a contemplation of Islam's past greatness, chiefly in other countries, and in the fact of the continuance of Turkey as an independent Moslem power,
practically the only one left. This feeling was not opposed
to or in conflict with Indian nationalism. Indeed many
Hindus admired and were well acquainted with Islamic history. They sympathized with Turkey because they looked
on the Turks as Asiatic victims of European aggression. Yet
the emphasis was different, and in their case that feeling

did not supply a psychological need as it did in the case of the Moslems.

After the Mutiny, the Indian Moslems had hesitated which way to turn. The British government had deliberately repressed them to an even greater degree than it had repressed the Hindus, and this repression had especially affected those sections of the Moslems from which the new middle class, the bourgeoisie, might have been drawn. They felt down-and-out and were intensely anti-British as well as conservative. British policy toward them underwent a gradual change in the seventies and became more favorable. This change was essentially due to the policy of balance and counterpoise which the British government had consistently pursued. Still, in this process Sir Syed Ahmad Khan played an important part. He was convinced that he could only raise the Moslems through co-operation with the British authorities. He was anxious to make them accept English education and thus to draw them out of their conservative shells. He had been much impressed by what he had seen of European civilization, and indeed some of his letters from Europe indicate that he was so dazed that he had rather lost his balance.

Sir Syed was an ardent reformer, and he wanted to reconcile modern scientific thought with Islam. This was to be done, of course, not by attacking any basic belief but by a rationalistic interpretation of scripture. He pointed out the basic similarities between Islam and Christianity. He attacked purdah, the seclusion of women, among the Moslems. He was opposed to any allegiance to the Turkish khalifat. Above all, he was anxious to push a new type of education. The beginnings of the national movement frightened him, for he thought that any opposition to the British authorities would deprive him of their help in his educational program. That help appeared to him to be essential, and so he tried to tone down anti-British sentiments among the Moslems and to turn away from the National Congress which was taking shape then. One of the declared objects of the Aligarh College he founded was "to make the Mussalmans of India worthy and useful subjects of the British Crown." He was not opposed to the National

Congress because he considered it predominantly a Hindu organization; he opposed it because he thought it was politically too agressive (though it was mild enough in those days), and he wanted British help and co-operation. He tried to show that Moslems as a whole had not rebelled during the Mutiny and that many had remained loyal to the British power. He was in no way anti-Hindu or communally separatist. Repeatedly he emphasized that religious differences should have no political or national significance. "Do you not inhabit the same land?" he said. "Remember that the words Hindu and Muhomedan are only meant for religious distinction—otherwise all persons, whether Hindu or Muhomedan, even the Christians who reside in this country are all in this particular respect belonging to one and the same nation."

Sir Syed Ahmad Khan's influence was confined to certain sections of the upper classes among the Moslems; he did not touch the urban or rural masses. These masses were almost completely cut off from their upper classes and were far nearer to the Hindu masses. While some among the Moslem upper classes were descendants of the ruling groups during Moghul times, the masses had no such background or tradition. Most of them had been converted from the lowest strata of Hindu society and were most unhappily situated, being among the poorest and the most exploited.

Sir Syed had a number of able and notable colleagues. In his rationalistic approach he was supported, among others, by Syed Chirag Ali and Nawab Mohsin-ul-Mulk. His educational activities attracted Munshi Karamat Ali, Munshi Zakaullah of Delhi, Dr. Nazir Ahmad, Maulana Shibli Nomani, and the poet Hali, who is one of the outstanding figures of Urdu literature. Sir Syed succeeded in so far as the beginnings of English education among the Moslems were concerned, and in diverting the Moslem mind from the political movement. A Mohammedan educational conference was started, and this attracted the rising Moslem middle class in the professions and services.

None the less many prominent Moslems joined the National Congress. British policy became definitely pro-

Moslem, or rather in favor of those elements among the Moslems who were opposed to the national movement. But early in the twentieth century the tendency toward nationalism and political activity became more noticeable among the younger generation of Moslems. To divert this and provide a safe channel for it, the Moslem League was started in 1906 under the inspiration of the British government and the leadership of one of its chief supporters, the Aga Khan. The League had two principal objects: loyalty to the British government and the safeguarding of Moslem interests.

It is worth noting that during the post-Mutiny period all the leading men among Indian Moslems, including Sir Syed Ahmad Khan, were products of the old traditional education, although some of them added knowledge of English later and were influenced by new ideas. The new Western education had yet produced no notable figure among them. The leading poet in Urdu and one of the outstanding literary figures of the century in India was Ghalib, who was in his prime before the Mutiny.

In the early years of the twentieth century there were two trends among the Moslem intelligentsia: one, chiefly among the younger element, was toward nationalism; the other was a deviation from India's past and even, to some extent, her present, and a greater interest in Islamic countries, especially Turkey, the seat of the khalifat. The pan-Islamic movement, encouraged by Sultan Abdul Hamid of Turkey, had found some response in the upper strata of Indian Moslems, and yet Sir Syed had opposed this and written against Indians interesting themselves in Turkey and the sultanate. The Young Turk movement produced mixed reactions. It was looked upon with some suspicion by most Moslems in India to begin with, and there was general sympathy for the sultan, who was considered a bulwark against the intrigues of European powers in Turkey. But there were others, among them Abul Kalam Azad, who eagerly welcomed the Young Turks and the promise of constitutional and social reform that they brought. When Italy suddenly attacked Turkey in the Tripoli war of 1911, and subsequently during the Balkan wars of 1912 and 1913, an astonishing wave of sympathy for Turkey roused Indian Moslems. All Indians felt that sympathy and anxiety, but in the case of Moslems this was keener and something almost personal. The last remaining Moslem power was threatened with extinction; the sheet anchor of their faith in the future was being destroyed. Dr. M. A. Ansari led a strong medical mission to Turkey and even the poor subscribed; money came more rapidly than for any proposal for the uplift of the Indian Moslems themselves. World War I was a time of trial for the Moslems because Turkey was on the other side. They felt helpless and could do nothing. When the war ended, their pent-up feelings were to break out in the Khalifat movement.

The year 1912 was notable also in the development of the Moslem mind in India because of the appearance of the two new weeklies—the *Al-Hilal* in Urdu and the *Comrade* in English. The *Al-Hilal* was started by Abul Kalam Azad (the present Congress president), then a brilliant young man of twenty-four, who had received his early education in Al Azhar University of Cairo, and while yet in his teens had become well known for his Arabic and Persian scholarship and deep learning. To this he added a knowledge of the Islamic world outside India and of the reform movements that were coursing through it, as well as of European developments. Rationalist in outlook and yet profoundly versed in Islamic lore and history, he interpreted scripture from a rationalist point of view. Soaked in Islamic tradition and with many personal contacts with prominent Moslem leaders and reformers in Egypt, Turkey, Syria, Palestine, Iraq, and Iran, he was powerfully affected by political and cultural developments in these countries. Because of his writings he was known in the Islamic countries more, probably, than any other Indian Moslem. The wars in which Turkey became involved aroused his intense interest and sympathy. And yet his approach was different from that of the older Moslem leaders. He had a wider and more rationalist outlook, which kept him away from the feudal and narrowly religious and separatist approach of these older leaders and inevitably made him an Indian nationalist. He had himself seen nationalism growing in

Turkey and the other Islamic countries, and he applied that knowledge to India and saw in the Indian national movement a similar development. Other Moslems in India were hardly aware of these movements elsewhere, and, wrapped up in their own feudal atmosphere, had little appreciation of what was happening there. They thought in religious terms only, and if they sympathized with Turkey it was chiefly because of that religious bond. In spite of that intense sympathy, they were not in tune with the nationalist and rather secular movements in Turkey.

Abul Kalam Azad spoke in a new language to them in his weekly *Al-Hilal*. It was not only a new language in thought and approach; even its texture was different, for Azad's style was tense and virile, though sometimes a little difficult because of its Persian background. He used new phrases for new ideas and was a definite influence in giving shape to the Urdu language as it is today. The older conservative leaders among the Moslems did not react favorably to all this, and criticized Azad's opinions and approach. Yet not even the most learned of them could easily meet Azad in debate and argument, even on the basis of scripture and old tradition, for Azad's knowledge of these happened to be greater than theirs. He was a strange mixture of medieval scholasticism, eighteenth-century rationalism, and the modern outlook.

There were a few among the older generation who approved of Azad's writings, among them being the learned Maulana Shibli Nomani, who had himself visited Turkey, and who had been associated with Sir Syed Ahmad Khan in Aligarh College. The tradition of Aligarh College was, however, different and conservative, both politically and socially. Its trustees came from among the princes and big landlords, typical representatives of the feudal order. Under a succession of English principals closely associated with government circles, it had fostered separatist tendencies and an antinationalist and anti-Congress outlook. The chief aim kept before its students was to enter government service in the subordinate ranks. For that a pro-government attitude was necessary, and no truck with nationalism and sedition. The Aligarh College group had become the leaders of the new Moslem intelligentsia and influenced sometimes openly, more often from behind the scenes, almost every Moslem movement. The Moslem League came into existence largely through their efforts.

Abul Kalam Azad attacked this stronghold of conservatism and antinationalism, not directly but by spreading ideas which undermined the Aligarh tradition. This very youthful writer and journalist created a sensation in Moslem intellectual circles, and though the elders frowned upon him, his words created a ferment in the minds of the younger generation. That ferment had already started because of events in Turkey, Egypt, and Iran, as well as the development of the Indian nationalist movement. Azad gave a definite trend to it by pointing out that there was no conflict between Islam and sympathy for Islamic countries, and Indian nationalism. This helped in bringing the Moslem League nearer to the Congress. Azad had himself joined the League, while yet a boy, at its first session in 1906.

The *Al-Hilal* was not approved of by the representatives of the British government. Securities were demanded from it under the Press Act, and ultimately its press was confiscated in 1914. Thus ended the *Al-Hilal* after a brief existence of two years. Azad thereupon brought out another weekly, the *Al-Balugh*, but this, too, ended in 1916 when Azad was interned by the British government. For nearly four years he was kept in internment, and when he came out at last, he took his place immediately among the leaders of the National Congress. Ever since then he has been continuously in the highest Congress executive, looked upon, in spite of his youthful years, as one of the elders of the Congress, whose advice both in national and political matters, as well as in regard to the communal and minority questions, is highly valued. Twice he has been Congress president, and repeatedly he has spent long terms in prison.

The other weekly that was started in 1912, some months before the *Al-Hilal*, was the *Comrade*. This was in English, and it influenced especially the younger English-educated generation of Moslems. It was edited by Maulana Mohammed Ali, who was an odd mixture of Islamic tradition and an Oxford education. He began as an adherent of the Aligarh tradition and was opposed to any aggressive politics. But he was far too able and dynamic a personality to remain confined in that static framework, and his language was always vigorous and striking. The annulment of the partition of Bengal in 1911 had given him a shock, and his faith in the *bona fides* of the British government had been shaken. The Balkan wars moved him, and he wrote passionately in favor of Turkey and the Islamic tradition it represented. Progressively he grew more anti-British, and the entry of Turkey in World War I completed the process. A famous and enormously long article of his (his speeches and writings did not err on the side of brevity or conciseness) in the *Comrade* entitled "The Choice of the Turks" put an end to the *Comrade*, which was stopped by the government. Soon after, the government arrested him and his brother Shaukat Ali and interned them for the duration of the war and a year after. They were released at the end of 1919, and both immediately joined the National Congress. The Ali brothers played a very prominent part in the khalifat agitation and in Congress politics in the early twenties, and suffered prison for it. Mohammed Ali presided over an annual session of the Congress and was for many years a member of its highest executive committee. He died in 1930.

The change that took place in Mohammed Ali was symbolic of the changing mentality of the Indian Moslems. Even the Moslem League, founded to isolate the Moslems from nationalist currents, and completely controlled by reactionary and semifeudal elements, was forced to recognize the pressure from the younger generation. It was drifting, though somewhat unwillingly, with the tide of nationalism and coming nearer to the Congress. In 1913 it changed its creed of loyalty to government to a demand for self-government for India. Maulana Abul Kalam Azad had advocated this change in his forceful writings in the *Al-Hilal*.

*Pandit Nehru provides a brief account of developments in India in the years prior to the first World War, emphasizing the development of separate electorates for the major religious communities and the activity of nationalist leaders such as Bal G. Tilak, with whose name is associated the growth of "extremism" in Indian political life. This brings the account up to the rise of Gandhi to prominence in the Congress Party.*

# VII. The Last Phase:
# (2) Nationalism Versus Imperialism

## I. HELPLESSNESS OF THE MIDDLE CLASSES
### GANDHI COMES

World War I came. Politics were at a low ebb, chiefly because of the split in the Congress between the two sections, the so-called Extremists and the Moderates, and because of wartime restrictions and regulations. Yet one tendency was marked: the rising middle class among the Moslems was growing more nationally minded and was pushing the Moslem League toward the Congress. They even joined hands.

Industry developed during the war and produced enormous dividends—100 to 200 per cent—from the jute mills of Bengal and the cotton mills of Bombay, Ahmadabad, and elsewhere. Some of these dividends flowed to the owners of foreign capital in Dundee and London; some went to swell the riches of Indian millionaires. And yet the workers who had created these dividends lived at an incredibly low level of existence—in "filthy, disease-ridden hovels" with no window or chimney, no light or water supply, no sanitary arrangements. This, near that so-called city of palaces, Calcutta, dominated by British capital. In Bombay, where Indian capital was more in evidence, an inquiry commission found in one room, 15 feet by 12, six families, in all thirty adults and children, living together. Three of these women were expecting a confinement soon, and each family had a separate oven in that one room. These are special cases, but they are not very exceptional. They describe conditions in the twenties and thirties of this century when some improvements had already been made.

What these conditions were like previous to these improvements staggers the imagination.[1]

I remember visiting some of these slums and hovels of industrial workers, gasping for breath there, and coming out dazed and full of horror and anger. I remember also going down a coal mine in Jharia and seeing the conditions in which our womenfolk worked there. I can never forget that picture or the shock that came to me that human beings should labor thus. Women were subsequently prohibited from working underground. But now they have been sent back there because, we are told, war needs require additional labor. And yet millions of men are starving and unemployed; there is no lack of men. But the wages are so low and the conditions of work so bad that they do not attract.

A delegation sent by the British Trade Union Congress visited India in 1928. In their report they said that "in Assam tea the sweat, hunger, and despair of a million Indians enter year by year." The director of public health in Bengal in his report for 1927–28 said that the peasantry of that province were "taking to a dietary on which even rats could not live for more than five weeks."

World War I ended at last and the peace, instead of bringing us relief and progress, brought us repressive legislation and martial law in the Punjab. A bitter sense of humiliation and a passionate anger filled our people. All the unending talk of constitutional reform and indianization of the services was a mockery and an insult when the manhood of our country was being crushed and the inexorable and continuous process of exploitation was deepening our poverty and sapping our vitality. We had become a derelict nation.

Yet what could we do, how change this vicious process? We seemed to be helpless in the grip of some all-powerful monster; our limbs were paralyzed, our minds deadened. The peasantry were servile and fear-ridden; the industrial workers were no better. The middle classes, the intelligent-

[1] These quotations and facts are taken from B. Shiva Rao's *The Industrial Worker in India* (Allen & Unwin, London, 1939), which deals with labor problems and workers' conditions in India.

sia, who might have been beacon lights in the enveloping darkness, were themselves submerged in this all-pervading gloom. In some ways their condition was even more pitiful than that of the peasantry. Large numbers of the *déclassé* intellectuals, cut off from the land and incapable of any kind of manual or technical work, joined the swelling army of the unemployed, and helpless, hopeless, sank ever deeper into the morass. A few successful lawyers or doctors or engineers or clerks made little difference to the mass. The peasant starved; yet centuries of an unequal struggle against his environment had taught him to endure, and even in poverty and starvation he had a certain calm dignity, a feeling of submission to an all-powerful fate. Not so the middle classes, more especially the new petty bourgeoisie, who had no such background. Incompletely developed, and frustrated, they did not know where to look, for neither the old nor the new offered them any hope. There was no adjustment to social purpose, no satisfaction of doing something worth while, even though suffering came in its train. Custom-ridden, they were born old, yet they were without the old culture. Modern thought attracted them, but they lacked its inner content, the modern social and scientific consciousness. Some tried to cling tenaciously to the dead forms of the past, seeking relief from present misery in them. But there could be no relief there, for, as Tagore has said, we must not nourish in our being what is dead, for the dead is death-dealing. Others made themselves pale and ineffectual copies of the West. So, like derelicts, frantically seeking some foothold of security for body and mind and finding none, they floated aimlessly in the murky waters of Indian life.

What could we do? How could we pull India out of this quagmire of poverty and defeatism which sucked her in? Not for a few years of excitement and agony and suspense, but for long generations our people had offered their "blood, toil, sweat and tears." And this process had eaten its way deep into the body and soul of India, poisoning every aspect of our corporate life, like that fell disease which consumes the tissues of the lungs and kills slowly but inevitably. Sometimes we thought that some swifter and more obvious process, resembling cholera or the bubonic plague, would have been better. But that was a passing thought, for adventurism leads nowhere, and the quack treatment of deep-seated diseases does not yield results.

And then Gandhi came. He was like a powerful current of fresh air that made us stretch ourselves and take deep breaths, like a beam of light that pierced the darkness and removed the scales from our eyes, like a whirlwind that upset many things but most of all the working of people's minds. He did not descend from the top; he seemed to emerge from the millions of India, speaking their language and incessantly drawing attention to them and their appalling condition. Get off the backs of these peasants and workers, he told us, all you who live by their exploitation; get rid of the system that produces this poverty and misery.

Political freedom took new shape then and acquired a new content. Much that he said we only partially accepted or sometimes did not accept at all. But all this was secondary. The essence of his teaching was fearlessness and truth and action allied to these, always keeping the welfare of the masses in view. The greatest gift for an individual or a nation, so we had been told in our ancient books, was *abhaya*, fearlessness, not merely bodily courage but the absence of fear from the mind. Chanakya and Yagnavalka had said, at the dawn of our history, that it was the function of the leaders of a people to make them fearless. But the dominant impulse in India under British rule was that of fear, pervasive, oppressing, strangling fear; fear of the army, the police, the widespread secret service; fear of the official class; fear of laws meant to suppress, and of prison; fear of the landlord's agent; fear of the moneylender; fear of unemployment and starvation, which were always on the threshold. It was against this all-pervading fear that Gandhi's quiet and determined voice was raised: Be not afraid.

Was it so simple as all that? Not quite. And yet fear builds its phantoms which are more fearsome than reality itself, and reality when calmly analyzed and its consequences willingly accepted loses much of its terror.

So, suddenly as it were, that black pall of fear was lifted

from the people's shoulders, not wholly, of course, but to an amazing degree. As fear is close companion to falsehood, so truth follows fearlessness. The Indian people did not become much more truthful than they were, nor did they change their essential nature overnight; nevertheless a sea change was visible as the need for falsehood and furtive behavior lessened. It was a psychological change, almost as if some expert in psychoanalytical method had probed deep into the patient's past, found out the origins of his complexes, exposed them to his view, and thus rid him of that burden.

There was that psychological reaction also, a feeling of shame at our long submission to an alien rule that had degraded and humiliated us, and a desire to submit no longer, whatever the consequences might be. We did not grow much more truthful, perhaps, than we had been previously, but Gandhi was always there as a symbol of uncompromising truth to pull us up and shame us into truth.

What is truth? I do not know for certain, and perhaps our truths are relative and absolute truth is beyond us. Different persons may and do take different views of truth, and each individual is powerfully influenced by his own background, training, and impulses. So also Gandhi. But truth is at least for an individual what he himself feels and knows to be true. According to that definition I do not know of any person who holds to the truth as Gandhi does. That is a dangerous quality in a politician, for he speaks out his mind and even lets the public see its changing phases.

Gandhi influenced millions of people in India in varying degrees; some changed the whole texture of their lives, others were only partly affected, or the effect wore off, and yet not quite, for some part of it could not be wholly shaken off. Different people reacted differently, and each will give his own answer to this question. Some might well say almost in the words of Alcibiades: "Besides, when we listen to any one else talking, however eloquent he is, we don't really care a damn what he says; but when we listen to you, or to someone else repeating what you've said, even if he puts it ever so badly, and never mind whether the person who is listening is man, woman, or child, we're absolutely staggered and bewitched. And speaking for myself, gentle-men, if I wasn't afraid you'd tell me I was completely bot-tled, I'd swear on oath what an extraordinary effect his words have had on me—and still do, if it comes to that. For the moment I hear him speak I am smitten by a kind of sacred rage, worse than any Corybant, and my heart jumps into my mouth and the tears start into my eyes—Oh, and not only me, but lots of other men.

"Yes, I have heard Pericles and all the other great ora-tors, and very eloquent I thought they were; but they never affected me like that; they never turned my whole soul up-side down and left me feeling as if I were the lowest of the low; but this latter day Maryas, here, has often left me in such a state of mind that I've felt I simply couldn't go on living the way I did. . . .

"And there is one thing I've never felt with anybody else —not the kind of thing you would expect to find in me, either—and that is a sense of shame. Socrates is the only man in the world that can make me feel ashamed. Because there's no getting away from it, I know I ought to do the things he tells me to; and yet the moment I'm out of his sight I don't care what I do to keep in with the mob. So I dash off like a runaway slave, and keep out of his way as long as I can: and then next time I meet him I remember all that I had to admit the time before, and naturally I feel ashamed. . . .

"Only I've been bitten by something much more poison-ous than a snake; in fact, mine is the most painful kind of bite there is. I've been bitten in the heart, or the mind, or whatever you like to call it. . . ."[2]


## II. THE CONGRESS BECOMES A DYNAMIC
## ORGANIZATION UNDER GANDHI'S LEADERSHIP

Gandhi for the first time entered the Congress organization and immediately brought about a complete change in its

[2] From *The Five Dialogues of Plato*, Everyman's Library.

constitution. He made it democratic and a mass organization. Democratic it had been previously also, but it had so far been limited in franchise and restricted to the upper classes. Now the peasants rolled in, and in its new garb it began to assume the look of a vast agrarian organization with a strong sprinkling of the middle classes. This agrarian character was to grow. Industrial workers also came in, but as individuals and not in their separate, organized capacity.

Action was to be the basis and objective of this organization, action based on peaceful methods. Thus far the alternatives had been: just talking and passing resolutions, or terroristic activity. Both of these were set aside, and terrorism was especially condemned as opposed to the basic policy of the Congress. A new technique of action was evolved which, though perfectly peaceful, yet involved nonsubmission to what was considered wrong, and as a consequence, a willing acceptance of the pain and suffering involved in this. Gandhi was an odd kind of pacifist, for he was an activist full of dynamic energy. There was no submission in him to fate or anything that he considered evil; he was full of resistance, though this was peaceful and courteous.

The call of action was twofold. There was of course the action involved in challenging and resisting foreign rules; there was also the action which led us to fight our own social evils. Apart from the fundamental objective of the Congress—the freedom of India—and the method of peaceful action, the principal planks of the Congress were national unity, which involved the solution of the minority problems, and the raising of the depressed classes and the ending of the curse of untouchability.

Realizing that the main props of British rule were fear, prestige, the co-operation, willing or unwilling, of the people, and certain classes whose vested interests were centered in British rule, Gandhi attacked these foundations. Titles were to be given up, and though the titleholders responded to this only in small measure, the popular respect for these British-given titles disappeared and they became symbols of degradation. New standards and values were set up, and the pomp and splendor of the viceregal court and the princes, which used to impress so much, suddenly appeared supremely ridiculous and vulgar and rather shameful, surrounded as they were by the poverty and misery of the people. Rich men were not so anxious to flaunt their riches; outwardly at least many of them adopted simpler ways, and in their dress became almost indistinguishable from humbler folk.

The older leaders of the Congress, nurtured in a different and more quiescent tradition, did not take easily to these new ways and were disturbed by the upsurge of the masses. Yet so powerful was the wave of feeling and sentiment that swept through the country that some of that intoxication filled them also. A very few fell away, and among them was Mr. M. A. Jinnah. He left the Congress not because of any difference of opinion on the Hindu-Moslem question but because he could not adapt himself to the new and more advanced ideology, and even more because he disliked the crowds of ill-dressed people, talking in Hindustani, who filled the Congress. His idea of politics was of a superior variety, more suited to the legislative chamber or to a committee room. For some years he felt completely out of the picture and even decided to leave India for good. He settled down in England and spent several years there.

It is said, and I think with truth, that the Indian habit of mind is essentially one of quietism. Perhaps old races develop that attitude to life; a long tradition of philosophy also leads to it. And yet Gandhi, a typical product of India, represents the very antithesis of quietism. He has been a demon of energy and action, a hustler, and a man who not only drives himself but drives others. He has done more than anyone I know to fight and change the pietism of the Indian people.

He sent us to the villages, and the countryside hummed with the activity of innumerable messengers of the new gospel of action. The peasant was shaken up and he began to emerge from his quiescent shell. The effect on us was different but equally far-reaching, for we saw, for the first time as it were, the villager in the intimacy of his mud hut and with the stark shadow of hunger always pursuing him. We learned our Indian economics more from these visits than from books and learned discourses. The emotional experience we had already undergone was emphasized and confirmed, and henceforward there could be no going back for us to our old life or our old standards, howsoever much our views might change subsequently.

Gandhi held strong views on economic, social, and other matters. He did not try to impose all of these on the Congress, though he continued to develop his ideas, and sometimes in the process varied them, through his writings. But some he tried to push into the Congress. He proceeded cautiously, for he wanted to carry the people with him. Sometimes he went too far for the Congress and had to retrace his steps. Not many accepted his views in their entirety; some disagreed with that fundamental outlook. But many accepted them in the modified form, in which they came to the Congress as being suited to the circumstances then existing. In two respects the background of his thoughts had a vague but considerable influence: the fundamental test of everything was how far it benefited the masses, and the means were always important and could not be ignored even though the end in view was right, for the means governed the end and varied it.

Gandhi was essentially a man of religion, a Hindu to the innermost depths of his being, and yet his conception of religion had nothing to do with any dogma or custom or ritual.[3] It was basically concerned with his firm belief in the moral law, which he calls the Law of Truth or Love. Truth and nonviolence appear to him to be the same thing or different aspects of one and the same thing, and he uses these words almost interchangeably.

Claiming to understand the spirit of Hinduism, he re-

[3] Gandhi told the Federation of International Fellowships in January 1928 that "after long study and experience I have come to these conclusions, that: (1) all religions are true, (2) all religions have some error in them, (3) all religions are almost as dear to me as my own Hinduism. My veneration for other faiths is the same as for my own faith. Consequently, the thought of conversion is impossible. . . . Our prayer for others ought never to be: 'God! give them the light thou hast given to me!' but: 'Give them all the light and truth they need for their highest development!' "

jects every text or practice which does not fit in with his idealist interpretation of what it should be, calling it an interpolation or a subsequent accretion. "I decline to be a slave," he has said, "to precedents or practice I cannot understand or defend on a moral basis." And so in practice he is singularly free to take the path of his choice, to change and adapt himself, to develop his philosophy of life and action, subject only to the overriding consideration of the moral law as he conceives this to be. Whether that philosophy is right or wrong may be argued, but he insists on applying the same fundamental yardstick to everything, and himself specially. In politics, as in other aspects of life, this creates difficulties for the average person, and often misunderstanding. But no difficulty makes him swerve from the straight line of his choosing, though within limits he is continually adapting himself to a changing situation. Every reform that he suggests, every advice that he gives to others, he straightway applies to himself. He is always beginning with himself, and his words and actions fit into each other like a glove on the hand. And so, whatever happens, he never loses his integrity and there is always an organic completeness about his life and work. Even in his apparent failures he has seemed to grow in stature.

What was his idea of India which he was setting out to mold according to his own wishes and ideals? "I shall work for an India in which the poorest shall feel that it is their country, in whose making they have an effective voice, an India in which there shall be no high class and low class of people, an India in which all communities shall live in perfect harmony. . . . There can be no room in such an India for the curse of untouchability or the curse of intoxicating drinks and drugs. . . . Women who will enjoy the same rights as men. . . . This is the India of my dreams."

Proud of his Hindu inheritance as he was, he tried to give to Hinduism a kind of universal attire and included all religions within the fold of truth. He refused to narrow his cultural inheritance. "Indian culture," he wrote, "is neither Hindu, Islamic nor any other, wholly. It is a fusion of all." Again he said: "I want the culture of all lands to be blown about my house as freely as possible. But I refuse to be blown off my feet by any. I refuse to live in other people's houses as an interloper, a beggar or a slave." Influenced by modern thought currents, he never let go of his roots and clung to them tenaciously.

And so he set about to restore the spiritual unity of the people and to break the barrier between the small westernized group at the top and the masses, to discover the living elements in the old roots and to build upon them, to waken these masses out of their stupor and static condition and make them dynamic. In his single-track and yet many-sided nature the dominating impression that one gathered was his identification with the masses, a community of spirit with them, an amazing sense of unity with the dispossessed and poverty-stricken not only of India but of the world. Even religion, as everything else, took second place to his passion to raise these submerged people. "A semi-starved nation can have neither religion nor art nor organization." "Whatever can be useful to starving millions is beautiful to my mind. Let us give today first the vital things of life, and all the graces and ornaments of life will follow. . . . I want art and literature that can speak to millions." These unhappy dispossessed millions haunted him, and everything seemed to revolve round them. "For millions it is an eternal vigil or an eternal trance." His ambition, he said, was "to wipe every tear from every eye."

It is not surprising that this astonishingly vital man, full of self-confidence and an unusual kind of power, standing for equality and freedom for each individual, but measuring all this in terms of the poorest, fascinated the masses of India and attracted them like a magnet. He seemed to them to link up the past with the future and to make the dismal present appear just as a steppingstone to that future of life and hope. And not the masses only, but intellectuals and others also, though their minds were often troubled and confused and the change-over for them from the habits of lifetimes was more difficult. Thus he effected a vast psychological revolution not only among those who followed his lead but also among his opponents and those many neutrals who could not make up their minds what to think and what to do.

Congress was dominated by Gandhi, and yet it was a peculiar domination, for the Congress was an active, rebellious, many-sided organization, full of variety of opinion, and not easily led this way or that. Often Gandhi toned down his position to meet the wishes of others; sometimes he accepted even an adverse decision. On some vital matters for him he was adamant, and on more than one occasion there came a break between him and the Congress. But always he was the symbol of India's independence and militant nationalism, the unyielding opponent of all those who sought to enslave her, and it was as such a symbol that people gathered to him and accepted his lead, even though they disagreed with him on other matters. They did not always accept that lead when there was no active struggle going on, but when the struggle was inevitable, that symbol became all-important and everything else was secondary.

Thus in 1920 the National Congress, and to a large extent the country, took to this new and unexplored path and came into conflict repeatedly with the British power. That conflict was inherent both in these methods and the new situation that had arisen; yet back of all this was not political tactics and maneuvering but the desire to strengthen the Indian people, for by that strength alone could they achieve independence and retain it. Civil disobedience struggles came one after the other, involving enormous suffering, but that suffering was self-invited and therefore strength-giving, not the kind which overwhelms the unwilling, leading to despair and defeatism. The unwilling also suffered, caught in the wide net of fierce governmental repression, and even the willing sometimes broke and collapsed. But many remained true and steadfast, harder for all the experience they had undergone. At no time, even when its fortunes were low, did Congress surrender to superior might or submit to foreign authority. It remained the symbol of India's passionate desire for independence and her will to resist alien domination. It was because of this that vast numbers of the Indian people sympathized with it and looked to it for leadership, even though many of them were too weak and feeble, or so circumstanced as to be unable to do anything themselves. The Congress was a party in some ways; it has also been a joint platform for several parties; but essentially it was something much more, for it represented the innermost desire of vast numbers of our people. The number of members on its rolls, large as this was, was only a feeble reflection of this widespread representative character, for membership depended not on the people's desire to join but on our capacity to reach remote villages. Often (as now) we have been an illegal organization, not existing at all in the eyes of the law, and our books and papers have been taken away by the police.

Even when there was no civil disobedience struggle going on, the general attitude of non-co-operation with the British apparatus of government in India continued, though it lost its aggressive character. That did not mean, of course, non-co-operation with Englishmen as such. When Congress governments were installed in many provinces, there was inevitably much co-operation in official and governmental work. Even then, however, that background did not change much, and instructions were issued regulating the conduct of Congressmen apart from official duties. Between Indian nationalism and an alien imperialism there could be no final peace, though temporary compromises and adjustments were sometimes inevitable. Only a free India could co-operate with England on equal terms.

## III. CONGRESS GOVERNMENTS IN THE PROVINCES

The British parliament, after some years of commissions, committees, and debates, passed a Government of India Act in 1935. This provided for some kind of provincial autonomy and a federal structure, but there were so many reservations and checks that both political and economic power continued to be concentrated in the hands of the British government. Indeed in some ways it confirmed and enlarged the powers of an executive responsible solely to that government. The federal structure was so envisaged as to make any real advance impossible, and no loophole was left for the representatives of the Indian people to interfere with or modify the system of British-controlled administration. Any change or relaxation of this could only come through the British parliament. Thus, reactionary as this structure was, there were not even any seeds in it of self-growth, short of some kind of revolutionary action. The act strengthened the alliance between the British government and the princes, landlords, and other reactionary elements in India. It added to the separate electorates, thus increasing the separatist tendencies. It consolidated the predominant position of British trade, industry, banking, and shipping, and laid down statutory prohibitions against any interference with this position—any "discrimination," it was called. It retained in British hands complete control over Indian finance, military, and foreign affairs. It made the viceroy even more powerful than he had been.[4]

In the limited sphere of provincial autonomy the transfer of authority was, or appeared to be, much greater. Nevertheless the position of a popular government was extraordinary. There were all the checks of viceregal powers and an irresponsible central authority, and even the governor of the province, like the viceroy, could intervene, veto, legislate on his own sole authority, and do almost anything he wanted to even in direct opposition to the popular ministers and the provincial legislature. A great part of the revenues were mortgaged to various vested interests and could not be touched. The superior services and the police were protected and could hardly be touched by the minis-

[4] The removal of these statutory prohibitions is still fiercely resisted by representatives of British industry and trade in India. In April 1945 a resolution demanding this removal was passed in the Central Assembly in spite of British opposition. Indian nationalism and indeed all Indian parties and groups are strongly in favor of this removal, and of course Indian industrialists are most anxious about it. And yet, it is significant to note, Indian businessmen in Ceylon are demanding exactly the same kind of protection in Ceylon which they rightly resent having been given to British business interests in India. Self-interest not only blinds one to justice and fair play but also to the simplest applications of logic and reason.

ters. They were wholly authoritarian in outlook and looked, as of old, to the governor for guidance and not to the ministers. And yet these were the very people through whom the popular government had to function.

The whole complicated structure of government remained as it was, from the governor down to the petty official and policeman; only somewhere in the middle a few ministers, responsible to a popularly elected legislature, were thrust in to carry on as best they could. If the governor (who represented British authority) and the services under him agreed and fully co-operated with the ministers, the apparatus of government might function smoothly. Otherwise—and this was much more likely, as the policy and methods of a popular government differed entirely from the old authoritarian, police-state ways—there was bound to be continuous friction. Even when the governor or the services were not openly at variance with or disloyal to the policy of the popular government, they could obstruct, delay, pervert, and undo what that government did or wished to do. In law there was nothing to prevent the governor and the viceroy from acting as they liked, even in active opposition to the ministry and the legislature; the only real check was fear of conflict. The ministers might resign, no others be able to command a majority in the legislature, and popular upheavals might follow. It was the old constitutional conflict between an autocratic king and parliament which had so often taken place elsewhere, leading to revolutions and the suppression of the king. Here the king was in addition a foreign authority supported by foreign military and economic power and the special interests and lap-dog breed it had created in the country.

The act of 1935 was bitterly opposed by all sections of Indian opinion. While the part dealing with provincial autonomy was severely criticized for its many reservations and the powers given to the governors and the viceroy, the federal part was even more resented. Federation as such was not opposed, and it was generally recognized that a federal structure was desirable for India; but the proposed federation petrified British rule and vested interests in India. Only the provincial autonomy part of it was applied, and the Congress decided to contest elections. But the question whether responsibility for provincial governments should be undertaken, within the terms of the act, led to fierce debate within the Congress. The success of the Congress in the elections was overwhelming in most of the provinces, but still there was hesitation in accepting ministerial responsibility unless it was made clear that there would be no interference by the governor or viceroy.

After some months some vague assurances were given to this effect, and Congress governments were established in July 1937. Ultimately there were such governments in eight of the eleven provinces, the three remaining ones being Sind, Bengal, and Punjab. Sind was a small, newly-created, and rather unstable province. In Bengal the Congress had the largest single party in the legislature, but as it was not in a majority, it did not participate in the government. Bengal (or rather Calcutta) being the principal headquarters of British capital in India, the European commercial element has been given astonishingly heavy representation. In numbers they are a mere handful (some thousands), and yet they have been given 25 seats as compared to the 50 seats for the general non-Moslem population consisting of about 17 millions (apart from the scheduled castes) of the whole province. This British group in the legislature thus plays an important part in Bengal politics and can make or unmake ministries.

The Congress could not possibly accept the act of 1935 as even a temporary solution of the Indian problem. It was pledged to independence and to combat the act. Yet a majority had decided to work provincial autonomy. It had thus a dual policy: to carry on the struggle for independence and at the same time to carry through the legislatures constructive measures of reform. The agrarian question especially demanded immediate attention.

The question of Congressmen joining other groups to form coalition governments was considered, although there was no necessity for this as the Congress had clear majorities. Still it was desirable to associate as many people as possible in the work of government. There was nothing inherently wrong about coalitions at all times, and indeed some form of a coalition was agreed to in the Frontier Province and in Assam. As a matter of fact the Congress itself was a kind of coalition or joint front of various groups tied together by the dominating urge for India's independence. In spite of this variety within its fold, it had developed a discipline, a social outlook, and a capacity to offer battle in its own peaceful way. A wider coalition meant a joining up with people whose entire political and social outlook was different, and who were chiefly interested in office and ministerships. Conflict was inherent in the situation, conflict with the representatives of British interests—the viceroy, the governor, the superior services; conflict also with vested interests in land and industry over agrarian questions and workers' conditions. The non-Congress elements were usually politically and socially conservative; some of them were pure careerists. If such elements entered government, they might tone down our whole social program or at any rate obstruct and delay it. There might even be intrigues with the governor over the heads of the other ministers. A joint front against British authority was essential. Any breach in this would be harmful to our cause. There would have been no binding cement, no common loyalty, no united objective, and individual ministers would have looked and pulled in different directions.

Our public life naturally included many who could be called politicians and nothing more, careerists both in the good and bad sense of the word. There were able, earnest, and patriotic men and women, as well as careerists, both in the Congress and in other organizations. But the Congress had been, ever since 1920, something much more than a constitutional political party, and the breath of revolutionary action, actual or potential, surrounded it and often put it outside the pale of the law. The fact that this action was not connected with violence, secret intrigue, and conspiracy, the usual accompaniments of revolutionary activity, did not make it any the less revolutionary. Whether it was right or wrong, effective or not, may be an arguable matter, but it is manifest that it involved cold-blooded courage and endurance of a high order. Perhaps it is easier to indulge in short, violent spurts of courage, even unto death, than to give up, under the sole compulsion of one's own mind, almost every thing that life offers and carry on in this way day after day, month after month, year after year. That is a test which few can survive anywhere, and it is surprising that so many in India have stood it successfully.

The Congress parties in the legislatures were anxious to pass measures in favor of the peasants and workers as soon as possible before some crisis overwhelmed them. That sense of impending crisis was always present; it was inherent in the situation. In nearly all the provinces there were second chambers elected on a very limited franchise and thus representing vested interests in land and industry. There were also other checks to progressive legislation. Coalition governments would add to all these difficulties, and it was decided not to have them to begin with, except in Assam and the Frontier Province.

This decision was itself by no means final, and the possibility of change was kept in view, but rapidly developing circumstances made any change in it more difficult, and the Congress governments in the provinces became entangled in the numerous problems that urgently demanded solution. In subsequent years there has been much argument about the wisdom of that decision, and opinions have differed. It is easy to be wise after the event, but I am still inclined to think that politically, and situated as we were then, it was a natural and logical decision for us. Nevertheless it is true that the consequences of it on the communal question were unfortunate, and it led to a feeling of grievance and isolation among many Moslems. This played into the hands of reactionary elements who utilized it to strengthen their own position among certain groups.

Politically or constitutionally, the new act or the establishment of Congress governments in the provinces made no vital difference to the British structure of government. Real power remained where it had so long been. But the psychological change was enormous, and an electric current seemed to run through the countryside. This change was noticeable more in the rural areas than in the cities, though in the industrial centers the workers also reacted in the same way. There was a sense of immense relief as of the lifting of a weight which had been oppressing the people; there was a release of long-suppressed mass energy which was evident everywhere. The fear of the police and the secret service agent vanished for a while at least, and even the poorest peasant added to his feeling of self-respect and self-reliance. For the first time he felt that he counted and could not be ignored. Government was no longer an unknown and intangible monster, separated from him by innumerable layers of officials, whom he could not easily approach and much less influence, and who were bent on extracting as much out of him as possible. The seats of the mighty were now occupied by men he had often seen and heard and talked to. Sometimes they had been in prison together, and there was a feeling of comradeship between them.

At the headquarters of the provincial governments, in the very citadels of the old bureaucracy, many a symbolic scene was witnessed. These provincial secretariats, as they were called, where all the high offices were congregated, had been the holy of holies of government, and out of them issued mysterious orders which none could challenge. Policemen and red-liveried orderlies, with shining daggers thrust in their waistbands, guarded the precincts, and only those who were fortunate or greatly daring or had a long purse could pass them. Now, suddenly, hordes of people from the city and the village entered these sacred precincts and roamed about almost at will. They were interested in everything; they went into the Assembly Chamber, where the sessions used to be held; they even peeped into the ministers' rooms. It was difficult to stop them, for they no longer felt as outsiders; they had a sense of ownership in all this, although it was all very complicated for them and difficult to understand. The policemen and the orderlies with shining daggers were paralyzed; the old standards had fallen; European dress, symbol of position and authority, no longer counted. It was difficult to distinguish between members of the legislatures and the peasants and townsmen who came in such large numbers. They were often dressed more or less alike, mostly in handspun cloth with the well-known Gandhi cap on their heads.

It had been very different in the Punjab and in Bengal, where ministries had come into existence several months earlier. There had been no impasse there, and the change-over had taken place quietly without ruffling the surface of life in any way. In the Punjab especially the old order continued and most of the ministers were not new. They had been high officials previously, and they continued to be so. Between them and the British administration there was no conflict or sense of tension, for politically that administration was supreme.

This difference between the Congress provinces and Bengal and the Punjab was immediately apparent in regard to civil liberties and political prisoners. In both Bengal and the Punjab there was no relaxation of the police and secret service raj and political prisoners were not released. In Bengal, where the ministry often depended on European votes, there were in addition thousands of *détenus*, that is, men and women kept indefinitely and for years and years in prison without charge or trial. In the Congress provinces, however, the very first step taken was the release of political prisoners. In regard to some of these, who had been convicted for violent activities, there was delay because of the governor's refusal to agree. Matters came to a head early in 1938 over this issue, and two of the Congress governments (U.P. and Bihar) actually offered their resignations. Thereupon the governor withdrew his objections and the prisoners were released.

## IV. INDIAN DYNAMISM VERSUS BRITISH CONSERVATISM IN INDIA

The new provincial assemblies had a much larger representation from the rural areas, and this inevitably led to a demand in all of them for agrarian reforms. In Bengal, because of the Permanent Settlement and for other reasons, the condition of the tenantry was worst of all. Next came the other big zamindari (landlord) provinces, chiefly Bihar and the United Provinces, and thirdly the provinces where originally some kind of peasant proprietorship had been established (Madras, Bombay, Punjab, etc.) but where big landed estates had also grown up. The Permanent Settlement came in the way of any effective reform in Bengal. Almost everybody is agreed that this must go, and even an official commission has recommended this, but vested interests still manage to prevent or delay change. The Punjab was fortunate in having fresh land at its disposal.

For the Congress the agrarian question was the dominating social issue, and much time had been given to its study and the formulation of policy. This varied in different provinces, as conditions were different and also the class composition of the provincial Congress organizations differed from one another. There was an all-India agrarian policy which had been formulated by the central organization, and each province added to it and filled in the details. The United Provinces Congress was in this respect the most advanced, and it had reached the conclusion that the zamindari (landlord) system should be abolished. This, however, was impossible under the Government of India Act of 1935, even apart from the special powers of the viceroy and the governor and the second chamber, which largely consisted of the landed class. Changes had thus to be made within the larger framework of this system, unless of course some revolutionary upheaval ended that system itself. This made reform difficult and terribly complicated, and it took much longer than was anticipated.

However, substantial agrarian reforms were introduced, and the problem of rural indebtedness was also attacked. So also labor conditions in factories, public health and sanitation, local self-government, education both in the lower stages and in the university, literacy, industry, rural development, and many other problems were tackled. All these social, cultural, and economic problems had been ignored and neglected by previous governments. Their function had been to make the police and the revenue departments efficient and to allow the rest to take their own course. Occasionally some little effort had been made and commissions and inquiry committees had been appointed, which produced huge reports after years of traveling about and labor. Then the reports had been put away in their respective pigeonholes and little was done. Even proper statistics had not been collected, in spite of insistent popular demand. This lack of statistics and surveys and necessary information has been a serious impediment in the way of progress in any direction. Thus the new provincial governments had, apart from the normal work of administration, to face a mountain of work, the result of years of neglect, and on every side urgent problems faced them. They had to change a police state into a socially guided state—never an easy job, but made much more difficult by the limitations on their power, the poverty of the people, and the divergence of outlook between these provincial governments and the central authority, which was completely autocratic and authoritarian, under the viceroy.

We knew all these limitations and barriers. We realized in our hearts that we could not do much till conditions were radically changed—hence our overwhelming desire for independence—and yet the passion for progress filled us, and the wish to emulate other countries which had gone so far ahead in many ways. We thought of the United States of America and even of some Eastern countries which were forging ahead. But most of all we had the example of the Soviet Union, which in two brief decades full of war and civil strife, and in the face of what appeared to be insurmountable difficulties, had made tremendous progress. Some were attracted to communism, others were not, but all were fascinated by the advance of the Soviet Union in education and culture and medical care and physical fitness and in the solution of the problem of nationalities—by the amazing and prodigious effort to create a new world out of the dregs of the old. Even Rabindranath Tagore, highly individualistic as he was and not attracted toward some aspects of the communistic system, became an admirer of this new civilization and contrasted it with present conditions in his own country. In his last deathbed message he referred to the "unsparing energy with which Russia has tried to fight disease and illiteracy, and has succeeded in steadily liquidating ignorance and poverty, wiping off the humiliation from the face of a vast continent. Her civilization is free from all invidious distinction between one class and another, between one sect and another. The rapid and astounding progress achieved by her made me happy and jealous at the same time. . . . When I see elsewhere some two hundred nationalities—which only a few years ago were at vastly different stages of development—marching ahead in peaceful progress and amity, and when I look about my own country and see a very highly evolved and intellectual people drifting into the disorder of barbarism, I cannot help contrasting the two systems of governments, one based on co-operation, the other on exploitation, which have made such contrary conditions possible."

If others could do it, why not we? We had faith in our capacity, our intelligence, our will to persevere, to endure and succeed. We knew the difficulties, our poverty and backwardness, our reactionary groups and classes, our divisions; yet we would face them and overcome them. We knew that the price was a heavy one, but we were prepared to pay for it, for no price could be greater than what we paid from day to day in our present condition. But how were we to begin on our internal problems when the external problem of British rule and occupation faced us at every turn and nullified our every effort?

The introduction of provincial autonomy without any change in the central government, which continued to be wholly irresponsible and authoritarian, was likely to lead to a growth of provincialism and diversity, and thus to a lessening of the sense of Indian unity. Probably the British government had this in view in furtherance of its policy of encouraging disruptive elements and tendencies. The Government of India, irremovable, irresponsible, and unresponsive, still representing the old tradition of British imperialism, stood as solid as a rock and of course pursued a uniform policy toward all the provincial governments. The governors, acting on instructions from New Delhi or Simla, did likewise. If the Congress provincial governments had reacted differently to this, each in its own way, they could have been disposed of separately. It was essential, therefore, for these provincial governments to hold together and present a united front to the Government of India. The Government of India, on the other hand, was equally anxious to prevent this co-operation and preferred to deal with each provincial government separately without reference to similar problems elsewhere.

In August 1937, soon after the formation of the Congress provincial governments, the Congress executive passed the following resolution:

"The Working Committee recommend to the Congress Ministers the appointment of a Committee of Experts to consider urgent and vital problems the solution of which is necessary to any scheme of national reconstruction and social planning. Such solution will require extensive surveys and the collection of data, as well as a clearly defined social objective. Many of these problems cannot be dealt with efficiently on a provincial basis and the interests of adjoining provinces are inter-linked. Comprehensive river surveys are necessary for the formulation of a policy to prevent disastrous floods, to utilize the water for the purposes of irrigation, to consider the problem of soil erosion, to eradicate malaria, and for the development of hydro-electric and other schemes. For this purpose the whole river valley will have to be surveyed and investigated, and large-scale State-planning resorted to. The development and control of industries require also joint and co-ordinate action on the part of several provinces. The Working Committee advise therefore that, to begin with, an inter-provincial committee of experts be appointed to consider the general nature of the problems to be faced, and to suggest how, and in what order, those should be tackled. This Expert Committee may suggest the formation of special committees or boards to consider each such problem separately and to advise the Provincial Governments concerned as to the joint action to be undertaken."

This resolution indicates the kind of advice that was sometimes tendered to the provincial governments. It shows also how desirous the Congress executive was to encourage co-operation between provincial governments in the economic and industrial sphere. That co-operation was not limited to the Congress governments, although the advice was necessarily addressed to them. A comprehensive river survey overlapped provincial boundaries; a survey of the Gangetic valley and the setting up of a Ganga River Commission, a work of the highest importance, which yet waits to be done, could only take place with the co-operation of three provincial governments—those of the United Provinces, Bihar, and Bengal.

The resolution also demonstrates the importance attached by the Congress to large-scale state planning. Such planning was impossible so long as the central government was not under popular control and the shackles on the provincial governments had not been removed. We hoped, however, that some essential preliminary work might be done and the foundations for future planning laid down. Unfortunately the provincial governments were so busy with their own problems that there was delay in giving effect to this resolution. Late in 1938 a National Committee was constituted and I became chairman of it.

I was often critical of the work of the Congress governments and fretted at the slowness of progress made. But looking back, I am surprised at their achievements during a brief period of two years and a quarter, despite the innumerable difficulties that surrounded them. Unfortunately some of their important work did not bear fruit, as it was on the point of completion when they resigned, and it was shelved afterward by their successor—that is, the British governor. Both the peasantry and industrial labor benefited and grew in strength. One of the most important and far-reaching achievements was the introduction of a system of mass education called Basic Education. This was not only based on the latest educational doctrine but was peculiarly suited to Indian conditions.

Every vested interest came in the way of progressive change. A committee appointed by the U. P. Government to inquire into labor conditions in the Cawnpore textile industry was treated by the employers (chiefly Europeans, but including some Indians) with the greatest discourtesy, and many of the facts and figures demanded were refused. Labor had long faced the organized opposition of both the employers and government, and the police had always been at the disposal of the employers. The change in policy introduced by the Congress governments was therefore resented by the employers. Of the tactics of employers in India, Mr. B. Shiva Rao, who has had long experience of the labor movement in India and belongs to the moderate wing of it, writes:

"The amount of resourcefulness and lack of scruple exhibited on such occasions (strikes, etc.) by the employers with the assistance of police would be incredible to one unacquainted with Indian condition." The government of most countries, constituted as it is, inclines toward the employers. In India, Mr. Shiva Rao points out, there is an additional reason for this. Apart from personal animosities, officials in India with rare exceptions have been obsessed with the fear that trade unions, if allowed to develop, would foster mass consciousness; and with the political struggle in India periodically flaring up into movements like non-co-operation and civil disobedience, they have felt presumably that no risks should be taken in regard to the organization of the masses."[5]

Governments lay down policy; legislatures pass laws; but the actual working out of this policy and the application of these laws depend ultimately on the services and the administrative personnel. The provincial governments had thus inevitably to rely on the permanent services, especially the Indian Civil Service and the police. These services, bred in a different and authoritarian tradition, disliked the new atmosphere, the assertive attitude of the public, the lessening of their own importance, and their subordination to persons whom they had been in the habit of arresting and imprisoning. They had been rather apprehensive at first as to what might happen. But nothing very revolutionary happened, and they gradually settled down to their old routine. It was not easy for the ministers to interfere with the man on the spot, and only in obvious cases could they do so. The services formed a close corporation and hung together,

[5] B. Shiva Rao, *The Industrial Worker in India* (London, 1939).

and if one man was transferred, his successor was likely to act in the same way. It was impossible to change suddenly the old reactionary and autocratic mentality of the services as a whole. A few individuals might change, some might make an effort to adapt themselves to the new conditions, but the vast majority of them thought differently and had always functioned differently; how could they undergo a sea change and emerge as crusaders of a new order? At the most they could give a passive and heavy-moving loyalty; there could not, in the very nature of things, be a flaming enthusiasm for the new kind of work to be done, in which they did not believe and which undermined their own vested interests. Unfortunately even this passive loyalty was often lacking.

Among the higher members of the civil service, long accustomed to authoritarian methods and unchecked rule, there was a feeling that these ministers and legislators were intruders in a domain reserved for them. The old conception that they, the permanent services and especially the British element in them, were India and all others were unimportant appendages died hard. It was not easy to suffer the newcomers, much less to take orders from them. They felt as an orthodox Hindu might feel if untouchables pushed their way into the sacred precincts of his own particular temple. The edifice of prestige and racial superiority which had been built with so much labor, and which had almost become a religion to them, was cracking. The Chinese are said to be great believers in "face," and yet I doubt if any among them are so passionately attached to "face" as the British in India. For the latter it is not only individual, racial, and national prestige; it is also intimately connected with their rule and vested interests.

Yet the intruders had to be tolerated; but the toleration grew progressively less as the sense of danger receded. This attitude permeated all departments of the administration, but it was especially in evidence away from headquarters, in the districts, and in matters relating to what is called law and order, which was the special preserve of the district magistrate and the police. The emphasis of the Congress governments on civil liberty gave the local officials and the police an excuse for allowing things to happen which, ordinarily, no government could have permitted. Indeed I am convinced that in some cases the initiative for these undesirable occurrences came from the local officials or the police. Many of the communal (religious) riots that took place were due to a variety of causes, but the magistrates and the police were certainly not always free from guilt. Experience showed that a quick and efficient handling of the situation put an end to the trouble. What we saw repeatedly was an astonishing slackness and a deliberate evasion of duty. It became obvious that the objective was to discredit the Congress governments. In the United Provinces the industrial city of Cawnpore offered the most glaring example of utter ineptitude and mismanagement on the part of the local officials, which could only be deliberate. Communal (religious) friction, leading sometimes to local riots, had been more in evidence in the late twenties and early thirties. After the Congress governments took office it was in many ways much less. It changed its nature and became definitely political and was deliberately encouraged and organized.

The civil service had a reputation, chiefly self-propagated, for efficiency. But it became evident that outside the narrow sphere of work to which they had been accustomed, they were helpless and incompetent. They had no training to function democratically and could not gain the good will and co-operation of the people, whom they both feared and despised; they had no conception of big and fast-moving schemes of social progress and could only hamper them by their red tape and lack of imagination. Apart from certain individuals, this applied to both British and Indian members of the higher services. It was extraordinary how unfitted they were for the new tasks that faced them.

There was, of course, a great deal of inefficiency and incompetence on the popular side. But it was counterbalanced by energy and enthusiasm, and close touch with masses, and a desire and capacity to learn from one's own mistakes. There was vitality there, a bubbling life, a sense of tension, a desire to get things done, all of which contrasted strangely with the apathy and conservatism of the British ruling class and their supporters. India, the land of tradition, thus offered a strange picture of reversal of roles. The British, who had come here as representatives of a dynamic society, were now the chief upholders of a static, unchanging tradition; among the Indians there were many who represented the new dynamic order and were eager for change, change not only political but also social and economic. Behind those Indians there were, of course, vast new forces at work which perhaps even they hardly realized. This reversal of roles was a demonstration of the fact that whatever creative or progressive role the British might have played in the past in India, they had long ceased to play it and were now a hindrance and an obstruction to all progress. The tempo of their official life was slow and incapable of solving any of the vital problems before India. Even their utterances, which used to have some clarity and strength, became turgid, inept, and lacking any real content.

There has long been a legend, propagated by British authorities, that the British government, through its higher services in India, was training us for the difficult and intricate art of self-government. We had managed to carry on, and with a considerable degree of success, for a few thousand years before the British came here and gave us the advantage of their training. No doubt we lack many of the good qualities that we should possess, and some misguided persons even say that this deficiency has grown under British rule. But whatever our failings might be, it seemed obvious to us that the permanent services here were totally incapable of leading India in any progressive direction. The very qualities they possessed made them unhelpful, for the qualities necessary in a police state are utterly different from those required in a progressive democratic community. Before they could presume to train others, it would be necessary for them to untrain themselves, and to bathe in the waters of Lethe so that they might forget what they had been.

The brief period during which the Congress governments functioned in the provinces confirmed our belief that the major obstruction to progress in India was the political and economic structure imposed by the British. It was perfectly true that many traditional habits and social forms and practices were barriers to progress and they had to go. Yet the inherent tendency of Indian economy to expand was not restricted so much by these forms and habits as by the political and economic stranglehold of the British. But for that steel framework, expansion was inevitable, bringing in its wake many social changes and the ending of outworn customs and ceremonial patterns. Hence attention had to be concentrated on the removal of that framework, and the energy spent on other matters bore little result and was often like plowing the sands. That framework was itself based on and protected the semi-feudal land tenure system and many other relics of the past. Any kind of democracy in India was incompatible with the British political and economic structure, and conflict between the two was inevitable. Hence the partial democracy of 1937–39 was always on the verge of conflict. Hence also the official British view that democracy in India had not been successful, because they could only consider it in terms of maintaining the structure and values and vested interests they had built up. As the kind of tame and subservient democracy of which they could have approved was not forthcoming, and all manner of radical changes were aimed at, the only alternative left to the British power was to revert to a purely authoritarian regime and put an end to all pretensions of democracy. There is a marked similarity in the development of this outlook and the birth and growth of fascism in Europe. Even the rule of law on which the British had prided themselves in India gave place to something in the nature of a state of siege and rule by ordinance and decree.

## V. THE QUESTION OF MINORITIES
### THE MOSLEM LEAGUE
### MR. M. A. JINNAH

The development and growth of the Moslem League during the last seven years has been an unusual phenomenon. Started in 1906 with British encouragement and in order to keep away the new generation of Moslems from the National Congress, it remained a small upper-class organization controlled by feudal elements. It had no influence on the Moslem masses and was hardly known by them. By its very constitution it was limited to a small group and a permanent leadership which perpetuated itself. Even so, events and the growing middle class among the Moslems pushed it in the direction of the Congress. World War I and the fate of the Turkish khalifat and the Moslem holy places produced a powerful impression on the Moslems of India and made them intensely anti-British. The Moslem League, constituted as it was, could not offer any guidance or leadership to these awakened and excited masses; indeed the League suffered from an attack of nerves and practically faded away. A new Moslem organization grew up, in close co-operation with the Congress—the Khalifat Committee. Large numbers of Moslems also joined the Congress and worked through it. After the first non-co-operation movement of 1920–23, the Khalifat Committee also began to fade away, as its very *raison d'être* had disappeared—the Turkish khalifat. The Moslem masses drifted away from political activity, as also the Hindu masses to a lesser extent. But a very considerable number of Moslems, chiefly of the middle classes, continued to function through the Congress.

During this period a number of petty Moslem organizations functioned spasmodically, often coming into conflict with each other. They had no mass affiliations, no political importance except such as was given to them by the British government. Their chief function was to demand special privileges and protection for the Moslems in the legislatures and services. In this matter they did represent a definite Moslem viewpoint, for there was a background of resentment and fear among the Moslems at the superior position of the Hindus in education, services, and industry, as well as numbers. Mr. M. A. Jinnah retired from Indian politics, and indeed from India, and settled down in England.

During the second civil disobedience movement of 1930 the response from the Moslems was very considerable, though less than in 1920–23. Among those who were jailed in connection with this movement there were at least ten thousand Moslems. The North-West Frontier Province, which is an almost entirely Moslem province (95% Moslems) played a leading and remarkable part in this movement. This was largely due to the work and personality of Khan Abdul Ghaffar Khan, the unquestioned and beloved leader of the Pathans in this province. Of all the happenings in India in recent times, nothing is more astonishing than the way in which Abdul Ghaffar Khan made his turbulent and quarrelsome people accept peaceful methods of political action, involving enormous suffering. That suffering was indeed terrible and has left a trail of bitter memories; and yet their discipline and self-control were such that no act of violence was committed by the Pathans against the government forces or others opposed to them. When it is remembered that a Pathan loves his gun more than his brother, is easily excited, and has long had a reputation for killing at the slightest provocation, this self-discipline appears little short of miraculous.

The Frontier Province, under Abdul Ghaffar Khan's leadership, stood firmly by the side of the National Congress; so also did a large number of politically conscious middle-class Moslems elsewhere. Among the peasantry and workers Congress influence was considerable, especially in provinces like the U.P., which had an advanced and workers' program. But it was none the less true that the Moslem masses as a whole were reverting vaguely to their old local and feudal leadership, which came to them in the guise of protectors of Moslem interests as against Hindus and others.

The communal problem, as it was called, was one of adjusting the claims of the minorities and giving them sufficient protection from majority action. Minorities in India, it must be remembered, are not racial or national minorities as in Europe; they are religious minorities. Racially India is a patchwork and a curious mixture, but no racial questions have arisen or can arise in India. Religion transcends these racial differences, which fade into one another and are often hard to distinguish. Religious barriers are obviously not permanent, as conversions can take place from one religion to another, and a person changing his religion does not thereby lose his racial background or his cultural and linguistic inheritance. Latterly religion, in any real sense of the word, has played little part in Indian political conflicts, though the word is often enough used and exploited. Religious differences, as such, do not come in the way, for there is a great deal of mutual tolerance for them. In political matters, religion has been displaced by what is called communalism, a narrow group mentality basing itself on a religious community but in reality concerned with political power and patronage for the group concerned.

Repeated efforts were made by the Congress as well as other organizations to settle this communal problem with the consent of the various groups concerned. Some partial success was achieved, but there was always a basic difficulty —the presence and policy of the British government. Naturally the British did not favor any real settlement which would strengthen the political movement—now grown to mass proportions—against them. It was a triangle, with the government in a position to play off one side against the other by giving special privileges. If the other parties had been wise enough, they could have overcome even this obstacle; but they lacked wisdom and foresight. Whenever a settlement was almost reached, the government would take some step which upset the balance.

There was no dispute about the usual provisions for minority protection such as the League of Nations used to lay down. All these were agreed to and much more. Religion, culture, language, the fundamental rights of the individual and the group were all to be protected and assured by basic constitutional provisions in a democratic constitution applying equally to all. Apart from this the whole history of India was witness of the toleration and even encouragement of minorities and of different racial groups. There is nothing in Indian history to compare with the bitter religious feuds and persecutions that prevailed in Europe. So we did not have to go abroad for ideas of religious and cultural toleration; these were inherent in Indian life. In regard to individual and political rights and civil liberties, we were influenced by the ideas of the French and American revolutions, as also by the constitutional history of the British parliament. Socialistic ideas, and the influence of the Soviet revolution, came in later to give a powerful economic turn to our thoughts.

Apart from full protection of all such rights of the individual and the group, it was common ground that every effort should be made by the state as well as by private agencies to remove all invidious social and customary barriers which came in the way of the full development of the individual as well as any group, and that educationally and economically backward classes should be helped to get rid of their disabilities as rapidly as possible. This applied especially to the depressed classes. It was further laid down that women should share in every way with men in the privileges of citizenship.

What remained? Fear that bigger numbers might politically overwhelm a minority. Normally speaking, numbers meant the peasantry and the workers, the masses of all religious faiths, who had long been exploited not only by foreign rule but by their own upper classes. Having assured the protection of religion and culture, etc., the major problems that were bound to come up were economic ones which had nothing to do with a person's religion. Class conflicts there might well be, but not religious conflicts, except in so far as religion itself represented some vested interest. Nevertheless people had grown so accustomed to think along lines of religious cleavage, and were continually being encouraged to do so by communal religious organizations and government action, that the fear of the major religious community, that is the Hindus, swamping others continued to exercise the minds of many Moslems. It was not clear how even a majority could injure the interests of a huge minority like the Moslems, concentrated mostly in certain parts of the country which would be autonomous. But fear is not reasonable.

Separate electorates for Moslems (and later for other and smaller groups) were introduced and additional seats were given to them in excess of their population. But even excess in representation in a popular assembly could not convert a minority into a majority. Indeed separate electorates made matters a little worse for the protected group, for the majority electorate lost interest in it and there was little occasion for mutual consideration and adjustment which inevitably take place in a joint electorate when a candidate has to appeal to every group. The Congress went further and declared that if there was any disagreement between the majority and a religious minority on any issue touching the special interests of that minority, it should not be decided by majority votes but should be referred to an impartial judicial tribunal, or even an international tribunal, whose decision should be final.

It is difficult to conceive what greater protection could be given to any religious minority or group under any democratic system. It must be remembered also that in some provinces Moslems were actually in a majority, and as the provinces were autonomous, the Moslem majority was more or less free to function as it chose, subject only to certain all-India considerations. In the central government Moslems would also inevitably have an important share. In the Moslem majority provinces this communal-religious problem was reversed, for there protection was demanded by the other minority groups (such as Hindu and Sikh) as against the Moslem majority. Thus in the Punjab there was a Moslem-Hindu-Sikh triangle. If there was a separate electorate for Moslems, then others claimed special protection for themselves also. Separate electorates having once been introduced, there was no end to the ramifications and compartments and difficulties that arose from them. Obviously the granting of weightage in representation to one group could only be done at the cost of some other group, which had its representation reduced below its population figures. This produced a fantastic result, especially in Bengal, where, chiefly because of excessive European representation, the seats allotted to the general electorate were absurdly reduced. Thus the intelligentsia of Bengal, which had played a notable part in Indian politics and the struggle for freedom, suddenly realized that it had a very weak position in the provincial legislature, and this fixed and limited by statute.

The Congress made many mistakes, but these were in relatively minor questions of approach or tactics. It was obvious that even for purely political reasons the Congress was eager and anxious to bring about a communal solution and thus remove a barrier to progress. There was no such eagerness in the purely communal organizations, for their chief reason for existence was to emphasize the particular demands of their respective groups, and this had led to a certain vested interest in the status quo. Though predominantly Hindu in membership, the Congress had large numbers of Moslems on its rolls, as well as all other religious groups—Sikhs, Christians, etc. It was thus forced to think in national terms. For it the dominating issue was national freedom and the establishment of an independent democratic state. It realized that in a vast and varied country like India, a simple type of democracy, giving full powers to a majority to curb or overrule minority groups in all matters, was not satisfactory or desirable, even if it could be established. We wanted unity, of course, and took it for granted, but we saw no reason why the richness and variety of India's cultural life should be regimented after a single pattern. Hence a large measure of autonomy was agreed to, as well as safeguards for cultural growth and individual and group freedom.

But on two fundamental questions the Congress stood firm: national unity and democracy. There were the foundations on which it had been founded and its very growth for half a century had emphasized these. The Congress organization is certainly one of the most democratic that I know of anywhere in the world, both in theory and practice. Through its tens of thousands of local committees spread out all over the country it had trained the people in democratic ways and achieved striking success in this. The fact that a dominating and very popular personality like Gandhi was connected with it did not lessen that essential democracy of the Congress. In times of crisis and struggle there was an inevitable tendency to look to the leader for guidance, as in every country, and such crises were frequent. Nothing is more absurd than to call the Congress an authoritarian organization, and it is interesting to note that such charges are usually made by high representatives of British authority, which is the essence of autocracy and authoritarianism in India.

We failed in finding a solution for the communal problem agreeable to all parties concerned, and certainly we must share the blame as we have to shoulder the consequences for this failure. But how does one get everybody to agree to any important proposition or change? There are always feudal and reactionary elements who are opposed to all change, and there are those who want political, economic, and social change; in between these are varying groups. If a small group can exercise a veto on change, then surely there can never be any change. When it is the policy of the ruling power to set up such groups and encourage them, even though they might represent an infinitesimal proportion of the population, then change can only come through successful revolution. It is obvious that there are any number of feudal and reactionary groups in India, some native to the soil and some created and nurtured by the British. In numbers they may be small, but they have the backing of the British power.

Among the Moslems various organizations grew up, apart from the Moslem League. One of the older and more important ones was the Jamiat-ul-Ulema, which consisted of divines and old-fashioned scholars from all over India. Traditional and conservative in its general outlook, and necessarily religious, it was yet politically advanced and anti-imperialist. On the political plane it often co-operated with the Congress, and many of its members were also members of the Congress and functioned through its organization. The Ahrar organization was founded later and was strongest in the Punjab. This represented chiefly lower-middle-class Moslems and had considerable influence on the masses also in particular areas. The Momins (principally the weaver class), though large in numbers, were the poorest and most backward among the Moslems and were weak and badly organized. They were friendly to the Congress and opposed to the Moslem League. Being weak, they avoided political action. In Bengal there was the Krishak (peasant) Sabha. Both the Jamiat-ul-Ulema and the Ahrars often co-operated with the Congress in its normal work and its more aggressive campaigns against the British government, and suffered for it. The chief Moslem organization which has never come into conflict, other than verbal, with the British authorities, is the Moslem League, which throughout subsequent changes and developments, and even when large numbers joined it, never shed its upper-class feudal leadership.

There were also the Shia Moslems organized separately, but rather vaguely, chiefly for the purpose of making political demands. In the early days of Islam in Arabia a bitter dispute about the succession to the khalifat led to a schism and two groups or sects emerged—the Sunnis and Shias. That quarrel perpetuated itself and still separates the two, though the schism ceased to have any political meaning. Sunnis are in a majority in India and in the Islamic countries except Iran, where Shias are in a majority. Religious conflicts have sometimes taken place between the two groups. The Shia organization in India as such kept apart and differed from the Moslem League. It was in favor of joint electorates for all. But there are many prominent Shias in the League.

All these Moslem organizations, as well as some others (but not including the Moslem League) joined hands to promote the Azad Muslim Conference, which was a kind of joint Moslem front opposed to the Moslem League. This conference held a very representative and successful first session in Delhi in 1940.

The chief Hindu communal organization is the Hindu Mahasabha, the counterpart of the Moslem League, but relatively less important. It is as aggressively communal as the League, but it tries to cover up its extreme narrowness of outlook by using some kind of vague national terminology, though its outlook is more revivalist than progressive. It is peculiarly unfortunate in some of its leaders who indulge in irresponsible and violent diatribes, as indeed some of the Moslem League leaders also do. This verbal warfare, indulged in on both sides, is a constant irritant. It takes the place of action.

The Moslem League's communal attitude was often difficult and unreasonable in the past, but no less unreasonable was the attitude of the Hindu Mahasabha. The Hindu minorities in the Punjab and Sind, and the dominant Sikh group in the Punjab, were often obstructive and came in the way of a settlement. British policy was to encourage and emphasize these differences and to give importance to communal organizations as against the Congress.

One test of the importance of a group or party, or at any rate of its hold on the people, is an election. During the general elections in India in 1937 the Hindu Mahasabha failed completely; it was nowhere in the picture. The Moslem League did better, but on the whole its showing was poor, especially in the predominantly Moslem provinces. In the Punjab and Sind it failed completely, in Bengal it met with only partial success. In the North-West Frontier Province, Congress formed a ministry later. In the Moslem minority provinces the League met with greater success on the whole, but there were also independent Moslem groups as well as Moslems elected as Congressmen.

Then began a remarkable campaign on behalf of the Moslem League against the Congress governments in the provinces and the Congress organization itself. Day after day it was repeated that these governments were committing "atrocities" on the Moslems. Those governments contained Moslem ministers also, but they were not members of the Moslem League. What these "atrocities" were it was not usually stated; or some petty local incidents, which had nothing to do with the government, were distorted and magnified. Some minor errors of some departments, which were soon rectified, became "atrocities." Sometimes entirely false and baseless charges were made. Even a report was issued, fantastic in its contents and having little to do with any facts. Congress governments invited those who made the charges to supply particulars for investigation or to come and inquire themselves with government help. No one took advantage of these offers. But the campaign continued unchecked. Early in 1940, soon after the resignation of the Congress ministries, the then Congress president, Dr. Rapendra Prasad, wrote to Mr. M. A. Jinnah and also made a public statement inviting the Moslem League to place any charges against the Congress governments before the federal court for inquiry and decision. Mr. Jinnah declined this offer and referred to the possibility of a royal commission being appointed for the purpose. There was no question of any such commission being appointed, and only the British government could do so. Some of the British governors who had functioned during the regime of the Congress governments declared that they had found nothing objectionable in the treatment of minorities. Under the act of 1935 they had been especially empowered to protect minorities if any such need arose.

I had made a close study of nazi methods of propaganda since Hitler's rise to power, and I was astonished to find something very similar taking place in India. A year later, in 1938, when Czechoslovakia had to face the Sudetenland crisis, the nazi methods employed there were studied and referred to with approval by Moslem League spokesmen. A comparison was drawn between the position of Sudetenland Germans and Indian Moslems. Violence and incitements in speeches and in some newspapers became marked. A Congress Moslem minister was stabbed, and there was no condemnation of this from any Moslem League leader; in fact it was condoned. Other exhibitions of violence frequently took place.

I was terribly depressed by these developments and by the general lowering of the standards of public life. Violence, vulgarity, and irresponsibility were on the increase, and it appeared that they were approved of by responsible leaders of the Moslem League. I wrote to some of these leaders and begged them to check this tendency, but with no success. So far as the Congress governments were concerned, it was obviously to their interest to win over every minority or other group, and they tried hard to do so. Indeed complaints arose from some quarters that they were showing undue favor to the Moslems at the expense of other groups. But it was not a question of a particular grievance which could be remedied, or a reasonable consideration of any matter. There was a regular rampage on the part of members or sympathizers of the Moslem League to make the Moslem masses believe that something terrible was happening and that the Congress was to blame. What that terrible thing was nobody seemed to know. But surely there must be something behind all this shouting and cursing, if not here then elsewhere. During by-elections the cry raised was "Islam in danger," and voters were asked to take their oaths on the holy book to vote for the Moslem League candidate.

All this had an undoubted effect on the Moslem masses. And yet it is surprising how many resisted it. The League won most by-elections, lost some; even when they won, there was a substantial minority of Moslem voters who went against them, being influenced more by the Congress agrarian program. But for the first time in its history the Moslem League got a mass backing and began to develop into a mass organization. Much as I regretted what was happening, I welcomed this development in a way, as I thought that this might lead ultimately to a change in the feudal leadership and more progressive elements would come forward. The real difficulty thus far had been the extreme political and social backwardness of the Moslems, which made them liable to exploitation by reactionary leaders.

Mr. M. A. Jinnah himself was more advanced than most of his colleagues of the Moslem League. Indeed he stood head and shoulders above them and had therefore become the indispensable leader. From public platforms he confessed his great dissatisfaction with the opportunism, and sometimes even worse failings, of his colleagues. He knew well that a great part of the advanced, selfless, and courageous element among the Moslems had joined and worked with the Congress. And yet some destiny or course of events had thrown him among the very people for whom he had no respect. He was their leader, but he could only keep them together by becoming himself a prisoner to their reactionary ideologies. Not that he was an unwilling prisoner, so far as the ideologies were concerned, for despite his external modernism, he belonged to an older generation which was hardly aware of modern political thought or developments. Of economics, which overshadow the world today, he appeared to be entirely ignorant. The extraordinary occurrences that had taken place all over the world since World War I had apparently had no effect on him. He had left the Congress when that organization had taken a political leap forward. The gap had widened as the Congress developed an economic and mass outlook. But Mr. Jinnah seemed to have remained ideologically in that identical place where he stood a generation ago, or rather he had gone further back, for now he condemned both India's unity and democracy. "They would not live," he has stated, "under any system of government that was based on the nonsensical notion of Western democracy." It took him a long time to realize that what he had stood for throughout a fairly long life was nonsensical.

When I was Congress president, I wrote to Mr. Jinnah on several occasions and requested him to tell us exactly what he would like us to do. I asked him what the League wanted and what its definite objectives were. I also wanted to know what the grievances of the League were against the Congress governments. The idea was that we might clarify matters by correspondence and then discuss personally the important points that had arisen in it. Mr. Jinnah sent me long replies but failed to enlighten me. It was extraordinary how he avoided telling me, or anyone else, exactly what he wanted or what the grievances of the League were. Repeatedly we exchanged letters, and yet always there was the same vagueness and inconclusiveness and I could get nothing definite. This surprised me very much and made me feel a little helpless. It seemed as if Mr. Jinnah did not want to commit himself in any way and was not at all eager for a settlement.

Subsequently Gandhiji and others among us met Mr. Jinnah several times. They talked for hours but never got beyond a preliminary stage. Our proposal was that representatives of the Congress and the League should meet and discuss all their mutual problems. Mr. Jinnah said that this could only be done after we recognized publicly that the Moslem League was the sole representative organization of the Moslems of India, and the Congress should consider itself a purely Hindu organization. This created an obvious difficulty. We recognized, of course, the importance of the League, and because of that we had approached it. But how could we ignore many other Moslem organizations in the country, some closely associated with us? Also there were large numbers of Moslems in the Congress itself and among our highest executives. To admit Mr. Jinnah's claim meant in effect to push out our old Moslem colleagues from the Congress and declare that the Congress was not open to them. It was to change the fundamental character of the Congress, and from a national organization, open to all, convert it into a communal body. That was inconceivable for us. If the Congress had not already been there, we would have had to build up a new national organization open to every Indian.

We could not understand Mr. Jinnah's insistence on this and refusing to discuss any other matter. Again we could only conclude that he did not want any settlement, nor did he want to commit himself in any way. He was satisfied in letting matters drift and in expecting that he could get more out of the British government this way.

Mr. Jinnah's demand was based on a new theory he had recently propounded—that India consisted of two nations, Hindu and Moslem. Why only two I do not know, for if nationality was based on religion, then there were many nations in India. Of two brothers one may be a Hindu, another a Moslem; they would belong to two different nations. These two nations existed in varying proportions in most of the villages of India. They were nations which had

no boundaries; they overlapped. A Bengali Moslem and a
Bengali Hindu, living together, speaking the same language
and having much the same traditions and customs, belonged to different nations. All this was very difficult to
grasp; it seemed a reversion to some medieval theory. What
a nation is it is difficult to define. Possibly the essential
characteristic of national consciousness is a sense of belonging together and of together facing the rest of mankind.
How far that is present in India as a whole may be a de-
batable point. It may even be said that India developed
in the past as a multinational state and gradually acquired
a national consciousness. But all these are theoretical ab-
stractions which hardly concern us. Today the most powerful states are multinational, but at the same time developing a national consciousness, like the U.S.A. or the
U.S.S.R.

From Mr. Jinnah's two-nation theory developed the conception of Pakistan, or splitting up of India. That of course
did not solve the problem of the "two nations," for they
were all over the place. But that gave body to a metaphysical conception. This again gave rise to a passionate
reaction among many in favor of the unity of India. Ordinarily national unity is taken for granted. Only when it is
challenged or attacked or attempts are made to disrupt it,
is unity really appreciated, and a positive reaction to maintain it takes place. Thus sometimes attempts at disruption
actually help to weld that unity.

There was a fundamental difference between the outlook of the Congress and that of the religious-communal
organizations. Of the latter the chief were the Moslem
League and its Hindu counterpart, the Hindu Mahasabha.
These communal organizations, while in theory standing
for India's independence, were more interested in claiming protection and special privileges for their respective
groups. They had inevitably to look to the British government for such privileges, and this led them to avoid conflict with it. The Congress outlook was so tied up with
India's freedom as a united nation that everything else was
secondary, and this meant ceaseless conflict or friction with
the British power. Indian nationalism, as represented by

the Congress, opposed British imperialism. The Congress had further developed agrarian, economic, and social programs. Neither the Moslem League nor the Hindu Mahasabha had ever considered any such question or attempted to frame a program. Socialists and Communists were of course intensely interested in such matters and had their own programs which they tried to push in the Congress as well as outside.

There was yet another marked difference between Congress policy and work and those of the religious-communal organizations. Quite apart from its agitational side and its legislative activity, when such existed, the Congress laid the greatest stress on certain constructive activities among the masses. These activities consisted in organizing and developing cottage industries, in raising the depressed classes, and later in the spread of basic education. Village work also included sanitation and some simple forms of medical relief. Separate organizations for carrying on these activities were created by the Congress, which functioned apart from the political plane, and which absorbed thousands of whole-time workers and a much larger number of part-time helpers. This quiet nonpolitical, constructive work was carried on even when political activities were at a low ebb; but even this was suppressed by government when there was open conflict with the Congress. The economic value of some of these activities was questioned by some people, but there could be no doubt of their social importance. They trained a large body of whole-time workers in intimate touch with the masses and produced a spirit of self-help and self-reliance among the people. Congressmen and -women also played an important part in trade-union and agrarian organizations, actually building up many of these. The largest and best organized trade union—that of the Ahmadabad textile industry—was started by Congressmen and worked in close co-operation with them.

All these activities gave a solid background to Congress work which was completely lacking in the religious-communal organizations. These latter functioned on the agitational plane only with fits and starts, or during elections. In them also was lacking that ever-present sense of risk and personal danger from government action which Congressmen had almost always to face. Thus there was a far greater tendency for careerists and opportunists to enter these organizations. The two Moslem organizations, the Ahrars and the Jamiat-ul-Ulema, however, suffered greatly from governmental repression because politically they often followed the same line as the Congress.

The beginning of World War II brought an internal crisis which resulted in the resignation of the Congress governments in the provinces. Before this occurred, however, the Congress made another attempt to approach Mr. M. A. Jinnah and the Moslem League. Mr. Jinnah was invited to attend the first meeting of the Congress executive after the commencement of the war. He was unable to join us. We met him later and tried to evolve a common policy in view of the world crisis. Not much progress was made, but nevertheless we decided to continue our talks. Meanwhile the Congress governments resigned on the political issue which had nothing to do with the Moslem League and the communal problem. Mr. Jinnah, however, chose that moment for a fierce attack on the Congress and a call on his League for the observance of a "Day of Deliverance" from Congress rule in the provinces. He followed this up by very unbecoming remarks on nationalist Moslems in the Congress and especially on the Congress president, Maulana Abul Kalam Azad, who was greatly respected among Hindus and Moslems alike. The "Day of Deliverance" was rather a flop, and counter demonstrations among Moslems took place in some parts of India. But it added to bitterness and confirmed the conviction that Mr. Jinnah and the Moslem League under his leadership had no intention whatever of coming to any settlement with the Congress, or of advancing the cause of Indian freedom. They preferred the existing situation.[6]

6 After I had finished writing this book, I read a book by a Canadian scholar, Wilfrid Cantwell Smith, who has spent some years in Egypt and India. This book, which is called *Modern Islam in India—A Social Analysis* (Lahore, 1943), is an able analysis and careful survey of the development of ideas among Indian Moslems since the Indian Mutiny of 1857. He deals with

## VI. THE NATIONAL PLANNING COMMITTEE

Toward the end of 1938 a National Planning Committee was constituted at the instance of the Congress. It consisted of fifteen members plus representatives of provincial governments and such Indian states as chose to collaborate with us. Among the members were well-known industrialists, financiers, economists, professors, scientists, as well as representatives of the Trade Union Congress and the Village Industries Association. The non-Congress provincial governments (Bengal, Punjab, and Sind), as well as some of the major states (Hyderabad, Mysore, Baroda, Travancore, Bhopal) co-operated with the committee. In a sense it was a remarkably representative committee cutting across political boundaries as well as the high barrier between official and nonofficial India—except for the fact that the Government of India was not represented and took up a non-co-operative attitude. Hardheaded big business was there as well as people who are called idealists and doctrinaires, and socialists and near-communists. Experts and directors of industries came from provincial governments and states.

It was a strange assortment of different types, and it was not clear how such an odd mixture would work. I accepted the chairmanship of the committee not without hesitation and misgiving; the work was after my own heart, and I could not keep out of it.

Difficulties faced us at every turn. There was not enough data for real planning, and few statistics were available. The government of India was not helpful. Even the provincial governments, though friendly and co-operative, did not seem to be particularly keen on all-India planning and took only a distant interest in our work. They were far too busy with their own problems and troubles. Important elements

the progressive and reactionary movements from Sir Syed Ahmad Khan's time onward, and the different phases of the Moslem League.

in the Congress, under whose auspices the committee had come into existence, rather looked upon it as an unwanted child, not knowing how it would grow up and rather suspicious of its future activities. Big business was definitely apprehensive and critical, and probably joined up because it felt that it could look after its interests better from inside the committee than from outside.

It was obvious also that any comprehensive planning could only take place under a free national government, strong enough and popular enough to be in a position to introduce fundamental changes in the social and economic structure. Thus the attainment of national freedom and the elimination of foreign control became an essential prerequisite for planning. There were many other obstacles— our social backwardness, customs, traditional outlook, etc. —but they had in any event to be faced. Planning, thus, was not so much for the present as for an unascertained future, and there was an air of unreality about it. Yet it had to be based on the present, and we hoped that this future was not a distant one. If we could collect the available material, co-ordinate it, and draw up blueprints, we would prepare the ground for the real, effective future planning, meanwhile indicating to provincial governments and states the lines on which they should proceed and develop their resources. The attempt to plan and to see the various national activities—economic, social, cultural—fitting into each other had also a highly educative value for ourselves and the general public. It made the people come out of their narrow grooves of thought and action, to think of problems in relation to one another and develop to some extent at least a wider co-operative outlook.

The original idea behind the Planning Committee had been to further industrialization—"the problems of poverty and unemployment, of national defence and of economic regeneration in general cannot be solved without industrialization. As a step towards such industrialization, a comprehensive scheme of national planning should be formulated. This scheme should provide for the development of heavy key industries, medium scale industries and cottage industries. . . ." But no planning could possibly ignore agriculture, which was the mainstay of the people. Equally important were the social services. So one thing led to another, and it was impossible to isolate anything or to progress in one direction without corresponding progress in another. The more we thought of this planning business, the vaster it grew in its sweep and range, till it seemed to embrace almost every activity. That did not mean that we intended regulating and regimenting everything, but we had to keep almost everything in view even in deciding about one particular sector of the plan. The fascination of this work grew upon me, and, I think, upon the other members of our committee also. But at the same time a certain vagueness and indefiniteness crept in; instead of concentrating on some major aspects of the plan we tended to become diffuse. This also led to delay in the work of many of our subcommittees which lacked the sense of urgency and of working for a definite objective within a stated time.

Constituted as we were, it was not easy for all of us to agree to any basic social policy or principles underlying social organization. Any attempt to discuss these principles in the abstract was bound to lead to fundamental differences of approach at the outset and possibly to a splitting up of the committee. Not to have such a guiding policy was a serious drawback, yet there was no help for it. We decided to consider the general problem of planning as well as each individual problem concretely and not in the abstract, and allow principles to develop out of such considerations. Broadly speaking, there were two approaches: the socialist one aiming at the elimination of the profit motive and emphasizing the importance of equitable distribution, and the big-business one striving to retain free enterprise and the profit motive as far as possible and laying greater stress on production. There was also a difference in outlook between those who favored a rapid growth of heavy industry and others who wanted greater attention to be paid to the development of village and cottage industries, thus absorbing the vast number of the unemployed and partially employed. Ultimately there were bound to be differences in the final conclusions. It did not very much matter even if there were two or more reports, provided that all the available facts were collected and co-ordinated, the common ground mapped out, and the divergences indicated. When the time would come for giving effect to the plan, the then existing democratic government would have to choose what basic policy to adopt. Meanwhile a great deal of essential preparation would have been made and the various aspects of the problem placed before the public and the various provincial and state governments.

Obviously we could not consider any problem, much less plan, without some definite aim and social objective. That aim was declared to be to insure an adequate standard of living for the masses; in other words, to get rid of the appalling poverty of the people. The irreducible minimum, in terms of money, had been estimated by economists at figures varying from Rs. 15 to Rs. 25 per capita per month. (These are all prewar figures.) Compared to Western standards this was very low, and yet it meant an enormous increase in existing standards in India. An approximate estimate of the average annual income per capita was Rs. 65. This included the rich and the poor, the town dweller and the villager. In view of the great gulf between the rich and the poor and the concentration of wealth in the hands of a few, the average income of the villager was estimated to be far less, probably about Rs. 30 per capita per annum. These figures bring home the terrible poverty of the people and the destitute condition of the masses. There was lack of food, of clothing, of housing, and of every other essential requirement of human existence. To remove this lack and insure an irreducible minimum standard for everybody, the national income had to be greatly increased, and in addition to this increased production there had to be a more equitable distribution of wealth. We calculated that a really progressive standard of living would necessitate the increase of the national wealth by 500 or 600 per cent. That was, however, too big a jump for us, and we aimed at a 200 to 300 per cent increase within ten years.

We fixed a ten-year period for the plan, with control figures for different periods and different sectors of economic life. Certain objective tests were also suggested:

(1) The improvement of nutrition—a balanced diet having a calorific value of 2400 to 2800 units for an adult worker.

(2) Improvement in clothing from the then consumption of about 15 yards to at least 30 yards per capita per annum.

(3) Housing standards to reach at least 100 square feet per capita.

Further, certain indices of progress had to be kept in mind:

(a) Increase in agricultural production
(b) Increase in industrial production
(c) Diminution of unemployment
(d) Increase in per capita income
(e) Liquidation of illiteracy
(f) Increase in public utility services
(g) Provision of medical aid on the basis of one unit for 1000 population
(h) Increase in the average expectation of life.

The objective for the country as a whole was the attainment, as far as possible, of national self-sufficiency. International trade was certainly not excluded, but we were anxious to avoid being drawn into the whirlpool of economic imperialism. We wanted neither to be victims of an imperialist power nor to develop such tendencies ourselves. The first charge on the country's produce should be to meet the domestic needs of food, raw materials, and manufactured goods. Surplus production would not be dumped abroad but be used for exchange of such commodities as we might require. To base our national economy on export markets might lead to conflicts with other nations and to sudden upsets when those markets were closed to us.

So, though we did not start with a well-defined social theory, our social objectives were clear enough and afforded a common basis for planning. The very essence of this planning was a large measure of regulation and co-ordination. Thus while free enterprise was not ruled out as such, its scope was severely restricted. In regard to defense industries it was decided that they must be owned and controlled by the state. Regarding other key industries, the majority were of opinion that they should be state-owned, but a substantial majority of the committee considered that state control would be sufficient. Such control of these industries, however, had to be rigid. Public utilities, it was also decided, should be owned by some organ of the state—either the central government, provincial government, or a local board. It was suggested that something of the nature of the London Transport Board might control public utilities. In regard to other important and vital industries no special rule was laid down, but it was made clear that the very nature of planning required control in some measure, which might vary with the industry.

In regard to the agency in state-owned industries it was suggested that as a general rule an autonomous public trust would be suitable. Such a trust would insure public ownership and control and at the same time avoid the difficulties and inefficiency which sometimes creep in under direct democratic control. Co-operative ownership and control were also suggested for industries. Any planning would involve a close scrutiny of the development of industry in all its branches and a periodical survey of the progress made. It would mean also the training of the technical staffs necessary for the further expansion of industry, and the state might call upon industries to train such staffs.

The general principles governing land policy were laid down: "Agricultural land, mines, quarries, rivers and forests are forms of national wealth, ownership of which must vest absolutely in the people of India collectively." The co-operative principle should be applied to the exploitation of land by developing collective and co-operative farms. It was not proposed, however, to rule out peasant farming in small holdings, to begin with at any rate, but no intermediaries of the type of taluqdars, zamindars, etc. should be recognized after the transition period was over. The rights and titles possessed by these classes should be progressively bought out. Collective farms were to be started immediately by the state on cultivable waste land. Co-operative farming could be combined either with individual or joint ownership. A certain latitude was allowed for various types to develop so that, with greater experience, particular types might be encouraged more than others.

We, or some of us at any rate, hoped to evolve a socialized system of credit. If banks, insurance, etc. were not to be nationalized, they should at least be under the control of the state, thus leading to a state regulation of capital and credit. It was also desirable to control the export and import trade. By these various means a considerable measure of state control would be established in regard to land as well as in industry as a whole, though varying in particular instances, and allowing private initiative to continue in a restricted sphere.

Thus, through the consideration of special problems, we gradually developed our social objectives and policy. There were gaps in them and occasional vagueness and even some contradiction; it was far from a perfect scheme in theory. But I was agreeably surprised at the large measure of unanimity achieved by us in spite of the incongruous elements in our committee. The big-business element was the biggest single group, and its outlook on many matters, especially financial and commercial, was definitely conservative. Yet the urge for rapid progress, and the conviction that only thus could we solve our problems of poverty and unemployment, were so great that all of us were forced out of our grooves and compelled to think on new lines. We had avoided a theoretical approach, and as each practical problem was viewed in its larger context, it led us inevitably in a particular direction. To me the spirit of co-operation of the members of the Planning Committee was peculiarly soothing and gratifying, for I found it a pleasant contrast to the squabbles and conflicts of politics. We knew our differences, and yet we tried and often succeeded, after discussing every point of view, in arriving at an integrated conclusion which was accepted by all of us or most of us.

## VII. THE CONGRESS AND INDUSTRY
### BIG INDUSTRY VERSUS COTTAGE INDUSTRY

The Congress, under Gandhiji's leadership, had long championed the revival of village industries, especially hand
spinning and hand weaving. At no time, however, had the
Congress been opposed to the development of big industries, and whenever it had the chance, in the legislatures
or elsewhere, it had encouraged this development. Congress provincial governments were eager to do so. In the
twenties when the Tata Steel and Iron Works were in difficulties, it was largely due to the insistence of the Congress
party in the central legislature that government aid was
given to help to tide over a critical period. The development of Indian shipbuilding and shipping services had long
been a sore point of conflict between nationalist opinion
and the government. The Congress, as all other sections of
Indian opinion, was anxious that every assistance should
be given to Indian shipping; the government was equally
anxious to protect the vested interests of powerful British
shipping companies. Indian shipping was thus prevented
from growing by official discrimination against it, although
it had both capital and technical and managerial ability
at its disposal. This kind of discrimination worked all along
the line whenever any British industrial, commercial, or
financial interests were concerned.

That huge combine, the Imperial Chemical Industries,
has been repeatedly favored at the expense of Indian industry. Some years ago it was given a long-term lease for
the exploitation of the minerals, etc. of the Punjab. The
terms of this agreement were, so far as I know, not disclosed, presumably because it was not considered "in the
public interest" to do so.

The Congress provincial governments were anxious to
develop a power alcohol industry. This was desirable from
many points of view, but there was an additional reason
in the U.P. and Bihar. The large numbers of sugar factories

there were producing as a by-product a vast quantity of molasses which was being treated as waste material. It was proposed to utilize this for the production of power alcohol. The process was simple, there was no difficulty, except one—the interests of the Shell and Burma Oil combine were affected. The Government of India championed these interests and refused to permit the manufacture of power alcohol. It was only in the third year of the present war, after Burma fell and the supplies of oil and petrol were cut off, that the realization came that power alcohol was necessary and must be produced in India. The American Grady Committee strongly urged this in 1942.

The Congress has thus always been in favor of the industrialization of India, and at the same time has emphasized the development of cottage industries and worked for this. Is there a conflict between these two approaches? Possibly there is a difference in emphasis, a realization of certain human and economic factors which were overlooked previously in India. Indian industrialists and the politicians who supported them thought too much in terms of the nineteenth-century development of capitalist industry in Europe and ignored many of the evil consequences that were obvious in the twentieth century. In India, because normal progress had been arrested for a hundred years, those consequences were likely to be more far-reaching. The kind of medium-scale industries that were being started in India, under the prevailing economic system, resulted not in absorbing labor but in creating more unemployment. While capital accumulated at one end, poverty and unemployment increased at the other. Under a different system and with a stress on big-scale industries absorbing labor, and with planned development, this might well have been avoided.

This fact of increasing mass poverty influenced Gandhi powerfully. It is true, I think, that there is a fundamental difference between his outlook on life generally and what might be called the modern outlook. He is not enamored of ever-increasing standards of living and the growth of luxury at the cost of spiritual and moral values. He does not favor the soft life; for him the straight way is the hard way, and the love of luxury leads to crookedness and loss of virtue. Above all he is shocked at the vast gulf that stretches between the rich and the poor, in their ways of living and their opportunities of growth. For his own personal and psychological satisfaction, he crossed that gulf and went over to the side of the poor, adopting, with only such improvements as the poor themselves could afford, their ways of living, their dress or lack of dress. This vast difference between the few rich and the poverty-stricken masses seemed to him to be due to two principal causes: foreign rule and the exploitation that accompanied it, and the capitalist industrial civilization of the West as embodied in the big machine. He reacted against both. He looked back with yearning to the days of the old autonomous and more-or-less self-contained village community where there had been an automatic balance between production, distribution, and consumption; where political or economic power was spread out and not concentrated as it is today; where a kind of simple democracy prevailed; where the gulf between the rich and the poor was not so marked; where the evils of great cities were absent and people lived in contact with the life-giving soil and breathed the pure air of the open spaces.

There was all this basic difference in outlook as to the meaning of life itself between him and many others, and this difference colored his language as well as his activities. His language, vivid and powerful as it often was, drew its inspiration from the religious and moral teachings of the ages, principally of India but also of other countries. Moral values must prevail; the ends can never justify unworthy means, or else the individual and the race perish.

And yet he was no dreamer living in some fantasy of his own creation, cut off from life and its problems. He came from Gujrat, the home of hardheaded businessmen, and he had an unrivaled knowledge of the Indian villages and the conditions of life that prevailed there. It was out of that personal experience that he evolved his program of the spinning wheel and village industry. If immediate relief was to be given to the vast numbers of the unemployed and partially employed, if the rot that was spreading throughout India and paralyzing the masses was to be stopped, if the villagers' standards were to be raised, however little, *en masse*, if they were to be taught self-reliance instead of waiting helplessly like derelicts for relief from others, if all this was to be done without much capital, then there seemed no other way. Apart from the evils inherent in foreign rule and exploitation, and the lack of freedom to initiate and carry through big schemes of reform, the problem of India was one of scarcity of capital and abundance of labor—how to utilize that wasted labor, that manpower that was producing nothing. Foolish comparisons are made between manpower and machine power; of course a big machine can do the work of a thousand or ten thousand persons. But if those ten thousand sit idly by or starve, the introduction of that machine is not a social gain, except in long perspective which envisages a change in social conditions. When the big machine is not there at all, then no question of comparison arises; it is a net gain both from the individual and the national point of view to utilize manpower for production. There is no necessary conflict between this and the introduction of machinery on the largest scale, provided that machinery is used primarily for absorbing labor and not for creating fresh unemployment.

Gandhiji's attitude to the use of machinery seemed to undergo a gradual change. "What I object to," he said, "is the craze for machinery, not machinery as such. . . . If we could have electricity in every village home, I shall not mind villagers plying their implements and tools with electricity." The big machine seemed to him to lead inevitably, at least in the circumstances of today, to the concentration of power and riches: "I consider it a sin and injustice to use machinery for the purpose of concentration of power and riches in the hands of the few. Today the machine is used in this way." He even came to accept the necessity of many kinds of heavy industries and large-scale key industries and public utilities, provided they were state-owned and did not interfere with some kinds of cottage industries which he considered essential. Referring to his own proposals, he said: "The whole of this program will be a structure on sand if it is not built on the solid foundation of economic equality."

Thus even the enthusiastic advocates for cottage and small-scale industries recognize that big-scale industry is, to a certain extent, necessary and inevitable; only they would like to limit it as far as possible. Superficially, then, the question becomes one of emphasis and adjustment of the two forms of production and economy. It can hardly be challenged that, in the context of the modern world, no country can be politically and economically independent, even within the framework of international interdependence, unless it is highly industrialized and has developed its power resources to the utmost. Nor can it achieve or maintain high standards of living and liquidate poverty without the aid of modern technology in almost every sphere of life. An industrially backward country will continually upset the world equilibrium and encourage the aggressive tendencies of more developed countries. Even if it retains its political independence, this will be nominal only and economic control will tend to pass to others. This control will inevitably upset its own small-scale economy which it has sought to preserve in pursuit of its own view of life. Thus an attempt to build up a country's economy largely on the basis of cottage and small-scale industries is doomed to failure. It will not solve the basic problems of the country or maintain freedom, nor will it fit in with the world framework, except as a colonial appendage.

Is it possible to have two entirely different kinds of economy in a country—one based on the big machine and industrialization, and the other mainly on cottage industries? This is hardly conceivable, for one must overcome the other, and there can be little doubt that the big machine will triumph unless it is forcibly prevented from doing so. Thus it is not a mere question of adjustment of the two forms of production and economy. One must be dominating and paramount, with the other complementary to it, fitting in where it can. The economy based on the latest technical achievements of the day must necessarily be the dominating one. If technology demands the big machine, as it does today in a large measure, then the big machine with all its implications and consequences must be accepted. Where it is possible, in terms of that technology, to decentralize production, this would be desirable. But in any event, the latest technique has to be followed, and to adhere to outworn and out-of-date methods of production, except as a temporary and stop-gap measure, is to arrest growth and development.

Any argument as to the relative merits of small-scale and large-scale industry seems strangely irrelevant today, when the world and the dominating facts of the situation that confront it have decided in favor of the latter. Even in India that decision has been made by these facts themselves, and no one doubts that India will be rapidly industrialized in the near future. She has already gone a good way in that direction. The evils of unrestricted and unplanned industrialization are well recognized today. Whether these evils are necessary concomitants of big industry or derive from the social and economic structure behind it, is another matter. If the economic structure is primarily responsible for them, then surely we should set about changing that structure, instead of blaming the inevitable and desirable developments in technique.

The real question is not one of quantitative adjustment and balancing of various incongruous elements and methods of production, but a qualitative change-over to something different and new, from which various social consequences flow. The economic and political aspects of this qualitative change are important, but equally important are the social and psychological aspects. In India especially, where we have been wedded far too long to past forms and modes of thought and action, new experiences, new processes, leading to new ideas and new horizons, are necessary. Thus we will change the static character of our living and make it dynamic and vital, and our minds will become active and adventurous. New situations lead to new experiences, as the mind is compelled to deal with them and adapt itself to a changing environment.

It is well recognized now that a child's education should be intimately associated with some craft or manual activity. The mind is stimulated thereby, and there is a co-ordination between the activities of the mind and the hands. So also the mind of a growing boy or girl is stimulated by the machine. It grows under the machine's impact (under proper conditions, of course, and not as an exploited and unhappy worker in a factory) and opens out new horizons. Simple scientific experiments, peeps into the microscope, and an explanation of the ordinary phenomena of nature bring excitement in their train, an understanding of some of life's processes and a desire to experiment and find out instead of relying on set phrases and old formulae. Self-confidence and the co-operative spirit grow, and frustration, arising out of the miasma of the past, lessens. A civilization based on ever-changing and advancing mechanical techniques leads to this. Such a civilization is a marked change, a jump almost, from the older type, and is intimately connected with modern industrialization. Inevitably it gives rise to new problems and difficulties, but it also shows the way to overcome them.

I have a partiality for the literary aspects of education and I admire the classics. But I am quite sure that some elementary scientific training in physics and chemistry and especially biology, as also in the applications of science, is essential for all boys and girls. Only thus can they understand and fit into the modern world and develop, to some extent at least, the scientific temper. There is something very wonderful about the high achievements of science and modern technology (which no doubt will be bettered in the near future), in the superb ingenuity of scientific instruments, in the amazingly delicate and yet powerful machines, in all that has flowed from the adventurous inquiries of science and its applications, in the glimpses into the fascinating workshop and processes of nature, in the fine sweep of science, through its myriad workers, in the realms of thought and practice, and above all in the fact that all this has come out of the mind of man.

# VIII. The Last Phase: (3) World War II

## I. THE CONGRESS DEVELOPS A FOREIGN POLICY

The National Congress, like all other political organizations in India, was for long entirely engrossed in internal politics and paid little attention to foreign developments. In the nineteen-twenties it began to take some interest in foreign affairs. No other organization did so except the small groups of socialists and communists. Moslem organizations were interested in Palestine and occasionally passed resolutions of sympathy for the Moslem Arabs there. The intense nationalism of Turkey, Egypt, and Iran was watched by them but not without some apprehension, as it was secular and was leading to reforms which were not wholly in keeping with their ideas of Islamic traditions. The Congress gradually developed a foreign policy which was based on the elimination of political and economic imperialism everywhere and the co-operation of free nations. This fitted in with the demand for Indian independence. As early as 1920 a resolution on foreign policy was passed by the Congress, in which our desire to co-operate with other nations and especially to develop friendly relations with all our neighboring countries was emphasized. The possibility of another large-scale war was later considered, and in 1927, twelve years before World War II actually started, the Congress first declared its policy in regard to it.

This was five or six years before Hitler came into power and before Japanese aggression in Manchuria had begun. Mussolini was consolidating himself in Italy but did not then appear as a major threat to world peace. Fascist Italy was on friendly terms with England and British statesmen expressed their admiration for the Duce. There were a number of petty dictators in Europe, also usually on good terms with the British government. Between England and Soviet Russia, however, there was a complete breach; there had been the Arcos raid and withdrawal of diplomatic representatives. In the League of Nations and the International Labor Office, British and French policy was definitely conservative.

In the interminable discussions on disarmament, when every other country represented in the League, as well as the U.S.A., was in favor of the total abolition of aerial bombardment, Britain made some vital reservations. For many years the British government had used aircraft, for "police purposes" it was called, for bombing towns and villages in Iraq and the North-West Frontier of India. This "right" was insisted upon, thus preventing any general agreement on this subject in the League and later in the Disarmament Conference.

Germany, the Germany of the Weimar republican constitution, had become a full member of the League, and Locarno had been hailed as a forerunner of perpetual peace in Europe and a triumph of British policy. Another view of all these developments was that Soviet Russia was being isolated and a joint front against her was being created in Europe. Russia had just celebrated the tenth anniversary of her revolution and had developed friendly ties with various Eastern countries—Turkey, Iran, Afghanistan, and Mongolia.

The Chinese revolution had also advanced with great strides and the nationalist armies had taken possession of half of China, coming into conflict with foreign and especially British interests in the port towns and the interior. Subsequently there had been internal trouble and a breakup of the Kuomintang into rival groups.

The world situation seemed to be drifting toward a major conflict, with England and France as heads of a European group of nations, and Soviet Russia associated with some Eastern nations. The United States of America held aloof from both these groups; their intense dislike of communism kept them away from Russia, and their distrust of

British policy and competition with British finance and industry prevented them from associating themselves with the British group. Over and above these considerations was the isolationist sentiment of America and the fear of being embroiled in European quarrels.

In this setting Indian opinion inevitably sided with Soviet Russia and the Eastern nations. This did not mean any widespread approval of communism, though a growing number were attracted to socialist thought. The triumphs of the Chinese revolution were hailed with enthusiasm as portents of the approaching freedom of India and of the elimination of European aggression in Asia. We developed an interest in nationalist movements in the Dutch East Indies and Indo-China, as well as in the western Asiatic countries and Egypt. The conversion of Singapore into a great naval base and the development of Trincomalee harbor in Ceylon appeared as parts of the general preparations for the coming war, in which Britain would try to consolidate and strengthen her imperialist position and crush Soviet Russia and the rising nationalist movements of the East.

It was with this background that the National Congress began to develop its foreign policy in 1927. It declared that India could be no party to an imperialist war, and in no event should India be made to join any war without the consent of her people being obtained. In the years that followed, this declaration was frequently repeated and widespread propaganda was carried on in accordance with it. It became one of the foundations of Congress policy and, as it was generally accepted, of Indian policy. No individual or organization in India opposed it.

Meanwhile changes were taking place in Europe, and Hitler and nazism had arisen. The Congress immediately reacted against these changes and denounced them, for Hitler and his creed seemed the very embodiment and intensification of the imperialism and racialism against which the Congress was struggling. Japanese aggression in Manchuria produced even stronger reactions because of sympathy for China. Abyssinia, Spain, the Sino-Japanese war, Czechoslovakia and Munich added to this strength of feeling and the tension of approaching war.

But this coming war was likely to be different from the one that had been envisaged before Hitler had arisen. Even so, British policy had been almost continuously pro-fascist and pro-nazi and it was difficult to believe that it would suddenly change overnight and champion freedom and democracy. Its dominant imperialist outlook and desire to hold on to its empire would continue despite other developments. Also its basic opposition to Russia and what Russia represented. But it became increasingly obvious that in spite of every desire to appease Hitler, he was becoming a dominating power in Europe, entirely upsetting the old balance and menacing the vital interests of the British Empire. War between England and Germany became probable; and if this broke out, what then would our policy be? How would we reconcile the two dominating trends of our policy: opposition to British imperialism and opposition to fascism and nazism? How would we bring in line our nationalism and our internationalism? It was a difficult question in the existing circumstances, difficult for us, but offering no difficulty if the British government took a step to demonstrate to us that they had given up their imperialist policy in India and wanted to rely on popular good will.

In a contest between nationalism and internationalism, nationalism was bound to win. That had happened in every country and in every crisis; in a country under foreign domination, with bitter memories of continuous struggle and suffering, that was an inevitable and unavoidable consequence. England and France had played false to republican Spain and betrayed Czechoslovakia, and thus sacrificed internationalism for what they considered—wrongly, as events proved—their national interests. The United States of America had clung to isolationism, in spite of their evident sympathy with England, France, and China, and their hatred of nazism and Japanese militarism and aggression. It was Pearl Harbor that flung them headlong into war. Soviet Russia, the very emblem of internationalism, had followed a strictly national policy, bringing confusion to many of its friends and sympathizers. It was the sudden and unannounced attack by the German armies that brought war to the U.S.S.R. The Scandinavian countries and Holland and Belgium tried to avoid war and entanglement in the vain hope of saving themselves, and yet were overwhelmed by it. Turkey sat precariously on the thin edge of a varying neutrality, governed solely by national considerations. Egypt, still a semicolonial country in spite of its apparent independence, itself one of the major battle areas, occupied a curious and anomalous position. For all practical purposes it was a belligerent country completely under the control of the armed forces of the United Nations, and yet apparently it was not a belligerent.

There may be justification or excuse for all these policies adopted by various governments and countries. A democracy cannot easily jump into war without preparing its people and gaining their co-operation. Even an authoritarian state has to prepare the ground. But whatever the reason or justification may be, it is clear that whenever a crisis has occurred, national considerations, or what were considered to be such, have been paramount, and all others which did not fit in with them have been swept away. It was extraordinary how, during the Munich crisis, the hundreds of international organizations, anti-fascist leagues, etc. in Europe were struck dumb and became powerless and ineffective. Individuals and small groups may become internationally minded and may even be prepared to sacrifice personal and immediate national interests for a larger cause, but not so nations. It is only when international interests are believed to be in line with national interests that they arouse enthusiasm. A few months ago the London *Economist*, discussing British foreign policy, wrote: "The only foreign policy that has any hope of being consistently pursued is one in which national interests are fully and obviously safeguarded. No nation puts the interests of the international community before its own. It is only if the two can be seen to coincide that there is any possibility of effective internationalism."

Internationalism can indeed only develop in a free country, for all the thought and energy of a subject country are directed toward the achievement of its own freedom. That subject condition is like a cancerous growth inside the body, which not only prevents any limb from becoming healthy but is a constant irritant to the mind and colors all thought and action. Conflict is inherent in it, and such conflict leads to a concentration of thought on it and prevents a consideration of wider issues. The history of a long succession of past conflicts and suffering becomes the inseparable companion of both the individual and the national mind. It becomes an obsession, a dominating passion, which cannot be exorcised except by removing its root cause. And even then, when the sense of subjection has gone, the cure is slow, for the injuries of the mind take longer to heal than those of the body.

All this background we have long had in India, and yet Gandhi gave a turn to our nationalist movement which lessened the feelings of frustration and bitterness. Those feelings continued, but I do not know of any other nationalist movement which has been so free from hatred. Gandhi was an intense nationalist; he was also, at the same time, a man who felt he had a message not only for India but for the world, and he ardently desired world peace. His nationalism, therefore, had a certain world outlook and was entirely free from any aggressive intent. Desiring the independence of India, he had come to believe that a world federation of interdependent states was the only right goal, however distant that might be. He had said: "My idea of nationalism is that my country may become free, that if need be the whole of the country may die, so that the human race may live. There is no room for race hatred here. Let that be our nationalism." And again: "I do want to think in terms of the whole world. My patriotism includes the good of mankind in general. Therefore, my service of India includes the service of humanity. . . . Isolated independence is not the goal of the world States. It is voluntary interdependence. The better mind of the world desires today not absolutely independent States, warring one against another, but a federation of friendly, interdependent States. The consummation of that event may be far off. I want to make no grand claim for our country. But I see nothing grand or impossible about our expressing our readiness for universal interdependence rather than independence. I desire the ability to be totally independent without asserting the independence."

As the nationalist movement grew in strength and self-confidence, many people began to think in terms of a free India, what she would be like, what she would do, and what her relations with other countries would be. The very bigness and potential strength and resources of the country made them think in big terms. India could not be a mere hanger-on of any country or group of nations; her freedom and growth would make a vital difference to Asia and therefore to the world. That led inevitably to the conception of full independence and a severance of the bonds that tied her to England and her empire. Dominion status, even when that status approached independence, seemed an absurd limitation and a hindrance to full growth. The idea behind dominion status, of a mother country closely connected with her daughter nations, all of them having a common cultural background, seemed totally inapplicable to India. It meant certainly a wider sphere of international co-operation, which was desirable, but it also meant at the same time lesser co-operation with countries outside that empire or commonwealth group. It thus became a limiting factor, and our ideas, full of the promise of the future, overstepped these boundaries and looked to a wider co-operation. In particular we thought of close relations with our neighbor countries in the east and west, with China, Afghanistan, Iran, and the Soviet Union. Even with distant America we wanted closer relations, for we could learn much from the United States as also from the Soviet Union. There was a feeling that we had exhausted our capacity for learning anything more from England, and in any event we could only profit by contact with each other after breaking the unhealthy bond that tied us and by meeting on equal terms.

When we talked of the independence of India, it was not in terms of isolation. We realized, perhaps more than many other countries, that the old type of complete national independence was doomed and there must be a new era of world co-operation. We made it repeatedly clear, therefore, that we were perfectly agreeable to limit that independence, in common with other nations, within some international framework. That framework should preferably cover the world or as large a part of it as possible, or be regional. The British Commonwealth did not fit in with either of these conceptions, though it could be a part of the larger framework.

It is surprising how internationally minded we grew in spite of our intense nationalism. No other nationalist movement of a subject country came anywhere near this, and the general tendency in such other countries was to keep clear of international commitments. In India also there were those who objected to our lining up with republican Spain and China, Abyssinia and Czechoslovakia. Why antagonize powerful nations like Italy, Germany, and Japan? they said; every enemy of Britain should be treated as a friend; idealism has no place in politics, which concerns itself with power and the opportune use of it. But these objectors were overwhelmed by the mass sentiment the Congress had created, and hardly ever gave public expression to their views. The Moslem League remained throughout discreetly silent and never committed itself on any such international issue.

In 1938 the Congress sent a medical unit consisting of a number of doctors and necessary equipment and material to China. For several years this unit did good work there. When this was organized, Subhas Bose was president of the Congress. He did not approve of any step being taken by the Congress which was anti-Japanese or anti-German or anti-Italian. And yet such was the feeling in the Congress and the country that he did not oppose this or many other manifestations of Congress sympathy with China and the victims of fascist and nazi aggression. We passed many resolutions and organized many demonstrations of which he did not approve during the period of his presidentship, but he submitted to them without protest because he realized the strength of feeling behind them. There was a big difference in outlook between him and others in the Congress executive, both in regard to foreign and internal matters, and this led to a break early in 1939. He then attacked Congress policy publicly, and early in August 1939 the Congress executive took the very unusual step of taking disciplinary action against him, who was an ex-president.

## II. THE CONGRESS APPROACH TO WAR

Thus the Congress laid down and frequently repeated a dual policy in regard to war. There was, on the one hand, opposition to fascism, nazism, and Japanese militarism, both because of their internal policies and their aggression on other countries; there was intense sympathy with the victims of that aggression; and there was a willingness to join up in any war or other attempt to stop this aggression. On the other hand there was an emphasis on the freedom of India, not only because that was our fundamental objective for which we had continuously labored, but also especially in relation to a possible war. For we reiterated that only a free India could take proper part in such a war; only through freedom could we overcome the bitter heritage of our past relations with Britain and arouse enthusiasm and mobilize our great resources. Without that freedom the war would be like any old war, a contest between rival imperialisms, and an attempt to defend and perpetuate the British Empire as such. It seemed absurd and impossible for us to line up in defense of that very imperialism against which we had been struggling for so long. And even if a few of us, in view of larger considerations, considered that a lesser evil, it was utterly beyond our capacity to carry our people. Only freedom could release mass energy and convert bitterness into enthusiasm for a cause. There was no other way.

The Congress specifically demanded that India should not be committed to any war without the consent of her people or their representatives, and that no Indian troops be sent for service abroad without such consent. The Central Legislative Assembly, consisting of various groups and parties, had also put forward this latter claim. It had long been a grievance of the Indian people that our armed forces were sent abroad for imperialist purposes and often to conquer or suppress other peoples with whom we had no quarrel whatever, and with whose efforts to regain their freedom we sympathized. Indian troops had been used as mercenaries for this purpose in Burma, China, Iran, and the Middle East, and parts of Africa. They had become symbols of British imperialism in all these countries and antagonized their peoples against India. I remember the bitter remark of an Egyptian: "You have not only lost your own freedom but you help the British to enslave others."

The two parts of this dual policy did not automatically fit into each other; there was an element of mutual contradiction in them. But that contradiction was not of our creation; it was inherent in the circumstances and was inevitably mirrored in any policy that arose from those circumstances. Repeatedly we pointed out the inconsistency of condemning fascism and nazism and maintaining imperialist domination. It was true that the former were indulging in horrid crimes while imperialism in India and elsewhere had stabilized itself. The difference was one of degree and of time, not of kind. And then the former were far away, about which some of us read; the latter was always at our doorstep, surrounding all of us and pervading the entire atmosphere. We emphasized the absurdity of holding aloft the banner of democracy elsewhere and denying it to us in India.

Whatever inconsistency there might have been in our dual policy, no question of the doctrine of nonviolence coming in the way of armed conflict for defense or against aggression arose.

I was in England and on the continent of Europe in the summer of 1938, and in speech, writing, and private conversation I explained this policy of ours, and pointed out the dangers of allowing matters to drift or to remain as they were. At the height of the Sudetenland crisis, anxious Czechs asked me what India was likely to do in case of war. Danger was too near and terrible for them to consider fine points and old grievances; nevertheless they appreciated what I said and agreed with the logic of it.

About the middle of 1939 it became known that Indian troops had been dispatched overseas, probably to Singapore and to the Middle East. Immediately there was an outcry at this having been done without any reference to the representatives of the people. It was recognized that troop movements during a period of crisis have often to be secret. Still there were many ways of taking representative leaders into confidence. There were the party leaders in the Central Assembly, and in every province there were popularly elected governments. In the normal course the central government had to consult and share confidence in many matters with these provincial ministries. But not even formal or nominal respect was shown to the people's representatives and the declared wishes of the nation. Steps were also being taken, through the British parliament, to amend the Government of India Act of 1935 under which the provincial governments were functioning, with a view to concentrating all power, in the event of a war emergency, in the central government. Normally, in a democratic country, this might have been a natural and reasonable step, if taken with the consent of the parties concerned. It is well known that federating states, provinces, or autonomous units in a federation are very jealous of their rights and do not easily agree to give them up to a central administration even in a period of crisis and emergency. This tug-of-war is continuous in the U.S.A., and as I write this, a referendum in Australia has rejected the proposal to add to the powers of the commonwealth government at the expense of the states even for the purposes and duration of the war. And yet both in the U.S.A. and Australia the central government and legislature are popularly elected and consist of representatives of those very states. In India the central government was, and is, wholly irresponsible and authoritarian, not elected and not in any way responsible to the people generally or to the provinces. It functioned completely as an agent of the British government. To add to its power at the expense of the provincial governments and legislatures meant weakening still further these popular provincial governments and striking at the very basis of provincial autonomy. This was deeply resented. It was felt that this was contrary to the assurances under which Congress governments had been formed, and indicated that, as previously, war would be imposed upon India without any reference to her chosen representatives.

The Congress executive expressed its strong dissent with this policy, which it considered a deliberate flouting of the declarations both of the Congress and the central legislature. It declared that it must resist any imposition of this kind and could not agree to India's being committed to far-reaching policies without the consent of her people. Again it stated (early in August 1939) that "in this world crisis the sympathies of the Working Committee are entirely with the peoples who stand for democracy and freedom and the Congress has repeatedly condemned fascist aggression in Europe, Africa and the Far East of Asia, as well as the betrayal of democracy by British Imperialism in Czechoslovakia and Spain." But, it was added, "the past policy of the British Government as well as recent developments, demonstrated abundantly that this Government does not stand for freedom and democracy and may at any time betray these ideals. India cannot associate herself with such a Government or be asked to give her resources for democratic freedom which is denied to her and which is likely to be betrayed." As a first step in protest against this policy, the Congress members of the Central Legislative Assembly were asked to refrain from attending the next session of the assembly.

This last resolution was passed three weeks before war actually broke out in Europe. It seemed that the Government of India, and the British government behind it, were bent on ignoring completely Indian opinion not only in regard to the major issues raised by the war crisis but also on many minor matters. This policy was reflected in the attitudes of the governors in the provinces and the civil service administration, which became more non-co-operative with the Congress governments. The position of these Congress provincial governments was becoming increasingly difficult, and strong sections of public opinion were excited and apprehensive. They feared that the British government would act as it had done a quarter of a century earlier in

1914, impose the war on India, ignoring the provincial governments and public opinion and everything that had happened during this period, and make the war a cloak for suppressing such limited freedom as India had obtained and exploiting her resources without check.

But much had happened during this quarter of a century, and the mood of the people was very different. The idea of a great country like India being treated as a chattel and her people utterly and contemptuously ignored was bitterly resented. Was all the struggle and suffering of the past twenty years to count for nothing? Were the Indian people to shame the land from which they sprung by quietly submitting to this disgrace and humiliation? Many of them had learned to resist what they considered evil and not to submit when such submission was considered shameful. They had willingly accepted the consequences of such nonsubmission.

War was declared in Europe, and immediately the Viceroy of India announced that India was also at war. One man, and he a foreigner and a representative of a hated system, could plunge four hundred millions of human beings into war, without the slightest reference to them. There was something fundamentally wrong and rotten in a system under which the fate of these millions could be decided in this way. In the dominions the decision was taken by popular representatives after full debate and consideration of various points of view. Not so in India, and it hurt.

## III. REACTION TO WAR

I was in Chungking when the war began in Europe. The Congress president cabled to me to return immediately and I hurried back. A meeting of the Congress executive was being held when I arrived, and to this meeting Mr. M. A. Jinnah was also invited, but he expressed his inability to come. The viceroy had not only committed India formally to the war but had issued a number of ordinances;

the British parliament had also passed the Government of India Amending Act. All these enactments circumscribed and limited the powers and activities of the provincial governments and were resented, especially as no effort had been made to consult the people's representatives. Indeed their oft-repeated wishes and declarations had been completely ignored.

On September 14, 1939, after long deliberation, the Congress Working Committee issued a lengthy statement on the war crisis. The steps the viceroy had taken and the new enactments and decrees were referred to, and it was stated that "the Working Committee must take the gravest view of these developments." Fascism and nazism were condemned, and particularly "the latest aggression of the Nazi Government in Germany against Poland," and sympathy was expressed for those who were resisting it.

While co-operation was offered, it was added that "any imposed decision . . . will necessarily have to be opposed by them. If co-operation is desired in a worthy cause, this cannot be obtained by compulsion and imposition, and the Committee cannot agree to the carrying out by the Indian people of orders issued by external authority. Co-operation must be between equals by mutual consent for a cause which both consider to be worthy. The people of India have, in the recent past, faced grave risks and willingly made great sacrifices to secure their own freedom and establish a free democratic State in India, and their sympathy is entirely on the side of democracy and freedom. But India cannot associate herself in a war said to be for democratic freedom when that very freedom is denied to her, and such limited freedom as she possesses, taken away from her.

"The Committee are aware that the Governments of Great Britain and France have declared that they are fighting for democracy and freedom and to put an end to aggression. But the history of the recent past is full of examples showing the constant divergence between the spoken word, the ideals proclaimed, and the real motives and objectives." Certain past events, during and after World War I, were referred to, and then: "Subsequent history has demonstrated afresh how even a seemingly fervent declaration of faith may be followed by an ignoble desertion. . . . Again it is asserted that democracy is in danger and must be defended and with this statement the Committee are in entire agreement. The Committee believe that the peoples of the West are moved by this ideal and objective and for these they are prepared to make sacrifices. But again and again the ideals and sentiments of the people and of those who have sacrificed themselves in the struggle have been ignored and faith has not been kept with them.

"If the war is to defend the status quo, imperialist possessions, colonies, vested interests and privilege, then India can have nothing to do with it. If, however, the issue is democracy and a world order based on democracy, then India is intensely interested in it. The Committee are convinced that the interests of Indian democracy do not conflict with the interests of British democracy or of world democracy. But there is an inherent and ineradicable conflict between democracy for India and elsewhere and imperialism and fascism. If Great Britain fights for the maintenance and extension of democracy, then she must necessarily end imperialism in her own possessions. . . . A free democratic India will gladly associate herself with other free nations for mutual defence against aggression and for economic co-operation. She will work for the establishment of a real world order based on freedom and democracy, utilising the world's knowledge and resources for the progress and advancement of humanity."

The Congress executive, nationalist as it was, took an international view and considered the war as something much more than a conflict of armed forces. "The crisis that has overtaken Europe is not of Europe only but of humanity and will not pass like other crises or wars leaving the essential structure of the present-day world intact. It is likely to refashion the world for good or ill, politically, socially and economically. This crisis is the inevitable consequence of the social and political conflicts and contradictions which have grown alarmingly since the last Great War, and it will not be finally resolved till these conflicts and contradictions are removed and a new equilibrium established. That equilibrium can only be based on the ending of the domination and exploitation of one country by another, and on a reorganization of economic relations on a juster basis for the common good of all. India is the crux of the problem, for India has been the outstanding example of modern imperialism and no refashioning of the world can succeed which ignores this vital problem. With her vast resources she must play an important part in any scheme of world reorganization. But she can only do so as a free nation whose energies have been released to work for this great end. Freedom today is indivisible and every attempt to retain imperialist domination in any part of the world will lead inevitably to fresh disaster."

The committee proceeded to refer to the offers of rulers of Indian states to support the cause of democracy in Europe, and suggested that it would be fitting if they introduced democracy within their own states, where undiluted autocracy prevailed.

The committee again stated their eagerness to help in every way but expressed their apprehension at the trend of British policy both in the past and present in which they failed "to find any attempt to advance the cause of democracy or self-determination or any evidence that the present war declarations of the British Government are being, or are going to be, acted upon." They added, however, that in view "of the gravity of the occasion and the fact that the pace of events during the last few days has often been swifter than the working of men's minds, the Committee desire to take no final decision at this stage, so as to allow for full elucidation of the issues at stake, the real objectives aimed at, and the position of India in the present and in the future." They invited therefore "the British Government to declare in unequivocal terms what their war aims are in regard to democracy and imperialism and the new order that is envisaged, in particular, how these aims are going to apply to India and to be given effect to in the present. Do they include the elimination of imperialism and the treatment of India as a free nation whose policy will be guided in accordance with the wishes of her

people? . . . The real test of any declaration is its application in the present, for it is the present that will govern
action today and give shape to the future. . . . It will be
infinite tragedy if even this terrible war is carried on in
the spirit of imperialism and for the purpose of retaining
this structure which is itself the cause of war and human
degradation."

This statement, issued after anxious deliberation, was an
attempt to overcome the barriers that had arisen between
India and England and poisoned their relations for a century and a half, to find some way to reconcile our eagerness
to join in this world struggle with popular enthusiasm behind us, and our passionate desire for freedom. That assertion of India's right to freedom was no new thing; it
was not the result of the war or the international crisis. It
had long been the very basis for all our thoughts and activities, round which we had revolved for many generations. There was no difficulty whatever in making a clear
declaration of India's freedom and then adapting this to
existing circumstances, keeping the needs of the war in
view. Indeed the very necessities of the war demanded it.
If England had the desire and the will to acknowledge
India's freedom, every major difficulty vanished and what
remained was capable of adjustment with the consent of
the parties concerned. In every province provincial governments were functioning. It was easy to evolve a popular
central apparatus of government for the war period which
would organize the war effort on an efficient and popular
basis, co-operate fully with the armed forces, and be a link
between the people and the provincial governments on the
one hand and the British government on the other. Other
constitutional problems could be postponed till after the
war, though of course it was desirable to attempt to solve
them even earlier. After the war the elected representatives
of the people would draw up the permanent constitution
and enter into a treaty with England in regard to our mutual interests.

It was no easy matter for the Congress executive to make
this offer to England when most of our people had little
appreciation of the international issues involved and were

expressing their resentment at recent British policy. We knew that longstanding distrust and suspicion on both sides could not vanish away by some magic word. Yet we hoped that the very stress of events would induce England's leaders to come out of their imperialist grooves, take a long view, and accept our offer, thus ending the long feud between England and India, and releasing India's enthusiasm and resources for the war.

But that was not to be, and their answer was a refusal of all we had asked for. It became clear to us that they did not want us as friends and colleagues but as a slave people to do their bidding. Both used the same word "co-operation," but a different meaning was attached to it by either party. For us co-operation was to be between comrades and equals; for them it meant their commanding and our obeying without demur. It was impossible for us to accept this position without abandoning and betraying everything that we had stood for and that had given some meaning to our lives. And even if some of us had been willing to do so, we could not have carried our people with us; we would have been stranded, isolated and cut off from the living currents of nationalism, as well as from the internationalism that we envisaged.

The position of our provincial governments became difficult, and the choice for them was submission to continuous interference by the governor and the viceroy, or conflict with them. The superior services were wholly on the governor's side and looked upon the ministers and the legislature, even more than before, as intruders. Again there was the old constitutional conflict between an autocratic king or his representatives and a parliament, with this addition, that the former were foreigners basing their rule on armed force. It was decided that the Congress governments in the eight provinces out of eleven (all except Bengal, Punjab, and Sind) should resign in protest. Some were of the opinion that instead of resigning they should carry on and thus invite dismissal by the governor. It was clear that in view of the inherent conflict, which was daily becoming more obvious, clashes between them and the governors were inevitable and if they did not resign, they would be dismissed from office. They took the strictly constitutional course of resigning and thus inviting a dissolution of the legislatures and fresh elections. As big majorities were behind them in the legislatures, no other ministries could be formed. The governors, however, were anxious to avoid new elections, as they knew well enough that these would result in the overwhelming triumph of the Congress. They did not dissolve the legislatures but merely suspended them, and assumed all the powers of the provincial governments and legislatures. They became completely autocratic heads of provinces, making laws, issuing decrees, and doing everything else they wanted to without the slightest reference to any elected body or public opinion.

## IV. ANOTHER CONGRESS OFFER AND ITS REJECTION BY THE BRITISH GOVERNMENT
### MR. WINSTON CHURCHILL

The change-over to autocratic and one-man rule in eight of the provinces was not a mere substitution of the people at the top, such as a change in ministries might indicate. It was a radical and organic change affecting the whole spirit, policy, and methods of the entire state organization. The legislatures and the various popular checks on the executive and the permanent services vanished, and the approach of the civil service, from the governor downward, and of the police service, toward the public became different. It was not merely a reversion and setback to the days before the Congress governments had come into power. It was much worse. In so-called law it was a going back to the unchecked autocracy of the nineteenth century. In practice it was harsher, as the old confidence and paternalism were absent, and all the fear and passion of a long-established vested interest which was breaking up pervaded the British element in the administration. The two and a quarter years of Congress governments had been hard to bear; the carrying out of the policy and orders of those who could always be sent to prison if they gave trouble had not been pleasant. Now there was a desire not only to resume the old thread but also to put these troublemakers in their proper places. Everyone, the peasant in the field, the worker in the factory, the artisans and the shopkeepers, the industrialists, the professional classes, the young men and women in colleges, the subordinate services, and even those Indians in the higher ranks of the services who had shown any enthusiasm for the popular governments must be made to realize that the British Raj still functioned and had to be reckoned with. It was that Raj that would determine their individual futures and their chances of preferment, and not some temporary intruders from outside. Those who had functioned as the secretaries of the ministers were now the bosses, acting under the governor, and spoke again in their old superior way; the district magistrates resumed their old functions of *gauleiters* for their respective areas; the police felt freer to revert to old habits, knowing well that they would be supported and protected from above, even when they misbehaved. The fog of war could be made to cover everything.

Many even of the critics of Congress governments viewed this prospect with dismay. They remembered now many of the virtues of those governments and expressed their strong displeasure at their resignation. According to them, they should have held on whatever the consequences. Curiously enough, even members of the Moslem League were apprehensive.

If this was the reaction on non-Congressmen and critics of the Congress governments, the reaction on the members and sympathizers of the Congress and the members of the legislatures can well be imagined. The ministers had resigned from their offices but not from membership of the legislature, nor had the speakers and the members of these legislatures resigned. Nevertheless they were pushed aside and ignored, and no fresh elections were held. Even from a purely constitutional point of view this was not easy to tolerate and would have produced a crisis in any country. A powerful, semirevolutionary organization like the Congress, representing the nationalist sentiment of the country, and with a long record of struggle for freedom behind it, could not passively accept this autocratic one-man rule. It could not just be a spectator of what was happening, more especially as this was directed against it. There were strong and repeated demands for positive action to counter this suppression of the legislatures and of public activity generally and the whole policy of the British government in regard to India.

After the refusal of the British government to state their war aims or to make any advance in India, the Congress Working Committee had declared: "The answer to this demand [of the Congress] has been entirely unsatisfactory and an attempt has been made on behalf of the British Government to create misunderstanding and to befog the main and moral issue. . . . The Committee can only interpret this attempt to avoid a statement of war aims and Indian freedom, by taking shelter under irrelevant issues, as a desire to maintain imperialist domination of India in alliance with the reactionary elements in the country. The Congress has looked upon the war crisis and the problems it raises as essentially a moral issue, and has not sought to profit by it in any spirit of bargaining. The moral and dominant issue of war aims and India's freedom has to be settled satisfactorily before any other subsidiary question can be considered. In no event can the Congress accept the responsibility of government, even in the transitional period, without real power being given to popular representatives."

The committee went on to say that because of the declarations made on behalf of the British government, the Congress had been compelled to dissociate itself from British policy, and as a first step in non-co-operation, the Congress governments in the provinces had resigned. The general policy of non-co-operation continued and would have to continue unless the British government revised its policy. "The Working Committee would, however, remind Congressmen that it is inherent in every form of Satyagraha that no effort is spared to achieve an honourable settlement with the opponent. . . . The Working Committee will, therefore, continue to explore the means of arriving at an honourable settlement, even though the British Government has banged the door in the face of the Congress."

In view of the excitement prevailing in the country and the possibility of young men taking to violent courses, the committee reminded the country of the basic policy of non-violence and warned it against any breach of it. Even if there was to be any civil resistance, it must be wholly peaceful. Further, that "Satyagraha means goodwill towards all, especially towards opponents." This reference to nonviolence had no connection with the war or with the defense of the country against aggression; it was meant to apply to any action that might be taken in the course of Indian freedom against British rule.

The situation in the country was deteriorating in many ways. Politically this was obvious. Even economically, while some among the peasantry and the workers were somewhat better off owing to war conditions, large numbers had been hit hard. The persons who were really prospering were the war profiteers, contractors, and a horde of officials, chiefly British, employed at fancy salaries for war work. The government's idea apparently was that the war effort would be best promoted by encouraging the motive for excessive profit. Corruption and nepotism were rampant, and there were no popular checks on them. Public criticism was considered a discouragement of war effort and hence to be put down by the all-embracing provisions of the Defence of India Act. It was a discouraging spectacle.

All these factors induced us to try our utmost once again to arrive at a settlement with the British government. What were the chances? Not very promising. The whole organization of the permanent services was enjoying a freedom from control and criticism such as they had not had for more than two generations. They could clap in prison any person they disapproved of, with or without trial. The governors enjoyed unrestrained power and authority over vast provinces. Why should they consent to a change unless they were forced to do so by circumstances? Over the top of the imperial structure sat the viceroy, Lord Linlithgow, surrounded by all the pomp and ceremony befitting his high position. Heavy of body and slow of mind, solid as a rock and with almost a rock's lack of awareness, possessing the qualities and failings of an old-fashioned British aristocrat, he sought with integrity and honesty of purpose to find a way out of the tangle. But his limitations were too many; his mind worked in the old groove and shrank back from any innovations; his vision was limited by the traditions of the ruling class out of which he came; he saw and heard through the eyes and ears of the civil service and others who surrounded him; he distrusted people who talked of fundamental political and social changes; he disliked those who did not show a becoming appreciation of the high mission of the British Empire and its chief representative in India.

In England there had been a change during the dark days of the German blitzkrieg over western Europe. Mr. Neville Chamberlain had gone, and that was a relief from many points of view. The Marquis of Zetland, that ornament of his noble order, had also departed from the India office without any tears being shed. In his place had come Mr. Amery about whom little was known, but this little was significant. He had vigorously defended in the House of Commons Japanese aggression over China, giving as an argument that if they condemned what Japan had done in China, they would have to condemn equally what Britain had done in India and Egypt. A sound argument used perversely for a wrong purpose.

But the person who really counted was Mr. Winston Churchill, the new prime minister. Mr. Churchill's views on Indian freedom were clear and definite and had been frequently repeated. He stood out as an uncompromising opponent of that freedom. In January 1930 he had said: "Sooner or later you will have to crush Gandhi and the Indian Congress and all they stand for." In December of that year he said: "The British nation has no intention whatever of relinquishing control of Indian life and progress. . . . We have no intention of casting away that most truly bright and precious jewel in the crown of the King, which more than all our Dominions and Dependencies, constitutes the glory and strength of the British Empire."

Later he explained what those magic words "dominion

status," so frequently thrown at us, really meant in relation to India. In January 1931 he said: "We have always contemplated it [dominion status] as the ultimate goal, but no one has supposed, except in a purely ceremonious sense in the way in which representatives of India attend Conferences during the war, that the principle and policy for India would be carried into effect in any time which it is reasonable or useful for us to foresee." And again, in December 1931: "Most of the leading public men—of whom I was one in those days—made speeches—I certainly did—about Dominion Status, but I did not contemplate India having the same constitutional rights and system as Canada in any period which we can foresee. . . . England, apart from her Empire in India, ceases for ever to exist as a great power."

That was the crux of the question. India was the empire; it was her possession and exploitation that gave glory and strength to England and made her a great power. Mr. Churchill could not conceive of England except as the head and possessor of a vast empire, and so he could not conceive of India free. And dominion status, which had so long been held out to us as something within our grasp, was explained to be a mere matter of words and ceremony, very far removed from freedom and power. Dominion status, even in its fullest sense, had been rejected by us, and we claimed independence. The gulf between Mr. Churchill and us was vast indeed.

Positive action became inevitable; for sometimes the only failure is in failing to act. That action could only be, in accordance with our established policy, in the nature of civil disobedience. Yet care was taken not to have any popular upheavals, and that civil disobedience was limited to chosen individuals. It was what is called individual civil disobedience as contrasted with the mass variety of it. It was really in the nature of a great moral protest. From a politician's point of view it seems odd that we should deliberately avoid any attempt to upset the administration, and make it easy for it to put the troublemakers in prison. That has not been the way of aggressive political action or revolution anywhere else. Yet that was Gandhi's way of combining morality with revolutionary politics, and he was always the inevitable leader when any such movement took place. It was his way of showing that while we refused to submit to British policy and showed our resentment and determination by voluntarily inviting suffering for ourselves, yet our object was not to create trouble.

This individual civil disobedience movement started in a very small way, each person having to pass some kind of a test and get permission before he or she could take part in it. Those who were chosen broke some formal order, were arrested and sentenced to imprisonment. As is usual with us, men at the top were chosen first—members of the Congress executive, ex-ministers of provincial governments, members of the legislatures, members of the all-India and provincial Congress committees. Gradually the circle grew till between twenty-five to thirty thousand men and women were in prison. These included the speakers and a large number of members of our provincial legislative assemblies, which had been suspended by government. Thus we demonstrated that if our elected assemblies were not allowed to function, they would not submit to autocratic rule and preferred prison to it.

Apart from those who offered formal civil disobedience, many thousands were arrested and sentenced for making speeches or some other activity, or detained without trial. I was arrested at an early stage and sentenced to four years' imprisonment for a speech.

From October 1940 for over a year all these persons remained in prison. We tried to follow, with such material as we could obtain, the course of the war and of events in India and the world. We read of the Four Freedoms of President Roosevelt, we heard of the Atlantic Charter, and, soon after, of Mr. Churchill's qualification that this charter had no application to India.

In June 1941 we were stirred by Hitler's sudden attack on Soviet Russia, and we followed with anxious interest the dramatic changes in the war situation.

On December 4, 1941, many of us were discharged. Three days later came Pearl Harbor and the Pacific war.

## V. AFTER PEARL HARBOR
### GANDHI AND NONVIOLENCE

When we came out of prison, the nationalist position, the question of India versus England, had changed in no way. Prison affects people in various ways: some break down or weaken, others grow harder and more confirmed in their convictions, and it is usually the latter whose influence is felt more by the mass of the people. But though nationally we remained where we were, Pearl Harbor and what followed it suddenly created a new tension and gave a new perspective. The Congress Working Committee met immediately after in this new atmosphere of tension. The Japanese had made no great advance till then, but major and stunning disasters had already taken place. The war ceased to be a distant spectacle and began to approach India and affect her intimately. Among Congressmen the desire to play an effective part in these perilous developments became strong, and the jail-going business seemed pointless in this new situation. But what could we do unless some door was open for honorable co-operation and the people could be made to feel some positive inspiration for action? A negative fear of threatening danger was not enough.

In spite of past history and all that had happened, we were eager to offer our co-operation in the war and especially for the defense of India, subject necessarily to a national government which would enable us to function in the co-operation with other elements in the country and to make the people feel that it was really a national effort and not an imposed one by outsiders who had enslaved us. There was no difference of opinion on this general approach among Congressmen as well as most others, but a vital difference of principle arose rather unexpectedly. Gandhi found himself unable to give up his fundamental principle of nonviolence even in regard to external war. The very nearness of that war became a challenge to him and a test of faith. If he failed at this critical moment, either non-violence was not the all-embracing and basic principle and course of action he had believed it to be, or else he was wrong in discarding it or compromising with it. He could not give up the faith of a lifetime on which he had based all his activities, and he felt that he must accept the necessary consequences and implications of that nonviolence.

When Gandhiji raised in 1940 the question of non-violence in relation to the war and the future of free India, the Congress Working Committee had to face the issue squarely. They made it clear to him that they were unable to go as far as he wanted them to go and could not possibly commit India or the Congress to future applications of this principle in the external domain. This led to a definite and public break with him on this issue. Two months later further discussions led to an agreed formula which was later adopted as part of a resolution by the All-India Congress Committee. That formula did not wholly represent Gandhiji's attitude; it represented what he agreed, perhaps rather unwillingly, for Congress to say on this subject. At that time the British government had already rejected the latest offer made by the Congress for co-operation in the war on the basis of a national government. Some kind of conflict was approaching, and, as was inevitable, both Gandhiji and Congress looked toward each other and were impelled by a desire to find a way out of the deadlock between them. The formula did not refer to the war, as just previously our offer of co-operation had been unceremoniously and utterly rejected. It dealt theoretically with the Congress policy in regard to nonviolence, and for the first time stated how, in the opinion of the Congress, the free India of the future should apply it in its external relations. That part of the resolution ran thus:

The All-India Congress Committee "firmly believes in the policy and practice of non-violence not only in the struggle for Swaraj, but also, in so far as this may be possible of application, in free India. The Committee is convinced, and recent world events have demonstrated, that complete world disarmament is necessary and the establishment of a new and juster political and economic order, if the world is not to destroy itself and revert to barbarism. A free India will, therefore, throw all her weight in favor of world disarmament and should herself be prepared to give a lead in this to the world. Such lead will inevitably depend on external factors and internal conditions, but the State would do its utmost to give effect to this policy of disarmament. Effective disarmament and the establishment of world peace by the ending of national wars, depend ultimately on the removal of the causes of wars and national conflicts. These causes must be rooted out by the ending of the domination of one country over another and the exploitation of one people or group by another. To that end India will peacefully labor, and it is with this objective in view that the people of India desire to attain the status of a free and independent nation. Such freedom will be the prelude to the close association with other countries within a comity of free nations for the peace and progress of the world." This declaration, it will be noticed, while strongly affirming the Congress wish for peaceful action and disarmament, also emphasized a number of qualifications and limitations.

The internal crisis within the Congress was resolved in 1940, and then came a year of prison for large numbers of us. In December 1941, however, the same crisis took shape again when Gandhiji insisted on complete nonviolence. Again there was a split and public disagreement, and the president of the Congress, Maulana Abul Kalam Azad, and others were unable to accept Gandhiji's view. It became clear that the Congress as a whole, including some of the faithful followers of Gandhiji, disagreed with him in this matter. The force of circumstances and the rapid succession of dramatic events influenced all of us, including Gandhiji, and he refrained from pressing his view on the Congress, though he did not identify himself with the Congress view.

At no other time was this issue raised by Gandhiji in the Congress. When later Sir Stafford Cripps came with his proposals, there was no question of nonviolence. His proposals were considered purely from the political point of view. In later months, leading up to August 1942, Gan-

dhiji's nationalism and intense desire for freedom made
him even agree to Congress participation in the war if
India could function as a free country. For him this was a
remarkable and astonishing change, involving suffering of
the mind and pain of the spirit. In the conflict between
that principle of nonviolence which had become his very
life blood and meaning of existence, and India's freedom,
which was a dominating and consuming passion for him,
the scales inclined toward the latter. That did not mean, of
course, that he weakened in his faith in nonviolence. But
it did mean that he was prepared to agree to the Congress
not applying it in this war. The practical statesman took
precedence over the uncompromising prophet.

## VI. TENSION

In India tension grew in those early months of 1942. The
theater of war came ever nearer, and there was now the
probability of air raids over Indian cities. What was going
to happen in those Eastern countries where war was raging? What new development would take place in the relations between India and England? Were we going to carry
on in the old way, glaring at each other, tied up and
separated by the bitter memories of past history, victims
of a tragic fate which none could avert? Or would common
perils help us to bridge that chasm? Even the bazaars woke
up from their normal lethargy; a wave of excitement passed
over them and they buzzed with all manner of rumors. The
monied classes were afraid of the future that was advancing so swiftly toward them, for that future, whatever else
it might be, was likely to upset the social structure they
were accustomed to and endanger their interests and special
position. The peasant and the worker had no such fear,
for he had little to lose and he looked forward to any change
from his present unhappy condition.

In India there had all along been much sympathy for
China, and as a consequence a certain antipathy to Japan.
The Pacific war, it was thought at first, would bring relief

to China. For four and a half years China had fought singlehanded against Japan; now she had powerful allies, and surely this must lighten her burden and lessen her danger. But those allies suffered blow after blow, and before the advancing Japanese armies the British colonial empire cracked up with amazing rapidity. Was this proud structure, then, just a house of cards with no foundations or inner strength? Inevitably, comparisons were made with China's long resistance to Japanese aggression in spite of her lack of almost everything required for modern war. China went up in people's estimation, and though Japan was not liked, there was a feeling of satisfaction at the collapse of old-established European colonial powers before the armed strength of an Asian power. That racial, Oriental-Asiatic feeling was evident on the British side also. Defeat and disaster were bitter enough, but the fact that an Oriental and Asiatic power had triumphed over them added to the bitterness and humiliation. An Englishman occupying a high position said that he would have preferred it if the *Prince of Wales* and the *Repulse* had been sunk by the Germans instead of by the yellow Japanese.

The visit of the Chinese leaders, Generalissimo and Mme. Chiang Kai-shek, was a great event in India. Official conventions and the wishes of the Government of India prevented them from mixing with the people, but their presence in India itself at that critical stage and their manifest sympathy for India's freedom helped to bring India out of her national shell and increased her awareness of the international issues at stake. The bonds that tied India and China grew stronger, and so did the desire to line up with China and other nations against the common adversary. The peril to India helped to bring nationalism and internationalism close together, the only separating factor being the policy of the British government.

The Government of India were no doubt very conscious of the approaching perils; there must have been anxiety in their minds and a sense of urgency. But such was the conventional existence of the British in India, so set were they in their established grooves, so wedded to the never-ending processes of bureaucratic red tape, that no marked change was visible in their outlook or activities. There was no sense of hurry and speed, of tension and getting things done. The system they represented had been built up for another age and with other objectives. Whether it was their army or their civil services, the objective in view was the occupation of India and the suppression of any attempts of the Indian people to free themselves. It was efficient enough for that purpose, but modern war against a powerful and ruthless adversary was a very different matter, and they found it exceedingly difficult to adapt themselves to it. Not only were they mentally not fitted for this, but a great part of their energies were absorbed in keeping down nationalism in India.

The collapse of the Burmese and Malayan administrations before new problems had been significant and revealing, yet it taught no lesson. Burma had been governed by the same kind of civil service as India; indeed till a few years ago it had been part of the Indian administration. The ways of government there were identical with those of India, and Burma had demonstrated how moribund this system was. But the system continued without change, and the Viceroy and his high officials functioned in the same way as before. They added to their number many of the higher officials who had failed so conspicuously in Burma; there was another Excellency sitting on the hilltop at Simla. As with the emigré governments in London, we were given the privilege of having in our midst emigré officials from British colonies. They fitted in like a glove into the British structure in India.

Like shadows on a stage these high officials continued to function in their old way, trying to impress us with their elaborate imperial ritual, their court ceremonies, their durbars and investitures, their parades, their dinners and evening dress, their pompous utterances. The Viceroy's House in New Delhi was the chief temple where the High Priest officiated, but there were many other temples and priests. All this ceremonial and display of imperial pomp was designed to impress, and it had impressed our people in the old days, for Indians also are given to ceremonial observances. But new standards had risen, different values had been created, and now this elaborate show was the subject of jest and ridicule. Indians are supposed to be a slow-moving people, disinclined to rush and hurry, but even they had developed a certain speed and vigor in their work, so strong was their desire to get things done. The Congress provincial governments, whatever their failings may have been, were anxious to achieve results and worked hard and continuously, disregarding many old-established routines. It was irritating to see the passivity and slowness of the Government of India and its many agents in the face of grave crisis and peril.

And then came the Americans. They were very much in a hurry, eager to get things done, ignorant of the ways and ceremonies of the Government of India and not particularly anxious to learn them. Intolerant of delay, they pushed aside obstructions and red-tape methods and upset the even tenor of life in New Delhi. They were not even careful of the dress they should wear on particular occasions and sometimes offended against the rigid rules of protocol and official procedure. While the help they were bringing was very welcome, they were not liked in the highest official circles and relations were strained. Indians liked them on the whole; their energy and enthusiasm for the work in hand were infectious and contrasted with the lack of these qualities in British official circles in India. Their forthrightness and freedom from official constraints were appreciated. There was much silent amusement at the underlying friction between the newcomers and the official class, and many true or imagined stories of this were repeated.

The approach of the war to India disturbed Gandhi greatly. It was not easy to fit in his policy and program of nonviolence with this new development. Obviously civil disobedience was out of the question in the face of an invading army or between two opposing armies. Passivity or acceptance of invasion were equally out of the question. What then? His own colleagues, and the Congress generally, had rejected nonviolence for such an occasion or as an alternative to armed resistance to invasion, and he had at last agreed that they had a right to do so. But he was none the less troubled, and for his own part, as an individual, he could not join any violent course of action. But he was much more than an individual; whether he had any official status or not in the nationalist movement, he occupied an outstanding and dominating position, and his word carried weight with large numbers of people.

Gandhiji knew India, and especially the Indian masses, as very few, if any, have known them in the past or the present. Not only had he widely traveled all over India and come into touch with millions of people, but there was something else which enabled him to come into emotional contact with those masses. He could merge himself with the masses and feel with them, and because they were conscious of this, they gave him their devotion and loyalty. And yet his view of India was to some extent colored by the outlook he had imbibed in his early days in Gujrat. The Gujratis were essentially a community of peaceful traders and merchants, influenced by the Jain doctrine of nonviolence. Other parts of India had been influenced much less by this, and some not at all. The widespread Kshatriya class of warriors certainly did not allow it to interfere with war or hunting wild animals. Other classes also, including the Brahmans, had been as a whole little influenced by it. But Gandhiji took an eclectic view of the development of Indian thought and history and believed that nonviolence had been the basic principle underlying it, even though there had been many deviations from it. That view appeared to be farfetched, and many Indian thinkers and historians did not agree with it. This had nothing to do with the merits of nonviolence in the present stage of human existence, but it did indicate a historical bias in Gandhiji's mind.

## VII. SIR STAFFORD CRIPPS COMES TO INDIA

With the fall of Penang and Singapore, and as the Japanese advanced in Malaya, there was an exodus of Indians and others and they poured into India. They had to leave very suddenly, carrying nothing with them except the clothes they were in. Then followed the flood of refugees from Burma, hundreds of thousands of them, mostly Indians. The story of how they had been deserted by civil and other authorities and left to shift for themselves spread throughout India. They trekked hundreds of miles across mountains and through dense forests, surrounded by enemies, many dying on the way, killed by dagger or disease or starvation. That was a horrible result of the war and had to be accepted. But it was not the war that caused the discrimination in treatment between Indian and British refugees. The latter were cared for as far as possible and arrangements were made for their transport and assistance. From one place in Burma where vast numbers of refugees were gathering there were two roads leading to India. The better one was reserved for Britishers or Europeans; it came to be known as the White Road.

Horrible stories of racial discrimination and suffering reached us, and as the famished survivors spread out all over India they carried these stories with them, creating a powerful effect on the Indian mind.

Just then Sir Stafford Cripps came to India with the proposals of the British war cabinet. Those proposals have been discussed fully during the past two and a half years, and they are past history already. It is a little difficult for one who took part in the negotiations that followed to deal with them in any detail without saying much that had better be left unsaid till some future time. As a matter of fact, all the relevant issues and considerations that arose have already been made public.

I remember that when I read those proposals for the first time I was profoundly depressed, and that depression was largely due to the fact that I had expected something more substantial from Sir Stafford Cripps as well as from the critical situation that had arisen. The more I read the proposals and considered their many implications, the greater was my feeling of depression. I could understand a person unacquainted with Indian affairs imagining that they went far to meet our demand. But, when analyzed, there were so many limitations, and the very acceptance of the principle of self-determination was fettered and circumscribed in such a way as to imperil our future.

The proposals dealt essentially with the future, after the cessation of hostilities, though there was a final clause which vaguely invited co-operation in the present. That future, while asserting the principle of self-determination, gave the right to provinces not to join the Indian union, and to form separate independent states. Further, the same right of nonaccession to the Indian union was given to the Indian states, and it should be remembered that there are over six hundred such states in India, some major ones, and the great majority tiny enclaves. These states, as well as the provinces, would all join in the constitution-making, would influence that constitution, and then could walk out of it. The whole background would be of separatism, and the real problems of the country, economic or political, would take secondary place. Reactionary elements, differing from each other in many ways, would unite to frustrate the evolution of a strong, progressive, unified national state. Under the constant threat of withdrawal, many undesirable provisions might be introduced into the constitution, the central government might be weakened and emasculated, and yet the withdrawal might still follow, and it would be difficult then to refashion the constitution and make it more workable for the remaining provinces and states. The elections in the provinces for the constitution-making body would take place under the existing system of separate religious electorates; that was unfortunate, as it would bring with it the old spirit of cleavage, and yet, in the circumstances, it was inevitable. But in the states there was no provision for elections, and their ninety million inhabitants were completely ignored. The semifeudal rulers of the states could nominate their own representatives in proportion to the population. These nominees might contain some able ministers, but as a whole they would inevitably represent, not the people of the states, but the feudal and autocratic ruler. They would form nearly one-quarter of the members of the constitution-making body, and would powerfully influence its decisions by their numbers, their socially backward attitude, and their threats of subsequent withdrawal. The constituent assembly or constitution-making body would be a curious mixture of elected and nonelected elements, the former chosen by separate religious electorates as well as by certain vested interests, the latter nominated by the rulers of the states. To this had to be added the fact that there would be no pressure to accept joint decisions, and the sense of reality which comes from evolving integrated and final decisions would be lacking. The tendency for many of its members would be to act in a wholly irresponsible manner, for they would feel that they could always withdraw and refuse to accept the responsibility for carrying out those decisions.

Any proposal to cut up India into parts was a painful one to contemplate; it went against all those deeply felt sentiments and convictions that move people so powerfully. The whole nationalist movement of India had been based on India's unity, but the sentiment was older and deeper than the present phase of nationalism; it went far back into the remote periods of Indian history. That belief and sentiment had been strengthened by modern developments till it had become an article of faith for vast numbers of people, something that could not be challenged or controverted. A challenge had come from the Moslem League, but few took it seriously, and there were certainly large numbers of Moslems who did not agree with it. Even the basis of that challenge was not really territorial, though it suggested a vague, undefined partition of territory. The basis was a medieval conception of nations based on religious differences, and according to it, therefore, in every village in India there were two or more nations. Even a partition of India could not get over these widespread and overlapping religious divisions. A partition would in fact add to the difficulty and increase the very problems it was intended to solve.

Apart from sentiment, there were solid reasons against partition. The social and economic problems of India had reached a crisis, chiefly because of the policy of the British government, which necessitated rapid and all-round progress if the gravest of disasters had to be averted. That progress could only take place with real and effective planning for the whole of India, for the various parts supplied each other's deficiencies. As a whole, India was to a large extent a powerful and self-sufficient unit, but each part by itself would be weak and dependent on others. If all these, and other, arguments were valid and sufficient in the past, they became doubly important by modern political and economic developments. Small states were disappearing everywhere as independent entities; they were becoming absorbed in, or economic appendages to, the larger states. There was an inevitable tendency for vast federations, or collections of many states functioning together, to grow up. The idea of the national state itself was giving place to the multinational state, and in the distant future there appeared a vision of a world federation. To think of partitioning India at this stage went against the whole current of modern historical and economic development. It seemed to be fantastic in the extreme.

And yet under stress of dire necessity or some compelling disaster one has to agree to many undesirable things. Circumstances may force a partition of what logically and normally must not be divided. But the proposals put forward on behalf of the British government did not deal with any definite and particular partition of India. They opened out a vista of an indefinite number of partitions both of provinces and states. They incited all the reactionary, feudal, and socially backward groups to claim partition. Probably none of them seriously wanted it, because they could not stand by themselves. But they could give a lot of trouble and obstruct and delay the formation of a free Indian state. If they were backed by British policy, as they well might be, it meant no freedom at all for a long time. Our experience of that policy had been bitter, and at every stage we had found that it encouraged fissiparous tendencies. What was the guarantee that it would not continue to do so and then claim that it could not fulfill its promise because the conditions for it were lacking? Indeed the probability was that this policy would continue.

Thus this proposal was not a mere acceptance of Pakistan or a particular partition, bad as that would have been, but something much worse, opening the door to the possibility of an indefinite number of partitions. It was a continuing menace to the freedom of India and a barrier to the fulfillment of the very promise that had been made.

The decision about the future of the Indian states was not going to be made by the people of those states or their chosen representatives but by their autocratic rulers. Our acceptance of this principle would have been a negation of our well-established and often repeated policy and a betrayal of the people of the states, who would have been condemned to autocratic rule for a much longer period. We were prepared to treat with the princes as gently as possible so as to gain their co-operation in the change-over to democracy, and if there had been no third party, like the British power, we would no doubt have succeeded. But with the British government supporting autocracy in the states, the princes were likely to keep out of the Indian union and rely on British military support for protection against their own people. Indeed, we were told that if such circumstances arose, foreign armed forces would be kept in the states. As these states were often likely to be isolated islands in the territory of the proposed Indian union, the question arose how foreign forces could reach them or communicate with the forces in some other similar state. That necessitated a right of way for foreign forces over the territory of the Indian union.

Gandhiji had repeatedly declared that he was no enemy of the princes. Indeed his attitude had been consistently a friendly one toward them, though he had often criticized their methods of government and their denial of even elementary rights to their people. For many years he had prevented the Congress from interfering directly with the affairs of the states, believing as he did that the people of the states should themselves take the initiative and thus develop self-confidence and strength. Many of us had disapproved of this attitude of his. Yet behind it lay one basic conviction, as he put it himself: "One fundamental element in my attitude is that I shall never be a party to the sale of the rights of the people of the States [even] for the sake of the freedom of the people of British India." Professor Berriedale Keith, the eminent authority on the British Commonwealth and Indian constitutions, supported Gandhiji's claim (which was the Congress claim) in regard to the states. Keith wrote: "It is impossible for the Crown's advisers to contend that the people of the States shall be denied the rights of Indians in the provinces, and it is their clear duty to advise the King-Emperor to use his authority to secure that the Princes shall enter into constitutional reforms which will result at no distant date in securing responsible government therein. No federation can be deemed in the interest of India, if in it representatives of the provinces are compelled to sit with the nominees of irresponsible rulers. There is, in fact, no answer to Mr. Gandhi's claim that the Princes are bound to follow the Crown in its transfer of authority to the people." Professor Keith had given this opinion in regard to the earlier proposal of the British government relating to federation, but it was even more applicable to the proposals brought by Sir Stafford Cripps.

The more one thought of these proposals, the more fantastic they grew. India became a checkerboard containing scores of nominally independent or semi-independent states, many of them relying on Britain for military protection of autocratic rule. There was to be neither political nor economic unity, and Britain might well continue to exercise dominating control, both politically and economically, through the many petty states it controlled.[1]

What the British war cabinet had in mind for the future I do not know. I think Sir Stafford Cripps meant well for India and hoped to see a free and united India. But this was not a matter of individual views or opinions or personal good will. We had to consider a state document, carefully drafted in spite of its deliberate vagueness, and we were told that we had to accept it or reject it as a whole. And

[1] The entire dependence of the Indian states on British power and protection is stressed by Sir Geoffrey de Montmorency in his *The Indian States and Indian Federation* (1942): The states "are still so numerous in India that they offer a grave conundrum in evolution to which no solution is at present forthcoming. . . . Their disappearance and absorption would, of course, be inevitable if Britain ever ceased to be the supreme power as regards India."

behind it lay the continuous, century-old policy of the British government, creating division in India and encouraging every factor that came in the way of national growth and freedom. Every forward step that had been taken in the past had always been hedged in by qualifications and limitations, which seemed innocuous enough at the beginning, and yet which proved to be formidable checks and breaks.

So it all came to this, that the existing structure of government would continue exactly as before, the autocratic powers of the viceroy would remain, and a few of us could become his liveried camp followers and look after canteens and the like. There was not an atom of difference between this and what Mr. Amery had offered eighteen months earlier and which had seemed to us then an affront to India. It was true that there would be a psychological change after all that had happened, and individuals make a difference. Strong and capable men would function differently from the servile breed that usually surrounded the viceregal throne.

But it was inconceivable and impossible for us to accept this position at any time and more specially at that time. If we had ventured to do so, we would have been disowned and rejected by our own people. As a matter of fact, when later the facts were known to the public, there was an outcry against the many concessions we had agreed to in the course of the negotiations.

In the whole course of our talks with Sir Stafford Cripps the so-called minority or communal issue was at no time raised or considered. Indeed it did not rise at that stage. It was an important issue in considering future constitutional changes, but these had been deliberately put aside after our initial reaction to the British proposals. If the principle of an effective transfer of power to a national government had been agreed to, then the question would no doubt have arisen as to the relative strengths of the various groups represented in it. But as we never reached the stage of agreement on that principle, the other question did not arise and was not considered at all. So far as we were concerned, we were so anxious to have an effective national government having the confidence of the principal parties that we felt that the question of proportions would not give much trouble. Maulana Abul Kalam Azad, the Congress president, in a letter to Sir Stafford Cripps had said: "We would point out to you that the suggestions we have put forward are not ours only but may be considered to be the unanimous demand of the Indian people. On these matters there is no difference of opinion among various groups and parties, and the difference is as between the Indian people as a whole and the British Government. Such differences as exist in India relate to constitutional changes in the future. We are agreeable to the postponement of this issue so that the largest possible measure of unity might be achieved in the present crisis for the defense of India. It would be a tragedy that even when there is this unanimity of opinion in India, the British Government should prevent a free National Government from functioning and from serving the cause of India as well as the larger causes for which millions are suffering and dying today."

In a subsequent and final letter of the Congress president it was stated: "We are not interested in the Congress as such gaining power, but we are interested in the Indian people as a whole having freedom and power. . . . We are convinced that if the British Government did not pursue a policy of encouraging disruption, all of us, to whatever party or group we belonged, would be able to come together and find a common line of action. But, unhappily, even in this grave hour of peril, the British Government is unable to give up its wrecking policy. We are driven to the conclusion that it attaches more importance to holding on to its rule in India, as long as it can, and promoting discord and disruption here with that end in view, than to an effective defence of India against the aggression and invasion that overhang us. To us, and to all Indians, the dominant consideration is the defence and safety of India, and it is by that test that we judge."

In this letter he also made clear our position in regard to defense. "No one has suggested any restrictions on the normal powers of the Commander-in-Chief. Indeed we went beyond this and were prepared to agree to further powers being given to him as War Minister. But it is clear that the British Government's conception and ours in regard to defence differ greatly. For us it means giving it a national character and calling upon every man and woman in India to participate in it. It means trusting our own people and seeking their full co-operation in this great effort. The British Government's view seems to be based on an utter lack of confidence in the Indian people and in withholding real power from them. You refer to the paramount duty and responsibility of His Majesty's Government in regard to defence. That duty and responsibility cannot be discharged effectively unless the Indian people are made to have and feel their responsibility, and the recent past stands witness to this. The Government of India do not realise that the war can only be fought on a popular basis."

Almost immediately after this last letter of the Congress president, Sir Stafford Cripps returned to England by air. But before he did so and on his return, he made certain statements to the public which were contrary to the facts and which were bitterly resented in India. In spite of contradiction by responsible persons in India, those statements were repeated by Sir Stafford and others.

The British proposals had been rejected not by the Congress only but by every single party or group in India. Even the most moderate of our politicians had expressed their disapproval of them. Apart from the Moslem League, the reasons for disapproval were more or less the same. The Moslem League, as has been its custom, waited for others to express their opinions and then, for its own reasons, rejected the proposals.

It was stated in the British parliament and elsewhere that the rejection by the Congress was due to the uncompromising attitude of Gandhi. This is wholly untrue. Gandhiji had strongly disapproved, in common with most others, of the indefinite and innumerable partitions that the proposals involved and of the way in which the ninety million people of Indian states had been allowed no say in their future. All the subsequent negotiations, which dealt with changes in the present and not with the future, took place in his absence, as he had to leave because of his wife's illness, and he had nothing whatever to do with them. The Congress Working Committee had, on several previous occasions, disagreed with him on the question of nonviolence, and was anxious to have a national government to co-operate in the war and especially in the defense of India.

The war was the dominant issue and thought in men's minds, and the invasion of India seemed imminent. And yet it was not the war that came in the way of agreement, for that war would inevitably have to be conducted by experts and not by laymen. On the conduct of the war itself it was easy to come to an agreement. The real question was the transfer of power to the national government. It was the old issue of Indian nationalism versus British imperialism, and on that issue, war or no war, the British governing class in England and in India was determined to hold on to what it held. Behind them stood the imposing figure of Mr. Winston Churchill.

## VIII. FRUSTRATION

The abrupt termination of the Cripps negotiations and Sir Stafford's sudden departure came as a surprise. Was it to make this feeble offer, which turned out to be, so far as the present was concerned, a mere repetition of what had been repeatedly said before, was it for this that a member of the British war cabinet had journeyed to India? Or had all this been done merely as a propaganda stunt for the people of the U.S.A.? The reaction was strong and bitter. There was no hope of a settlement with Britain; no chance was to be given to the people of India even to defend their country against invasion as they wanted to.

Meanwhile the chances of that invasion were growing, and hordes of starving Indian refugees were pouring across the eastern frontiers of India. In eastern Bengal, in a panicky state of mind in anticipation of an invasion tens of thousands of riverboats were destroyed. (It was subsequently stated that this had been done by a mistaken interpretation of an official order.) That vast area was full of waterways, and the only transport possible was by these boats. Their destruction isolated large communities, destroyed their means of livelihood and transport, and was one of the contributory causes of the Bengal famine. Preparations were made for large-scale withdrawals from Bengal, and a repetition of what had happened in Rangoon and lower Burma seemed probable. In the city of Madras a vague and unconfirmed (and, as it turned out, a false) rumor of the approach of a Japanese fleet led to the sudden departure of high government officials and even to a partial destruction of harbor facilities. It seemed that the civilian administration of India was suffering from a nervous breakdown. It was strong only in its suppression of Indian nationalism.

What were we to do? We could not tolerate any part of India submitting tamely to invasion. So far as armed resistance was concerned, that was a matter for the army and air force, such as they were. American help was pouring in, especially in the shape of aircraft, and was slowly changing the military situation. The only way we could have helped was by changing the whole atmosphere of the home front, by creating enthusiasm in the people and a fierce desire to resist at all costs, by building up citizen forces for this purpose and home guards and the like. That had been made terribly difficult for us by British policy. Even on the eve of invasion no Indian outside the regular army could be trusted with a gun, and even our attempts to organize unarmed self-defense units in villages were disapproved and sometimes suppressed. Far from encouraging the organization of popular resistance, the British authorities were afraid of this, for they had long been accustomed to look upon all popular self-defense organizations as seditious and dangerous to British rule. They had to follow their old policy, for the only alternative was to accept a national government relying on the people and organizing them for defense. This alternative had been definitely rejected by them, and there was no middle course or halfway house.

Inevitably they were led to treat the people as chattels who were to be allowed no initiative and were to be used and disposed of entirely according to their own wishes. The All-India Congress Committee, which met at the end of April 1942, declared its deep resentment of this policy and treatment and said that it could never accept a position which involved our functioning as slaves of foreign authority.

Nevertheless we could not remain silent and inert spectators of the tragedy that seemed to be imminent. We had to advise the people, the vast masses of the civilian population, as to what they should do in case of invasion. We told them that in spite of their indignation against British policy, they must not interfere in any way with the operations of the British or Allied armed forces, as this would be giving indirect aid to the enemy aggressor; further, that they must on no account submit to the invader, or obey his orders or accept any favors from him. If the invading forces sought to take possession of the people's homes and fields, they must be resisted even unto death. This resistance was to be peaceful; it was to be the completest form of non-co-operation with the enemy.

Many people criticized with considerable sarcasm what seemed to them the absurd notion of resisting an invading army with these methods of nonviolent non-co-operation. Yet far from being absurd, it was the only method, and a very brave method, left to the people. The advice was not offered to the armed forces, nor was peaceful resistance put forward as an alternative to armed resistance. That advice was meant only for the unarmed civilian population which almost invariably submits to the invader when its armed forces are defeated or withdrawn. Apart from the regular armed forces, it is possible to organize guerrilla units to harass the enemy. But this was not possible for us, for it requires training, arms, and the full co-operation of the regular army. And even if some guerrilla units could have been trained, the rest of the population remained. Normally the civilian population is expected to submit to enemy occupation. Indeed it was known that directions had been issued by British authorities in certain threatened areas advising submission, even by some of the petty officials, to the enemy when the army and the higher officials withdrew.

We knew perfectly well that peaceful non-co-operation could not stop an advancing enemy force. We knew also that most of the civilian inhabitants would find it difficult to resist even if they wanted to do so. Nevertheless we hoped that some leading personalities in the towns and villages occupied by the enemy would refuse to submit or carry out the enemy's orders, or help in getting provisions or in any other way. That would have meant swift punishment for them, very probably death as well as reprisals. We expected this nonsubmission and resistance unto death of even a limited number of persons to have a powerful effect on the general population not only in the area concerned but in the rest of India. Thus we hoped that a national spirit of resistance might be built up.

While this struggle was going on in India's mind and a feeling of desperation was growing, Gandhiji wrote a number of articles which suddenly gave a new direction to people's thoughts, or, as often happens, gave shape to their vague ideas. Inaction at that critical stage and submission to all that was happening had become intolerable to him. The only way to meet that situation was for Indian freedom to be recognized and for a free India to meet aggression and invasion in co-operation with allied nations. If this recognition was not forthcoming, then some action must be taken to challenge the existing system and wake up the people from the lethargy that was paralyzing them and making them easy prey for every kind of aggression.

There was nothing new in this demand, for it was a repetition of what we had been saying all along, but there was a new urgency and passion in his speech and writing. And there was the hint of action. There was no doubt that he represented at the moment the prevailing sentiment in India. In a conflict between the two, nationalism had triumphed over internationalism, and Gandhiji's new writings created a stir all over India. And yet that nationalism was at no time opposed to internationalism and indeed was trying its utmost to find some opening to fit in with that larger aspect, if only it could be given an opportunity to do so honorably and effectively. There was no necessary conflict between the two, for unlike the aggressive nationalisms of Europe it did not seek to interfere with others but rather to co-operate with them to their common advantage. National freedom was seen as the essential basis of true internationalism and hence as the road to the latter, as well as the real foundation for co-operation in the common struggle against fascism and nazism. Meanwhile that internationalism which was being so much talked about was beginning to look suspiciously like the old policy of the imperialist powers, in a new, and yet not so new attire; indeed it was itself an aggressive nationalism which, in the name of empire or commonwealth or mandatory, sought to impose its will on others.

Some of us were disturbed and upset by this new development, for action was futile unless it was effective action, and any such effective action must necessarily come in the way of the war effort at a time when India herself stood in peril of invasion. Gandhiji's general approach also seemed to ignore important international considerations and appeared to be based on a narrow view of nationalism. During the three years of war we had deliberately followed a policy of nonembarrassment, and such action as we had indulged in had been in the nature of symbolic protest. That symbolic protest had assumed huge dimensions when thirty thousand of our leading men and women were sent to prison in 1940–41. And yet even that prison-going was a selected individual affair and avoided any mass upheaval or any direct interference with the governmental apparatus. We could not repeat that, and if we did something else it had to be of a different kind and on a more effective scale. Was this not bound to interfere with the war on India's borders and encourage the enemy?

These were obvious difficulties, and we discussed them at length with Gandhiji without converting each other. The difficulties were there, and risks and perils seemed to follow any course of action or inaction. It became a question of balancing them and choosing the lesser evil. Our mutual discussions led to a clarification of much that had been vague and cloudy, and to Gandhiji's appreciating many international factors to which his attention had been drawn. His subsequent writings underwent a change, and he himself emphasized these international considerations and looked at India's problem in a wider perspective. But his fundamental attitude remained: his objection to a passive submission to British autocratic and repressive policy in India and his intense desire to do something to challenge this. Submission then, according to him, meant that India would be broken in spirit, and whatever shape the war might take, whatever its end might be, her people would act in a servile way and their freedom would not be achieved for a long time. It would mean also submission to an invader and not continuing resistance to him regardless even of temporary military defeat or withdrawal. It would mean the complete demoralization of our people and their losing all the strength that they had built up during a quarter of a century's unceasing struggle for freedom. It would mean that the world would forget India's demand for freedom and the postwar settlement would be governed by the old imperialist urges and ambitions. Passionately desirous of India's freedom as he was, India was to him something more than his loved homeland; it was the symbol of all the colonial and exploited peoples of the world, the acid test whereby any world policy must be judged. If India remained unfree, then also the other colonial countries and subject races would continue in their present enslaved condition and the war would have been fought in vain. It was essential to change the moral basis of the war. The armies and the navies and air forces would function in their respective spheres and they might win by superior methods of violence; but to what end was their victory? And even armed warfare requires the support of morale; had not Napoleon said that in war "the moral is to the physical as three to one"? The moral factor of hundreds of millions of subject and exploited people all over the world realizing and believing that this war was really for their freedom was of immense importance even from the narrower viewpoint of the war, and much more so for the peace to come. The very fact that a crisis had arisen

in the fortunes of the war necessitated a change in outlook
and policy and the conversion of these sullen and doubting
millions into enthusiastic supporters. If this miracle could
take place, all the military might of the Axis powers would
be of little avail and their collapse was assured. Many of
the peoples of the Axis countries might themselves be affected by this powerful world sentiment.

In India it was better to convert the sullen passivity of
the people into a spirit of nonsubmission and resistance.
Though that nonsubmission would be, to begin with, to
arbitrary orders of the British authorities, it could be
turned into resistance to an invader. Submissiveness and
servility to one would lead to the same attitude toward
the other and thus to humiliation and degradation.

We were familiar with all these arguments; we believed
them and had ourselves used them frequently. But the
tragedy was that the policy of the British government prevented that miracle from taking place, and all our attempts
to solve the Indian problem even temporarily during the
course of the war had failed, and all our requests for a
declaration of war aims had been turned down. It was certain that a further attempt of this kind would also fail.
What then? If it was to be conflict, howsoever much it
might be justified on moral or other grounds, there could
be no doubt that it would tend to interfere greatly with
the war effort in India at a time when the danger of invasion was considerable. There was no getting away from
that fact. And yet, oddly enough, it was that very danger
that had brought this crisis in our minds. For we could
not remain idle spectators of it and see our country mis-
managed and ruined by people whom we considered incompetent and wholly incapable of shouldering the burden
of a people's resistance which the occasion demanded. All
our pent-up passion and energy sought some outlet, some
way of action.

On August 7 and 8, 1942, in Bombay the All-India Congress Committee considered and debated in public the
resolution, which has since come to be known as the "Quit
India Resolution." That resolution was a long and comprehensive one, a reasoned argument for the immediate

recognition of Indian freedom and the ending of British rule in India "both for the sake of India and for the success of the cause of the United Nations. The continuation of that rule is degrading and enfeebling India and making her progressively less capable of defending herself and of contributing to the cause of world freedom. . . . The possession of empire, instead of adding to the strength of the ruling power, has become a burden and a curse. India, the classic land of modern Imperialism, has become the crux of the question, for by the freedom of India will Britain and the United Nations be judged, and the peoples of Asia and Africa be filled with hope and enthusiasm." The resolution went on to suggest the formation of a provisional government which would be composite and would represent all important sections of the people, and whose "primary function must be to defend India and resist aggression with all the armed as well as the non-violent forces at its command, together with its Allied Powers." This government would evolve a scheme for a constituent assembly which would prepare a constitution for India acceptable to all sections of the people. The constitution would be a federal one, with the largest measure of autonomy for the federating units and with the residuary powers vesting in those units. "Freedom will enable India to resist aggression effectively with the people's united will and strength behind it."

This freedom of India must be the symbol of and prelude to the freedom of all other Asiatic nations. Further, a world federation of free nations was proposed, of which a beginning should be made with the United Nations.

The committee stated that it was "anxious not to embarrass in any way the defence of China and Russia, whose freedom is precious and must be preserved, or to jeopardize the defensive capacity of the United Nations." (At that time the dangers to China and Russia were the greatest.) "But the peril grows both to India and these nations, and inaction and submission to a foreign administration at this stage is not only degrading India and reducing her capacity to defend herself and resist aggression but is no answer to that growing peril and is no service to the peoples of the United Nations."

The Committee again appealed to Britain and the United Nations "in the interest of world freedom." But —and there came the sting of the resolution—"the Committee is no longer justified in holding the nation back from endeavouring to assert its will against an imperialist and authoritarian Government which dominates over it and prevents it from functioning in its own interest and in the interest of humanity. The Committee resolves therefore to sanction, for the vindication of India's inalienable right to freedom and independence, the starting of a mass struggle on non-violent lines" under the inevitable leadership of Gandhiji. That sanction was to take effect only when Gandhi so decided. Finally, it was stated that the Committee had "no intention of gaining power for the Congress. The power, when it comes, will belong to the whole people of India."

In their concluding speeches Maulana Abul Kalam Azad, the Congress president, and Gandhiji made it clear that their next steps would be to approach the viceroy, as representing the British government, and to appeal to the heads of the principal United Nations for an honorable settlement, which, while recognizing the freedom of India, would also advance the cause of the United Nations in the struggle against the aggressor Axis powers.

The resolution was finally passed late in the evening of August 8, 1942. A few hours later, in the early morning of August 9, a large number of arrests were made in Bombay and all over the country. And so to Ahmadnagar Fort.

# IX. Ahmadnagar Fort Again

## I. THE CHAIN OF HAPPENING

Ahmadnagar Fort. August thirteenth, nineteen forty-four.
It is just over two years since we came here, two years of
a dream life rooted in one spot, with the same few individuals to see, the same limited environment, the same
routine from day to day. Sometime in the future we shall
wake up from this dream and go out into the wider world
of life and activity, finding it a changed world. There will
be an air of unfamiliarity about the persons and things we
see; we shall remember them again and past memories will
crowd into our minds, and yet they will not be the same,
nor will we be the same, and we may find it difficult to
fit in with them. Sometimes we may wonder whether this
renewed experience of everyday living is not itself a sleep
and a dream from which we may suddenly wake up. Which
is the dream and which is the waking? Are they both real,
for we experience and feel them in all their intensity, or
are they both unsubstantial and of the nature of fleeting
dreams which pass, leaving vague memories behind?

Prison and its attendant solitude and passivity lead to
thought and an attempt to fill the vacuum of life with
memories of past living, of one's own life, and of the long
chain of history of human activity. So during the past four
months, in the course of this writing, I have occupied my
mind with India's past records and experiences, and out
of the multitude of ideas that came to me I have selected
some and made a book out of them. Looking back at what
I have written, it seems inadequate, disjointed and lack-

ing in unity, a mixture of many things, with the personal
element dominant and giving its color even to what was
intended to be an objective record and analysis. That personal element has pushed itself forward almost against
my will; often I checked it and held it back, but sometimes I loosened the reins and allowed it to flow out of
my pen, and mirror, to some extent, my mind.

By writing of the past I have tried to rid myself of the
burden of the past. But the present remains with all its
complexity and irrationality, and the dark future that lies
beyond, and the burden of these is no less than that of the
past. The vagrant mind, finding no haven, still wanders
about restlessly, bringing discomfort to its possessor as well
as to others. There is some envy for those virgin minds
which have not been soiled or violated by thought's assault,
and on which doubt has cast no shadow nor written a line.
How easy is life for them in spite of its occasional shock
and pain.

Events take place one after the other and the uninterrupted and unending stream of happenings goes on. We
seek to understand a particular event by isolating it and
looking at it by itself, as if it were the beginning and the
end, the resultant of some cause immediately preceding it.
Yet it has no beginning and it is but a link in an unending
chain, caused by all that has preceded it, and resulting
from the wills, urges, and desires of innumerable human
beings coalescing and conflicting with each other, and producing something which is different from what any single
individual intended to happen. Those wills, urges, and desires are themselves largely conditioned by previous events
and experiences, and the new event in its turn becomes
another conditioning factor for the future. The man of destiny, the leader who influences the multitude, undoubtedly
plays an important part in this process, and yet he himself
is the product of past events and forces and his influence
is conditioned by them.

*The discussion turns to the chain of events in India after
the August 8 "Quit India" resolution passed by the Congress. The internment of many Congress leaders, followed*

*by mass unrest and sporadic rioting, is described along with
the reaction to trends in India among Americans. Mr.
Nehru also reports the tragic Bengal famine of 1943. The
frustration of the wartime political scene leads to reflec-
tions on India's arrested growth.*

## II. INDIA'S GROWTH ARRESTED

A nation, like an individual, has many personalities, many
approaches to life. If there is a sufficiently strong organic
bond between these different personalities, it is well; otherwise those personalities split up and lead to disintegration
and trouble. Normally, there is a continuous process of adjustment going on and some kind of an equilibrium is established. If normal development is arrested, or sometimes
if there is some rapid change which is not easily assimilated, then conflict arises between those different personalities. In the mind and spirit of India, below the surface
of our superficial conflicts and divisions, there has been
this fundamental conflict due to a long period of arrested
growth. A society, if it is to be both stable and progressive,
must have a certain more or less fixed foundation of principles as well as a dynamic outlook. Both appear to be necessary. Without the dynamic outlook there is stagnation
and decay; without some fixed basis of principle there is
likely to be disintegration and destruction.

In India from the earliest days there was a search for
those basic principles, for the unchanging, the universal,
the absolute. Yet the dynamic outlook was also present and
an appreciation of life and the changing world. On these
two foundations a stable and progressive society was built
up, though the stress was always more on stability and security and the survival of the race. In later years the dynamic aspect began to fade away, and in the name of eternal principles the social structure was made rigid and
unchanging. It was, as a matter of fact, not wholly rigid,
and it did change gradually and continuously. But the ideology behind it and the general framework continued un-

changed. The group idea as represented by
autonomous castes, the joint family, and the
self-governing life of the village were the mai
this system, and all these survived for so long because, in
spite of their failings, they fulfilled some essential needs of
human nature and society. They gave security and stability
to each group and a sense of group freedom. Caste survived
because it continued to represent the general power relationships of society, and class privileges were maintained,
not only because of the prevailing ideology, but also because they were supported by vigor, intelligence, and ability, as well as a capacity for self-sacrifice. That ideology was
not based on a conflict of rights but on the individual's
obligations to others and a satisfactory performance of his
duties, on co-operation within the group and between different groups, and essentially on the idea of promoting
peace rather than war. While the social system was rigid,
no limit was placed on the freedom of the mind.

Indian civilization achieved much that it was aiming at,
but in that very achievement life began to fade away, for
it is too dynamic to exist for long in a rigid, unchanging
environment. Even those basic principles, which are said
to be unchanging, lose their freshness and reality when they
are taken for granted and the search for them ceases. Ideas
of truth, beauty, and freedom decay, and we become prisoners following a deadening routine.

The very thing India lacked, the modern West possessed
and possessed to excess. It had the dynamic outlook. It
was engrossed in the changing world, caring little for ultimate principles, the unchanging, the universal. It paid little attention to duties and obligations, and emphasized
rights. It was active, aggressive, acquisitive, seeking power
and domination, living in the present and ignoring the future consequences of its actions. Because it was dynamic,
it was progressive and full of life, but that life was a fevered one and the temperature kept on rising progressively.

If Indian civilization went to seed because it became
static, self-absorbed, and inclined to narcissism, the civilization of the modern West, with all its great and manifold
achievements, does not appear to have been a conspicuous

success or to have thus far solved the basic problems of life. Conflict is inherent in it, and periodically it indulges in self-destruction on a colossal scale. It seems to lack something to give it stability, some basic principles to give meaning to life, though what these are I cannot say. Yet because it is dynamic and full of life and curiosity, there is hope for it.

India, as well as China, must learn from the West, for the modern West has much to teach, and the spirit of the age is represented by the West. But the West is also obviously in need of learning much, and its advances in technology will bring it little comfort if it does not learn some of the deeper lessons of life, which have absorbed the minds of thinkers in all ages and in all countries.

India had become static, and yet it would be utterly wrong to imagine that she was unchanging. No change at all means death. Her very survival as a highly evolved nation shows that there was some process of continuous adaptation going on. When the British came to India, though technologically somewhat backward she was still among the advanced commercial nations of the world. Technical changes would undoubtedly have come and changed India as they had changed some Western countries. But her normal development was arrested by the British power. Industrial growth was checked, and as a consequence social growth was also arrested. The normal power relationships of society could not adjust themselves and find an equilibrium, as all power was concentrated in the alien authority, which based itself on force and encouraged groups and classes which had ceased to have any real significance. Indian life thus progressively became more artificial, for many of the individuals and groups who seemed to play an important rôle in it had no vital functions left and were there only because of the importance given to them by the alien power. They had long ago finished their rôle in history and would have been pushed aside by new forces if they had not been given foreign protection. They became straw-stuffed symbols or protégés of foreign authority, thereby cutting themselves further away from the living currents of the nation. Normally they would have

2

been weeded out or diverted to some more appropriate function by revolution or democratic process. But so long as foreign authoritarian rule continued, no such development could take place. And so India was cluttered up with these emblems of the past and the real changes that were taking place were hidden behind an artificial façade. No true social balances or power relationships within society could develop or become evident, and unreal problems assumed an undue importance.

## III. RELIGION, PHILOSOPHY, AND SCIENCE

India must break with much of her past and not allow it to dominate the present. Our lives are encumbered with the dead wood of this past; all that is dead and has served its purpose has to go. But that does not mean a break with, or a forgetting of, the vital and life-giving in that past. We can never forget the ideals that have moved our race, the dreams of the Indian people through the ages, the wisdom of the ancients, the buoyant energy and love of life and nature of our forefathers, their spirit of curiosity and mental adventure, the daring of their thought, their splendid achievements in literature, art, and culture, their love of truth and beauty and freedom, the basic values that they set up, their understanding of life's mysterious ways, their toleration of other ways than theirs, their capacity to absorb other peoples and their cultural accomplishments, synthesize them and develop a varied and mixed culture; nor can we forget the myriad experiences which have built up our ancient race and lie embedded in our subconscious minds. We will never forget them or cease to take pride in that noble heritage of ours. If India forgets them, she will no longer remain India and much that has made her our joy and pride will cease to be.

It is not this that we have to break with, but all the dust and dirt of ages that have covered her up and hidden her inner beauty and significance, the excrescences and abortions that have twisted and petrified her spirit, set it in rigid frames, and stunted her growth. We have to cut away these excrescences and remember afresh the core of that ancient wisdom and adapt it to our present circumstances. We have to get out of traditional ways of thought and living which, for all the good they may have done in a past age, and there was much good in them, have ceased to have significance today. We have to make our own all the achievements of the human race and join up with others in the exciting adventure of Man, more exciting today perhaps than in earlier ages, realizing that this has ceased to be governed by national boundaries or old divisions and is common to the race of man everywhere. We have to revive the passion for truth and beauty and freedom which gives meaning to life, and develop afresh that dynamic outlook and spirit of adventure which distinguished those of our race who, in ages past, built our house on these strong and enduring foundations. Old as we are, with memories stretching back to the early dawns of human history and endeavor, we have to grow young again, in tune with our present time, with the irrepressible spirit and joy of youth in the present and its faith in the future.

Truth as ultimate reality, if such there is, must be eternal, imperishable, unchanging. But that infinite, eternal, and unchanging truth cannot be apprehended in its fullness by the finite mind of man which can only grasp, at most, some small aspect of it limited by time and space, and by the state of development of that mind and the prevailing ideology of the period. As the mind develops and enlarges its scope, as ideologies change and new symbols are used to express that truth, new aspects of it come to light, though the core of it may yet be the same. And so, truth has ever to be sought and renewed, reshaped and developed, so that, as understood by man, it may keep in line with the growth of his thought and the development of human life. Only then does it become a living truth for humanity, supplying the essential need for which it craves, and offering guidance in the present and for the future.

But if some one aspect of the truth has been petrified by dogma in a past age, it ceases to grow and develop and adapt itself to the changing needs of humanity; other aspects of it remain hidden, and it fails to answer the urgent questions of a succeeding age. It is no longer dynamic but static, no longer a life-giving impulse but dead thought and ceremonial and a hindrance to the growth of the mind and of humanity. Indeed, it is probably not even understood to the extent it was understood in that past age when it grew up and was clothed in the language and symbols of that age. For its context is different in a later age, the mental climate has changed, new social habits and customs have grown up, and it is often difficult to understand the sense, much less the spirit, of that ancient writing. Moreover, as Aurobindo Ghose has pointed out, every truth, however true in itself, yet, taken apart from others which at once limit and complete it, becomes a snare to bind the intellect and a misleading dogma; for in reality each is one thread of a complex weft, and no thread must be taken apart from the weft.

Religions have helped greatly in the development of humanity. They have laid down values and standards and have pointed out principles for the guidance of human life. But with all the good they have done, they have also tried to imprison truth in set forms and dogmas, and encouraged ceremonials and practices which soon lose all their original meaning and become mere routine. While impressing upon man the awe and mystery of the unknown that surrounds him on all sides, they have discouraged him from trying to understand not only the unknown but what might come in the way of social effort. Instead of encouraging curiosity and thought, they have preached a philosophy of submission to nature, to the established church, to the prevailing social order, and to everything that is. The belief in a supernatural agency which ordains everything has led to a certain irresponsibility on the social plane, and emotion and sentimentality have taken the place of reasoned thought and inquiry. Religion, though it has undoubtedly brought comfort to innumerable human beings and stabilized society by its values, has checked the tendency to change and progress inherent in human society.

As knowledge advances, the domain of religion, in the narrow sense of the word, shrinks. The more we understand life and nature, the less we look for supernatural causes. Whatever we can understand and control ceases to be a mystery. The processes of agriculture, the food we eat, the clothes we wear, our social relations, were all at one time under the dominion of religion and its high priests. Gradually they have passed out of its control and become subjects for scientific study. Yet much of this is still powerfully affected by religious beliefs and the superstitions that accompany them. The final mysteries still remain far beyond the reach of the human mind and are likely to continue to remain so. But so many of life's mysteries are capable of and await solution, that an obsession with the final mystery seems hardly necessary or justified. Life still offers not only the loveliness of the world but also the exciting adventure of fresh and never-ceasing discoveries, of new panoramas opening out and new ways of living, adding to its fullness and ever making it richer and more complete.

It is therefore with the temper and approach of science, allied to philosophy, and with reverence for all that lies beyond, that we must face life. Thus we may develop an integral vision of life which embraces in its wide scope the past and the present, with all their heights and depths, and look with serenity toward the future. The depths are there and cannot be ignored, and always by the side of the loveliness that surrounds us is the misery of the world. Man's journey through life is an odd mixture of joy and sorrow; thus only can he learn and advance. The travail of the soul is a tragic and lonely business. External events and their consequences affect us powerfully, and yet the greatest shocks come to our minds through inner fears and conflicts. While we advance on the external plane, as we must if we are to survive, we have also to win peace with ourselves and between ourselves and our environment, a peace which brings satisfaction not only to our physical and material needs but also to those inner imaginative urges and adventurous spirit that have distinguished man ever since he started on his troubled journey in the realms of thought and action. Whether that journey has any ultimate purpose or not we do not know, but it has its compensations, and it points to many a nearer objective which appears attainable and which may again become the starting point for a fresh advance.

Science has dominated the Western world and everyone there pays tribute to it, and yet the West is still far from having developed the real temper of science. It has still to bring the spirit and the flesh into creative harmony. In India in many obvious ways we have a greater distance to travel. And yet there may be fewer major obstructions on our way, for the essential basis of Indian thought for ages past, though not its later manifestations, fits in with the scientific temper and approach, as well as with internationalism. It is based on a fearless search for truth, on the solidarity of man, even on the divinity of everything living, and on the free and co-operative development of the individual and the species, ever to greater freedom and higher stages of human growth.

## IV. THE IMPORTANCE OF THE NATIONAL IDEA
### CHANGES NECESSARY IN INDIA

A blind reverence for the past is bad and so also is a contempt for it, for no future can be founded on either of these. The present and the future inevitably grow out of the past and bear its stamp, and to forget this is to build without foundations and to cut off the roots of national growth. It is to ignore one of the most powerful forces that influence people. Nationalism is essentially a group memory of past achievements, traditions, and experiences, and nationalism is stronger today than it has ever been. Many people thought that nationalism had had its day and must inevitably give place to the ever-growing international tendencies of the modern world. Socialism with its proletarian background derided national culture as something tied up with a decaying middle class. Capitalism itself became progressively international with its cartels and combines and overflowed national boundaries. Trade and commerce, easy communications and rapid transport, the radio and cinema all helped to create an international atmosphere and to produce the delusion that nationalism was doomed.

Yet whenever a crisis has arisen, nationalism has emerged again and dominated the scene, and people have sought comfort and strength in their old traditions. One of the remarkable developments of the present age has been the rediscovery of the past and of the nation. This going back to national traditions has been most marked in the ranks of labor and the proletarian elements, who were supposed to be the foremost champions of international action. War or similar crisis dissolves their internationalism and they become subject to nationalist hates and fears even more than other groups. The most striking example of this is the recent development of the Soviet Union. Without giving up in any way its essential social and economic structure, it has become more nationalist-minded and the appeal of the fatherland is now much greater than the appeal of the international proletariat. Famous figures in national history have again been revived and have become heroes of the Soviet people. The inspiring record of the Soviet people in this war, the strength and unity they have shown, are no doubt due to a social and economic structure which has resulted in social advances on a wide front, in planned production and consumption, in the development of science and its functions, and in the release of a vast quantity of new talent and capacity for leadership, as also in brilliant leadership. But it may also be partly due to a revival of national memories and traditions and a new awareness of the past, of which the present was felt to be a continuation. It would be wrong to imagine that this nationalist outlook of Russia is just a reversion to old-style nationalism. It is certainly not that. The tremendous experiences of the revolution and all that followed it cannot be forgotten, and the changes that resulted from it in social structure and mental adjustment must remain. That social structure leads inevitably to a certain international outlook. Nevertheless nationalism has reappeared in such a way as to fit in with the new environment and add to the strength of the people.

It is a curious and significant fact that in spite of all

modern scientific progress and talk of internationalism, racialism and other separating factors are at least as much in evidence today, if not more so, than at any previous time in history. There is something lacking in all this progress, which can neither produce harmony between nations nor within the spirit of man. Perhaps more synthesis and a little humility toward the wisdom of the past, which after all is the accumulated experience of the human race, would help us to gain a new perspective and greater harmony. That is especially needed by those peoples who live a fevered life in the present only and have almost forgotten the past. But for countries like India a different emphasis is necessary, for we have too much of the past about us and have ignored the present. We have to get rid of that narrowing religious outlook, that obsession with the supernatural and metaphysical speculations, that loosening of the mind's discipline in religious ceremonial and mystical emotionalism, which come in the way of our understanding ourselves and the world. We have to come to grips with the present, this life, this world, this nature which surrounds us in its infinite variety. Some Hindus talk of going back to the Vedas; some Moslems dream of an Islamic theocracy. Idle fancies, for there is no going back to the past; there is no turning back even if this was thought desirable. There is only one-way traffic in Time.

India must therefore lessen her religiosity and turn to science. She must get rid of the exclusiveness in thought and social habit which has become like a prison to her, stunting her spirit and preventing growth. The idea of ceremonial purity has erected barriers against social intercourse and narrowed the sphere of social action. The day-to-day religion of the orthodox Hindu is more concerned with what to eat and what not to eat, whom to eat with and from whom to keep away, than with spiritual values. The rules and regulations of the kitchen dominate his social life. The Moslem is fortunately free from these inhibitions, but he has his own narrow codes and ceremonials, a routine which he rigorously follows, forgetting the lesson of brotherhood which his religion taught him. His view of life is perhaps even more limited and sterile than the

Hindu view, though the average Hindu today is a poor representative of the latter view, for he has lost that traditional freedom of thought and the background that enriches life in many ways.

Caste is the symbol and embodiment of this exclusiveness among the Hindus. It is sometimes said that the basic idea of caste might remain but its subsequent harmful development and ramifications should go; that it should not depend on birth but on merit. This approach is irrelevant and merely confuses the issue. In a historical context a study of the growth of caste has some value, but obviously we cannot go back to the period when caste began; in the social organization of today it has no place left. If merit is the only criterion and opportunity is thrown open to everybody, then caste loses all its present-day distinguishing features and, in fact, ends. Caste has in the past not only led to the suppression of certain groups but to a separation of theoretical and scholastic learning from craftsmanship and a divorce of philosophy from actual life and its problems. It was an aristocratic approach based on traditionalism. This outlook has to change completely, for it is wholly opposed to modern conditions and the democratic ideal. The functional organization of social groups in India may continue, but even that will undergo a vast change as the nature of modern industry creates new functions and puts an end to many old ones. The tendency today everywhere is toward a functional organization of society, and the concept of abstract rights is giving place to that of functions. This is in harmony with the old Indian ideal.

The spirit of the age is in favor of equality, though practice denies it almost everywhere. We have got rid of slavery in the narrow sense of the word, that a man can be the property of another. But a new slavery, in some ways worse than the old, has taken its place all over the world. In the name of individual freedom, political and economic systems exploit human beings and treat them as commodities. And again, though an individual cannot be the property of another, a country and a nation can still be the property of another nation, and thus group slavery is tolerated. Racialism also is a distinguishing feature of our times, and we have not only master nations but also master races.

Yet the spirit of the age will triumph. In India, at any rate, we must aim at equality. That does not and cannot mean that everybody is physically or intellectually or spiritually equal or can be made so. But it does mean equal opportunities for all and no political, economic, or social barrier in the way of any individual or group. It means a faith in humanity and a belief that there is no race or group that cannot advance and make good in its own way, given the chance to do so. It means a realization of the fact that the backwardness or degradation of any group is not due to inherent failings in it but principally to lack of opportunities and long suppression by other groups. It should mean an understanding of the modern world wherein real progress and advance, whether national or international, have become very much a joint affair and a backward group pulls back others. Therefore not only must equal opportunities be given to all, but special opportunities for educational, economic, and cultural growth must be given to backward groups so as to enable them to catch up to those who are ahead of them. Any such attempt to open the doors of opportunity to all in India will release enormous energy and ability and transform the country with amazing speed.

If the spirit of the age demands equality, it must necessarily also demand an economic system which fits in with it and encourages it. The present colonial system in India is the very antithesis of it. Absolutism is not only based on inequality but must perpetuate it in every sphere of life. It suppresses the creative and regenerative forces of a nation, bottles up talent and capacity, and discourages the spirit of responsibility. Those who have to suffer under it lose their sense of dignity and self-reliance. The problems of India, complicated as they seem, are essentially due to an attempt to advance while preserving the political and economic structure more or less intact. Political advance is made subject to the preservation of this structure and existing vested interests. The two are incompatible.

Political change there must be, but economic change is

equally necessary. That change will have to be in the direction of a democratically planned collectivism. "The choice," says R. H. Tawney, "is not between competition and monopoly, but between monopoly which is irresponsible and private and a monopoly which is responsible and public." Public monopolies are growing even in capitalist states, and they will continue to grow. The conflict between the idea underlying them and private monopoly will continue till the latter is liquidated. A democratic collectivism need not mean an abolition of private property, but it will mean the public ownership of the basic and major industries. It will mean the co-operative or collective control of the land. In India especially it will be necessary to have, in addition to the big industries, co-operatively controlled small and village industries. Such a system of democratic collectivism will need careful and continuous planning and adaptation to the changing needs of the people. The aim should be the expansion of the productive capacity of the nation in every possible way, at the same time absorbing all the labor power of the nation in some activity or other and preventing unemployment. As far as possible there should be freedom to choose one's occupation. An equalization of income will not result from all this, but there will be far more equitable sharing and a progressive tendency toward equalization. In any event, the vast differences that exist today will disappear completely, and class distinctions, which are essentially based on differences in income, will begin to fade out.

Such a change would mean an upsetting of the present-day acquisitive society based primarily on the profit motive. The profit motive may still continue to some extent, but it will not be the dominating urge, nor will it have the same scope as it has today. It would be absurd to say that the profit motive does not appeal to the average Indian, but it is nevertheless true that there is no such admiration for it in India as there is in the West. The possessor of money may be envied but he is not particularly respected or admired. Respect and admiration still go to the man or woman who is considered good and wise, and especially to those who sacrifice themselves or what they possess for the public good. The Indian outlook, even of the masses, has never approved of the spirit of acquisitiveness.

## V. REALISM AND GEOPOLITICS
### WORLD CONQUEST OR WORLD ASSOCIATION
### THE U.S.A. AND THE U.S.S.R.

The war enters on its final stage in Europe and the nazi power collapses before the advancing armies in the east and west. Paris, that lovely and gracious city, so tied up with freedom's struggle, is itself free again. The problems of peace, more difficult than those of war, rise up to trouble men's minds, and behind them lies the disturbing shadow of the great failure of the years that followed World War I. Never again, it is said. So they said also in 1918.

Fifteen years ago, in 1929, Mr. Winston Churchill said: "It is a tale that is told, from which we may draw the knowledge and comprehension needed for the future. The disproportion between the quarrels of nations and the suffering which fighting out those quarrels involves; the poor and barren prizes which reward sublime endeavour on the battlefield; the fleeting triumph of war; the long, slow rebuilding; the awful risks so hardily run; the doom missed by a hair's breadth, by the spin of a coin, by the accident of an accident—all this should make the prevention of another great war the main preoccupation of mankind."

Mr. Churchill should know, for he has played a leading part in war and peace, led his country with extraordinary courage at a time of distress, peril, and in victory nursed great ambitions on its behalf. After World War I, British armies occupied the whole of western Asia from the borders of India across Iran and Iraq and Palestine and Syria right up to Constantinople. Mr. Churchill saw then a vision of a new Middle Eastern empire for Britain, but fate decided otherwise. What dream does he cherish now for the future? "War is a strange alchemist," so wrote a gallant and distinguished colleague of mine, now in prison, "and in its hidden chambers are such forces and powers brewed and distilled that they tear down the plans of the victorious and vanquished alike. No peace conference at the end of the last war decided that four mighty empires of Europe and Asia should fall into dust—the Russian, the German, the Austrian and the Ottoman. Nor was the Russian, the German, the Turkish Revolution decreed by Lloyd George, Clemenceau or Wilson."

What will the leaders of the victorious nations say when they meet together after success in war has crowned their efforts? How is the future taking shape in their minds, and how far do they agree or differ between themselves? What other reactions will there be when the passion of war subsides and people try to return to the scarce-remembered ways of peace? What of the underground resistance movements of Europe and the new forces they have released? What will the millions of war-hardened soldiers, returning home much older in mind and experience, say and do? How will they fit into the life which has gone on changing while they were away? What will happen to devastated and martyred Europe, and what to Asia and Africa? What of the "overpowering surge for freedom of Asia's hundreds of millions," as Mr. Wendell Willkie describes it? What of all this and more? And what, above all, of the strange trick that fate so often plays, upsetting the well-laid schemes of our leaders?

The two outstanding facts emerging from the war are the growth in power and actual and potential wealth of the U.S.A. and the U.S.S.R. The Soviet Union actually is probably poorer than it was prior to the war, owing to enormous destruction, but its potential is tremendous and it will rapidly make good and go further ahead. In physical and economic power there will be none to challenge it on the Eurasian continent. Already it is showing an expansionist tendency and is expanding its territories more or less on the basis of the tsar's empire. How far this process will go it is difficult to say. The socialist economy does not necessarily lead to expansion, for it can be made self-sufficient. But other forces and old suspicions are at play, and again we notice the fear of so-called encirclement. In any event the U.S.S.R. will be busy for many years in repairing the ravages of war. Yet the tendency to expand if not in territory then in other ways, is evident. No other country today presents such a politically solid and economically well-balanced picture as the Soviet Union, though some of the developments there in recent years have come as a shock to many of its old admirers. Its present leaders have an unchallengeable position, and everything depends on their outlook for the future.

Much will inevitably depend on American and Soviet policy, and on the degree of co-ordination or conflict between the two and Britain. Everybody talks loudly about the necessity for the Big Three to pull together in the interests of world peace and co-operation, yet rifts and differences peep out at every stage even during the course of the war. Whatever the future may hold, it is clear that the economy of the U.S.A. after the war will be powerfully expansionist and almost explosive in its consequences. Will this lead to some new kind of imperialism? It would be yet another tragedy if it did so, for America has the power and opportunity to set the pace for the future.

The future policy of the Soviet Union is yet shrouded in mystery, but there have been some revealing glimpses of it already. It aims at having as many friendly and dependent or semidependent countries near its borders as possible. Though working with other powers for the establishment of some world organization, it relies more on building up its own strength on an unassailable basis. So, presumably, do other nations also, in so far as they can. That is not a hopeful prelude to world co-operation. Between the Soviet Union and other countries there is not the same struggle for export markets as between Britain and the U.S.A. But the differences are deeper, their respective viewpoints further apart, and mutual suspicions have not been allayed even by the joint effort in the war. If these differences grow, the U.S.A. and Britain will tend to seek each other's company and support as against the U.S.S.R. group of nations.

Where do the hundreds of millions of Asia and Africa come in this picture? They have become increasingly conscious of themselves and their destiny, and at the same time have become world-conscious. Large numbers of them follow world events with interest. For them, inevitably, the test of each move or happening is this: Does it help toward our liberation? does it end the domination of one country over another? will it enable us to live freely the life of our choice in co-operation with others? does it bring equality and equal opportunity for nations as well as groups within each nation? does it hold forth the promise of an early liquidation of poverty and illiteracy and bring better living conditions? They are nationalistic, but this nationalism seeks no dominion over or interference with, others. They welcome all attempts at world co-operation and the establishment of an international order, but they wonder and suspect if this way may not be another for continuing the old domination. Large parts of Asia and Africa consist of awakened, discontented, seething humanity no longer prepared to tolerate existing conditions. Conditions and problems differ greatly in the various countries of Asia, but throughout this vast area, in China and India, in southeast Asia, in western Asia and the Arab world run common threads of sentiment and invisible links which hold them together.

For a thousand years or more, while Europe was backward and often engulfed in its Dark Ages, Asia represented the advancing spirit of man. Epoch after epoch of a brilliant culture flourished there, and great centers of civilization and power grew up. About five hundred years ago Europe revived and slowly spread eastward and westward till, in the course of centuries, it became the dominant continent of the world in power, wealth, and culture. Was there some cycle about this change, and is that process now being reversed? Certainly power and authority have shifted more to America in the far West and to eastern Europe, which was organically hardly a part of the European heritage. And in the East also there has been tremendous growth in Siberia, and other countries of the East are ripe for change and rapid advance. Will there be conflict in the future, or a new equilibrium between the East and the West?

But only the distant future will decide that, and it serves little purpose to look so far ahead. For the present we have to carry the burden of the day and face the many problems which afflict us. Behind these problems in India, as in many other countries, lies the real issue, which is not merely the establishment of democracy of the nineteenth-century European type but also far-reaching social revolution. Democracy has itself become involved in that seemingly inevitable change, and hence among those who disapprove of the latter, doubts and denials arise about the feasibility of democracy, and this leads to fascist tendencies and the continuation of an imperialist outlook. All our present-day problems in India—the communal or minority problem, the Indian princes, vested interest of religious groups and the big landowners, and the entrenched interests of British authority and industry in India—ultimately resolve themselves into opposition to social change. And because any real democracy is likely to lead to such change, therefore democracy itself is objected to and considered unsuited to the peculiar conditions of India. So the problems of India, for all their seeming variety and difference from others, are of the same essential nature as the problems of China or Spain or many other countries of Europe and elsewhere, which the war has brought to the surface. Many of the resistance movements of Europe reflect these conflicts. Everywhere the old equilibrium of social forces has been upset, and till a new equilibrium is established there will be tension, trouble, and conflict. From these problems of the moment we are led to one of the central problems of our time: how to combine democracy with socialism, how to maintain individual freedom and initiative and yet have centralized social control and planning of the economic life of the people, on the national as well as the international plane.

## VI. FREEDOM AND EMPIRE

The United States and the Soviet Union seem destined to play a vital part in the future. They differ from each other almost as much as any two advanced countries can differ,

and even their faults lie in opposite directions. All the evils
of a purely political democracy are evident in the U.S.A.;
the evils of the lack of political democracy are present in
the U.S.S.R. And yet they have much in common—a
dynamic outlook and vast resources, a social fluidity, an
absence of a medieval background, a faith in science and
its applications, and widespread education and opportunities for the people. In America, in spite of vast differences
in income, there are no fixed classes as in most countries,
and there is a sense of equality. In Russia the outstanding
event of the past twenty years has been the tremendous
education and cultural achievements of the masses. Thus
in both countries the essential basis for a progressive, democratic society is present, for no such society can be based
on the rule of a small intellectual elite over an ignorant
and apathetic people. Nor can such an elite long continue
to dominate over an educationally and culturally advanced
people.

A hundred years ago de Tocqueville, discussing the
Americans of those days, said: "If the democratic principle
does not, on the one hand, induce men to cultivate science
for its own sake, on the other, it does enormously increase
the number of those who do cultivate it. . . . Permanent
inequality of conditions leads men to confine themselves
to the arrogant and sterile researches of abstract truths,
whilst the social condition and institutions of democracy
prepare them to seek the immediate and useful practical
results of the sciences. The tendency is natural and inevitable." Since then America has developed and changed and
become an amalgam of many races, but its essential characteristics continue.

Yet another common characteristic of both Americans
and Russians is that they do not carry that heavy burden
of the past which has oppressed Asia and Europe, and conditioned to a great extent their activities and conflicts.
They cannot, of course, escape, as none of us can, the terrible burden of this generation. But they have a clearer
past, so far as other people are concerned, and are less
encumbered for their journey into the future.

As a result of this they can approach other peoples without that background of mutual distrust which always accompanies the contacts of well-established imperialist nations with others. Not that their past is free of spots and stains and suspicions. Americans have their Negro problem which is a continuing reproach to their professions of democracy and equality. Russians have yet to wipe out memories of past hatreds in eastern Europe, and the present war is adding to them. Still, Americans make friends easily in other countries. Russians are almost totally devoid of racialism.

Most of the European nations are full of their mutual hatreds and past conflicts and injustices. The imperialist powers have inevitably added to this the intense dislike for them of the people they have ruled over. Because of England's long record of imperialist rule, her burden is the greatest. Because of this, or because of racial characteristics, Englishmen are reserved and exclusive and do not easily make friends with others. They are unfortunately judged abroad by their official representatives, who are seldom the standard-bearers of their liberalism or culture, and who often combine snobbery with an apparent piety. These officials have a peculiar knack of antagonizing others. Some months ago a secretary to the Government of India wrote an official letter to Mr. Gandhi (in detention) which was an example of studied insolence, and which was looked upon by large numbers of people as a deliberate insult to the Indian people. For Gandhi happens to be a symbol of India.

Another era of imperialism, or an age of international co-operation, or world commonwealth: which is it going to be in the future? The scales incline toward the former, and the old arguments are repeated but not with the old candor. The moral urges of mankind and its sacrifices are used for base ends, and rulers exploit the goodness and nobility of man for evil purposes and take advantage of the fears, hatreds, and false ambitions of the people. They used to be more frank about empire in the old days. Speaking of the Athenian empire, Thucydides wrote: "We make no fine profession of having a right to our Empire because we overthrew the Barbarian single-handed, or because we risked our existence for the sake of our dependents and of civilization. States, like men, cannot be blamed for providing for their proper safety. If we are now here in Sicily, it is in the interest of our own security. . . . It is Fear that forces us to cling to our Empire in Greece, and it is Fear that drives us hither, with the help of our friends, to order matters in Sicily." And again, when he referred to the tribute of the Athenian colonies: "It may seem wickedness to have won it; but it is certainly folly to let it go."

The history of Athens is full of lessons of the incompatibility of democracy with empire, of the tyranny of a democratic state over its colonies, and the swift deterioration and fall of that empire. No upholder of freedom and empire today could state his case so well and so eloquently as Thucydides did: "We are the leaders of civilization, the pioneers of the human race. Our society and intercourse is the highest blessing man can confer. To be within the circle of our influence is not dependence but a privilege. Not all the wealth of the East can repay the riches we bestow. So we can work on cheerfully, using the means and the money that flow into us, confident that, try as they will, we shall still be creditors. For through effort and suffering and on many a stricken field we have found the secret of human power, which is the secret of happiness. Men have guessed at it under many names; but we alone have learnt to know it and to make it at home in our city. And the name we know it by is Freedom, for it has taught us that to serve is to be free. Do you wonder why it is that alone among mankind we confer our benefits, not on conditions of self-interest, but in the fearless confidence of Freedom?"

All this has a familiar ring in these days when freedom and democracy are so loudly proclaimed and yet limited to some only. There is truth in it and a denial of truth. Thucydides knew little of the rest of mankind, and his vision was confined to the Mediterranean countries. Proud of the freedom of his famous city, praising this freedom as the secret of happiness and human power, yet he did not realize that others also aspired to this freedom. Athens, lover of freedom, sacked and destroyed Melos and put to death all the grown men there and sold the women and children for slaves. Even while Thucydides was writing of the empire and freedom of Athens, that empire had crumbled away and that freedom was no more.

For it is not possible for long to combine freedom with domination and slavery; one overcomes the other, and only a little time divides the pride and glory of empire from its fall. Today, much more than ever before, freedom is indivisible. The splendid eulogy of Pericles for his beloved city was followed soon after by that city's fall, and a Spartan garrison occupied the Acropolis. And yet his words move us still for their love of beauty and wisdom and freedom and courage, not merely in their application to the Athens of his day, but in the larger context of the world: "We are lovers of beauty without extravagance, and lovers of wisdom without unmanliness. Wealth to us is not mere material for vainglory but an opportunity for achievement; and poverty we think it no disgrace to acknowledge but a real degradation to make no effort to overcome. . . . Let us draw strength, not merely from twice-told arguments— how fair and noble a thing it is to show courage in battle— but from the busy spectacle of our great city's life as we have it before us day by day, falling in love with her as we see her, and remembering that all this greatness she owes to men with the fighter's daring, the wise man's understanding of his duty, and the good man's self-discipline in its performance—to men who, if they failed in any ordeal, disdained to deprive the city of their services, but sacrificed their lives as the best offerings on her behalf. So they gave their bodies to the commonwealth and received, each for his own memory, praise that will never die, and with it the grandest of all sepulchres, not that in which their mortal bones are laid, but a home in the minds of men, where their glory remains fresh to stir to speech or action as the occasion comes by. For the whole earth is a sepulchre of famous men; and their story is not graven only on stone over their native earth, but lives on far away, without visible symbol, woven into the stuff of other men's lives. For you now it remains to rival what they have done and, knowing the secret of happiness to be freedom and the secret of freedom a brave heart, not idly to stand aside from the enemy's onset."[1]

## VII. THE MODERN APPROACH TO AN OLD PROBLEM

The modern mind, that is to say the better type of the modern mind, is practical and pragmatic, ethical and social, altruistic and humanitarian. It is governed by a practical idealism for social betterment. The ideals which move it represent the spirit of the age, the Zeitgeist, the *Yugadharma*. It has discarded to a large extent the philosophic approach of the ancients, their search for ultimate reality, as well as the devotionalism and mysticism of the medieval period. Humanity is its god and social service its religion. This conception may be incomplete, as the mind of every age has been limited by its environment, and every age has considered some partial truth as the key to all truth. Every generation and every people suffer from the illusion that their way of looking at things is the only right way, or is, at any rate, the nearest approach to it. Every culture has certain values attached to it, limited and conditioned by that culture. The people governed by that culture take these values for granted and attribute a permanent validity to them. So the values of our present-day culture may not be permanent and final; nevertheless they have an essential importance for us for they represent the thought and spirit of the age we live in. A few seers and geniuses, looking into the future, may have a completer vision of humanity and the universe; they are of the vital stuff out of which all real advance comes. The vast majority of people do not even catch up to the present-day values, though they may talk about them in the jargon of the day, and they live imprisoned in the past.

We have therefore to function in line with the highest

[1] The quotations from Thucydides have been taken from Alfred Zimmern's *The Greek Commonwealth* (1924).

ideals of the age we live in, though we may add to them
or seek to mold them in accordance with our national
genius. Those ideals may be classed under two heads:
humanism and the scientific spirit. Between these two
there has been an apparent conflict, but the great upheaval
of thought today, with its questioning of all values, is removing the old boundaries between these two approaches,
as well as between the external world of science and the
internal world of introspection. There is a growing synthesis between humanism and the scientific spirit, resulting in
a kind of scientific humanism. Science also, while holding
on to fact, is on the verge of other domains, or at any rate
has ceased to deny them contemptuously. Our five senses
and what they can perceive, obviously, do not exhaust the
universe. During the past twenty-five years there has been
a profound change in the scientist's picture of the physical
world. Science used to look at nature as something almost
apart from man. But now Sir James Jeans tells us that the
essence of science is that "man no longer sees nature as
something distinct from himself." And then the old question arises which troubled the thinkers of the Upanishads:
How can the knower be known? How can the eyes that
can see external objects see themselves? And if the external
is part and parcel of the internal, what we perceive or conceive is but a projection of our minds, and the universe
and nature and the soul and mind and body, the transcendent and the immanent are all essentially one, how
then are we, within the limited framework of our minds, to
understand this mighty scheme of things objectively? Science has begun to touch these problems, and though they
may elude it, still the earnest scientist of today is the prototype of the philosopher and the man of religion of earlier
ages. "In this materialistic age of ours," says Professor Al-
bert Einstein, "the serious scientific workers are the only
profoundly religious people."[2]

In all this there appears to be a firm belief in science
and yet an apprehension that purely factual and purpose-

[2] Fifty years ago, Vivekananda regarded modern science as a
manifestation of the real religious spirit, for it sought to understand truth by sincere effort.

less science is not enough. Was science, in providing so much of life's furniture, ignoring life's significance? There is an attempt to find a harmony between the world of fact and the world of spirit, for it was becoming increasingly obvious that the overemphasis on the former was crushing the spirit of man. The question that troubled the philosophers of old has come up again in a different form and context: How to reconcile the phenomenal life of the world with the inner spiritual life of the individual. The physicians have discovered that it is not enough to treat the body of the individual or of society as a whole. In recent years, medical men familiar with the finding of modern psychopathology have abandoned the antithesis between "organic" and "functional" diseases, and lay greater stress on the psychological factor. "This is the greatest error in the treatment of sickness," wrote Plato, "that there are physicians for the body and physicians for the soul, and yet the two are one and indivisible."

Einstein, most eminent among scientists, tells us that "the fate of the human race is more than ever dependent on its moral strength today. The way to a joyful and happy state is through renunciation and self-limitation everywhere." He takes us back suddenly from this proud age of science to the old philosophers, from the lust for power and the profit motive to the spirit of renunciation with which India has been so familiar. Probably most other scientists of today will not agree with him in this, or when he says: "I am absolutely convinced that no wealth in the world can help humanity forward, even in the hands of the most devoted workers in the cause. The example of great and pure characters is the only thing that can produce fine ideas or noble deeds. Money only appeals to selfishness and always tempts its owners irresistibly to abuse it."

In facing this question, that is as old as civilization itself, modern science has many advantages denied to the old philosophers. It possesses stores of accumulated knowledge and a method which has abundantly justified itself. It has mapped and charted many regions which were unknown to the ancients. As it has enlarged man's understanding and control over many things, they have ceased to be mysteries to be exploited by the priests of religion. But it has some disadvantages also. The very abundance of its accumulated knowledge has made it difficult for man to take a synthetic view of the whole, and he loses himself in some part of it, analyzes it, studies it, partly understands it, and fails to see its connection with the whole. The vast forces science has released overwhelm him and carry him forward relentlessly, and often an unwilling victim, to unknown shores. The pace of modern life, the succession of crisis after crisis, comes in the way of a dispassionate search for truth. Wisdom itself is hustled and pushed about and cannot easily discover that calm and detached outlook which is so necessary for true understanding. "For still are the ways of wisdom and her temper trembleth not."

Perhaps we are living in one of the great ages of mankind and have to pay the price for that privilege. For the great ages have been full of conflict and instability, of an attempt to change over from the old to something new. There is no permanent stability and security and changelessness, for then life itself would cease. At the most we can seek a relative stability and a moving equilibrium. Life is a continuous struggle of man against man, of man against his surroundings, a struggle on the physical, intellectual, and moral plane out of which new things take shape and fresh ideas are born. Destruction and construction go side by side, and both aspects of man and nature are ever evident. Life is a principle of growth, not of standing still, a continuous becoming which does not permit of static conditions.

Today in the world of politics and economics there is a search for power, and yet when power is attained much else of value has gone. Political trickery and intrigue take the place of idealism, and cowardice and selfishness the place of disinterested courage. Form prevails over substance, and power, so eagerly sought after, somehow fails to achieve what it aimed at. For power has its limitations, and force recoils on itself. Neither can control the spirit, though they may harden and coarsen it. "You can rob an army of its general," says Confucius, "but not the least of men of his will."

John Stuart Mill wrote in his autobiography: "I am now convinced that no great improvements in the lot of mankind are possible, until a great change takes place in the fundamental constitution of their modes of thought." And yet that a fundamental change in the modes of thought itself comes from a changing environment and the pain and suffering that accompany life's unceasing struggles. And so, though we may try to change those modes of thought directly, it is even more necessary to change the environment in which they grew and found sustenance. Each depends on the other and influences it. There is an endless variety of men's minds, and each sees the truth in its own way and is often unable to appreciate the other's viewpoint. Out of that comes conflict. Out of that interaction also a fuller and more integrated truth emerges. For we have to realize that truth is many-sided and is not the monopoly of any group or nation. So also the way of doing things. There may be different ways for different people in different situations. India and China, as well as other nations, evolved their own ways of life and gave them an enduring foundation. They imagined, and many among them vainly imagine still, that their way was the only way. Today Europe and America have evolved their own way of life, which is dominant in the world, and which, their people imagine, is the only way. But probably none of these ways is the one and only desirable way and each may learn something from the other. Certainly India and China must learn a great deal, for they had become static and the West not only represents the spirit of the age but is dynamic and changing and has the capacity for growth in it, even though this functions through self-destruction and periodical human sacrifice.

In India, and perhaps in other countries also, there are alternating tendencies for self-glorification and self-pity. Both are undesirable and ignoble. It is not through sentimentality and emotional approaches that we can understand life but by a frank and courageous facing of realities. We cannot lose ourselves in aimless and romantic quests unconnected with life's problems, for destiny marches on and does not wait for our leisure. Nor can we concern ourselves with externals only, forgetting the significance of the inner life of man. There has to be a balance, an attempt at harmony between them. "The greatest good," wrote Spinoza in the seventeenth century, "is the knowledge of the union which the mind has with the whole of nature. . . . The more the mind knows, the better it understands its forces and the order of nature; the more it understands its forces or strength, the better it will be able to direct itself and lay down rules for itself; and the more it understands the order of nature, the more easily it will be able to liberate itself from useless things; this is the whole method."

In our individual lives also we have to discover a balance between the body and the spirit, and between man as part of nature and man as part of society. "For our perfection," says Tagore, "we have to be vitally savage and mentally civilized; we should have the gift to be natural with nature and human with human society." Perfection is beyond us for it means the end, and we are always journeying, trying to approach something that is ever receding. And in each one of us are many different human beings with their inconsistencies and contradictions, each pulling in a different direction. There is the love of life and the disgust with life, the acceptance of all that life involves and the rejection of much of it. It is difficult to harmonize these contrary tendencies, and sometimes one of them is dominant and sometimes another. "Oftentimes," says Laotze,

> "Oftentimes, one strips oneself of passion
>     In order to see the Secret of Life;
> Oftentimes, one regards life with passion,
>     In order to see its manifold results."

For all our powers of reason and understanding and all our accumulated knowledge and experience, we know little enough about life's secrets, and can only guess at its mysterious processes. But we can always admire its beauty and, through art, exercise the godlike function of creation. Though we may be weak and erring mortals, living a brief and uncertain span of life, yet there is something of the stuff of the immortal gods in us. "We must not," therefore, says Aristotle, "obey those who urge us, because we are human and mortal, to think human and mortal thoughts; in so far as we may we should practice immortality, and omit no effort to live in accordance with the best that is in us."

## VIII. EPILOGUE

Nearly five months have gone by since I took to this writing and I have covered a thousand handwritten pages with this jumble of ideas in my mind. For five months I have traveled in the past and peeped into the future and sometimes tried to balance myself on that "point of intersection of the timeless with time." These months have been full of happenings in the world and the war has advanced rapidly toward a triumphant conclusion, so far as military victories go. In my own country also much has happened of which I could only be a distant spectator, and waves of unhappiness have sometimes temporarily swept over me and passed on. Because of this business of thinking and trying to give some expression to my thoughts, I have drawn myself away from the piercing edge of the present and moved along the wider expanses of the past and the future.

But there must be an end to this wandering. If there were no other sufficient reason for this, there is a very practical consideration which cannot be ignored. I have almost exhausted the supply of paper that I had managed to secure after considerable difficulty, and it is not easy to get more of it.

The discovery of India—what have I discovered? It was presumptuous of me to imagine that I could unveil her and find out what she is today and what she was in the long past. Today she is four hundred million separate individual men and women, each differing from the other, each living in a private universe of thought and feeling. If this is so in the present, how much more difficult is it to grasp that multitudinous past of innumerable successions of human beings. Yet something has bound them together and binds them still. India is a geographical and economic entity, a cultural unity amidst diversity, a bundle of contradictions held together by strong but invisible threads. Overwhelmed again and again, her spirit was never conquered, and today when she appears to be the plaything of a proud conqueror, she remains unsubdued and unconquered. About her there is the elusive quality of a legend of long ago; some enchantment seems to have held her mind. She is a myth and an idea, a dream and a vision, and yet very real and present and pervasive. There are terrifying glimpses of dark corridors which seem to lead back to primeval night, but also there is the fullness and warmth of the day about her. Shameful and repellent she is occasionally, perverse and obstinate, sometimes even a little hysteric, this lady with a past. But she is very lovable and none of her children can forget her wherever they go or whatever strange fate befalls them. For she is part of them in her greatness as well as her failings, and they are mirrored in those deep eyes of hers that have seen so much of life's passion and joy and folly and looked down into wisdom's well. Each one of them is drawn to her, though perhaps each has a different reason for that attraction or can point to no reason at all, and each sees some different aspect of her many-sided personality. From age to age she has produced great men and women, carrying on the old tradition and yet ever adapting it to changing times. Rabindranath Tagore, in line with that great succession, was full of the temper and urges of the modern age and yet was rooted in India's past, and in his own self built up a synthesis of the old and the new. "I love India," he said, "not because I cultivate the idolatry of geography, not because I have had the chance to be born in her soil, but because she has saved through tumultuous ages the living words that have issued from the illuminated consciousness of her great ones." So many will say, and yet others will explain their love for her in some different way.

The old enchantment seems to be breaking today and she is looking around and waking up to the present. But

however she changes, as change she must, that old witchery
will continue and hold the hearts of her people. Though
her attire may change, she will continue as of old, and her
store of wisdom will help her to hold on to what is true
and beautiful and good in this harsh, vindictive, and grasp-
ing world.

The world of today has achieved much, but for all its
declared love for humanity, it has based itself far more on
hatred and violence than on the virtues that make man
human. War is the negation of truth and humanity. War
may be unavoidable sometimes, but its progeny are terrible
to contemplate. Not mere killing, for man must die, but
the deliberate and persistent propagation of hatred and
falsehood, which gradually become the normal habits of
the people. It is dangerous and harmful to be guided in
our life's course by hatreds and aversions, for they are
wasteful of energy and limit and twist the mind and prevent it from perceiving the truth. Unhappily there is hatred
in India and strong aversions, for the past pursues us and
the present does not differ from it. It is not easy to forget
repeated affronts to the dignity of a proud race. Yet, fortunately, Indians do not nourish hatred for long; they re-
cover easily a more benevolent mood.

India will find herself again when freedom opens out
new horizons and the future will then fascinate her far
more than the immediate past of frustration and humiliation. She will go forward with confidence, rooted in herself
and yet eager to learn from others and co-operate with
them. Today she swings between a blind adherence to her
old customs and a slavish imitation of foreign ways. In
neither of these can she find relief or life or growth. It
is obvious that she has to come out of her shell and take
full part in the life and activities of the modern age. It
should be equally obvious that there can be no real cultural or spiritual growth based on imitation. Such imitation
can only be confined to a small number who cut themselves
off from the masses and the springs of national life. True
culture derives its inspiration from every corner of the
world, but it is home-grown and has to be based on the
wide mass of the people. Art and literature remain lifeless

if they are continually thinking of foreign models. The day of a narrow culture confined to a small fastidious group is past. We have to think in terms of the people generally and their culture must be a continuation and development of past trends, and must also represent their new urges and creative tendencies.

Emerson, over a hundred years ago, warned his country-men in America not to imitate or depend too much cul-turally on Europe. A new people as they were, he wanted them not to look too much on their European past but to draw inspiration from the abounding life of their new country. "Our day of dependence, our long apprenticeship to the learning of other lands, draws to a close. The mil-lions that around us are rushing into life cannot always be fed on the sere remains of foreign harvests. Events, actions arise, that must be sung, that will sing themselves . . . there are creative manners, there are creative actions and creative words . . . that is, indicative of no custom or au-thority, but springing spontaneous from the mind's own sense of good and fair." And again in his essay on self-reliance: "It is for want of self-culture that the supersti-tion of Traveling, whose idols are Italy, England, Egypt, retains its fascination for all educated Americans. They who made England, Italy, or Greece venerable in the im-agination did so by sticking fast where they were, like an axis of the earth. In manly hours we feel that duty is our place. The soul is no traveler; the wise man stays at home, and when his necessities, his duties, on any occasion call him from his house, or into foreign fields, he is at home still, and shall make men sensible by the expression of his countenance that he goes the missionary of wisdom and virtue, and visits cities and men like a sovereign and not like an interloper or a valet."

"I have no churlish objection," continues Emerson, "to the circumnavigation of the globe, for the purposes of art, of study, and benevolence, so that man is first domesti-cated, or does not go abroad with the hope of finding some-thing greater than he knows. He who travels to be amused, or to get somewhat which he does not carry, travels away from himself, and grows old even in youth among old things. In Thebes, in Palmyra, his will and mind have become old and dilapidated as they. He carries ruins to ruins.

"But the rage for traveling is a symptom of a deeper unsoundness affecting the whole intellectual action. . . . We imitate. . . . Our houses are built with foreign taste; our shelves are garnished with foreign ornaments; our opinions, our tastes, our faculties, lean on and follow the past and the distant. The Soul created the arts wherever they have flourished. It was in his own mind that the artist sought his model. It was an application of his own thought to the thing to be done and the conditions to be observed. . . . Insist on yourself; never imitate. Your own gift you can present every moment with the cumulative force of a whole life's cultivation; but of the adopted talent of another you have only an extemporaneous half possession."

We in India do not have to go abroad in search of the Past and the Distant. We have them here in abundance. If we go to foreign countries it is in search of the Present. That search is necessary, for isolation from it means backwardness and decay. The world of Emerson's time has changed and old barriers are breaking down; life becomes more international. We have to play our part in this coming internationalism and for this purpose to travel, meet others, learn from them and understand them. But a real internationalism is not something in the air without roots or anchorage. It has to grow out of national cultures, can only flourish today on a basis of freedom and equality and true internationalism. Nevertheless Emerson's warning holds today as it did in the past, and our search can only be fruitful in the conditions mentioned by him. Not to go anywhere as interlopers but only if we are welcomed as equals and as comrades in a common quest. There are countries, notably in the British dominions, which try to humiliate our countrymen. They are not for us. We may, for the present, have to suffer the enforced subjection to an alien yoke and to carry the grievous burdens that this involves, but the day of our liberation cannot be distant.

We are citizens of no mean country and we are proud

of the land of our birth, of our people, our culture and traditions. That pride should not be for a romanticized past to which we want to cling; nor should it encourage exclusiveness or a want of appreciation of other ways than ours. It must never allow us to forget our many weaknesses and failings or blunt our longing to be rid of them. We have a long way to go and much leeway to make up before we can take our proper station with others in the van of human civilization and progress. And we have to hurry, for the time at our disposal is limited and the pace of the world grows ever swifter. It was India's way in the past to welcome and absorb other cultures. That is much more necessary today, for we march to the One World of tomorrow where national cultures will be intermingled with the international culture of the human race. We shall therefore seek wisdom and knowledge and friendship and comradeship wherever we can find them, and co-operate with others in common tasks, but we are no suppliants for others' favors and patronage. Thus we shall remain true Indians and Asiatics, and become at the same time good internationalists and world citizens.

My generation has been a troubled one in India and the world. We may carry on for a little while longer, but our day will be over and we shall give place to others, and they will live their lives and carry their burdens to the next stage of the journey. How have we played our part in this brief interlude that draws to a close? I do not know. Others of a later age will judge. By what standards do we measure success or failure? That too I do not know. We can make no complaint that life has treated us harshly, for ours has been a willing choice, and perhaps life has not been so bad to us after all. For only those can sense life who stand often on the verge of it, only those whose lives are not governed by the fear of death. In spite of all the mistakes that we might have made, we have saved ourselves from triviality and an inner shame and cowardice. That, for our individual selves, has been some achievement. "Man's dearest possession is life, and since it is given to him to live but once, he must so live as not to be seared with the shame of a cowardly and trivial past, so live as not to be tortured for years without purpose, so live that dying he can say: 'All my life and my strength were given to the first cause in the world—the liberation of mankind.' "[3]

[3] Lenin.

# ACKNOWLEDGMENTS

Acknowledgment is hereby made for permission to use in this book quotations from the following books:

Charles and Mary Beard, *The Rise of American Civilization*, New York, The Macmillan Company.

*Cambridge History of India*, New York, The Macmillan Company; Cambridge, Cambridge University Press.

Gordon Childe, *What Happened in History*, New York, Penguin Books.

*The Five Dialogues of Plato*, New York, E. P. Dutton & Company; London, J. M. Dent & Sons.

B. H. Liddell Hart, *The Strategy of Indirect Approach*, London, Faber & Faber.

*Hindu Scriptures*, New York, E. P. Dutton & Company; London, J. M. Dent & Sons (Everyman edition, credited therein to E. J. Lazarus & Company).

Lancelot Hogben, *Mathematics for the Million*, New York, W. W. Norton & Company; London, George Allen & Unwin.

Gilbert Murray, translator, *Alcestis of Euripides* and *The Bacchae of Euripides*, New York, Oxford University Press.

Edward Thompson, *The Making of the Indian Princes*, London, Oxford University Press.

I. Tsing, *A Record of the Buddhist Religions as Practiced in India and Malay Archipelago*, translated by T. Takakusu, London, Oxford University Press.

# INDEX